Architectural Detailing

Architectural Detailing

Function • Constructability • Aesthetics

Fourth Edition

Patrick Rand | Jason Miller | Edward Allen

WILEY

Copyright © 2025 by John Wiley & Sons, Inc. All rights reserved, including rights for text and data mining and training of artificial technologies or similar technologies.

Published by John Wiley & Sons, Inc., Hoboken, New Jersey.
Published simultaneously in Canada.

No part of this publication may be reproduced, stored in a retrieval system, or transmitted in any form or by any means, electronic, mechanical, photocopying, recording, scanning, or otherwise, except as permitted under Section 107 or 108 of the 1976 United States Copyright Act, without either the prior written permission of the Publisher, or authorization through payment of the appropriate per-copy fee to the Copyright Clearance Center, Inc., 222 Rosewood Drive, Danvers, MA 01923, (978) 750-8400, fax (978) 750-4470, or on the web at www.copyright.com. Requests to the Publisher for permission should be addressed to the Permissions Department, John Wiley & Sons, Inc., 111 River Street, Hoboken, NJ 07030, (201) 748-6011, fax (201) 748-6008, or online at http://www.wiley.com/go/permission.

Trademarks: Wiley and the Wiley logo are trademarks or registered trademarks of John Wiley & Sons, Inc. and/or its affiliates in the United States and other countries and may not be used without written permission. All other trademarks are the property of their respective owners. John Wiley & Sons, Inc. is not associated with any product or vendor mentioned in this book.

Limit of Liability/Disclaimer of Warranty: While the publisher and author have used their best efforts in preparing this book, they make no representations or warranties with respect to the accuracy or completeness of the contents of this book and specifically disclaim any implied warranties of merchantability or fitness for a particular purpose. No warranty may be created or extended by sales representatives or written sales materials. The advice and strategies contained herein may not be suitable for your situation. You should consult with a professional where appropriate. Further, readers should be aware that websites listed in this work may have changed or disappeared between when this work was written and when it is read. Neither the publisher nor authors shall be liable for any loss of profit or any other commercial damages, including but not limited to special, incidental, consequential, or other damages.

For general information on our other products and services or for technical support, please contact our Customer Care Department within the United States at (800) 762-2974, outside the United States at (317) 572-3993 or fax (317) 572-4002.

Wiley also publishes its books in a variety of electronic formats. Some content that appears in print may not be available in electronic formats. For more information about Wiley products, visit our web site at www.wiley.com.

Library of Congress Cataloging-in-Publication Data Applied for:

Paperback ISBN: 9781119912705
ePDF ISBN: 9781119912729
epub ISBN: 9781119912712

Cover Design: Wiley
Cover Images: © Patrick Rand and Jason Miller

Set in 9.5/12 pts and Times LT Std by Straive, Chennai, India.

SKY10082565_082124

CONTENTS

Acknowledgments   xi
Introduction   xiii

PART I – DETAIL PATTERNS   1

SECTION 1 FUNCTION   3

CHAPTER 1 Controlling Water   5

- Wash   7
- Overlap   12
- Overhang and Drip   15
- Drain and Weep   19
- Unobstructed Drainage   21
- Ventilated Cold Roof   22
- Foundation Drainage   24
- Moisture Break   25
- Capillary Break   26
- Labyrinth   28
- Rainscreen Assembly and Pressure Equalization   29
- Upstand   34
- Sealant Joints and Gaskets   36

CHAPTER 2 Controlling Air   45

- Air Barrier System   47
- Weatherstripped Crack   49

CHAPTER 3 **Controlling Heat Flow** 51

 Thermal Insulation 52

 Thermal Break 54

 Multiple Glazing 59

 White and Bright Surfaces 60

 Reflective Glazing 61

 Reflective Surface and Airspace 62

 Outside-Insulated Thermal Mass 64

CHAPTER 4 **Controlling Water Vapor** 67

 Warm Interior Surfaces 68

 Warm-Side Vapor Retarder 70

 Vapor Ventilation 75

 Condensate Drainage 78

CHAPTER 5 **Controlling Sound** 79

 Airtight, Heavy, Limp Partition 80

 Cushioned Floor 83

 Quiet Attachments 85

 Sound-Absorbing Surfaces 86

CHAPTER 6 **Accommodating Movement** 89

 Seasoning and Curing 91

 Vertical-Grain Lumber 94

 Equalizing Cross Grain 96

 Relieved Back 98

 Foundation below Frost Line 99

 Structure/Enclosure Joint 100

 Abutment Joint 102

 Expansion Joint 103

 Control Joint 106

 Sliding Joint 109

 Building Separation Joint 111

CHAPTER 7 **Providing Structural Support** 113

 Small Structures 114

 Connecting Dissimilar Materials 116

 Distributing Loads 118

CHAPTER 8 **Providing Passages for Building Services** 121

 Vertical Chase 122

 Horizontal Plenum 125

CHAPTER 9 **Health and Safety** 129

 Safe Footing 130

 Fall Protection 132

 Safe Edges 134

 Safe Glazing 135

 Nontoxic Materials 136

 Fire-Safe Materials 137

 Fire-Resistant Assemblies 138

 Barrier-Free Design 140

 Universal Design 141

CHAPTER 10 **Providing for the Aging of the Building** 145

 Life Cycle 146

 Expected Life 148

 Surfaces That Age Gracefully 150

 Repairable Surfaces 152

 Cleanable Surfaces 153

 Maintenance Access 154

 Dry Wood 156

 Protected and Similar Metals 158

 Less Absorbent Materials 161

 Robust Assemblies 163

 Building Armor 164

 Extreme Event Protection 166

SECTION 2 CONSTRUCTABILITY   169

CHAPTER 11 Ease of Assembly   171

 Uncut Units 172

 Minimum Number of Parts 174

 Parts That Are Easy to Handle 176

 Repetitious Assembly 179

 Simulated Assemblies 181

 Observable Assemblies 183

 Accessible Connections 184

 Detailing for Disassembly 186

 Installation Clearance 188

 Nonconflicting Systems 189

CHAPTER 12 Forgiving Details   191

 Dimensional Tolerance 192

 Sliding Fit 197

 Adjustable Fit 201

 Reveal 204

 Butt Joint 206

 Clean Edge 209

 Progressive Finish 211

 Forgiving Surface 213

CHAPTER 13 Efficient Use of Construction Resources   215

 Factory and Site 216

 Repetitious Fabrication 218

 Rehearsing the Construction Sequence 220

 Off-the-Shelf Parts 223

 Local Skills and Resources 224

 Aligning Forms with Forces 226

 Refining the Detail 229

 All-Weather Construction 230

 Pride of Craftsmanship 232

 Accepted Standards 233

SECTION 3 AESTHETICS — 235

CHAPTER 14 Aesthetics — 237

- *Contributive Details*   237
- *Timeless Features*   240
- *Geometry and Proportion*   241
- *Hierarchy of Refinement*   243
- *Intensification and Ornamentation*   245
- *Sensory Richness*   247
- *Formal Transitions*   248
- *Didactic Assemblies*   251
- *Composing the Detail*   252

PART II – DETAIL DEVELOPMENT — 253

SECTION 1 APPLYING THE DETAIL PATTERNS — 255

CHAPTER 15 Detailing a Building in Wood Light Framing — 257

CHAPTER 16 Detailing a Building in Architectural Concrete — 291

CHAPTER 17 Detailing a Building in Masonry on a Concrete Frame — 313

SECTION 2 GETTING STARTED — 349

APPENDIX A: The Detailer's Reference Shelf — 351

APPENDIX B: Formulating Exercises for Self-Study, Studio, or Classroom Use — 359

INDEX — 361

ACKNOWLEDGMENTS

Patrick Rand thanks Edward Allen, generous mentor to a generation of architectural educators, for the opportunity to collaborate with him on previous editions of this book. Ed showed us all how to make the most important aspects of our craft vivid and accessible, empowering countless young designers to make architecture that is functional, constructable, and aesthetically pleasing.

Ed Allen understood that excellence in architectural design and building technologies were inseparable. He often said that any pedagogy based on a separation of design from technology was a flawed pedagogy. Students must never come upon a book, a faculty member, a course, or a curriculum based on the belief that architectural design could be disengaged from technology, or that technology could be engaged without a healthy dose of design.

Ed once answered the key question, What is the Essence of Building Technology? "The primary focus of all of our courses is **getting the form right!** With the right form, the rest is easy."

Pat is also grateful to his many excellent students spanning more than four decades; whose ambitious designs and probing questions helped him grow. Students in his graduate detailing seminars explored the breadth and depth of the principles in this book as they used them to analyze existing buildings and to design their own new projects. Work by these students provoked revisions of nearly all the patterns in this edition.

Pat found this collaboration with Jason Miller brought refreshing new insights to every pattern in this book. Jason's revisions to text and drawings substantially improve the content for today's readers. He also thanks Christine Nalepa for her patience, support, and candid critiques of word and image.

At John Wiley & Sons, Inc., Todd Green, executive editor, guided all phases of the preparation and publication of this edition of this book with wisdom, patience, and good humor. Many thanks especially to our managing editors: first Amy Odum and then Monica Chandra Sekar, who provided valuable guidance and judgment in this new edition.

We acknowledge the compatibility between this and other publications with which the authors have been involved. Most notably, the widely used text *Fundamentals of Building Construction: Materials and Methods*, 7th ed. (2019) by Iano and Allen, which shares similar concepts, terminology, and graphic approach. *Detailing for Landscape Architects* (2011) by Ryan, Allen, and Rand transforms the detailing patterns approach to the realm of landscape architecture. Both volumes are by John Wiley & Sons, Inc.

PATRICK RAND, FAIA, DPACSA
Distinguished Professor of Architecture

To work in the footsteps of Edward Allen and Patrick Rand continues to be a truly humbling experience.

Jason Miller thanks Patrick Rand for providing the opportunity to participate in the making of a fourth edition of this book. The clarity of thought Ed and Pat have committed to many publications regarding the design process and its resulting constructed product has deeply influenced Jason's thought and work in both professional and academic settings.

With knowledge, skill, and patience, Pat has mentored generations of architecture students, empowering them to contribute to the built environment in significant ways. Pat possesses a unique capacity to instill belief in others. Collaborating with Pat on this edition has offered Jason an important reminder: Joy is found in the asking of good questions and the discovery of new things.

Jason would like to recognize the aggregate contributions of his students who, in myriad ways, have helped shape a pedagogic perspective about the importance of connecting architectural education with architectural practice. In the studio, in the shop, or on a jobsite, work by these students has consistently reinforced the timelessness – and timeliness – of the design detailing principles discussed in this book.

Jason also thanks his family for their abiding love and support in his "chasing of butterflies" that make projects like this one possible.

JASON MILLER, AIA
Professor of Building Sciences

INTRODUCTION

This book is about making architectural details. The process of turning architectural idea into constructed reality is built, decision by decision and layer upon layer, amid a landscape of ever-changing circumstances. Details deliver more than mere illustrations of prescriptive or performance-based code requirements. Details provide far more than iconic elements or decorative embellishments. A good detail, and good architectural detailing, reveals a synthesis between creative and critical thinking. They make functional, buildable, and aesthetic solutions, informed by experience, precedent, and research.

Architects design, draw, and document for each building a set of details that clearly describe its assembly. Architects retain primary responsibility for the detailing in buildings, a fact that architectural curricula often underappreciate and underserve. The process and products of detailing should be at least as prominent in architecture curricula as the study of structures and building services: two areas in which consulting engineers often have primary responsibility.

This book is intended as a resource to help students and young professionals become proficient with the principles of architectural detailing by (a) describing ***what*** needs to be considered, (b) demonstrating ***how*** those needs might be met, and (c) explaining ***why*** those needs matter to the creation of quality works of architecture in the built environment.

The act of detailing asks questions of the architect: How does the architect know if a detail, or family of details, will achieve the intended result and perform appropriately? Will the building they depict go together – or come apart – easily and economically? Will it shed and manage water responsibly? Will it be easy and cost-effective to heat and cool? Will the details coordinate with one another? With the overall form and space of the building? Will the building age gracefully? Will it last for the requisite period and adapt readily to changes in technology or use over time? Will the building support the health, safety, and welfare of its occupants? Many more questions of similar importance might be asked. A key skill of detailing is to ask the questions and search for the solutions.

An experienced architect does not leave those solutions to chance. Each detail, no matter how unique or unprecedented, conforms through design with timeless and universal patterns. When coupled with competent execution in the factory or on the construction site, well-developed details virtually guarantee acceptable building performance. ***These detail patterns are the subject of this book***.

Detail patterns are principles present in all successful building details. They represent an accumulation of knowledge about what works in building construction and what does not. Many patterns are firmly grounded in scientific fact. Others are based just as solidly on common sense and the realities of human performance. Patterns evolve and expand with advances in the means and methods of design and construction. An experienced architect employs all these patterns automatically and instinctually when designing details.

Good detailing is an opportunity to advance the concepts and aesthetic strategies of the basic design for a building project. Detail patterns can be used to edit and refine the schematic design, celebrating its strengths and eliminating features that do not contribute to the central ideas.

Detail patterns are tools. ***The patterns present and clarify issues relevant to a particular detail but avoid stating what the specific solution should be. They are meant instead to provoke the designer to consider their potential implications, to discover many possible solutions, and to provide a clear process through which each can be assessed.*** When learning about a new tool, the best teacher is practice.

Architectural details are rarely designed from scratch, as a pure response to a situation, as if it had never existed before. More often, details are built on precedents that model solutions similar to the circumstance or condition needed. The architect uses the detail patterns as a reliable means of analyzing and understanding existing details. They are beneficial when reviewing one's own work, when checking the work of other detailers in the office, when judging the quality of manufactured building components, and when diagnosing problems in existing buildings. The absence of attention to a particular detail pattern or the presence of a feature that contradicts a pattern usually indicates a problem or a potential problem that should be corrected.

The detail patterns are straightforward and easy to learn. This book establishes slightly more than 100 of them. Each is irreducibly simple.

The first part of this book introduces each pattern, explains it, and illustrates examples of its use. These illustrations are drawn purposefully by hand, as sketching maximizes retention of principles and concepts – reinforcing a critical and meaningful skill for architects and designers. Each pattern is given a descriptive name and a graphic icon for visual recognition of its core detailing principle.

The patterns are arranged in three main groups: **Function**, **Constructability**, and **Aesthetics**, corresponding with the three major design concerns of the detailer. The order of presentation of these groups does not imply their hierarchy or their sequence in the design process. Within each group, the patterns are further categorized by similarity of intent. The first category of patterns under Function, for example, is Controlling Water, containing 13 detail patterns that offer a comprehensive strategy for accomplishing this important task.

The second part of this book, Detail Development, demonstrates the use of the detail patterns during the process of designing details for three different – and hypothetical – buildings: one in wood light frame, one in architectural concrete, and one in brick veneer over a reinforced concrete frame.

The third and final part of this book closes with an annotated listing of publications and a list of websites recommended for the detailer's own reference shelf. Exercises for self-study or classroom use are also provided.

Approximately 500 original sketches and drawings by the authors are intended to illustrate the building elements and natural phenomena addressed. These are not and should not be confused with architectural working drawings. Almost all the drawings are freehand sketches because this manual process remains an appropriate one for designers to use as they begin creating details. Designing details is a creative act that begins with sketches that are quick tools for exploring the problem and possible solutions. Like designing the building plan or the elevation, multiple iterations are typically used to get a viable solution.

Some information has been intentionally deleted or added to make the drawings effective instructional tools. For instance, anchors securing a masonry veneer to the backup are drawn in these sections; in practice, they might be identified only in specifications or in a large-scale detail in a set of working drawings. By including them in the sketches, readers can engage the visual reality in more complete terms.

It is assumed that the reader has a general background in the materials and methods of building construction and is familiar with the conventions of architectural drawing.

In the detail drawings throughout the book, **the exterior is located to the left or top of the drawing.** The number in the lower-left corner of each detail drawing corresponds with the numbered text passage describing a specific example of the detail pattern.

PART I

DETAIL PATTERNS

SECTION 1
FUNCTION

For a building to function well, its details – all its details – must function well. Each detail must perform individually and collectively with other details. When designing details for a building, the detailer has seemingly endless options to assess and decisions to make with no prescribed pathway toward the most appropriate solution. This section of the book guides the detailer by describing and illustrating factors that affect the functional performance of details.

In architecture, function includes the technical performance of the details that contribute to making a building safe and secure for its occupants. But function also includes features that impact the qualities of the forms, surfaces, and spaces that compose the building. In other words, function affects experience and well-being. For instance, an interior space supported by a solid structure and protected by a well-sealed building envelope – but that allows a reverberating echo or provides glaring light – does not function as well as it could.

The detailer faces many challenges: Controlling the flow of water, air, or heat. Managing sound and accommodating movement. Providing supplemental structural support or passages for building services. Mitigating risks to health and safety. The detailer is challenged to begin by addressing these, and other, functional needs of the building when it is new. But they must also address these needs long into the future and beyond the lifetime of those who designed or constructed it. Buildings change constantly in response to natural forces, such as the daily cycles of temperature and light or because of longer or more extreme seasonal patterns. A fundamental grasp of physics and of biological and chemical processes is an integral part of the architectural detailing process. Other functions concern the people who engage with the building every day, altering it internally, externally, and incrementally through countless actions.

The detail patterns that relate to function address the breadth of these topics. They are organized into thematic groups to focus the detailer's attention on each topic individually. But it is important to note that each topic does not exist alone. Topics connect to and integrate with other topics. Each pattern within a particular topic builds awareness of the issue and includes directions toward possible solutions. The patterns describe the natural processes involved, as well as the codes, standards, and conventional practices that are relevant to discovering appropriate detailing solutions.

Architectural Detailing: Function Constructability Aesthetics. Fourth Edition. Patrick Rand, Jason Miller, and Edward Allen.
© 2025 John Wiley & Sons, Inc. Published 2025 by John Wiley & Sons, Inc.

CHAPTER 1 Controlling Water

Water must be controlled in order to prevent leakage, which is the penetration of water through a building assembly. Water intrusion is the most common detailing problem encountered in buildings. For water to penetrate through a building assembly, three conditions must all occur at the same time:

1. There must be an opening through the assembly.
2. There must be water present at the opening.
3. There must be a force to move the water through the opening.

If any one of these three conditions is not met, water will not penetrate the assembly. In developing any exterior detail, therefore, the designer can pursue one or more of three strategies:

1. Try to eliminate openings in building assemblies.
2. Try to keep water away from openings in building assemblies.
3. Try to neutralize forces that move water through openings in building assemblies.

Complete success in any one of these three strategies will result in the complete elimination of water leaks, but in detailing it is sometimes necessary to pursue two of these strategies or even all three of them at the same time. This approach gives added security in case one of the strategies fails as a result of poor workmanship or building deterioration. Each of these strategies is considered briefly here with a corresponding list of detail patterns that relate to each. All of the patterns listed are explained later in this chapter.

1. Eliminating Openings in Building Assemblies

Every building is full of openings. A shingled roof has an opening under each shingle. A wall has cracks around windows and doors, and around joints between the units of material from which the wall is made. Additional cracks and holes may form as the building ages and deteriorates. The designer can attempt to eliminate all these openings by using preformed gaskets and sealants; however, this is an unreliable strategy for the life cycle performance of the building. Gaskets may not seal securely if they are the wrong size or resiliency, or if the surfaces they touch are rough or unclean. Sealants may fail to adhere properly if the materials to which they are applied are not scrupulously clean and properly primed, or if the installer does not compress the sealant fully into the seam. Both sealants and gaskets can deteriorate from weathering and from the flexing and stretching they may undergo as the building ages. A building envelope that relies on sealants and gaskets alone for watertightness will leak sooner or later. Even a small defect in a sealant or gasket that is exposed to the weather can leak very large amounts of water, just as a small hole in a bathtub can create a very large puddle.

Sealants and preformed gaskets are still extremely useful as components of an overall strategy for making a building envelope watertight. Therefore, it is important to know how to detail sealant joints and gasket joints correctly and how to incorporate them into more complex schemes for controlling water penetration. The detail pattern that relates to eliminating openings in building assemblies is:

Sealant Joints and Gaskets (p. 36)

2. Keeping Water Away from Openings in Building Assemblies

There are a number of effective ways to keep water away from openings. Often it is useful to keep most water away from an opening simply to reduce the volume of water that must be dealt with at the opening itself. In many cases we can easily and securely keep all water away from an opening.

The detail patterns that relate to keeping water away from openings in building assemblies are the following:

Wash (p. 7)
Overlap (p. 12)
Overhang and Drip (p. 15)
Drain and Weep (p. 18)
Ventilated Cold Roof (p. 22)
Foundation Drainage (p. 24)

3. Neutralizing Forces That Move Water through Openings in Building Assemblies

There are five forces that can move water through an opening in a wall or a roof: (1) gravity, (2) surface tension, (3) capillary action, (4) momentum, and (5) air pressure differentials. In most cases, it is surprisingly easy to detail a building assembly so that all five of these forces are neutralized, and the most secure strategies for keeping water out of a building are based on this approach.

Architectural Detailing: Function Constructability Aesthetics. Fourth Edition. Patrick Rand, Jason Miller, and Edward Allen.
© 2025 John Wiley & Sons, Inc. Published 2025 by John Wiley & Sons, Inc.

The force of gravity is neutralized by two previously encountered detail patterns useful in keeping water away from openings in buildings:

> *Wash* (p. 7)
> *Overlap* (p. 12)

Surface tension, a force that causes water to cling to the underside of a surface where it can run into an opening, is neutralized by:

> *Overhang and Drip* (p. 15)

The patterns for neutralizing the other three forces are the following:

> *Moisture Break* (p. 25)
> *Capillary Break* (p. 26)
> *Labyrinth* (p. 28)
> *Rainscreen Assembly and Pressure Equalization* (p. 29)
> *Upstand* (p. 34)

The capillary break neutralizes capillary action. The labyrinth neutralizes momentum, and the rainscreen assembly and the upstand neutralize air pressure differentials. By combining these seven patterns in each exterior joint of a building, we can make a building entirely waterproof.

When conceived as a well-coordinated group, these features combine to form the water control layer of the building envelope. The designer should be able to draw an uninterrupted line in plan and section representing the water control layer. A building with a continuous water control layer is entirely waterproof.

Wash

A *wash* is the slope given to a surface to drain water away from vulnerable areas of a building. In general, every external, nearly horizontal surface of a building should have a wash. More permeable materials should have a steeper slope to shed water more quickly.

1. A window or door sill, whether made of stone, concrete, wood, or metal, always has a wash to keep water from accumulating next to the door or sash. A minimum slope for this type of wash is about 1 in. per foot (1:10 or 1:12). A steeper slope drains water faster and is more secure, because the more quickly water is removed from a surface, the less time it has to leak through. It is also more difficult for wind to drive water up a steeper slope.

2. The wash on this concrete chimney cap keeps water away from the vulnerable crack between the clay flue tile and the concrete. The slope should be at least 1:12. The outer edge of the cap should have a thickness of at least 3 in. (75 mm) to discourage cracking of the concrete, not the feather edge that is commonly used (see **Clean Edge**, Chapter 12). The cricket on the upslope side of the chimney consists of two washes that divert water around the shaft of the chimney. ▷

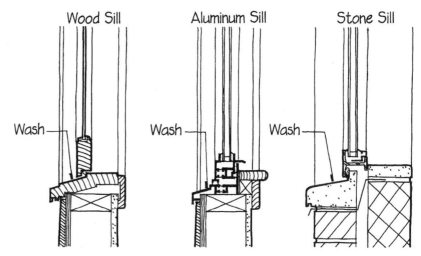

1. Washes on Window Sills

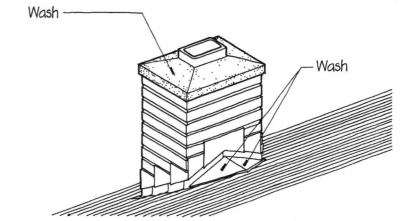

2. Wash on Chimney Cap and Cricket

3. The coping on a building parapet has a wash to keep standing water away from the seams in the parapet. Usually, the wash drains toward the roof to minimize water staining of building façades. The cant strip at the base of the parapet slopes steeply toward the roof membrane to direct water away from the joint between the parapet and the roof deck.

4. The bottom surface in a horizontal joint between wall panels should have a wash to drain water to the outside. Even if the joint will be closed at the outside face with sealant, the wash should be provided to discourage leaking if the sealant should fail.

5. The sloping roof is a special case of the wash. A shingled roof will not shed water unless it has a considerable slope. If the slope were too shallow, water would linger on the roof, flow around and under the shingles, and penetrate the gaps beneath. Each type of shingle material has its own recommended minimum slope. A slope steeper than the minimum is advisable on exposed sites where rain is often driven against the building by wind. A good rule of thumb is to avoid roof slopes less than 4:12. Wood shingles, asphalt shingles, and unsoldered metal roofing can function on a slope as shallow as 3:12 with a special underlayment (consult appropriate literature from trade associations or manufacturers for more information). Steeper slopes shed water faster and thus are less prone to problems; however, they may be more expensive because the roof area is increased, and workers will have greater difficulty moving about the steeper surface. Many roofing materials can be installed at a very steep slope, even on vertical surfaces.

6. So-called flat roofs are seldom flat. They are given a positive slope toward points where water is removed by roof drains or scuppers, because standing water on a roof can cause deterioration of the roof membrane and even structural collapse. The correct name for "flat" roofs, in fact, is "low-slope" roofs. These roof membranes may be exposed to the sky or may be covered with pavers, vegetated roof treatments, solar panels, and other permeable or discontinuous coverings. Drains in a low-slope roof should be located either at points of maximum structural deflection (usually the midspan of a beam or joist) or

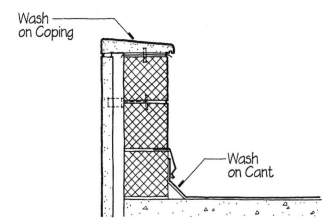

3. Washes at Parapet

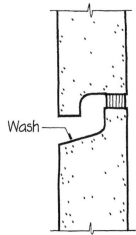

4. Horizontal Panel Joint

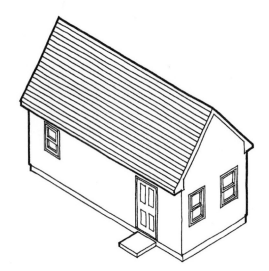

5. Sloping Roof

at low points purposely created by sloping the structure that supports the roof.

Tapered insulation or roof fill should be used if necessary to create an additional slope that will cause water to drain properly from a roof. If a drain is located at a point of maximum structural deflection, the minimum recommended slope for membrane roofs is ¼ in. per foot (1:50), and more slope than this is desirable. If a drain is located at a low point created by sloping a beam, the overall rise along the length of the beam should be at least twice the expected maximum deflection in the beam, plus another ⅛ in. per foot (1:100) of the length of the beam, to be sure water cannot be trapped by the curvature of the beam. The detailer should work closely with the structural engineer to design a system of roof drainage that complies with these guidelines. This is especially important if the roof is composed of cambered elements such as precast concrete planks or beams.

It is desirable (and mandatory under some building codes) to provide a complete, independent set of auxiliary roof drains or scuppers to take over in case the primary drains become clogged with debris. The auxiliary drains or scuppers are usually located 2 in. (51 mm) higher in elevation than the primary drains and must be served by their own network of piping.

7. A rooftop terrace is usually drained through open joints between its dead-level paving stones or tiles. The water drops through the joints and is funneled to a system of roof drains by the low-slope roof membrane below. The same recommended slopes apply to this membrane as to any low-slope roof. The terrace paving is held level by small, adjustable-height pedestals that stand on the roof membrane and support the paving units at each intersection. These pedestals are marketed in several proprietary designs and are usually made of plastic.

Vegetated roofs – either extensive or intensive assemblies – are designed to retain some water and drain excess water slowly. The slope and drain considerations are similar to other low-slope roofs; however, the installation application is different. Because the roof or parapet drain serves an overflow function, the drain access is

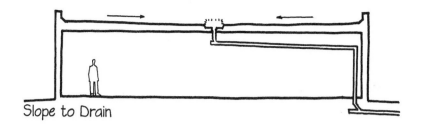

Slope to Drain

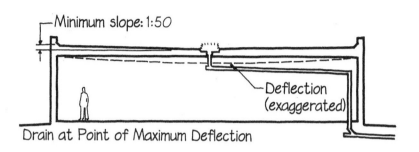

Drain at Point of Maximum Deflection

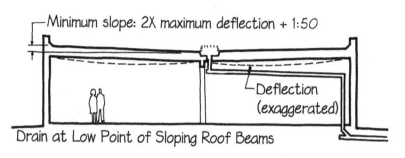

Drain at Low Point of Sloping Roof Beams

6. Low-Slope Roofs

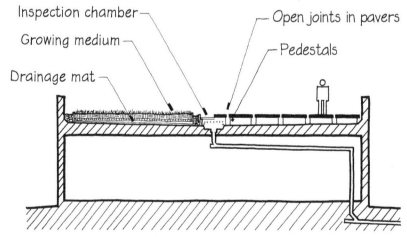

7. Vegetated Roof and Rooftop Terrace

located above the prescribed water line of the drainage and retention mat that serves as the vegetation substrate in the assembly. The drain is protected by a band of gravel – which is itself separated from the vegetated areas by a profiled strip – and capped with an inspection chamber for routine maintenance operations. ▷

8. Another special case of the wash is indicated on architectural drawings by the note "pitch to drain." The rain gutter at the eave of a roof is usually pitched (sloped) to drain water toward the nearest downspout. Common slopes used for gutters are ⅛ in. or ¼ in. per foot (1:100 or 1:50). A steeper slope gives a greater capacity to handle water in a heavy rainstorm, and is recommended where precipitation volumes are large. Rainwater collected by gutters can continue to flow by gravity toward cisterns, planters, or vegetated surfaces, or it can be discharged into a stormwater collection system.

9. An industrial or basement floor slab is often pitched toward floor drains to eliminate puddles of standing water. A rule-of-thumb pitch for slab drainage is ¼ in. per foot (1:50), but to prevent puddles, this should be increased for surfaces that are not very flat, and can be decreased for very smooth surfaces. In the case of a floor or paving, however, pitches should not become too steep, or they will be awkward for pedestrians and vehicles to navigate.

10. If there is no interior floor drain, a residential garage floor is usually pitched so water dripping off a car will run under the garage door and out. Minimum pitch recommendations are the same as for industrial and basement slabs.

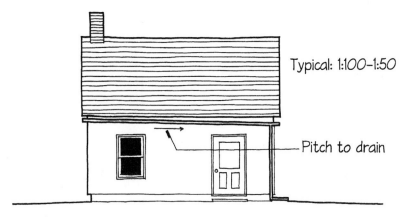

8. Pitched Gutter

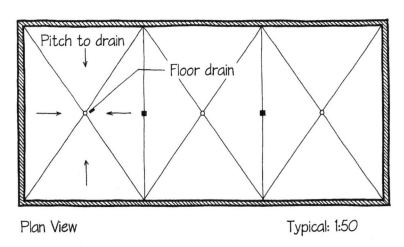

9. Floor Slab Pitched to Drain

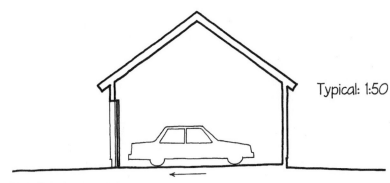

10. Slab Pitched to Drain

11. Roads, driveways, and walks are usually crowned, to shed water in both directions and to avoid puddling. The slope on each side of the crown should be at least 1:200. Parking lots should slope at least 1:100 to shed water, but not more than 5:100.

12. The ground surrounding a building should slope away from the building at a rate of at least 2:100 for at least 6 ft. (1.83 m). This helps keep water from puddling against the foundation and leaking into basements and crawl spaces.

A wash ensures that gravity will act to keep water away from an opening, but its action can be overcome by strong wind currents. Thus, a wash that is contained within a joint is often combined with an air barrier and a pressure equalization chamber to form a rainscreen joint (see **Rainscreen Assembly and Pressure Equalization**, later in this chapter). ■

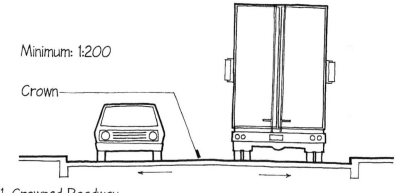

11. Crowned Roadway

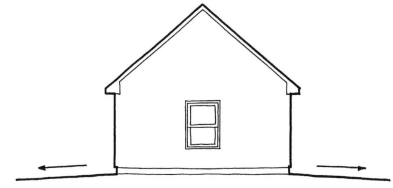

12. Slope Away From Building

Overlap

In an *overlap*, a higher surface is extended over a lower surface so water moved by the force of gravity cannot run behind or beneath them. For an overlapping detail to work, the surfaces must be sloping or vertical. Porous materials need a greater overlap and steeper slope to be effective. The overlap detail pattern is useful to consider when applying off-site panelized and volumetric elements to on-site assemblies.

1. Roof shingles and tiles keep water out by overlapping in such a way that there is no descending path through or between them. Each unit covers a joint between units in the course below. The overlap only works if the roof surface slopes steeply enough so that water runs off before it can find its way around the reverse side of the shingles or tiles to the open cracks beneath.

2. Wood bevel siding sheds water by overlapping each board over the one below. The weak spots in wood siding are the end joints, which should be caulked and flashed to prevent water penetration.

3. Flashings keep water out and protect other materials in a building assembly by overlapping. Flashing is used to create overlap wherever the overlap or slope of base materials is insufficient to prevent water intrusion. This simple Z-flashing of sheet metal or thin plastic keeps water from coming through the crack above a window or door frame.

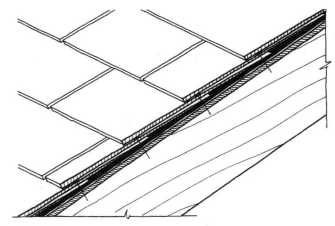

1. Wood Shingle Roofing

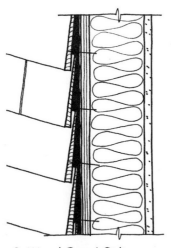

2. Wood Bevel Siding

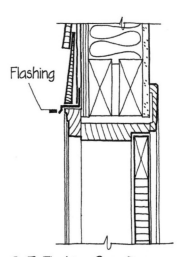

3. Z-Flashing Over Door

4. This lintel flashing in a masonry cavity wall is another example of overlapping. Any water that penetrates the outer brick facing is caught by the metal or synthetic flashing sheet and is conducted through weep holes to the outdoors. Notice the overhang and drip on the outside edge of the flashing. These keep water out of the crack between the flashing and the steel lintel (see *Overhang and Drip*, later in this chapter).

5. A reglet is an upward-sloping slot in a vertical surface into which a flashing or the edge of a roof membrane may be inserted. The slope (wash) acts to prevent water from being forced into the vulnerable joint by gravity, and the overlap of the upper lip of the reglet over the flashing keeps water from reaching the joint between the two components. The reglet shown in this drawing is a traditional type that is largely obsolete, but it may still be encountered when older buildings are renovated. It is molded into glazed terra-cotta tiles that are built into a parapet wall by masons. Shims and/or a sealant bead must be inserted into the reglet to hold the flashing or membrane in place.

6. This contemporary reglet is created in a concrete wall or spandrel beam by using a preformed strip of metal or plastic that is nailed lightly to the formwork before the concrete is poured. The opening in the reglet is usually closed temporarily with an adhesive tape or a strip of plastic foam to prevent its being accidentally clogged with concrete. A variety of patented profiles for this type of reglet are intended to interlock securely with a folded edge on the top of the flashing. Careful inspection is needed just prior to concrete pouring to be sure that the reglet is installed right side up.

If a reglet is wetted, water may find its way through by *capillary action*. (see *Capillary Break*, later in this chapter). Capillary action is associated with surface tension, meaning water can travel horizontally or vertically against the force of gravity in spaces within or between materials. A continuous bead of sealant between the flashing and the reglet can be helpful in preventing this water movement. ▷

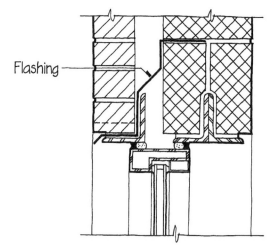

4. Lintel Flashing

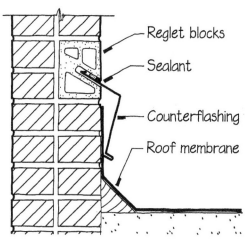

5. Traditional Terra-Cotta Reglet

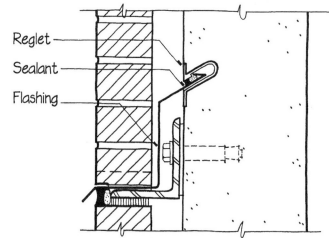

6. Preformed Reglet in Concrete

SECTION 1 ■ FUNCTION 13

7. There are also a number of patented designs of surface-mounted reglets made of plastic or metal. A bead of sealant is intended to keep water from behind the reglet. This is somewhat risky, because the success of the detail is entirely dependent on perfect workmanship in installing the sealant and perfect adhesion of the sealant to the wall.

8. The ridge of a standing seam metal roof uses a continuous cap assembly to overlap all of the standing seams, producing covered openings through which water cannot enter, but hot air can escape.

An overlap is generally very effective in preventing entry of water driven by the force of gravity. If wind is allowed to blow through an overlap, however, it may carry water with it. An overlap is useless against standing water, so it cannot be used on a level surface.

9. Panelized wall assemblies provided by off-site fabricators can use substrate and trim materials to overlap and cap the vulnerable seam between individual panels. A prefabricated wall panel – including primary structure, sheathing, insulation, fenestration, and exterior finish materials – simplifies the construction process (see Chapter 13) and reduces potential points of weakness in the building envelope. ■

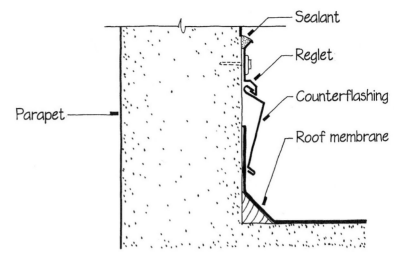

7. Surface-Mounted Reglet

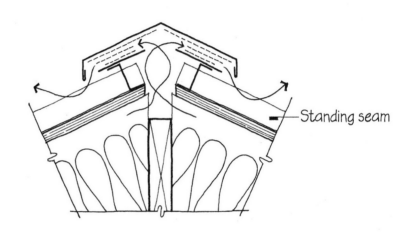

8. Continuous Ridge Vent with Standing Seam Metal Roof

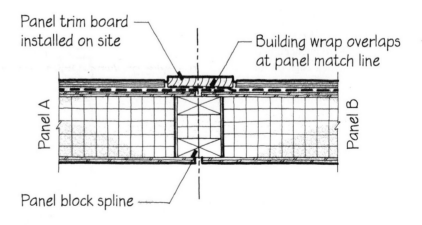

9. Panelized Wall Assemblies

Overhang and Drip

Drops or streams of water adhering to and running down the wall of a building can be kept away from an opening in the wall by a twofold strategy: (1) creating a projecting profile (an *overhang*) just above the opening and (2) creating a continuous groove or ridge in the underside of the projection (a *drip*) so that gravity will pull the adhering water free of the overhang.

1. The size of an overhang is determined by its function. The width of an overhang that protects a seam or joint does not need to extend far from the face of the surface it is protecting. An overhang meant to protect a tall exterior wall must be much wider to be effective. The wider the overhang, the greater the wall area below that will be protected, because wind-driven rain falls at an angle, not straight down.

The angle of falling rain during a storm is difficult to predict accurately, but a good rule of thumb is to add 20 to the wind speed (in mph) at the time of the rain. The sum is the approximate angle from the vertical of the falling rain. Rain falling with a 20 mph (32 kph) wind would fall at an angle of about 40 degrees off of vertical; at 40 mph (64 kph) it would fall at approximately 60 degrees off of vertical. Greater overhang width also moves the splash of the water on the ground below farther from the wall face, decreasing secondary wetting and soiling of the wall surface. ▷

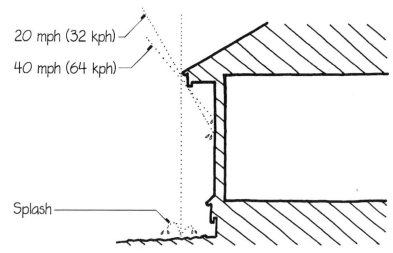

1a. Overhang and Wind-Driven Rain

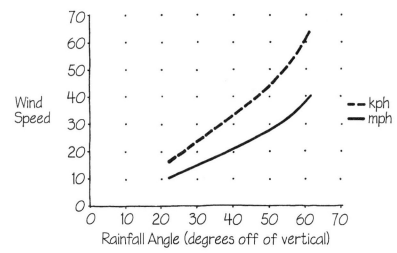

1b. Angle of Wind-Driven Rainfall

2. These are two versions of a door sill detail: one executed entirely in wood and the other in a combination of wood and aluminum components. There are two openings that must be protected in either case: the crack between the door and the sill, and the joint between the sill and the wall of the building. The door cannot fit tightly to the sill because a generous clearance is required to allow free operation of the door. We would certainly weatherstrip this crack, but the weatherstrip is intended only as a barrier to the passage of air (see Chapter 2) and should not be relied upon to prevent water from passing. We would want the installer to bed the sill in sealant, but the sealant work might be imperfect, and it would deteriorate over time. The overhang and drip is a simple, economical, and highly effective detailing element that shows up in many kinds of details.

In these two drawings, we see it used to protect the two openings beneath a door. In the lower part of both these details, the sill overhangs the wall below. In the wood sill detail (2a), the drip is simply a groove milled into the bottom of the wooden sill. The groove must be wide enough and deep enough so that a drop of water cannot bridge it: Usually a width of ¼ in. (6 mm) and a depth of ⅛ in. (3 mm) are about right. In the aluminum sill detail (2b), the drip is formed by the downturned outer edge of the extrusion. In either case, adhering drops of water cannot move across the drip. To do so, they would have to move uphill, against the force of gravity. Therefore, they collect at the outer edge of the drip and fall free. Notice in both cases that the sill has a wash to drain water away from the door.

On the bottom of the door in both details is a second type of overhang and drip that protects the crack between the door and the sill. The overhang is provided by a wooden or aluminum drip strip that is screwed tightly to the door. The underside of the drip strip is configured so that water must drip free at the outer edge, well clear of the crack between the door and the sill. The top of the drip strip, of course, has a steep wash in each case.

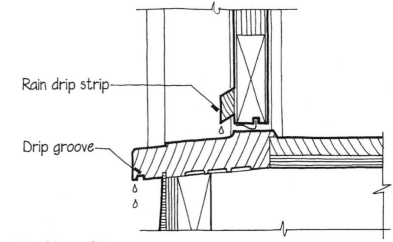

2a. Wood Door Sill

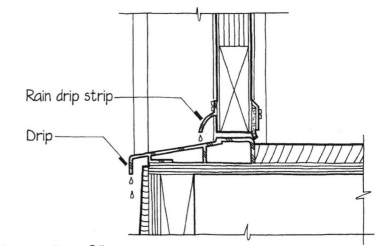

2b. Aluminum Door Sill

3. Standard exterior details of wood frame buildings contain several examples of the overhang and drip principle. Roof shingles overhang the fascia board and slope upward so that water will drip clear of the joint between the fascia and the shingles. The lower edge of the fascia projects below the horizontal soffit so that water running down the fascia will drip free of the crack between the fascia and the soffit. The whole eave is a large overhang and drip that keeps water off the vulnerable upper edge of the wall and adds some protection to window and door openings. At the base of the wall, a traditional water table detail consists of an overhang and drip designed to keep water out of the crack between the wood wall and the foundation. Whether or not a water table is used, the bottom edge of the siding should be spaced away from the foundation wall to create another overhang and drip.

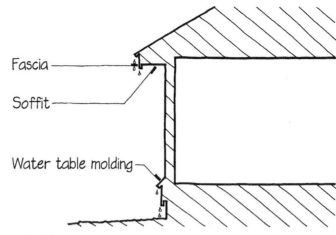

3. Wood Frame Wall

4. The stone or concrete coping atop a masonry parapet wall is sloped toward the inside of the building to help prevent staining and leaking of the outer surface of the wall. A generous overhang and a drip are provided to keep water out of the mortar joint immediately beneath the coping. Additionally, the metal flashing in this mortar joint projects outward and downward to provide another overhang and drip.

The seam between the metal counterflashing and roof membrane, where the roof joins the parapet wall, is potentially troublesome. The counterflashing and roof membrane often fit closely enough that water entering the seam would be pulled into it by capillary action. The overhang and drip in the counterflashing profile keeps the seam dry. As a backup precaution, the counterflashing is also folded out to create a **Capillary Break** (see information later in this chapter). For ease of installation, the counterflashing is often made in two pieces, as shown. The first piece is embedded in the wall by the masons and the second piece is inserted into the first and screwed to it by the roofing installers. ▷

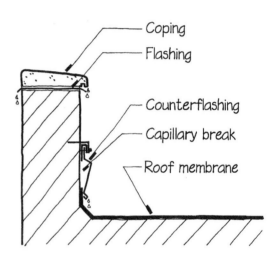

4. Masonry Parapet

5. A drip should always be provided under the outer edge of an overhanging story of a building. In a wood building, the bottom edge of the siding can usually be projected below the soffit to provide a drip. In a concrete or stone building, a drip groove around the outer edge of the soffit will prevent leakage and staining of the soffit area.

6. Internal flashings in masonry veneers sometimes catch and divert relatively large volumes of water as the mortar joints in the veneer above age and deteriorate. Each flashing should project completely through the outer face of the masonry by roughly ¾ in. (19 mm) and turn down at 45 degrees to keep the draining water from wetting the mortarless horizontal joint beneath the flashing. The detailer should resist the urge to recess the outer edge of the flashing into the mortar joint. This might look better than a projecting flashing, but it can lead to serious leakage and deterioration problems beneath the flashing. Flashing is most effective when it overlaps seams in the substrate.

7. A larger-scale overhang and drip in the form of a porch roof or marquee offers the building user the opportunity to leave a door or a window open for ventilation or access even during moderately severe rainstorms.

The problems in making the cracks around exterior doors waterproof are significant: A reasonable solution is to provide a small protective roof above every exterior door in a building. ■

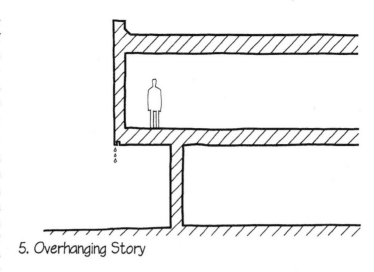
5. Overhanging Story

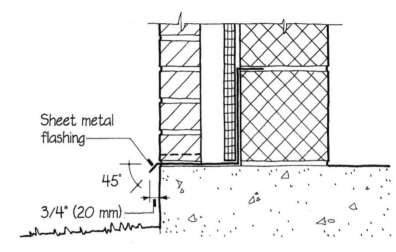
6. Flashing Drip Detail

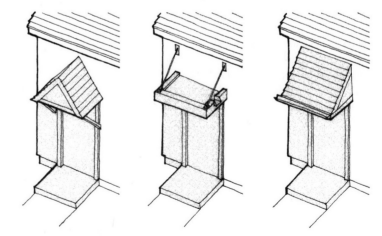
7. Roof Over Door

Drain and Weep

Drain and *weep* details collect and conduct away any water that may leak through the outer layer of a building cladding system. An internal drainage system acknowledges that things can go wrong in sealants, glazing compounds, gaskets, mortar joints, and metal connections – whether the problem is caused by faulty materials, inadequate workmanship, building movement, or deterioration of materials over time. This type of drainage system also releases any water that condenses inside the assembly or is introduced from interior sources. It is inexpensive insurance against the damage that can be caused by uncontrolled leakage and the expense of rebuilding a wall of flawed design. An internal drainage system is composed of spaces or channels that conduct water by gravity to weep holes or other openings that direct the water away from the building.

1. The rafter detail of a basic wood- or metal-framed greenhouse is extremely simple. Sheets of polycarbonate glazing that bear on the rafter are secured with rubber gaskets and aluminum extrusions that are held on with screws. This is not a rainscreen detail; any defect in the rubber gaskets will result in water leakage between the glazing and the rafter. Because of surface tension, water that has leaked through may cling to the rafter and run down its sides. This detail furnishes small drainage gutters in the upper surface of the gasket, located below the polycarbonate glazing. These gutters will catch this water and conduct it to the bottom of the rafter, where it weeps to the outdoors (see also **Condensate Drainage**, Chapter 4). Contemporary manufactured skylight assemblies use similar integral drainage features.

2. The outer wythe of a masonry cavity wall is expected to leak water, especially as the mortar joints age and deteriorate. The leakage drains down the cavity until it encounters an interruption of the cavity, such as a window, door lintel, or the base of the wall. At each of these conditions, continuous flashing collects the water and drains it through weep holes that are provided at horizontal intervals of from 8 to 32 in. (203 to 813 mm). ▷

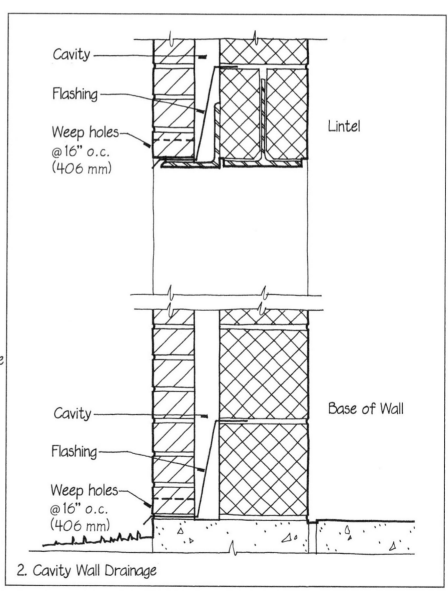

1. Greenhouse Rafter

2. Cavity Wall Drainage

3. The horizontal mullion of an aluminum curtain wall acts as a gutter to accumulate leakage if the seal between the glass and the glazing gasket is imperfect. Weep holes discharge this leakage back to the outdoors. A window of average width might have three weep holes distributed across its sill. Refer to manufacturers for weep hole recommendations. Wind can drive water back through a weep hole if there is not an adequate air barrier between the weep hole and the interior of the building. This possibility can be minimized by locating the weep hole in a sheltered location unlikely to get wet and by inserting a baffle behind the weep hole. The baffle is made of a nondecaying, noncorroding open-celled material that allows water to filter out by gravity, but slows entering air currents through the opening. A typical baffle material is a nonwoven mat composed of stiff plastic filaments.

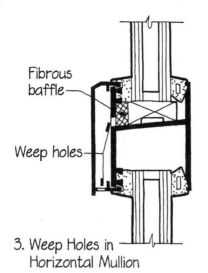

3. Weep Holes in Horizontal Mullion

4. In detailing a rainscreen panel system (see **Rainscreen Assembly and Pressure Equalization**, later in this chapter), it is important to design a three-dimensional system for draining the open joints. Especially crucial is the design of the intersections of the horizontal and vertical joints, which need to be detailed carefully for ease of assembly and for rain-tightness. Any cavity between rainscreen panels and the air barrier wall must also be drained, using a detail similar to that used in a masonry cavity wall (see detail 2). ■

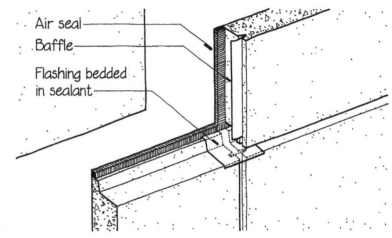

4. Rainscreen Panel Joint Intersection

Unobstructed Drainage

Water sometimes leaks into an assembly because of an inadequate or poorly maintained drainage mechanism. To achieve *unobstructed drainage*, designers must trace the path of water from where it first contacts the building to its point of discharge, to be sure that the path will be effective. The best drainage mechanisms remove water swiftly and directly. Gutterless overhangs and scuppers release water to fall by gravity, without a continuous drainage mechanism. Special attention is called for when drainage lines are concealed inside of roof or wall assemblies, because they are difficult to detect and expensive to repair.

1. Water collected in a drainage system needs to move smoothly to the discharge point by avoiding flat or circuitous paths. Paths should consist of fluid shapes, even though they may be made of sheet metal or rigid plastic. Even short distances where water is stationary can allow waterborne sediment to collect, possibly slowing or blocking the flow of water. Transitions, such as a roof drain junction in a low-slope roof, intersecting sloped roofs, and bends in the leader that carries water down through the building, are all points where turbulence is expected. Careful detailing and installation are needed to avoid obstructions and leaks at conditions like these.

2. Anticipate where obstructions may occur and include features that minimize threats to effective performance. Use rainfall intensity data from the relevant plumbing code – such as the International Plumbing Code / Storm Drainage – for the building location to calculate the volume of water to be carried by the drainage system. Include a safety factor to accommodate unusual weather, ice damming, or poor maintenance. The safety factor should double if multiple adverse factors are expected. Scale gutters, leaders, and scuppers generously, and avoid abrupt reductions in the size of the channel that carries the water. Provide accessible cleanouts at the locations where

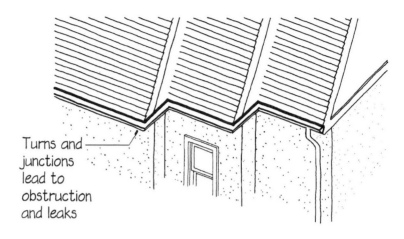

1. Irregular Gutter Configuration

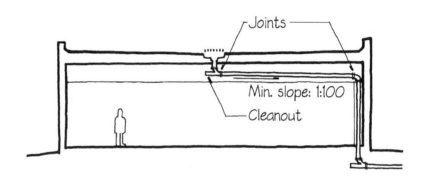

2. Concealed Roof Drain

obstruction is most likely. Where possible, include details that separate waterborne debris from the moving water. Filters or strainers at the point where water enters a roof drain, gutter, or leader are a common solution but require periodic maintenance to remove debris.

3. Joints in water drainage systems that carry precipitation, snowmelt, and condensation typically are not sealed as tightly as plumbing pipes that contain water under pressure. When drainage channels are obstructed, water may collect and cause leakage at joints. Drainage lines concealed within a wall cavity or roof assembly should be watertight to prevent leaks that are difficult to find and correct. Concealed drains are subject to testing by code inspectors. In one such test, the drain lines are filled with water and must remain watertight for at least 15 minutes.

Ventilated Cold Roof

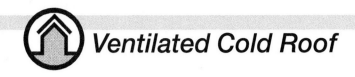

In a traditional ventilated wood-framed attic assembly, the outer surface of a roof in a snowy climate should be kept cold in winter to prevent snow from melting. Roof drainage systems often become clogged with snow and ice during cold winter weather. When meltwater runs down the roof and reaches ice-clogged gutters, drains, or eaves, pools can form that are deep enough to back up around flashings and shingles and thereby leak into the building assembly. Ventilating the underside of the roof deck with outdoor air can keep the roof cold enough so that the snow will not melt, except in above-freezing outdoor temperatures that will also melt the snow and ice in the drainage system.

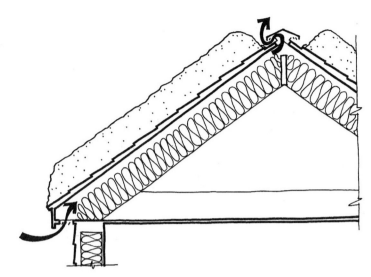

1. Ventilated Eave and Ridge

1. For cold roofs, most building codes require a prescribed minimum amount of net free ventilation area at eave and ridge in a sloping roof – commonly 1/300 of the area of the space to be ventilated. A building with a ceiling area of 3,000 square feet (279 sq. m), for example, would require a total of at least 10 square feet (0.93 sq. m) of net free ventilation opening. Half this amount should be distributed along the ridge or high in the gable ends and the other half should be distributed along the eaves. These high and low ventilation openings allow convection to work efficiently to remove heat from the roof space or attic. Appropriate ventilation louvers for this purpose are available from a number of manufacturers, which list the net free ventilation area for each product.

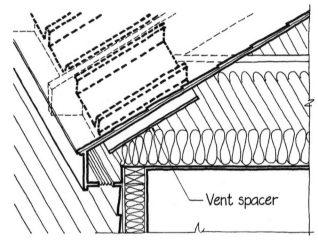

2. Vent Spacers

2. It is important to detail the cold roof so that all ventilation takes place above the thermal insulation in the roof. Most building codes require that ventilated roof assemblies have a minimum of 1 in. (25 mm) of air space between the insulation and the roof sheathing. In any situation where insulation might accidentally block the ventilating cavities beneath the roof sheathing, vent spacer channels made of foam plastic or paper-board should be used to maintain open air passages. These channels are especially appropriate when loose fill, batt insulation, or spray-in-place foam insulation is used.

Roof ventilation also serves to carry away any water vapor that may pass through defects in the vapor retarder or through ceiling penetrations, such as light fixtures and attic hatches.

3. In cold climates, the required amount of insulation may exceed the available depth provided by ceiling joists or roof rafters. In this case, a raised-heel truss may be the best means to provide plenty of space for attic insulation and ventilation at the eave.

4. In snowy environments, some buildings with low-slope roofs are furnished with a strong horizontal lattice construction several feet above the roof that catches and holds snow, keeping the roof membrane below free of snow and ice. When the weather is warm enough to melt the snow, the water drips through the lattice and is carried away by the membrane and roof drains. The space between the roof membrane and the lattice is open to the air and tall enough for inspection and maintenance. ■

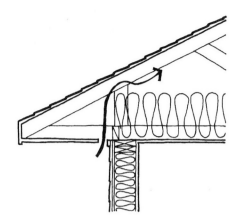

3. Raised-Heel Truss

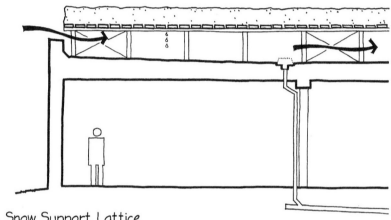

4. Snow Support Lattice

Foundation Drainage

Basements tend to leak. Water is almost always present in the surrounding soil. There are always openings in basement walls: Concrete and masonry foundation walls are full of cracks, pores, and utility line penetrations, and the joint between a basement floor slab and a foundation wall is difficult to make waterproof. Strong forces to move any water through the openings are also present, especially hydrostatic pressure. Removing water from the soil around a basement by means of foundation drainage is the surest way to keep the basement from leaking. Foundation drainage has the added benefit of reducing or eliminating the water pressure that tends to collapse the basement walls. These principles also apply to buildings without basements because groundwater can harm slabs on grade and crawl space foundation systems.

1. Slopes and swales are a first line of defense against water around a basement. They provide a simple system of sloping surfaces (see **Wash**, earlier in this chapter) of earth or paving that encourage surface water to drain away from the basement rather than toward it. Gradients of 2–10% are recommended for a distance of at least 6 ft. (1.83 m) from the house.

Roof drainage systems, including perimeter gutters or internal roof drains, collect roof water so that it can be directed away from the foundation and basement.

2. The second line of defense against water around a basement consists of perforated drain piping that is laid in porous material at the base of the basement wall. On very wet sites drain piping is sometimes laid under the floor slab as well. The porous material against the wall may be either crushed stone (of uniform particle size, for maximum porosity) and/or a thick panel or mat of synthetic material that contains large internal passages for water. When water moves through the ground toward the basement wall, it first reaches the porous layer, where gravity pulls it rapidly downward.

As water accumulates at the base of the wall, it enters the open drain piping and flows by gravity either to an outlet down the slope from the building or to a sump in the basement floor, from which it is ejected by an automatic pump.

The drain piping has a line of holes or slots in it to allow water to enter. The pipe provides an unobstructed lateral passage for water through the crushed stone. Provided the pipe is placed lower than the slab of the basement it is protecting, it makes no difference whether the holes face up, down, or sideways, except that downward-facing holes allow water to enter the pipe at a lower elevation than the other orientations.

Fine soil particles can be carried into the drainage layer by water percolating through the soil. Eventually, these particles may clog the pores of the drainage material. To prevent this, it is good practice to provide a synthetic filter fabric between the drainage material and the soil. The fabric allows water to pass freely, while straining out the soil particles. ∎

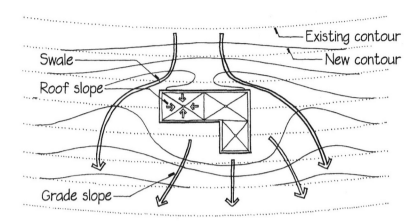

1. Plan of Surface Drainage

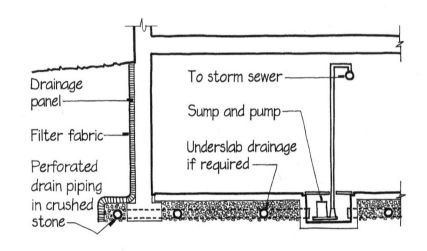

2. Foundation Drainage

Moisture Break

Most exterior building materials are not completely waterproof. When water comes in contact with permeable exterior materials, such as wood, concrete, stucco, and masonry, moisture may migrate into the material and may continue to move through the assembly, using porous materials as its path. Moisture can be prevented from moving through assemblies by using a cavity, an impermeable barrier, or both.

1. A cavity is a void that interrupts a path through one or more porous materials. Moisture reaching a cavity may evaporate or drain down into the cavity and be directed by a flashing through weeps to the exterior. Cavities are often used in vertical assemblies, such as behind stone or masonry veneers. Only metal ties bridge the cavity, These ties do not compromise the moisture break, because they are not water permeable. A reliable continuous water barrier is applied to the interior face of the cavity.

At the bottom of all cavities, an impermeable barrier may be made using a durable flashing material, such as a compatible sheet metal or flexible synthetic flashing.

At the base of the wall, continuous through-wall flashing prevents groundwater from migrating through the concrete and masonry foundation materials This

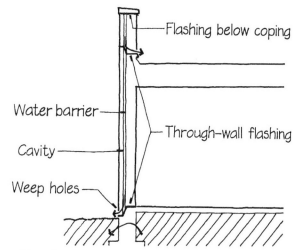

1. Moisture Breaks

flashing is installed near the elevation of finish grade, where the foundation meets the superstructure of the building.

Some of the precipitation that falls on the coping of this building may enter the assembly, either through the coping material or through its joints. Through-wall flashing is installed below the coping to isolate its moisture from the wall below. Parapet materials below the coping may also get wet, and condensation may occur in the upper portion of the wall cavity when temperatures fall below the dew point.

Through-wall flashing is also installed near the base of the parapet to prevent moisture from these sources from entering the lower portions of the wall or the roof assembly.

Through-wall flashing at the base of a cavity will also need weeps, but these are not required when through-wall flashing is not located below a cavity. Through-wall flashing enhances resistance to moisture intrusion, but it may compromise the structural integrity of the wall, so consultation with the structural engineer is recommended.

Capillary Break

Water can pull itself by capillary action across and even upward through a narrow crack but not a wide one. To prevent capillary entry of water, create a capillary break by enlarging the crack internally to a dimension large enough so that a drop of water cannot bridge across it, at least ¼ in. (6 mm).

1. This drawing shows a vertical edge between two exterior cladding panels that we want to place only ⅛ in. (3 mm) apart. If this edge is wetted, water will be drawn into the narrow opening by capillary action. When the water reaches the capillary break, however, it will be unable to bridge it, and it will not pass farther toward the interior of the building unless pushed by wind forces.

2. In this horizontal joint between wall panels, a capillary break is created by enlarging the clear dimension of the labyrinth joint in the center of the panels.

3. Traditional detailing of the sill of a wood window shows a capillary break created by milling a groove in the under edge of the sash.

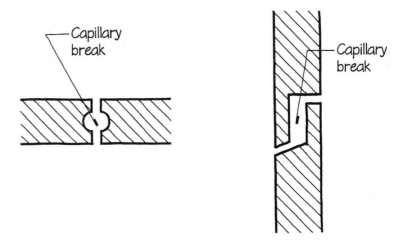

1. Vertical Panel Joint

2. Horizontal Panel Joint

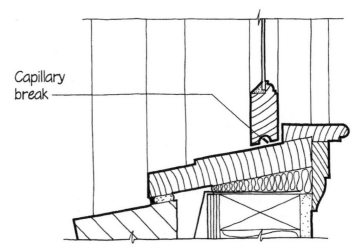

3. Wood Window Sash at Sill

4. There are two capillary breaks in this detail of an aluminum window: one between the sash and the frame, and another between the aluminum frame and the stone sill.

5. A parapet counterflashing can pull water by capillary action through the narrow crack between itself and the upturned edge of the roofing membrane underneath. This possibility can be avoided by bending the sheet metal flashing so that it creates a capillary break.

A capillary break serves only to neutralize capillary action as a force that can move water through a building assembly. It is a reliable and useful component of an overall strategy for making an assembly watertight, but it is not capable of resisting water penetration caused by gravity, momentum, or wind.

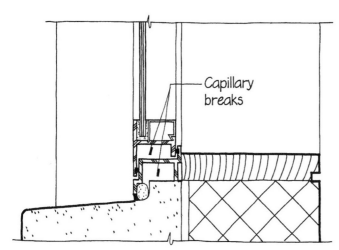

4. Metal Sash at Sill

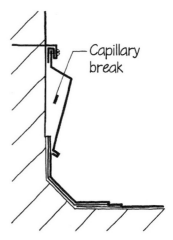

5. Counterflashing

Labyrinth

When a joint is designed so that no straight line may pass through it without striking solid material, then a raindrop or a snowflake cannot pass through the joint by its own momentum.

1. A windblown raindrop or snowflake possesses momentum that can move it through an opening in a building wall. A raindrop striking this open horizontal joint between two stone or precast concrete wall panels, for example, will splatter water through the joint toward the interior of the building, unless the joint is configured as a simple labyrinth.

2. This is a labyrinth design for the vertical joints in metal-clad foam composite panels.

3. A labyrinth can also be executed in extruded aluminum or other metal.

4. This rigid metal or plastic baffle is another approach to designing a vertical labyrinth joint. It is intended only to block water driven by momentum, so it fits loosely in the grooves. In this type of joint, the panel edges are not as fragile as in some of the other kinds of labyrinth joints, and there are no left-hand and right-hand panel edges to keep track of – both vertical edges of every panel are the same.

5. The astragal is a traditional labyrinth design that is used to keep water drops from being blown through the vertical crack between a pair of swinging doors.

    A labyrinth is a very useful part of an overall strategy for preventing water penetration into a building, but it is not sufficient to prevent the passage of windblown water or snow; it must be combined with an air barrier and a pressure equalization chamber (see the following section). ■

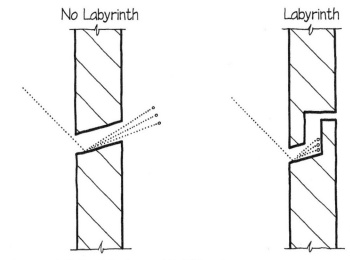

1. Horizontal Joint Between Wall Panels

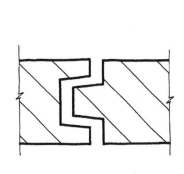

2. Vertical Labyrinth Joint Between Wall Panels

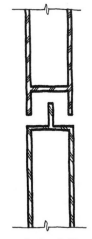

3. Aluminum Labyrinth Joint

4. Baffle in Vertical Joint   5. Astragal

Rainscreen Assembly and Pressure Equalization

A detail that blocks air currents from passing through a joint will resist water being pushed through the joint by air pressure differentials. For the same reason that you cannot blow much air into an empty soft drink bottle, wind and water cannot readily enter a joint made in this way.

1. By using a combination of *Wash, Labyrinth, Capillary Break,* and *Overhang and Drip*, designing a low-maintenance wall or window joint is achievable. Such a joint will resist the entry of water driven by the forces of gravity, momentum, capillary action, and surface tension. If this joint is wetted, however, and if a current of air is passing through from outside to inside, the air current can blow or pump water and vapor through the joint.

To look at it another way, the passage of the air current indicates the air pressure outside the joint is higher than the air pressure inside. This difference in pressure represents potential energy that can move water from outside to inside. Such differences in pressure exist on every building exposed to wind, which is why most water leaks in building skins occur in windy, rainy weather.

2. Air currents can force water through even circuitous joints, so an air barrier is used behind an outer rainscreen to limit the penetration of even storm-force winds. The wall panels themselves are referred to as a rainscreen, meaning that they act to screen out rainwater except at the joints. A rainscreen also deflects the kinetic force of wind-driven rain and reduces air pressure in the cavity by reducing the wind's velocity.

In projects where wind-driven precipitation is of greater concern, a pressure equalization chamber (PEC) can be created. A PEC is a container of air maintained at the same pressure as the air outside the wall by means of tiny movements of air in and out of the PEC vents.

The smaller the volume of air in the chamber, the more quickly the air pressure in the chamber equalizes the outside wind's air pressure. Quickly equalizing air pressure allows less water to be driven by wind into the assembly. The pressure equalization strategy can be applied to small joints, and to the wall as a whole. The entire assembly of rainscreen, air barrier, and PEC is known as a rainscreen assembly, and the principle by which it works is known as the rainscreen principle. ▷

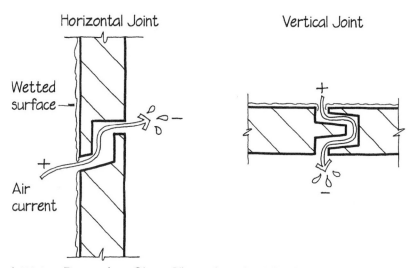

1. Water Pumped or Blown Through a Joint by Air Currents

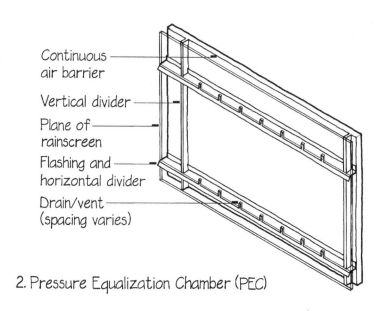

2. Pressure Equalization Chamber (PEC)

SECTION 1 ■ FUNCTION 29

3. This is the same pair of details as in the first drawing, with the addition of a bead of sealant along the interior edge of the joint. We will assume for the moment that the sealant is perfectly airtight. Now air can pass in and out of the joint, but it can no longer pass through it. If a sudden gust of wind raises the pressure on the outside of the wall, air will be forced into the open interior of the joint by the increased external pressure. After only a very small amount of air has moved into the joint, however, the air pressure inside the joint will equal the air pressure outside, and air movement will cease. Because the two air pressures are equal, there is no energy available to pump water, so water will not penetrate past the joint. Damp-tolerant materials (see **Robust Assemblies**, Chapter 10) must be used to make the joint. The sealant joint in this detail never becomes wet; it serves only as an air barrier. The large capillary break inside the joint has now taken on a second function: It works also as a pressure equalization chamber.

4. The location of the sealant in the joint is important, especially if there is a defect in the sealant. Perhaps the sealant never adhered properly to one of the panels, or perhaps it has grown old and cracked, creating a small opening through which air or water can pass. Unless the sealant falls completely out of the joint, however, it will prevent most air from passing, and the small amount of air that does pass will not be sufficient to disrupt seriously the automatic pressure-equalizing action that prevents the pumping of water through the joint. As a rule of thumb, if the total area of leaks in the air barrier is no larger than $\frac{1}{10}$ of the total area of the openings that the air barrier protects, leakage is unlikely.

Contrast this with a defective sealant installation on the outside of the same joint instead of on the inside. The sealant will be bathed with water during a rainstorm, and water will be forced through the defect by even small differences in air pressure between the inside and outside. This demonstrates that the outside of a joint is not the place to install an air barrier, because in this position the air barrier only works if it is perfect. The proper location for an air barrier is on the inside of the joint, where it is always dry and where small holes, cracks, or other defects will not impair its action.

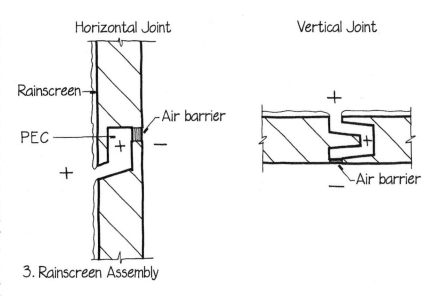

3. Rainscreen Assembly

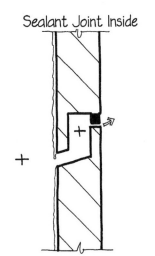
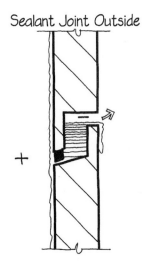

4. Effect of Defective Sealant Joints

5. This is the sill of an ordinary wood window. The detail to the left incorporates all the principles we have identified so far for keeping water from penetrating: There is a wash on the sill to prevent water entry by gravity, and an overhang and drip beneath it to prevent water entry by surface tension. The L-shaped crack between the sash and the sill is a labyrinth that eliminates momentum as a force that can move water through the window unit. The groove in the bottom of the sash is a capillary break. With the addition of a reasonably airtight weatherstrip at the inside end of the crack, the groove becomes a pressure equalization chamber (PEC), and wind forces are neutralized. This detail represents a complete strategy for keeping water out – a true rainscreen detail.

The detail to the right differs from the one to the left only in the location of the weatherstrip. If the weatherstrip in this example has even a small leak, water can be forced through it during wind-driven rainstorms and can easily be pumped up onto the window stool inside.

6. To the left is a door sill that illustrates a complete rainscreen strategy for preventing water penetration. The PEC is the space under the aluminum drip strip. The air barrier is a weatherstrip on the inside face of the door (it could also be inside the crack). The rainscreen is the door itself.

The sill detail to the right shows an available type of drip strip that incorporates a synthetic rubber weatherstrip. The weatherstrip is placed just to the inside of the PEC and will remain dry and effective in this location. If it were placed, instead, at the outside edge of the drip strip, the entire detail would be unreliable.

7. The left-hand detail represents a horizontal joint between two composite metal panels of a curtain wall system. It includes a wash, a labyrinth, and an internal drip. An air barrier is provided by two synthetic rubber gaskets that are inserted into a narrow aluminum channel just behind the metal panel. This is a simple rainscreen detail. Even if the gasket does not seal perfectly, this detail will not leak.

The right-hand detail is not a rainscreen detail. It relies completely on the integrity of the sealant joint. It is much simpler and less expensive to install, but it is unreliable, because any defect in the sealant will cause a water leak. An improved two-stage drained sealant joint, which creates a PEC in the small chamber between the two sealants, is shown in ***Sealant Joints and Gaskets***, later in this chapter.

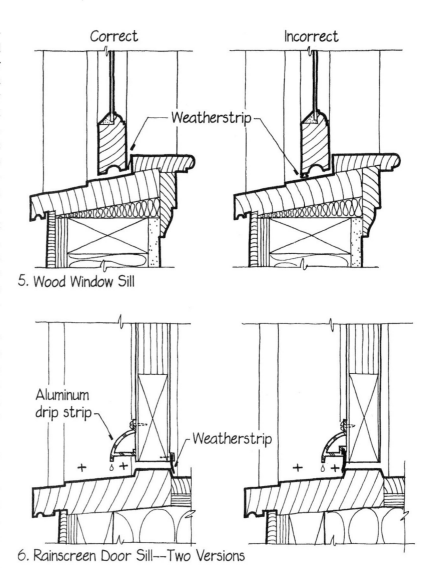

5. Wood Window Sill

6. Rainscreen Door Sill—Two Versions

7. Horizontal Panel Joints

8. This is a typical sill detail from an aluminum-and-glass curtain wall system. It has a synthetic rubber gasket that is located on the outside of the glass. If the gasket is slightly defective, water will move past it and into the interior aluminum channel beneath the glass. The manufacturer of the wall system has anticipated this possibility, however, and has provided weep holes that will allow the leakage to drain back to the outdoors. There is also a gasket on the inside face of the glass that acts as an air barrier, preventing the water from being pumped farther toward the inside of the building.

In other words, if the external gasket leaks, this detail functions as a rainscreen detail. In a detail like this, the external gasket is called a "deterrent seal," because its role is only to deter the passage of as much water as possible, and not to act as a perfect seal against all water penetration. The internal gasket is called an "air seal" to indicate that it functions as an air barrier in a rainscreen detail.

9. The traditional masonry cavity wall is a rainscreen design. The outer wythe of masonry is the rainscreen. The cavity is the pressure equalization chamber – if it is compartmented. The sealed inner wythe of masonry is the air barrier, and the weep holes provide not only for drainage but also for the passage of air to equalize air pressure between the cavity and the outdoors.

10. This drawing illustrates an adaptation of the cavity wall rainscreen design to a building faced with story-high panels of aluminum composite material (ACM). The air barrier wall is composed of steel studs, sheathing, and rigid insulation, covered with a rubberized asphalt mastic coating to make it airtight and water resistant.

In looking at these last two rainscreen designs with their large PECs, there are three important observations to keep in mind.

First, the air barrier, whether it is a backup wall, a gasket, or a bead of sealant, supports all the wind load on its portion of the face of the building. Every air barrier must be engineered to support full wind load. In a masonry cavity wall, the backup wall, not the facing, supports the wind load. In the

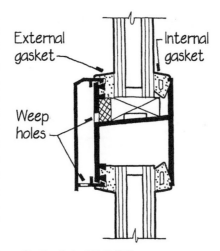

8. Curtain Wall Sill

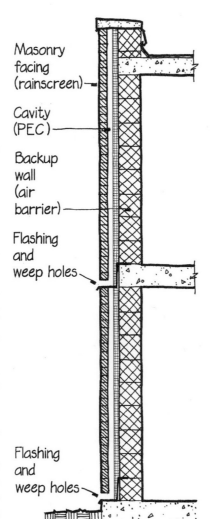

9. Masonry Cavity Wall

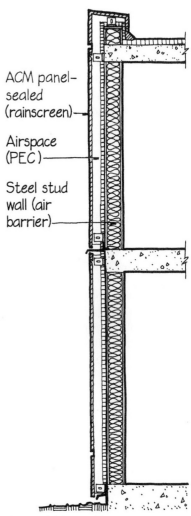

10. ACM Panel Rainscreen Wall

32 PART I ■ DETAIL PATTERNS

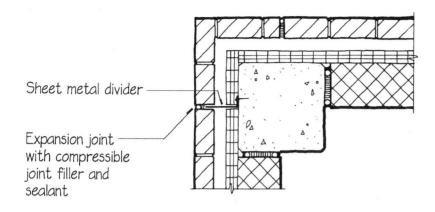

Sheet metal divider

Expansion joint with compressible joint filler and sealant

11. Vertical PEC Divider

ACM panel wall shown in drawing 10 of this section, the metal studs must be engineered to withstand the full wind load regardless of the stiffness of the panels. At a door sill, the weatherstrip must be sufficiently stiff to resist the force of wind upon it. The area of the weatherstrip is small, so the total wind force on it is similarly small, but the backup wall is large in area and must absorb a large load.

Second, wind pressure varies considerably across the face of a building. In a freestanding tall building, pressures are much higher at upper stories of the building than at lower stories, and pressures near the edges of a facade are much different from those in the middle. Some areas of a wall are subject to suctions rather than positive pressures because of the aerodynamics of a building. Buildings in urban settings often have highly variable pressure gradients near adjoining buildings. Because of this, it is important to divide building facades into compartments. Compartments may be larger in the central portion of a facade, but they should be relatively small at building edges and parapets. Air pressure in a smaller compartment equalizes more quickly with the outside air pressure, reducing the volume of air and water entering. The largest compartments may be up to two stories high and one structural bay in width.

Drawing 11 illustrates a vertical PEC divider made of sheet metal that is economically installed into a vertical expansion joint near the corner of a building. If the chamber behind the rainscreen is not compartmented, then air pressure is reduced but not equalized. Air can rush from one part of the building facade to another within the chamber and cause localized pressure differentials that may result in water leakage. The divisions between the compartments need not be absolutely airtight, but they should be designed to choke off most airflow. The dividers can be made of masonry, sheet metal, compressible foam, or any other material appropriate to the wall construction system.

Third, every pressure equalization chamber, no matter the size, must be drained and wept to the outdoors to dispose harmlessly of any water that may enter (see **Drain and Weep**, earlier in this chapter).

The rainscreen approach cannot be applied to solid walls because a solid wall, by definition, cannot contain a pressure equalization chamber. Solid masonry or concrete exterior walls are thought of as face-sealed "barrier walls," meaning they are so thick and so well constructed that leaking is unlikely. The barrier wall approach is far from foolproof, however, because a single crack can allow water to enter the building. ∎

Upstand

An *upstand* is a dam. The principle of the upstand is that wind pressure can drive water uphill only to a height at which the hydrostatic pressure of the standing water retained by the dam is equal to the pressure exerted by the wind. An upstand is used in detailing when it is impractical to provide a reliable air barrier to prevent water from being driven through a horizontal crack by air pressure differentials. This can happen in situations where installation access to the proper location for an air barrier is blocked by a spandrel beam or a column. It can happen at the sill of a door or a window as a gasket or weatherstrip ages, wears, and begins to leak large volumes of air. The upstand reduces pressure that might force water through an imperfect weatherstrip. In any of these cases, a simple upstand can serve to prevent wind pressure from pushing water through a horizontal joint, even if the joint is totally unsealed against air leakage.

The required height of an upstand is determined by the maximum expected wind pressure. To find the wind pressure, find the design wind speed for the building location in the appropriate building code. (Note: Building and site configurations may create local wind speeds that exceed the general wind loads stated in building codes.) Then determine the necessary height of the upstand according to Table 1-1, interpolating as necessary.

TABLE 1-1: Minimum Heights of Upstands

Approximate Wind Speed	Wind Pressure	Upstand Height
45 mph (70 km/h)	5 psf (240 Pa)	1″ (25 mm)
60 mph (100 km/h)	10 psf (480 Pa)	2″ (51 mm)
90 mph (145 km/h)	20 psf (960 Pa)	4″ (102 mm)
110 mph (175 km/h)	30 psf (1,440 Pa)	6″ (152 mm)
125 mph (200 km/h)	40 psf (1,920 Pa)	8″ (203 mm)
140 mph (225 km/h)	50 psf (2,400 Pa)	10″ (254 mm)

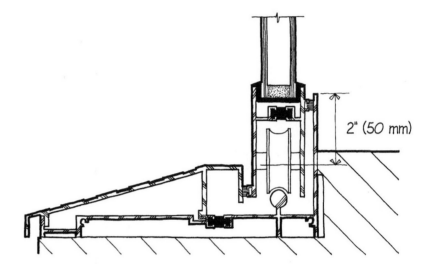

1. Sill of Sliding Glass Door

1. A manufacturer of sliding glass doors recognizes that if the interior weatherstrip becomes sufficiently worn with years of use, the rainscreen action of the sill detail may become inoperative. A 2 in. (51 mm) upstand at the interior side of the door offers a degree of backup protection by preventing leakage up to a maximum wind pressure of 10 psf (480 Pa), equivalent to a 60-mph wind (100 km/h). A taller upstand would offer even more protection against leakage, but this advantage must be weighed against the increased tripping hazard of a taller sill.

2. This horizontal joint between metal curtain wall panels has a 3 in. (75 mm) upstand, giving protection against water penetration at wind pressures as high as 15 psf (720 Pa), even if the gasket has been inadvertently omitted during installation.

3. To prevent water being pumped back through a weep hole by wind pressure, the hole can be drained through a vertical weep tube that exits the wall a distance below the point that is being drained. If there is a vertical distance of 10 in. (254 mm) between the inlet and outlet of a weep tube, for example, it would take a wind of approximately 140 mph (225 km/h) to pump water up and into the building through the tube. This is the upstand principle applied in a different way, using the same table to equate heights of water to pressures of air. The tube diameter must be at least ⅜ in. (9.5 mm) for good drainage; this is also large enough to prevent capillary entry of water.

When detailing an upstand, its ends must be dammed carefully at vertical joints, or the water will simply drain out of the ends to become unwanted leakage. In aluminum cladding details, end dams are often plugs molded of synthetic rubber. ■

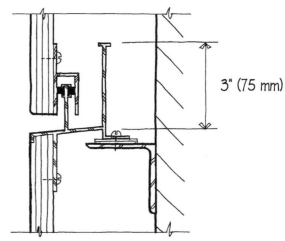

2. Horizontal Joint Between Curtain Wall Panels

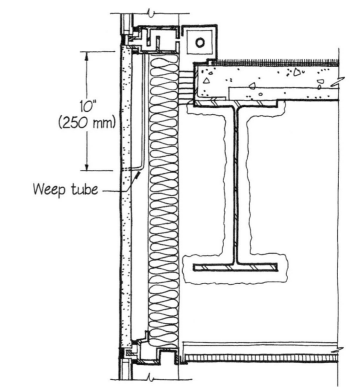

3. Weep Tube in Curtain Wall

Sealant Joints and Gaskets

Sealants and *gaskets* are elastic materials placed in a joint to block the passage of air and/or water, while allowing for relative movement between the two sides of the joint. A gasket is a strip of elastomeric rubber that is compressed into the joint. Most sealants are mastic materials injected into the joint and then cure to a rubberlike state. A gasket seals a surface by compressing tightly against it. A sealant seals by adhering tightly to the surface.

1. The width and depth of a sealant joint must never be left to chance; they should be determined in accordance with the procedure shown in **Expansion Joint** (see Chapter 6). The plastic-foam backer rod is a critical part of every sealant joint: It limits the depth of the sealant to the predetermined dimension, provides a firm surface against which to tool the sealant, and imparts to the sealant bead the 1:2 hourglass shape that optimizes the strength and elasticity of the sealant. The backer rod should be at least 20% larger than the maximum joint width.

2. If the sealant joint is too narrow, normal amounts of movement between the adjoining components can overstretch the sealant and tear it. This can also happen if the sealant joint is too shallow in proportion to its width.

3. If the sealant bead is too deep, stresses in the bead will be excessive, and tearing is likely.

4. Tooling forces the sealant material to fill the joint, assume the desired profile, and adhere to the adjoining components.

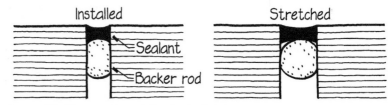

1. Correctly Proportioned Sealant Joint

2. Incorrect: Joint Too Narrow

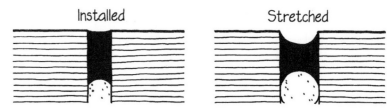

3. Incorrect: Sealant Bead Too Deep

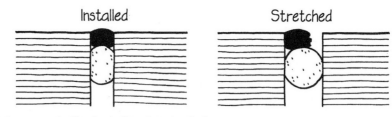

4. Incorrect: Sealant Bead Untooled

5 and 6. In a three-sided sealant joint, bond-breaker tape should be applied against the back of the joint to allow for full extension of the sealant bead when the joint opens.

7. If a sealant joint is too narrow, the sealant may become overcompressed, squeezing it out of the joint and tearing it.

8. Sealant should be applied at an air temperature that is neither too hot nor too cold. If application at very hot or very cold temperatures is anticipated, the initial joint width should be adjusted to compensate for the seasonal overstressing that might otherwise occur. ▷

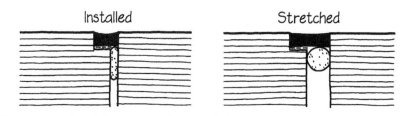

5. Correct: Bond Breaker in Three-Sided Joint

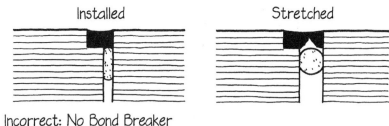

6. Incorrect: No Bond Breaker

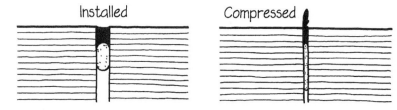

7. Incorrect: Joint Too Narrow

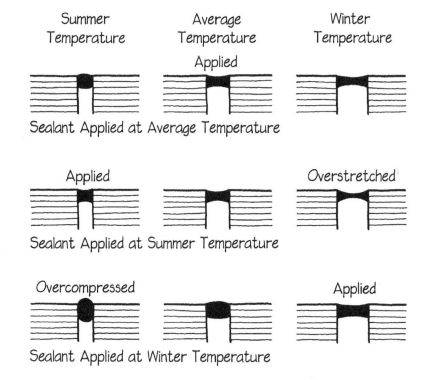

8. Sealant Application and Temperature

SECTION 1 ■ FUNCTION 37

9. A sealant lap joint may be dimensioned using the same procedures as for a normal butt joint, such as those illustrated previously in this section.

10. Even if perfectly installed, sealant joints are likely to fail as the material ages and becomes less elastic. Added protection and durability can be provided by a two-stage drained sealant joint. This consists of the careful installation of backer rod and sealant within the joint and recessed behind the outer sealant joint to produce a small cavity. Two-stage joints require a minimum joint width of ¾ in. (19 mm) for sufficient access by the installer. Vertical two-stage joints must be detailed to drain any water at the bottom of the joints. The cavity between sealants can also be pressure-equalized if the inner seal is airtight.

11. There are many types of glazing details that include wet (gunnable) sealants. In general, these incorporate synthetic rubber spacers that regulate the depth and thickness of the sealant, according to the principles laid out earlier. In the detail to the left in the drawing, the glass is set on synthetic rubber blocks and centered in the metal frame with the aid of compressible spacer strips that also serve as backer rods. This detail minimizes the number of different components needed to install the glass by eliminating any gaskets. The detail to the right uses a preformed synthetic rubber gasket on the interior side for easy installation and a neat appearance. The outside is sealed with a gunnable sealant for maximum security against leakage.

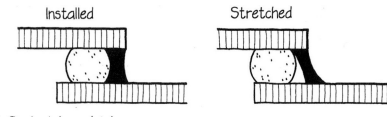

9. Sealant Lap Joint

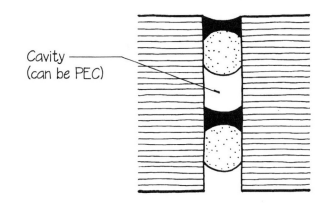

10. Two-Stage Sealant Joint

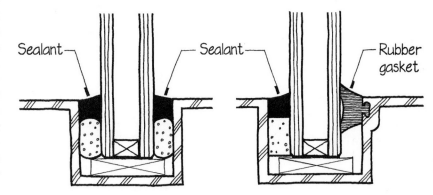

11. Glazing Details Using Wet Sealants

12. This is an example of a preformed synthetic rubber gasket used to close a movement joint in a high-traffic horizontal surface, such as a roadway or a parking garage. The gasket is slightly wider than the joint and must be compressed during installation.

13. Preformed gaskets are widely used to seal between window glass and metal framing. In this example, a closed-cell sponge gasket is inserted first; then the glass is inserted. Finally, a dense gasket in a roll-in wedge profile is forced between the inside face of the glass and the frame, compressing the sponge gasket and holding the entire assembly together. For additional security against water penetration, a bead of gunnable sealant is sometimes placed over the outside gasket. This is called a cap sealant. Gaskets are typically miter-cut to fit snugly at corners.

14. There are many types of synthetic rubber lockstrip gaskets that are useful in glazing applications. This example incorporates a pine tree spline that is inserted into a slot in a concrete sill or jamb. The glass is installed in the gasket, and then the synthetic rubber lockstrip is inserted with a special tool, to make the gasket rigid and lock the glass in place. Lockstrip gaskets are simple and secure but have been found to be vulnerable to water leakage, perhaps because they do not exert sustained pressure on the lip of the gasket against the glass. This vulnerability does not limit their use in interior or sheltered settings. ▷

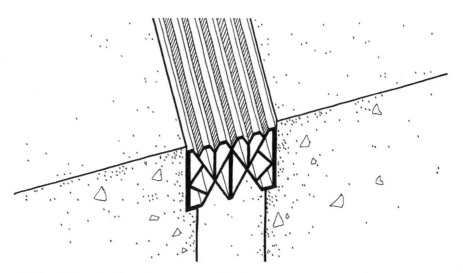

12. Synthetic Rubber Compression Seal

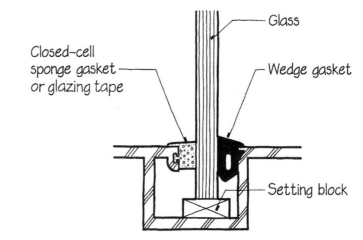

13. Preformed Gasket Glazing

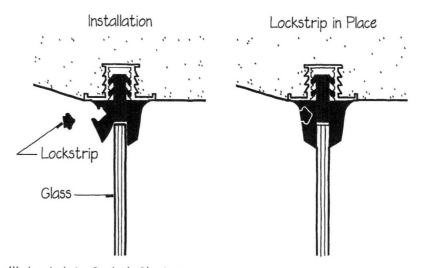

14. Lockstrip Gasket Glazing

15. Preformed solid tape sealants are made to be compressed between components of nonworking joints. The tape is thick and very sticky. The semirigid shim rod in the center of the tape controls the thickness of the joint and limits the tendency of the surrounding mastic to squeeze out.

16. The waterstop is a preformed synthetic rubber gasket used to seal pour joints and movement joints in concrete foundation walls. The example shown here features a center tube that allows the waterstop to stretch or compress considerably in response to movement in the concrete walls. Many other shapes of synthetic rubber waterstops are also manufactured, along with alternative designs made of rigid plastic, metal, mastic, and even bentonite clay, which expands and seals when wetted.

Glazing and cladding details are usually developed by manufacturers of glazing and cladding systems, rather than by detailers in architectural offices. However, it is important for designers and detailers to have a good grasp of detailing principles so that they are able to assess manufacturers' systems and installed work in the field.

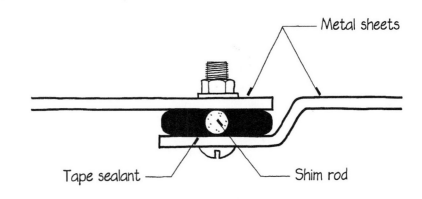

15. Preformed Solid Tape Sealant

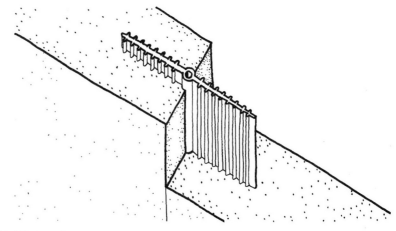

16. Waterstop

PROPORTIONING SEALANT JOINTS

Sealant joints should be provided at frequent enough intervals in a surface so that the expected overall movement in the surface is divided into an acceptably small amount of movement in each joint. Usually, sealant joint spacing is determined by the desired sizes of the panels or sheet materials that make up a wall.

Generally, a sealant joint should not be narrower than ¼ in. (6 mm). A joint narrower than this is difficult to make and has little ability to absorb movement. Joints can be as wide as 1–2 in. (25–51 mm), depending on the ability of the sealant not to sag out of the joint before it has cured. The depth of sealant in a joint should be equal to half the width of the joint, but not less than ¼ in. (6 mm) or more than ½ in. (13 mm). Thus, a ¼-in.-wide joint should be ¼ in. deep (6 × 6 mm), a ¾-in.-wide joint should be ⅜ in. deep (19 × 9 mm), and a 1¼-in.-wide joint should be ½ in. deep (32 × 13 mm).

To determine the required width for a sealant joint in a particular location in a building, many factors must be considered. The spacing between movement joints, the particular materials used, and the climate at the building location are some of these factors.

A complete discussion of this topic, including example calculations of sealant joints, follows in the section "Determining Widths of Sealant Joints."

Determining Widths of Sealant Joints

Calculations of expansion joint intervals and sealant joint widths are interdependent. The width of a sealant joint should be determined by the designer of the building, the detailer, the specifications writer, the suppliers of the components or materials on either side of the joint, and the structural engineer. These collaborators work together using all available information on temperature extremes at the building site, the time of year when the sealant will be installed, the properties of the materials on either side of the joint, the properties of the sealant itself, and the structural characteristics of the frame and skin of the building. For preliminary purposes, the following equation may be used to determine the width of any sealant joint:

$$W = \frac{100}{X}(\varepsilon L \Delta T + M_o) + t$$

where

W = required width of sealant joint

X = % plus or minus movement capability of sealant, expressed as a whole number

ε = coefficient of expansion of skin material

L = length of building skin between joints

ΔT = annual range between extreme high and low temperatures. If specific temperature data is lacking, assume that ΔT is 130°F (54°C)

M_o = anticipated movement due to such nonthermal factors as structural deflections, creep, or moisture expansion and contraction

t = construction tolerance

This formula may be used with either conventional or SI units. Following are three examples of its use.

TABLE 1-2: Coefficients of Linear Thermal Expansion of Common Building Materials (verify properties of specific materials used)

		in./in./°F	mm/mm/°C
Wood (seasoned)			
Douglas fir	parallel to grain	0.0000021	0.0000038
	perpendicular to grain	0.0000320	0.0000580
Pine	parallel to grain	0.0000030	0.0000054
	perpendicular to grain	0.0000190	0.0000340
Oak	parallel to grain	0.0000027	0.0000049
	perpendicular to grain	0.0000300	0.0000540
Maple	parallel to grain	0.0000036	0.0000065
	perpendicular to grain	0.0000270	0.0000486
Masonry and Concrete			
Limestone		0.0000044	0.0000079
Granite		0.0000047	0.0000085
Marble		0.0000073	0.0000131
Brick and terra-cotta		0.0000036	0.0000065
Concrete masonry units, normal aggregate		0.0000052	0.0000094
Concrete masonry units, lightweight aggregate		0.0000043	0.0000077
Concrete		0.0000055	0.0000099
Autoclaved aerated concrete		0.0000045	0.0000081
Metals			
Steel		0.0000065	0.0000117
Stainless steel, Type 304		0.0000099	0.0000173
Aluminum		0.0000128	0.0000231
Copper		0.0000093	0.0000168
Lead		0.0000151	0.0000272
Tin		0.0000161	0.0000290
Titanium		0.0000050	0.0000090
Zinc		0.0000172	0.0000310
Finish Materials			
Gypsum board		0.0000090	0.0000162
Gypsum plaster, sand		0.0000070	0.0000126
Fiber cement panel		0.0000076	0.0000142
Glass		0.0000050	0.0000090
Acrylic glazing sheet		0.0000410	0.0000742
Polycarbonate glazing sheet		0.0000440	0.0000796
Polyethylene		0.0000850	0.0001530
Polyvinyl chloride		0.0000400	0.0000720
Polyester, glass fiber reinforced		0.0000140	0.0000250

Sealant Joint Width Calculations

Example 1 Calculate the required width of a horizontal sealant joint for an all-aluminum curtain wall panel, dark gray in color, that is 6 ft. 8 in. or 80 in. (2032 mm) high. The temperature ranges annually between −40° and +100°F (−40° and +38°C). The building is framed with steel. A sealant with a movement capability of 125% is recommended by the wall panel manufacturer.

The annual range of air temperature is 100° to −40°F = 140°F (78°C), but the sun will heat the dark-colored panel to well above the air temperature. As an estimate, we will add 40°F (22°C) to the temperature to account for this phenomenon, making a total temperature range of up to 180°F (100°C).

The structural engineer estimates that deflections of the spandrel beams and columns under live and wind loadings can total as much as 0.04 in. (1 mm) per panel.

The construction tolerance, the accuracy of the aluminum panels as installed on the building, is estimated by the curtain wall contractor to be ±⅛ in. (3.2 mm). From Table 1-2, we determine that the coefficient of thermal expansion of aluminum is 0.0000128 in./in./°F.

Starting with the given equation:

$$W = \frac{100}{X}(\varepsilon L \Delta T + M_o) + t$$

and substituting,

$$W = \frac{100}{25}[(0.0000128 \text{ in./in./°F})(80 \text{ in.})(180°F) + 0.04 \text{ in.}] + 0.125 \text{ in.}$$

we have $W = 1.02$ in.; use a 1-in.-wide sealant joint or 1⅛ in., if we wish to be conservative. The depth should be ½ in.

This example may be worked in SI (metric) units using the same formula and procedure, so long as all the units of length are consistent and the temperature is converted from Fahrenheit to Celsius.

$$W = \frac{100}{25}[(0.0000231 \text{ mm/mm/°C})(2032 \text{ mm})(100°C) + 1 \text{ mm}] + 3.2 \text{ mm}$$

we have $W = 25.98$ mm; use a 26 mm wide sealant joint. The depth should be 13 mm.

Example 2 Calculate the required width of a sealant joint between white granite wall panels that are 4 ft. 7 in. or 55 in. (1397 mm) in maximum dimension. The annual range of air temperature is from −10° to 110°F (−23° to 43°C). The building structure will be of reinforced concrete, and the structural engineer estimates that creep in the frame will eventually reach about 0.03 in. (0.76 mm) per panel, but that structural deflections will be insignificant. The sealant will have a movement capability of ±25%. The supplier and installer of the granite panels expect to work to an accuracy of ±³⁄₁₆ in. (4.76 mm).

From Table 1-2 in Example 1, we find a coefficient of thermal expansion for granite of 0.0000047 in./in./°F. Starting with the given equation:

$$W = \frac{100}{X}(\varepsilon L \Delta T + M_o) + t$$

and substituting,

$$W = \frac{100}{25}[(0.0000047 \text{ in./in./°F})(55 \text{ in.})(120°F) + 0.03 \text{ in.}] + \frac{3}{16} \text{ in.}$$

we have $W = 0.43$ in.; use a ½-in. joint. A depth of ¼ in. is suitable.

Working in SI (metric) units:

$$W = \frac{100}{25}[(0.0000085 \text{ mm/mm/°C})(1397 \text{ mm})(66°C) + 0.76 \text{ mm}] + 4.76 \text{ mm}$$

we have $W = 10.93$ mm; use a 11-mm joint. A depth of 6 mm is suitable.

Example 3 Calculate the required width of a vertical sealant joint in a brick wall with a joint spacing of 21 ft. 4 in. or 256 in. (6.5 m or 6500 mm). The air temperature range is up to 108°F (60°C). The contractor would like to use a sealant that has a movement capability of ±12.5%. According to *Technical Note No. 18* of the Brick Industry Association, brickwork will expand over time by about ²⁄₁₀₀ of 1% due to moisture absorption. A construction tolerance of ±¼ in. (6 mm) is expected.

According to Table 1-2, the coefficient of thermal expansion of brick masonry is about 0.0000036 in./in./°F (0.0000065 mm/mm/°C). Starting with the given equation:

$$W = \frac{100}{X}(\varepsilon L \Delta T + M_o) + t$$

and substituting,

$$W = \frac{100}{12.5}[(0.0000036 \text{ in./in./°F})(256 \text{ in.})(108°F) + (256 \text{ in.})(0.0002)] + \frac{1}{4} \text{ in.}$$

we have $W = 1.45$ in.

Working in SI (metric) units:

$$W = \frac{100}{12.5}[(0.0000065 \text{ mm/mm/°C})(6500 \text{ mm})(60°C) + (6500 \text{ mm})(0.0002)] + 6 \text{ mm}$$

we have $W = 36.7$ mm

This is very wide, nearly 1½ in. – which would make sealant installation difficult. If a sealant with a ±25% movement capability was used instead, the joint would only need to be ⅞ in. (22 mm) wide, which could be rounded up to 1 in. (25 mm). If a narrower joint is desired, then another sealant with even greater movement capability could be selected. ■

CHAPTER 2 Controlling Air

Controlling air through a building assembly has to do with allowing or preventing air movement. Natural ventilation systems use air pressure differences between outside and inside to move fresh air through buildings. In appropriate climates, natural ventilation of building interiors offers many tangible benefits, such as providing comfort, low installation costs, low maintenance demands, no energy costs, and often improved indoor air quality. Natural ventilation is most viable when:

1. The building is oriented perpendicular to the prevailing wind direction for anticipated cross ventilation.
2. The building width is narrow.
3. The building contains vents or other openings that occupants can operate easily.

Many configurations are possible to encourage desirable air movement through a building. Options such as stack effect may increase effectiveness of natural ventilation even if ambient wind speeds are low.

On the other hand, leaking air, often called *infiltration,* can cause uncomfortable drafts and introduce problems to building performance. Heated and cooled air wasted by leaks through the building envelope represents lost energy. Air leaks are also sound leaks that can destroy the acoustical effectiveness of building enclosures. Air leaks can transmit a fire's heat and smoke from one part of a building to another. Air leaks can bring pollutants, dust, mold spores, and insects into a building. And air is not always dry. Leaking air can transport humidity and rainwater through a wall, window, door, or roof. Leaking air can cause condensate or frost to form in winter, when warmer, more humid indoor air leaks into cold building cavities (see **Warm Interior Surfaces**, Chapter 4).

Air leaks are uncontrolled airflow through the exterior assembly of a building; leaks are driven by pressure differentials between the air inside and outside. Air pressure differences can be created by wind, by a thermal stack effect in a tall building, and by the building mechanical ventilation systems.

Controlled ventilation must not be confused with air leakage. For instance, controlled ventilation of a cold roof assembly is not air leakage, because it is carefully introduced to control temperature and humidity in the roof assembly. A naturally ventilated cavity behind a rainscreen helps the wall control moisture and temperature. Similarly, controlled ventilation of the soil in a residential crawl space below a vapor barrier can carry away radon gasses escaping from the soil in some areas. In all of these examples, ventilation takes place *outside* of the building's air barrier envelope.

To maintain interior air quality some amount of fresh air must enter a building, but we should never rely on air leaks to supply this air. The correct strategy is to seal the building envelope as tightly as possible and ventilate by means of operable windows and vents or through the building's mechanical system.

The principle behind airtight detailing is similar to that for watertight detailing: In order for air to penetrate through a building assembly, three conditions must all occur at the same time:

1. There must be an opening through the assembly.
2. There must be air present at the opening.
3. There must be a force to move the air through the opening.

If any one of these three conditions is not met, air will not penetrate the assembly.

Despite the similarity in principle, however, the detailing strategy for controlling air leakage is rather different from that for controlling water leakage. We are surrounded by air, so we cannot keep it away from openings. Of the forces that move air through openings, convection and wind pressure are largely beyond the control of the building designer. Pressure differentials caused by heating, cooling, and ventilating equipment within the building are consciously regulated in some large buildings, to minimize the loss of conditioned air to the outdoors, but this is not the case in most buildings. Therefore, airflow through a building assembly must be controlled primarily by closing openings in the building assembly to the best of our ability. The detail patterns that relate to this are the following (see the corresponding sections later in this chapter):

Air Barrier System (p. 47)
Weatherstripped Crack (p. 49)

Architectural Detailing: Function Constructability Aesthetics. Fourth Edition. Patrick Rand, Jason Miller, and Edward Allen.
© 2025 John Wiley & Sons, Inc. Published 2025 by John Wiley & Sons, Inc.

In addition to these two patterns, we have already considered in Chapter 1, "Controlling Water," other patterns useful in controlling air leakage:

Ventilated Cold Roof (p. 22)
Rainscreen Assembly and Pressure Equalization (p. 29)
Sealant Joints and Gaskets (p. 36)

Detail selection and development for controlling airflow must consider the durability and expected service life of the system solution. It is important to recognize that air barrier surfaces, weatherstrips, sealant joints, and gaskets are all elements that must withstand wind forces. Therefore, they must be designed with sufficient structural strength and stiffness to withstand, at minimum, the wind loads specified for the cladding of the building. Furthermore, they must reliably do so for the life of the building, because they cannot be readily inspected or repaired. Issues related to detailing for building longevity are addressed in Chapter 10, "Providing or the Aging of the Building":

Life Cycle (p. 146)
Expected Life (p. 148)

When conceived as a well-coordinated group, these features combine to form the air-control layer of the building. As with all control layers in a building – those managing the flows of water, heat, and water vapor – the designer should be able to draw an uninterrupted line in plan and section representing the air control layer.

Air Barrier System

The conditioned spaces of a building should be wrapped in a thin yet durable air barrier system to reduce air leakage through the many different types of small openings that are commonly present in the bottom floor, exterior walls, and roof. From a detailing perspective, achieving appropriate air barrier continuity over the entire building envelope is at once important and complex. A properly installed air barrier system can reduce building energy consumption, control condensation/vapor intrusion, improve interior air quality, and increase the overall durability of the building.

1. The exterior surfaces of a building of wood light frame construction are riddled with openings, primarily the cracks between sheathing panels and the cracks around window and door units. These allow air to filter through electrical boxes, baseboards, and door and window casings into or out of a building. The air leakage along these paths can be reduced greatly by covering the sheathing beneath the siding or roofing with an airtight sheet material or coating. Different material and installation choices impact the level of airtightness in a light wood frame building.

A traditional and inexpensive, but ultimately ineffective, form of air barrier surface consists of asphalt-saturated paper. Because the paper (usually referred to as "felt," "building paper," or "tar paper") is furnished in rolls only 36 in. (900 mm) wide, it is easy to install; however, the resulting air barrier has numerous seams that can leak air.

A contemporary solution is an air barrier sheet made of nonwoven polypropylene or spun-bonded polyolefin (SBPO) fibers. This sheet, sometimes referred to as "housewrap," is manufactured in such a way that water vapor can pass through, but air and liquid water cannot. It is so thin and lightweight that it is usually furnished in rolls that are 9 ft. (2.7 m) wide, allowing each story of a simple residential-scale building to be wrapped in a single horizontal band. This greatly reduces the number of seams. Remaining seams at penetrations and perimeters are carefully sealed with a durable tape or sealants, often provided for this purpose by the housewrap manufacturer. The structural resistance to wind loading is furnished not by the air barrier sheet itself, but by the materials between which it is sandwiched – for example, the wall sheathing on one side and the rigid insulation or siding on the other.

Integrated water-resistive barrier/air barrier (WRB/AB) sheathing combines control layers and engineered wood or gypsum panels into a single product. WRB/AB sheathing is usually furnished in 4 ft. × 8 ft. (1.2 m × 2.4 m) panels, $7/16$ in. or $5/8$ in. (11 mm × 16 mm) thick. Seams at panel joints, corners, or openings are sealed with a durable tape, liquid flashing, or transition membranes. These flexible joint seals establish a continuous plane of airtightness for the air barrier system. Integrated WRB/AB sheathing reduces the number of installation layers in light wood frame construction.

2. In masonry-faced buildings of cavity wall construction, the air barrier is generally placed on the outside of the inner, structural layer of the wall. Although this structural layer is very strong, if it is made of plain concrete masonry units, it will not be an air barrier, because the concrete masonry units are not airtight. The wall's air permeability exceeds code-stipulated levels [0.004 cfm/sq. ft. @ 1.57 psf (0.02L/second/sq. m @ 75 Pa)]. Concrete masonry was traditionally parged with a $5/8$ in. (16 mm) thick layer of portland cement plaster on the side facing the continuous wall cavity, to reduce air leakage. In current work, this surface is typically coated with a fluid-applied, vapor-permeable mastic, or with horizontal strips of a manufactured membrane that are cemented to the wall and to one another at the seams. Because these materials are flexible, mastics and membranes are more likely to remain airtight if the substrate moves or cracks.

In any of these cases, it is very important to maintain the integrity of the air barrier by sealing carefully at all seams and transitions. See specific code provisions regarding air barrier installation around

▷

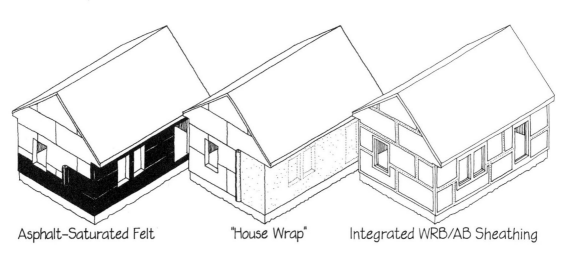

Asphalt-Saturated Felt   "House Wrap"   Integrated WRB/AB Sheathing

1. Air Barriers for Wood Light Frame Construction

the edges of the backup wall where it joins columns, spandrel beams, slabs, window openings, roof edges, recessed lighting, and electrical boxes. Codes also describe procedures for testing completed buildings to verify that the air barrier assembly performs as expected.

Some mastics and membranes used as air barriers also act as water barriers and/or vapor barriers. There is no harm in installing multiple air barriers within one assembly, but at most one vapor retarder layer should exist. See *Controlling Water Vapor* (Chapter 4) for a discussion of this related issue.

3. If the masonry facing is backed up by a wall of steel studs and gypsum sheathing, the minimum air barrier that should be detailed is a thin SBPO membrane applied to the outside of the sheathing before the masonry ties are attached. It will serve as both the air barrier and as a secondary water barrier. For greater security against air and water leaks, the sheathing can be coated instead with a fiber-containing asphaltic mastic or strips of manufactured membrane. These transform the sheathing into a highly effective air barrier and provide excellent protection against water for the materials in the backup wall. The fibers in the mastic help it bridge cracks and holes in the sheathing and adjust to small amounts of movement in the sheathing. ■

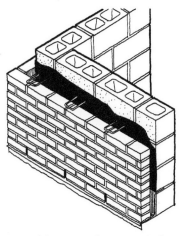

2. Mastic Air Barrier on a Masonry Backup Wall

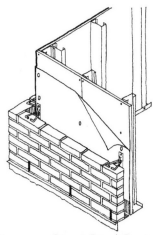

3. Membrane Air Barrier on a Steel Stud Backup Wall

Weatherstripped Crack

Cracks around door openings and window sashes need to be wide enough to allow an operating clearance. To keep air from blowing through, various kinds of weatherstrip are installed in the cracks. Manufactured windows, doors, and skylights must conform to limits set forth by codes regarding air leakage. Site-built openings should also be detailed to limit air leaks.

1. One of the oldest and simplest kinds of weatherstrip is spring weatherstrip of bronze or plastic, which adjusts automatically to the width and contour of a crack.

2. The interlocking weatherstrip is more effective and much more laborious to install than spring weatherstrip. It is made of thin strips of spring bronze.

3. Interlocking weatherstrip details have been updated with the use of rigid components made of extruded aluminum. With the addition of a synthetic rubber tubular compression gasket, a high degree of airtightness can be achieved.

4. Compression gaskets of synthetic rubber have many uses in weatherstripping. They can be designed to seal very large cracks or very small ones, and adaptations are available for every conceivable type of door, including overhead garage doors and airplane hangar doors. Two types are shown here: a tubular gasket of solid rubber and a solid gasket of sponge rubber.

▷

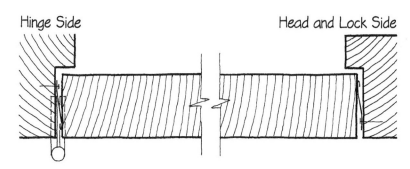

1. Spring Weatherstrip: Bronze or Plastic

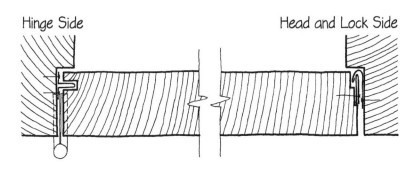

2. Spring Bronze Interlocking Weatherstrip

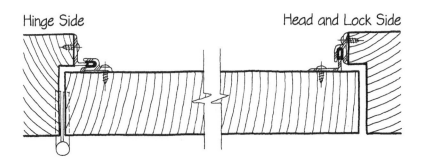

3. Rigid Aluminum Interlocking Weatherstrip

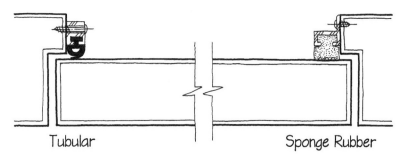

4. Rubber Compression Gaskets

5. Pile weatherstrip resembles a small, continuous brush with very dense, fine bristles. The pile is usually made from a synthetic fiber with excellent wear characteristics, but eventually it will require replacement as a result of abrasion or compression of the fibers. Pile weatherstrip, because of its low friction, is one of the few types that work well in joints of sliding windows and doors. The pile is generally very short and cannot tolerate much dimensional variation in the crack compared with spring bronze or synthetic rubber weatherstripping.

6. Door bottom weatherstrip may be of any of the types already shown. In addition to the three examples shown here, aluminum thresholds that interlock with weatherstrip on the door bottom are also available. In particularly demanding applications, an automatic door bottom may be used. This is a mechanism that lifts the weatherstrip above the sill when the door is opened and presses it down against the sill just as the door is closed, reducing friction and wear and ensuring a very tight seal. It is actuated by a small plunger that bears against the jamb when the door is closed.

Weatherstripping devices are manufactured in a wide range of materials and configurations, often using combinations of the types shown here to meet particular demands for differing door and window types, and for sealing against wind, smoke, or sound.

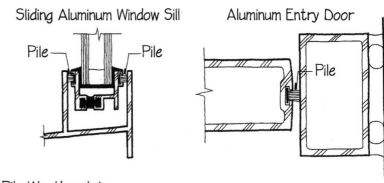

5. Pile Weatherstrip

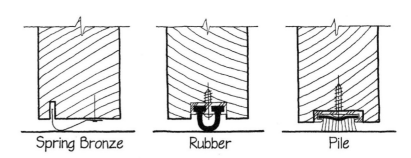

6. Door Bottom Weatherstrip

Window and door manufacturers carefully detail the weatherstrips between frames and movable doors and sash. Air infiltration in swinging door assemblies cannot exceed 0.5 cfm/sq. ft. (2.6 L/second/ sq. m.). All other types of openings are limited to 0.3 cfm/sq. ft. (1.5 L/second/sq. m). Manufacturers' catalogs and official websites are the best source of up-to-date information. ∎

CHAPTER 3: Controlling Heat Flow

Excessive heat flow through a building assembly results in wasted energy, unnecessarily high investment in oversized heating and cooling equipment, water damage in winter from condensation and frost on interior surfaces, and discomfort for the occupants of the building. In detailing a building, there are three basic ways to minimize heat transmission and maximize thermal comfort:

1. Control the conduction of heat through the building envelope.
2. Control the radiation of heat onto and through the building envelope.
3. Utilize thermal mass to regulate the flow of heat through the building envelope.

Each of these generates its own detail patterns. The patterns will be introduced here, and each will be more fully described later in this chapter.

1. Control the Conduction of Heat

Most building materials are dense and conduct heat rapidly. In assembling layers of material to make a wall, roof, floor, foundation, window, or door, we almost always include one or more low-density materials with low thermal conductivities.

Detailing patterns that relate to controlling conduction of heat include:

> *Thermal Insulation* (p. 52)
> *Thermal Break* (p. 54)
> *Multiple Glazing* (p. 59)

When conceived as a well-coordinated group, these features combine to form the thermal control layer of the building envelope. The designer should be able to draw an uninterrupted line in plan and section representing the thermal control layer. A building with a continuous thermal control layer will likely be comfortable, efficient, and sustainable to operate. The line may even be made wider or darker in locations where thermal control is high, and thinner or lighter where it is low. Unlike water and air control, thermal control is not a yes / no condition; it usually is a gradient. Varying the line weight illustrates subtle differences in thermal control.

2. Control the Radiation of Heat

There are two very different sources of radiated heat that must be controlled in a building. One is the sun and the other is warm surfaces and objects within and around the building.

Radiant heat from the sun strikes the building from a single direction at any given moment; however, that direction changes constantly with the time of day and time of year in a predictable pattern. Solar radiation is transmitted across a broad spectrum of wavelengths. Most of its energy lies within the visible spectrum and the shorter infrared wavelengths. These wavelengths can be reflected efficiently by both white surfaces and bright metallic surfaces. Solar radiation can also be blocked effectively with simple shading devices.

The detail patterns that relate to controlling the radiation of solar heat include:

> *White and Bright Surfaces* (p. 60)
> *Reflective Glazing* (p. 61)

Warm surfaces and objects in and around buildings radiate heat in all directions, primarily in the longer infrared wavelengths. These wavelengths are reflected efficiently only by bright metallic surfaces. The detail pattern that relates to controlling radiation from warm building surfaces and objects is:

> *Reflective Surface and Airspace* (p. 62)

3. Utilize Thermal Mass

When exposed to warm air or solar radiation, large masses of dense materials, such as soil, masonry, concrete, and water, absorb and store considerable quantities of heat. They do so over a period of time that depends on the thickness of the material and its thermal properties; in a building, this period typically can be as much as 12 hours. In hot climates with large temperature differences between day and night, this delay may be turned to the designer's advantage. Detailing the building in such a way that its thermal mass absorbs heat during the day and gives it off at night maintains a comfortable temperature range inside the building, while the outside air temperature fluctuates over a much wider range.

Thermal mass can also be useful in allowing a building to receive large amounts of heat (from solar radiation or internal sources such as lighting and machinery) during the day without overheating. The thermal mass can then give this heat back to the interior spaces at night when they would otherwise tend to become too cool. The detail pattern that relates to utilizing thermal mass is:

> *Outside-Insulated Thermal Mass* (p. 64)

Architectural Detailing: Function Constructability Aesthetics. Fourth Edition. Patrick Rand, Jason Miller, and Edward Allen.
© 2025 John Wiley & Sons, Inc. Published 2025 by John Wiley & Sons, Inc.

Thermal Insulation

More energy is used worldwide to heat and cool buildings than for any other single purpose. Reduction of energy consumption is an important means of reducing the economic and environmental costs of building maintenance and operations. In recent revision cycles, code requirements regarding thermal insulation have increased substantially, a trend that will likely continue. In some cases, owners and designers avoid high future operating costs by intentionally exceeding minimum thermal insulation requirements.

Thermal insulating materials are used as components of walls, ceilings, and floors of a building to reduce energy consumption and to maintain interior surfaces at comfortable temperatures.

1. A material's thermal conductivity often correlates directly with its density, so building insulating materials are almost always very low in density. This makes them fragile and easily damaged; many are also unattractive to the eye. Foam plastic insulations are often combustible and may give off toxic gasses when burned, requiring that they be covered with fire-resistant materials. Foam plastics also degrade rapidly when exposed to ultraviolet light. For these reasons, when detailing building assemblies these insulating materials are sandwiched in the middle, protected and hidden from view by exterior and interior finish layers.

2. Insulating materials vary in their efficiencies: An inch of phenolic foam has a much higher resistance to heat flow than an inch of lightweight concrete. The accompanying table lists the thermal resistances of common insulating materials. The thermal resistance for an insulation material also varies according to its particular formulation, the density of the installation, and the specific temperature at which its thermal resistance is being measured. These variables are represented by the range in the table. The detailer's task includes selecting insulating materials that can furnish the required thermal resistance in the amount of space available within the building assembly being detailed.

3. The least expensive insulating materials, measured in terms of units of thermal resistance per dollar of installed cost, are generally those made of glass fibers. These can be used only in dry locations, because they lose their insulating value when they become wet. Glass fiber batts should not be compressed, because their effectiveness depends on their thickness and fluffiness.

4. Thermal resistance of installed insulation may change over time. Loose fill insulations tend to settle, and some rigid foam insulations demonstrate slightly lower R values as they age. Detailers should base their analyses on values that account for anticipated aging and settling of insulation materials (see Table 3-1).

5. Insulation is often required in wet locations, such as on the outside of a foundation wall, inside a masonry cavity wall, or in

TABLE 3-1: Thermal Resistance of Common Insulating Materials (includes effects of aging and settling). Use Data for a Particular Manufacturer's Product

	Range		Use for Analysis	
	(ft^2-hr-°F/BTU-in.)	(m^2-°K/W-m)	(ft^2-hr-°F/BTU-in.)	(m^2-°K/W-m)
Cellulose fibers, loose fill or sprayed	3.1–4.0	22–28	3.5	25
Concrete, low-density 30 lb/ft^3 (480 kg/m^3)	1.0–1.5	7–10	1.1	7.7
Glass fibers, normal batts	2.9–3.8	20–27	3.2	22
Glass fibers or mineral wool, high-density batts	3.7–4.3	26–30	4.1	29
Glass fibers, boards	2.7–2.9	19–20	2.9	20
Glass fibers, sprayed	3.1–4.0	22–28	3.5	25
Glass foam board, 7.5 lb/ft^3 (120 kg/m^3)	3.4–4.0	25–28	3.4	24
Perlite, loose fill	2.4–3.7	17–26	2.7	19
Polystyrene foam, extruded board (XPS)	4.5–5.0	32–35	5.0	35
Polystyrene foam, expanded board (EPS)	3.6–4.2	25–29	3.8	27
Polyisocyanurate board	5.0–6.0	35–42	6.0	42
Polyisocyanurate board, foil faced	5.8–7.8	40–53	6.5	46
Polyicynene or polyurethane, low-density, foam	3.6–4.0	25–28	3.6	25
Polyurethane, high-density, foam	5.0–7.0	35–49	6.0	42
Aerogel silica gel, blanket	8.0–10.0	55–69	9.0	63

a protected membrane roof assembly. Closed-cell extruded polystyrene (XPS) foam is one material that retains most of its insulating value when wetted over very long periods of time. Another is glass foam board insulation, which is not hygroscopic and is composed of countless tiny hermetically sealed glass cells.

6. Some foam-in-place insulation can serve as the building envelope's air barrier and vapor retarder if installed properly. Some rigid foam boards can also serve these additional functions if reliably sealed at edges. If the thermal insulation is not also the vapor retarder, then the designer must correctly position the vapor retardant layer in relation to the thermal insulation, matched with the requirements of the local climate. For instance, in climates with cold winters, thermal insulation should generally be installed with a vapor retarder on its interior side; in hot, humid climates, the vapor retardant layer may be placed on the outside of the insulation or even omitted from the assembly. See **Warm-Side Vapor Retarder** (Chapter 4).

7. Aerogel insulation is an extremely low-density silica gel. It can be imbedded in a flexible glass fiber fabric to form a 0.2-in. or 0.4-in. 5- or 10-mm thick blanket; multiple layers can be installed to achieve the intended insulation levels. Aerogel insulation can provide a given thermal resistance with an exceptionally thin and lightweight product, but it is very costly and fragile. ∎

Thermal Break

A thermal break is a strip of insulating material inserted into a building assembly to prevent rapid heat conduction through dense, highly conductive materials such as metal, concrete, and masonry. Thermal breaks must be included, not only in wall and roof assemblies, but also in any elements that pass through them to the outside, such as structural elements or utility lines. Thermal breaks save energy and lower the risk of condensation occurring on cool surfaces inside wall and roof assemblies. Try to limit the elements that bridge the thermal break when detailing to small elements, such as fasteners, wires, and small pipes.

1. The spaces between steel studs and steel rafters can be insulated effectively and economically with glass fiber batts, but these steel framing members will continue to conduct heat through the wall or roof at a very high rate. The framing members in this case are referred to as thermal bridges, meaning that they furnish a way for heat to flow easily through an otherwise well-insulated assembly, much as a road bridge allows traffic to flow readily across an otherwise impassable obstacle. In detailing, we block a potential thermal bridge with a thermal break, which is made of a material with low thermal conductivity.

In the example shown here, the thermal bridges are steel studs in a wall, and the thermal breaks consist of 1 in. (25 mm) thick strips of plastic foam placed between the exterior cladding material and the studs. Although one of these thermal breaks may not insulate the framing member to the same thermal resistance value as the insulated space between the members, it greatly reduces the flow of heat through it, and it raises the temperature of the indoor side of the member enough so that moisture will not condense on it. The steel screws that pass through the thermal break constitute another set of thermal bridges, but they are so small in cross section that little heat flows through them.

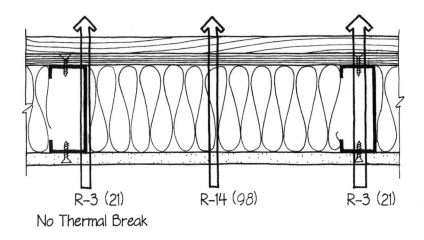

No Thermal Break

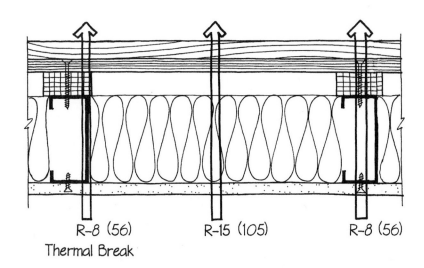

Thermal Break

1. Thermal Resistance of a Steel Stud Wall

2. Although wood is not highly conductive of heat – as compared to metals – wood studs and rafters do conduct heat much more rapidly than the insulated cavities between them. Approximately 15 percent of the area of a light frame wall is wood framing, not insulated cavity. A continuous plane of rigid plastic foam insulation may be added across either the outside or the inside of the framing members as a thermal break to improve energy efficiency. The additional layer provides thermal breaks over each framing member and increases the overall thermal resistance of the assembly. It also serves as continuous insulation where called for by building or energy codes.

3. Aluminum conducts heat even more readily than steel. This can be a problem in aluminum window frames, door frames, and cladding components in cold climates. Where aluminum passes continuously from outdoors to indoors in these components, large quantities of water and frost often condense on the cold inner surface in winter. To prevent this from happening, several types of thermal breaks have been developed for use in aluminum members. In the example shown here, a hard plastic is cast into a groove in the aluminum member during manufacture. Then the groove is debridged (the thermal bridge is removed) by milling away the aluminum at the bottom of the groove. This leaves only the relatively low-conductivity plastic thermal break to connect the indoor side of the member to the outdoor side.

4. A second type of thermal break for an aluminum cladding assembly is a simple plastic or rubber strip that is inserted between the outer and inner layers of a mullion during assembly. The aluminum screws remain as thermal bridges, but they are too small in area to conduct much heat. A third type of thermal break for an aluminum assembly is the use of small, intermittent plastic clips that mount the interior cover components to the mullion. ▷

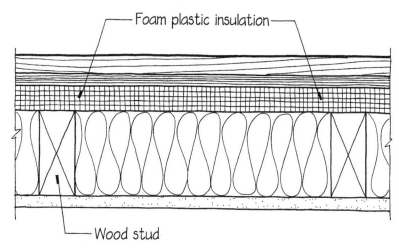

2. Foam Plastic Insulation Across Wood Studs

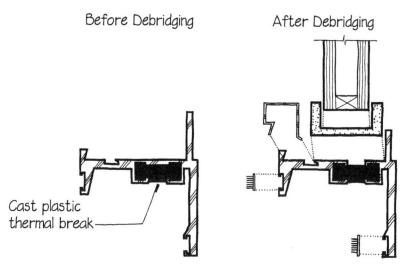

3. Thermal Break in Aluminum Window Frame

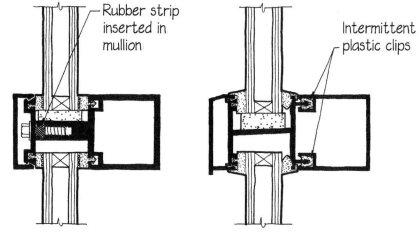

4. Thermal Breaks in Aluminum Cladding Systems

5. If more thermal insulation in a wood light frame wall is required, alternative insulation and framing strategies can be used. One strategy is to apply horizontal furring strips and a second layer of insulating batts across the outside or inside face of the studs. Another is to construct another stud wall just outside the first, leaving a small airspace between the studs to act as a thermal break. The first method reduces the thermal bridging caused by wood framing to only about 4 percent of the wall area. The second method can lower the bridging area to less than 1 percent.

6. Hollow concrete masonry units can be insulated by filling their cores with either a granular fill insulation or plastic foam, but the webs of the units act as thermal bridges. Many different schemes have been invented to minimize these bridges. Several kinds of proprietary masonry units have been designed with webs that are as small in cross section as is structurally feasible, to reduce the thermal bridging effect.

7. A common approach to the thermal bridging problem in concrete masonry is to furr the masonry wall on the inside and to insulate between the furring strips. This method can also be used on concrete walls. Placing insulation inside of the masonry or concrete wall nullifies the value of the thermal mass of those materials; see **Outside-Insulated Thermal Mass**, later in this chapter, for a complete discussion.

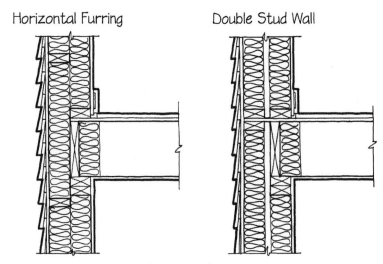

5. Thermally Broken Wood Stud Walls

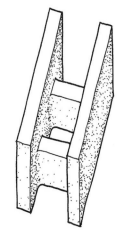

6. Concrete Masonry Unit With Minimal Webs

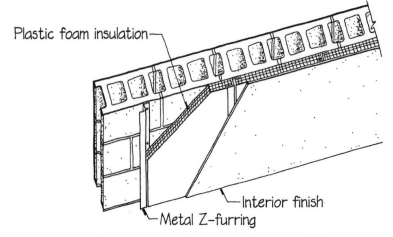

7. Inside Furring and Insulation on Concrete Masonry Wall

8. Another common approach is to clad the outside of the masonry wall with an exterior insulation and finish system (EIFS) consisting of a continuous layer of plastic foam board insulation adhered to the outside of the masonry wall and coated with a synthetic stucco finish. The moisture-trapping potential of this cladding system is of less concern when over a masonry substrate rather than one made of cellulosic materials.

9. In a masonry cavity wall construction, a continuous layer of foam insulation can be placed on the inner face of the cavity, to eliminate thermal bridges in the concrete masonry units and limit overall thermal bridging to just the metal joint reinforcement between the two wythes (see Chapter 17).

10. In sitecast concrete wall construction in which both faces of the concrete will be seen, a thermal break is very difficult to achieve. To make a thermal break in such a wall, the concrete can be cast in two layers simultaneously, with a continuous layer of plastic foam board insulation firmly secured between them inside the formwork. The concrete must be placed evenly on both sides of the insulation to avoid moving the insulation. Typically, the concrete on the interior side is the primary structural element, with the outer layer acting primarily as the exterior wall finish. Alternatively, the concrete layers can be formed and cast separately.

A similar assembly can be produced more easily in insulated precast concrete panels. In this case, the layers are cast in sequence horizontally at the factory, with a short delay between placements of the layers. Offsite fabrication of the precast panels may also achieve higher quality control and dimensional accuracy (See **Factory and Site** and **Dimensional Tolerances**, Chapter 13).

In both cases, steel ties or reinforcement are the only thermal bridges that pass through the thermal break, but they are a very small portion of the wall's area. ▷

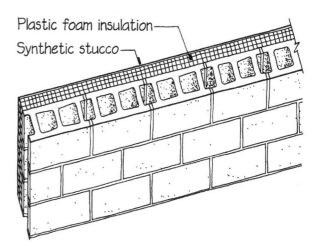

8. Exterior Insulation and Finish System (EIFS) on Concrete Masonry Wall

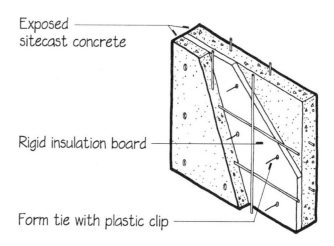

10. Insulated Sitecast Concrete Wall

11. Thermal breaks can be used at joints in steel frames where the dense, thermally conductive structural element passes through the building's thermal envelope. Examples could be as large as a cantilevered steel beam that supports an entry canopy, or as small as a steel shelf angle that passes through the insulation layer to support a masonry veneer.

Proprietary off-the-shelf solutions for these important connections can be used to comply with stringent thermal insulation requirements, without sacrificing structural capability. In the example shown, special stainless steel hardware and bushings transfer loads with relatively small cross sections, minimizing the breach of the otherwise continuous plane of thermal insulation. Stainless steel is used because its thermal resistance is about three times greater than that of carbon steel. Proprietary connections like these are expensive but can be justified with a thorough life cycle analysis and lower operating costs, especially in hot or cold climates. ■

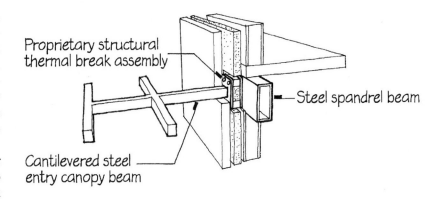

11. Thermal Break Where Structure Crosses Thermal Envelope

Multiple Glazing

Glass is a poor thermal insulator. For more thermally efficient windows, two or more layers of glass can be assembled with spaces between them. Innovations in multiple glazing assemblies can help meet energy efficiency criteria in the rating systems used to certify sustainable, high-performance buildings. The principles discussed here apply to both glass and polymer glazing products, such as polycarbonate and acrylic.

1. A single sheet of glass conducts heat about 20 times as rapidly as an adequately insulated wall. If a second sheet of glass is added, with an airspace between the two sheets (double glazing), this rapid heat flow is cut in half. If a third sheet of glass and a second airspace are added (triple glazing), the overall flow is about a third of what it was for a single sheet of glass. The thickness of the airspace, if at least ⅜ in. (9 mm), makes relatively little difference in its insulating ability.

Multiple glazing can be created by adding a removable sheet of glass on the outside (a storm window) or inside the window. In most cases, however, it is more satisfactory to use double or triple insulating glass units (IGUs) that have been assembled at the factory. These units have a hermetic seal around the edge, a fill of dry air or low-conductivity gas between the panes of glass, and an insert of silica gel crystals in the edge seal to remove any stray moisture from the trapped air. This avoids problems of dust and condensation between the panes, which is important because it is impossible to wash the interior surfaces.

2. The major problem with conventional multiple glazing units is that they are still highly heat conductive when compared with a well-insulated wall. More sheets of glass and more airspaces may be added, but the glazing unit becomes thick and heavy, and each successive layer added to the assembly contributes less additional insulation value than the one before. Therefore, several other strategies are often followed to increase the thermal resistance of multiple glazing units.

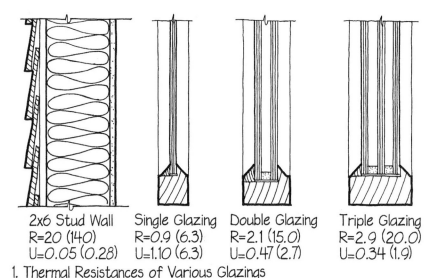

1. Thermal Resistances of Various Glazings

Prescriptive residential building codes limit the U-factor of window assemblies to 0.32 to 0.40, depending on the climate zone. To comply, manufacturers supplement multiple glazing with additional detailing strategies. Many manufacturers of window and skylight assemblies utilize one or more of the following:

- Interior glazing sheets of very thin, durable, highly transparent plastic film. These add static airspaces, while adding little thickness and almost no weight.
- Low-conductivity, nontoxic gas fills, usually argon or krypton, instead of dry air between the panes.
- Low-emissivity (low-E) coatings on inside surfaces of glass. These microscopically thin coatings are usually formulated for use in cold climates, to be highly transparent to solar wavelengths of light and heat but to reflect the longer infrared wavelengths that are characteristic of heat radiated from the interior of a building. For use in buildings where summer cooling is the primary problem, other formulas are used, to produce coatings that reflect most solar heat. Sunny exposures on a building may require a slightly different coating than those not exposed to direct sunlight. Manufacturers can accommodate subtle differences in the specification of the coating, with no noticeable change in the appearance of the window. Note that reflected solar heat may harm nearby surfaces and spaces, as discussed later in this chapter.
- Edge spacer details between the sheets of glass that are less conductive of heat than the conventional metal spline.
- Fiberglass thermal breaks within sash, window frames and curtain wall mullions.
- Vacuum insulated glass is an emerging technology that promises up to R-10 (70) performance by sealing and substantially evacuating the cavity between glass panels.

Currently, the most thermally efficient multiple glazing units, by utilizing a combination of these devices, achieve a whole-product insulating value of up to R-10 (70) or U-0.10 (0.57) – about 50 percent of a well-insulated wall. See manufacturers' literature for more information regarding advancements in windows and glazing. When evaluating alternative types of windows for their thermal resistances, it is important to compare test values for entire window units, rather than for the center of glazing alone. Whole-product values include the effects of the glass, edge seal, and frame, while center-of-glazing values relate only to the glass itself. ■

White and Bright Surfaces

Bright metallic surfaces and bright white surfaces are very effective in reflecting the heat of the sun from the exterior of a building. Inversely, dark surfaces absorb radiant energy from the sun and convert it to heat. Building surfaces exposed to sunlight should be chosen with consideration for the building's overall objectives for lighting, heating, and cooling.

1. Table 3-2 indicates the ability of various surfaces to reflect solar heat. A whitewashed or white-painted building will remain substantially cooler in summer than a dark-colored building. A roof covering that is bright white or bright metal will be very helpful in keeping the sun's heat out of a building, especially when compared with a black or dark-colored roof. A curtain wall that has a white or bright metallic finish will not be subject to as great a range of temperatures as a darker one, making it less subject to extremes of expansion and contraction. Very light colors are somewhat effective in reflecting solar heat. Medium to dark colors tend to absorb solar heat rather than reflect it. White or metallic surfaces that have oxidized, chalked, or grown dirty become absorptive rather than reflective, so regular cleaning and recoating are important.

Light-colored materials tend to diffuse energy in many directions, but highly reflective planar surfaces may direct radiant energy toward nearby landscapes or other buildings, causing glare or increasing the temperature in public spaces, on surfaces, and even inside nearby buildings. It is prudent to verify that reflected energy will do no harm on nearby landscapes or buildings.

TABLE 3-2: Approximate Percentage of Solar Reflectance by Various Surfaces

Surface	Reflectance
White thermoplastic cool roof membrane, new	90%
White thermoplastic cool roof membrane, weathered	85%
Aluminum, polished, new	85%
Aluminum paint, new	80%
White paint	80%
White rubber roof membrane, TPO, new	75%
Copper or brass, polished, new	70%
White Kynar® PVDF film on metal, new	65%
White concrete	60%
White marble	55%
Stainless steel, 301, 316	55%
Aluminum paint, weathered	50%
Red brick	45%
Copper or brass, weathered	35%
Steel, galvanized, new	35%
Concrete, natural gray, unweathered	35%
Red clay tiles	30%
Brown, red, green, dark gray paint	30%
White asphalt shingles	25%
Vegetation	25%
Steel, galvanized, weathered	20%
Sand	20%
Black rubber roof membrane, built-up roof	15%
Unpainted wood, pine, unweathered	10%
Water	10%
Black paint	10%

In some jurisdictions, adopted regulations limit solar reflectance of roof surfaces as a means of mitigating the heat island effect. One such standard calls for a minimum 3-year aged roof surface to have a solar reflectance of at least 30 percent if the roof is sloped greater than 2:12, and at least 55 percent if sloped 2:12 or less. ∎

Reflective Glazing

Windows that are reflective can turn away most solar heat before it enters a building. Glass and polymer glazing products can be formulated or coated to provide the desired views and levels of daylighting and heating without bringing in excessive amounts of heat or glare.

1. Clear glass transmits most of the sunlight and most of the solar heat that shines on it. Standard uncoated float glass reflects approximately 8% of the sunlight that strikes it. Antireflective coatings can be applied to glass to reduce this to only 2%, which might be desired for glass over solar collectors, where maximum energy transmission is desired. However, clear glass windows that are poorly oriented and unshaded can be major sources of summertime discomfort and high cooling costs in buildings. Tinted glass, also called "heat-absorbing" glass, can reduce the solar heat transmission of a window by a quarter to a half, but much of the absorbed heat is passed on to the interior room air. Reflective glass, which has a metallic coating on one surface, can reflect solar heat before it enters the building and is extremely effective in maintaining comfortable interior temperatures at a low cooling cost. Glazing products can be made that are reflective to specific portions of the visible portion of the spectrum, as well as those outside of this range. Invisible low-emissivity (low-E) coatings (see **Multiple Glazing**, earlier in this chapter) can also reflect radiant energy, but they allow more of it to enter than most types of reflective glass.

2. When choosing glass, use the solar heat gain coefficient (SHGC) figures from manufacturers' catalogs or official websites to evaluate the relative abilities of various types of glass to control solar heat gain (Table 3-3). The SHGC accounts for heat both from the sunlight that passes through the glass and for the heat conducted from the outside through the glass to the room air. A low SHGC indicates that less heat enters the building. Building codes stipulate maximum SHGC values for each climate zone.

The manufacturer's shading coefficient figure is a ratio of heat gain due to sunlight passing through a product compared with a single lite of ⅛ in. (3 mm) clear glass. It does not include heat conducted through the glass. A shading coefficient of 0.35, for example, means that the glass will admit only 35 percent as much solar heat as double-strength (⅛ in. thick, or 3 mm) clear glass, and half as much heat as glass that has a shading coefficient of 0.70. The shading coefficient of reflective glazing depends mostly on the density of its metallic coating.

3. Some coatings that make a glazing product reflective to solar energy are hard and durable. Many others are vulnerable to scratching; therefore, coatings should be located on the cavity side of a multiglazed unit. Follow the manufacturers' recommendations regarding which glass surface receives the coating. Some coatings are available only with insulating glass units, because the coatings would be damaged if they were on surfaces that were repeatedly cleaned.

4. The detailer should keep in mind some potential problems that are often associated with reflective glazing. Reflective glass can reflect the sun into the eyes of pedestrians and motorists. Reflective glass and low-E glass can cause solar overheating problems in adjacent buildings and outdoor spaces by reflecting sunlight onto surfaces that would not otherwise receive it. If they create too perfect a reflection of natural surroundings, reflective glass surfaces can be mistaken by birds as a safe flight path. Special frits and patterns can be used when making reflective glass products, to make the façade evident to birds flying near the building. Reflective glass gives complete privacy to the interior of the building during the day, but at night, when interior lights are on, it appears from the outside as dark but transparent glass, and the interior of the building is fully visible to passersby. ∎

TABLE 3-3: Approximate Solar Heat Gain and Shading Coefficients of Common Glazing Materials

All glazing products are ¼ in. (6 mm) thick except where noted.	Number of Layers	Solar Heat Gain Coefficient	Shading Coefficient
Clear glass	1	0.85	0.65–0.94
	2	0.70	0.55–0.80
	3	0.52	0.50–0.60
Tinted glass, gray, range of tinting options	1	0.43–0.78	0.48–0.68
	2	0.41–0.62	0.38–0.55
Clear glass, low-E coating, range of coating options	1	0.17–0.50	0.19–0.57
	2	0.27–0.63	0.30–0.65
	3	0.24–0.60	0.25–0.55
Reflective glass, range of coating options	1	0.10–0.30	0.15–0.35
	2	0.20–0.60	0.29–0.41
Polycarbonate sheet, corrugated, clear, 0.04 in. (1 mm)	1	0.85–1.00	0.70–0.86
corrugated, tinted, 0.04 in. (1 mm)	1	0.49–0.75	0.42–0.79
multiwall sheet, clear, 0.33 in. (8 mm)	3	0.69	0.77
multiwall sheet, tinted, 0.33 in. (8 mm)	3	0.49–0.67	0.30–0.52
multiwall sheet, tinted, 0.33 in. (8 mm)	3	0.39	0.45

Reflective Surface and Airspace

A bright metal sheet or foil is an excellent reflector of radiant heat energy at any wavelength, and it can be used within a roof or wall assembly to reduce the flow of heat into the building. To be effective, however, it must face a clear airspace that is at least ½ in. (13 mm) thick, and it must remain clean.

1. A bright aluminum foil in a wall or roof construction with a 1 in. (25 mm) airspace on one side has an insulating value of approximately R-2 (R-14 in SI units).

If the foil is bright on both faces and has airspaces on both sides, its insulating value is approximately twice as great.

2. A bright metal foil sandwiched tightly between two pieces of building material has no insulating value. A reflective foil used as a facing on an insulating batt has no insulating value if it is installed tightly against the back of the interior wall finish material. If the wall finish is furred out to provide an airspace, however, the foil facing adds considerably to the thermal resistance of the insulating batt. Similarly, foil-backed gypsum wallboard gains no insulating value from the foil if the board is installed tightly against batts of insulation. If the board is spaced away from the insulation on furring strips, or if there is space behind the board between the wall studs, the foil becomes effective.

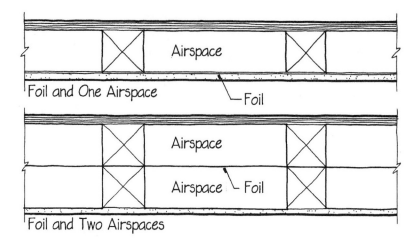

1. Metal Foil Used As Insulation

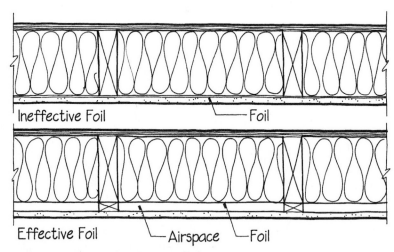

2. Ineffective Foil and Effective Foil

3. In well-insulated roof assemblies, the radiant barrier only slightly improves overall thermal performance. The cost of installing the radiant barrier in such buildings is better directed toward additional thermal insulation. However, in older lightly insulated assemblies, or in an uninsulated roof, such as a garage or outbuilding, a bright foil surface makes an excellent radiant heat barrier between rafters. Several products of this type are commercially available.

The one illustrated here is a bright aluminum foil laminated to a cardboard backing, configured so that it forms an air passage just beneath the roof sheathing of a wood light frame building. This is particularly effective in keeping solar heat from being transmitted from the roof into the spaces below, blocking as much as 40 percent of summer heat gain. The airspace between the foil and the sheathing serves both as (1) a clear space into which one side of the foil can reflect, and (2) a ventilated airspace to carry away solar heat. In winter, the foil acts as additional insulation to retard the heat flow out of the building into the cold outside air. It does this, not only because foil is a poor absorber (that is, a good reflector) of radiant energy, but also because it is a poor emitter, meaning

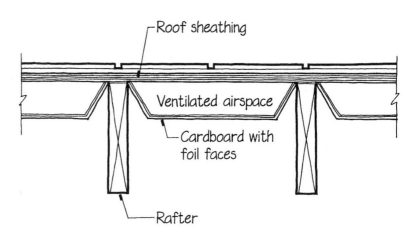

3. Radiant Barrier in Roof Construction

that it does not radiate heat effectively into space. In fact, its rate of absorbance and its rate of emittance are the same, which means that it does not make any difference which way heat is flowing through a foil that faces an airspace; the foil will be equally effective in blocking heat flow in either direction.

4. The reflective qualities of a bright metal surface diminish rapidly as the surface becomes dusty or tarnished. A foil in a static, dry airspace will generally stay cleaner and retain its thermal effectiveness better than one in a circulating stream of air.

5. Metal foils are excellent vapor retarders, and in cold climates they can be installed on the warm side of a wall or roof assembly to fulfill both functions see ***Warm-Side Vapor Retarder***, Chapter 4. If a reflective foil surface must be used where no vapor retarder is desired, it should be perforated to allow water vapor to pass freely. ■

Outside-Insulated Thermal Mass

The ability of massive materials such as concrete, masonry, and earth to store large quantities of heat can be harnessed to create buildings that are easy to heat and cool.

1. The thick walls and heavy roof of a traditional uninsulated adobe building in a desert climate absorb large quantities of heat during the day, both from the sun and from the hot outdoor air. This heat warms the adobe material layer by layer, starting from the outside and working its way slowly toward the inside. After the sun sets, however, the outside air quickly cools off, the night sky becomes an absorber of heat, and the outside of the adobe structure begins to radiate and convect its stored heat back to the outdoors. If the wall or roof is thick enough, this happens before the heat of the day has traveled all the way through the adobe to the interior of the building. Much of the stored heat that is advancing through the walls and roof does a slow U-turn and dissipates to the outdoors during the cold night. The interior of the building stays within a relatively narrow and comfortable range of air temperatures. The adobe functions as thermal mass, a large volume of heat-absorbing material that can be used to moderate interior temperatures.

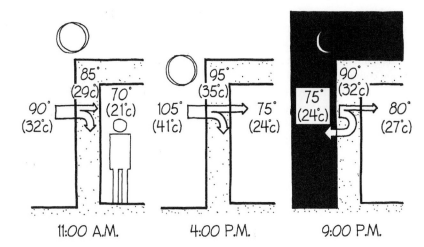

1. Heat Flow and Temperatures in a Thick Adobe Wall

2. In a hot, humid climate, the outdoor air does not cool off very much at night, and an uninsulated thermal mass is of little use. An uninsulated thermal mass is also useless in a winter climate that is cold both day and night. It is most effective in a climate that features warm days and cool nights year-round.

3. If a layer of thermal insulation is added to the outside of a massive building, such as an ordinary masonry or concrete structure, the mass becomes effective in almost any climate, because it becomes a thermal "flywheel" that stabilizes the interior temperature of the building despite short-term inputs of heat.

A building with outside-insulated thermal mass can receive large amounts of solar heat through windows during a winter day and still maintain comfortable indoor air temperatures, because the concrete and masonry absorb and store much of the heat. When the interior air cools down at night, the mass slowly gives back this stored heat to stabilize the indoor temperature. Heat-producing machinery such as equipment that runs for only part of the day can be operated without overheating the building; much of the excess heat is saved in the thermal mass of the structure for use when the building needs it.

The outside layer of insulation also has the advantage of stabilizing the thermal movements in the frame and surfaces of the building, eliminating most of the expansion and contraction that are characteristic of building structures exposed to outdoor air.

One example of outside-insulated thermal mass is a reinforced concrete frame building that is completely enclosed by well-insulated curtain wall panels. Another is a masonry bearing wall building that is clad with an exterior insulation and finish system (EIFS). A third example is a wood-frame house with large masonry fireplaces or heavy ceramic tile floors.

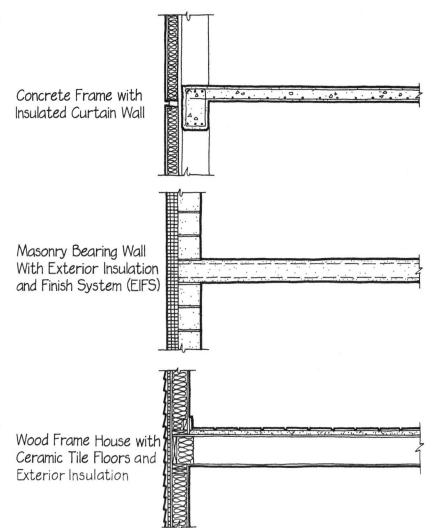

3. Buildings with Outside-Insulated Thermal Mass

4. A thermal mass can be utilized best in a building's passive heating strategy when the sun's radiant energy charges the mass directly. This "direct gain" strategy generally involves positioning and orienting windows so that sunlight passes through them and strikes thermal mass floor or wall surfaces.

In this example, the concrete floor slabs and concrete masonry wall are both exposed to direct sunlight coming through the tall windows. Vents in the masonry wall permit occupants to circulate room air into the zone between the window and masonry wall as needed to make the room comfortable.

The basement wall and ground slab in this example also contribute to the thermal mass of the building. A continuous layer of rigid foam insulation outside of the foundation wall isolates the mass of the building from fluctuating outside temperatures. Except in permafrost climate zones, energy codes only require that foundation walls be thermally insulated to a depth of 10 ft. (3 m), because the deep earth is far enough away from fluctuating temperatures and can become part of the thermal mass of the building. In this example, the vegetated roof is not calculated as part of the thermal mass, because it is outside of the building's thermal insulation envelope and is exposed to fluctuating outside temperatures.

5. As a passive system, thermal mass will not control interior air temperature as closely as a thermostat and a mechanical heating and cooling system, but during the spring and the fall, it can maintain a daily temperature swing of only a few degrees in either direction from an optimum temperature, and it will help the building's comfort control system maintain comfortable temperatures during the rest of the year.

6. A building with outside-insulated thermal mass should be designed in close

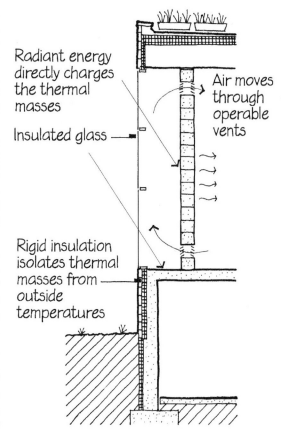

4. Direct Gain of Energy by Thermal Mass

collaboration with the designer of the building's heating and cooling system. A thermally massive design may be inappropriate for a building that is heated or cooled intermittently – such as a house of worship, which may only be heated one day per week, or a weekend cottage – because the thermal mass makes the building very slow to warm up.

7. To be fully effective, thermal mass must be exposed directly to the indoor air; it is best if also exposed to sunlight that has entered the space. Secondary or tertiary building elements like carpets, suspended ceilings, and furred walls all reduce the effectiveness of a massive building. ■

CHAPTER Controlling Water Vapor

Water vapor is a colorless, odorless gas that is always present in the air. Water vapor interests the detailer because of the problems created if it condenses on or within building components. Condensation occurs when moist air is cooled below its dew point temperature, by either mixing with colder air or contacting cold surfaces. Condensation can cause fogging or frosting of the surfaces of glass- and metal-cladding components. It can saturate insulating materials in walls and roofs and render them ineffective. It can create drips, puddles, water stains, fungal growth, and metal corrosion inside a building. Chronic dampness can cause some building materials to weaken and disintegrate. It can blister and rupture paint coatings and roof membranes on the outside of a building. In short, condensation can greatly impact building performance over time if not accounted for in detailing.

Water vapor inside a building is produced mainly by cooking, bathing, washing, industrial processes, and human metabolic activity such as respiration. In a new building, water vapor may also come from wood, concrete, plaster, and masonry or other materials that are still giving off excess moisture. Residences generally produce more interior humidity than commercial or institutional buildings. Optimum interior relative humidity for human comfort and health is 40–60%. A building's mechanical system is often designed to reduce the amount of water vapor inside a building by ventilation, by dehumidifying the air with an air-conditioning system, or both. In warm, humid locations, interior air pressure should be slightly higher than outside to reduce the inflow of humid air. But whether or not such mechanical systems are installed, there are four precautions to take when detailing to avoid water vapor problems in a building:

1. Use thermal insulation, multiple glazing, and thermal breaks to keep interior surfaces at temperatures above the dew point of the air.
2. Use a warm-side vapor retarder to keep air and water vapor from reaching surfaces and spaces cool enough to cause condensation to occur.
3. In every building assembly, ventilate the portion that lies on the cold side of a vapor retarder to ensure no moisture is trapped there.
4. Where condensation is likely to occur despite any such precautions, provide a gravity-driven system to catch and remove condensate before it can create problems.

These actions translate into four detail patterns (see the corresponding sections later in this chapter):

Warm Interior Surfaces (p. 68)
Warm-Side Vapor Retarder (p. 70)
Vapor Ventilation (p. 75)
Condensate Drainage (p. 78)

Architectural Detailing: Function Constructability Aesthetics. Fourth Edition. Patrick Rand, Jason Miller, and Edward Allen.
© 2025 John Wiley & Sons, Inc. Published 2025 by John Wiley & Sons, Inc.

Warm Interior Surfaces

To prevent condensation, surfaces inside a building's thermal envelope should be detailed so that their temperatures will always remain above the dew point temperature of the air. This detailing pattern is especially important in humid regions or where interior air is not dehumidified.

1. When interior air humidity is high, moisture condenses on the outside of a cold water pipe and drips onto whatever is below. To prevent this, the pipe is wrapped with thermal insulation. The outside of the thermal insulation is at a temperature that is very close to room temperature, so condensation does not occur. However, it is also important to cover the outside of the pipe insulation with a vapor retarder, such as plastic sheeting or metal foil, to prevent water vapor from moving through the insulation to condense on the cold surface of the pipe. Without the vapor retarder, vapor can migrate through vapor-permeable insulation or through gaps between pieces of insulation. Once the insulation is saturated with water, the dripping would begin again (see **Warm-Side Vapor Retarder**, later in this chapter).

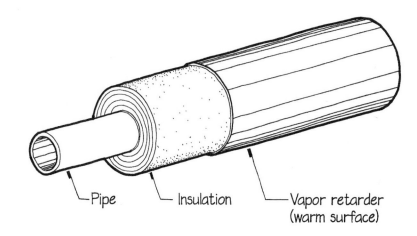

1. Insulated Cold Water Pipe

2. In a similar fashion, the tank or cistern on the back of a toilet becomes cold because of the temperature of the water that it contains, and drips condensate onto the floor under humid conditions. This is messy and can cause decay of the floor structure. There are two ways of tackling this problem: One is to install a mixing valve on the pipe that supplies water to the water closet. The mixing valve adds enough hot water to keep the temperature of the outside of the tank above the dew point of the air. The other approach is not as wasteful of energy: Add an insulating liner of plastic foam to the inside of the tank. This isolates the cold water from the wall of the tank so that the wall stays at a temperature above the dew point of the air. The tank wall is made of porcelain or plastic, neither of which is permeable to water vapor. Thus, the tank itself serves as a vapor retarder.

2. Insulated Tank on Water Closet

3. Air-conditioning supply ducts that pass through unconditioned space often have surface temperatures below the dew point of the surrounding air. They must be wrapped with insulation and an outside vapor retarder to prevent condensation. Ducts that run within the conditioned space carry air that is only slightly cooler than the room air, so condensation seldom occurs, and insulation is not required. As part of a regular operations and maintenance cycle, maintenance staff should periodically inspect the interiors of supply ducts nearest to the cooling equipment to confirm condensation and biological growth are not present.

4. A basement wall of concrete or masonry stays cool in the summer because of the vast thermal mass of soil outside. Even a basement that is in dry soil will often become damp and musty because of water condensing on the cool interior side of the walls. The best answer to this problem is to use plastic foam to insulate the basement wall on the outside, between the wall and the soil. This allows the interior surface of the wall to stay near the interior air temperature so condensation will not occur.

However, if it is necessary to insulate a basement wall on the inside, especially when retrofit or remodeling work is being done, this can be done by furring the wall and adding thermal insulation between the furring strips. A vapor retarder should be installed just beneath the interior wall finish to keep moist basement air out of the insulation. Unfortunately, this leaves a potential problem unsolved: Basements also tend to leak water from the soil outside, and any leakage will be trapped behind the vapor retarder and insulation, where it can cause decay, rust, and mildew. There is no good answer to this problem. The only option that remains is to damp-proof and drain the foundation carefully on the outside (see **Foundation Drainage**, Chapter 1), and hope for the best.

5. Exterior walls, roofs, window frames, and glass can become cold enough in winter to condense moisture on their interior surfaces. Three detailing patterns in Chapter 3 – **Thermal Insulation**, **Thermal Break**, and **Multiple Glazing** – are often used to keep these interior surfaces warm enough to prevent condensation. There are standard calculation procedures for finding the temperature at which condensation is likely to occur in a building and for determining the amount of thermal resistance necessary in a wall, window, or roof to maintain its interior surface above this temperature. While relatively simple, these procedures are beyond the scope of this book. They are presented in any standard reference book on the heating and cooling of buildings. The detailer may perform these procedures directly or consult with the engineer who is designing the mechanical systems for the building. ■

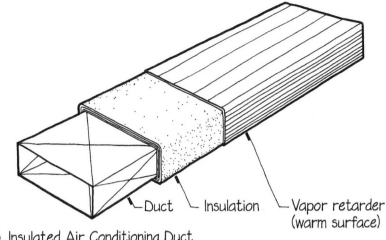

3. Insulated Air Conditioning Duct

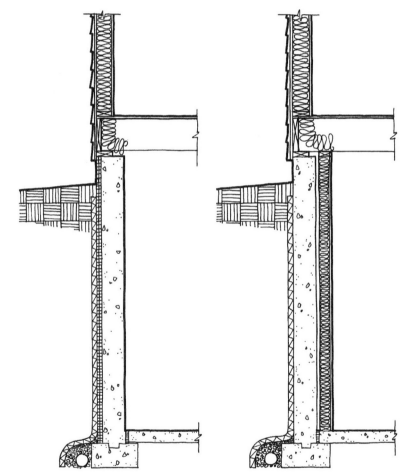

Best: Polystyrene foam insulation on cold side of the wall

Questionable: Furring and insulation inside the wall

4. Basement Wall Insulation

Warm-Side Vapor Retarder

In many climates, a vapor retarder sheet should be installed on the warm side of any insulating material to prevent condensation of moisture within the assembly. There should be only one vapor retarder, which should be at least five times more resistant to vapor than the total vapor resistance of all materials on the cool side of the retarder. This allows the small amount of vapor on the cool side to breathe or escape to the exterior. The vapor retarder prevents water vapor from entering the assembly, and the vapor-permeable side lets any water vapor exit.

The vapor retarder layer should be another of the continuous control layers making up the building envelope. The designer should be able to draw a single uninterrupted line in plan and section representing the vapor retarder layer. A building with one continuous and correctly located vapor retarder layer will not have harmful condensation within the assemblies. Using this single-line test, it is also important to confirm that no more than one vapor retardant layer is present; otherwise, vapor may be trapped with no way to be safely released.

1. Because warm air generally contains more water vapor than cool air, water vapor almost always enters a layer of thermal insulation from the warm side. Somewhere within the layer of insulation, this vapor is likely to condense if there is a large difference in temperature between the indoors and the outdoors. To prevent thermal insulation from becoming saturated with condensate, a vapor retarder should be installed on the warm side of the insulation. Building codes stipulate for each climate zone the class of vapor retarder that is required, and where this control layer should be placed in the assembly. The particular solution for a given project must be carefully selected in collaboration with consultant engineers and with the owner, because it is influenced by the particular locality and by assumptions regarding the building's heating and cooling parameters.

The vapor retarder keeps water vapor from entering the insulation. In the preceding detail pattern, *Warm Interior Surfaces*, a warm-side vapor retarder was shown on the outside of pipe insulation, air-conditioning ductwork insulation, and toilet tank insulation. In walls, floors, and roofs of buildings in climatic areas with cool and cold winters, the warm side is the interior side of the insulation. In hot, humid climates, the warm side is the outside of the insulation, if the building is artificially cooled. In some very mild climates, condensation is unlikely at any time of year under normal climatic conditions, and no vapor retarder is needed. Except for warm, damp climates (climate zones 1–3), the safe thing to do in North America and similar continental locations is to provide a vapor retarder of the appropriate type (see Table 4-1) on the interior side of any thermal insulation in the shell of a building. Refer to Table 4-2 for recommendations for each climate zone.

It is important to avoid leaks in the vapor retarder. Although many types of insulating batts are furnished with a vapor retarder sheet already attached to the interior side, the seams between the batts furnish paths for major leakage of air and water vapor. In most cases, it is preferable to use unfaced batts and to detail a seamless vapor retarder sheet between the insulation and the interior finish layer. The vapor retarder must be sealed around any penetrations, such as window and door frames, electric switches, and receptacles. Closed-cell spray foams are sometimes used to seal minor leaks in these locations.

To detail the exterior envelope of a building, the designer must be aware of how each material in the assembly affects the flow of vapor. The following tables provide general guidelines, and a sample of vapor permeance data for some of the most common building materials. Refer to manufacturers' literature for the properties of particular products being used. Note that some vapor retarders, shown in boldface type in Table 4-3, are more permeable to vapor when the humidity is

TABLE 4-1: Vapor Retarder Classifications

	Permeability	US Perms grains/hr-ft^2-in. Hg
Class I	impermeable	<0.1
Class II	semi-impermeable	0.1–1.0
Class III	semi-permeable	1.0–10.0
(not classified)	permeable	>10.0

TABLE 4-2: Vapor Retarder Use in Various Climate Zones

	Recommended Class on the Interior of Wall Assemblies		
IECC and IRC Climate Zone	If Exterior Sheathing is < 0.1 perm (Class I)	If Exterior Sheathing is 0.1–1.0 perm (Class II)	If Exterior Sheathing is 1.0–10.0 perm (Class III)
1	not required	not required	not required
2	not required	not required	not required
3	not required	not required	not required
4 (not marine)	Class III	Class III	Class III
4 (marine)	Class III or lower	Class II or I	Class III
5	Class II or I	Class II or I	Class III or lower
6	Class II or I	Class II or I	Class II or I
7	Class II or I	Class II or I	Class II or I

Adapted from "Understanding Vapor Barriers," by Joseph Lstiburek, *Building Science Press*, October 2006 (rev. April 2011).

TABLE 4-3: Vapor Permeance of Common Building Materials

	Vapor Permeance		IECC and IRC Class
	US Perms grains/ hr-ft²-in. Hg	Metric Perms ng/s-m²-Pa	
Aluminum foil, 1 mil (0.025 mm)	0	0	I
Roofing felt, double-ply, with hot asphalt	0.005	0.29	I
Bituminous flashing and waterproof membranes, self-adhered	0.05	2.8	I
Polyethylene sheet, 4 mil (0.08 mm)	0.08	4.6	I
Vapor retarder under concrete slab on grade	0.3	17	II
Paint, exterior alkyd (oil), three coats over wood	0.3–1.0	17–57	II
Kraft paper facing for glass fiber batt insulation			
low humidity	0.4–1.0	23–57	II
high humidity	8.0	460	III
Paint, latex vapor barrier primer	0.4	23	II
EPDM single-ply roofing, 45 mil (1.1 mm)	0.4	23	II
Polyurethane, closed-cell spray foam, high density, 2 in. (51 mm)	0.6	34	II
OSB, exterior glue, ½ in. (13 mm), unpainted	0.7	40	II
Plywood, exterior glue, ½ in. (13 mm), unpainted			
low humidity	0.5	29	II
high humidity	3.0–10.0	170–570	III
Brick masonry, 4 in. (102 mm)	0.8–1.1	46–63	II
Proprietary variable-permeance sheet, paper based			
low humidity	0.8	46	II
high humidity	5.5	314	III
Proprietary variable-permeance sheet, nylon or polyethylene based			
low humidity	<1.0	<57	II
high humidity	>10.0	>570	not classified
Paint, interior alkyd (oil), primer and one finish coat over plaster	1.6–3.0	92–172	III
Gypsum wallboard, ½ in. (13 mm)			
unpainted	25.0	1400	not classified
painted, interior latex	2.0–3.0	110–172	III
Building paper, asphalt impregnated	3.3	190	III
Housewraps, SBPO			
low permeance	5.0–10.0	290–570	III
high permeance	>10.0	>570	not classified
Plaster on metal lath, ¾ in. (19 mm)	15.0	860	not classified
Polyicynene, low-density spray foam, 3½ in. (90 mm)	16.0	914	not classified
Polyurethane, open-cell spray foam, 2 in. (51 mm)	17.0	970	not classified

high and less permeable when it is low. These are sometimes called "smart" vapor retarders because they permit greater vapor diffusion when drying is desired, and they retard vapor diffusion in less humid conditions. These variable-permeability membranes are best suited to climate zones that experience substantial swings in temperature and humidity conditions from summer to winter.

2. A low-slope roof is made waterproof by an impervious membrane made of synthetic rubber, plastic, or asphalt laminated with felt. This membrane is also an effective vapor retarder. If insulation is installed below it in a cool or cold climate, two precautions should be taken: A vapor retarder should be installed on the underside (warm side) of the insulation, and a ventilated space should be provided between the insulation and the roofing membrane. This illustration shows how this can be done for insulation below the roof deck.

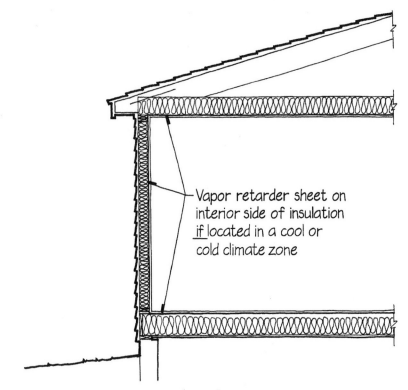

1. Vapor Retarder in Wood Frame Building

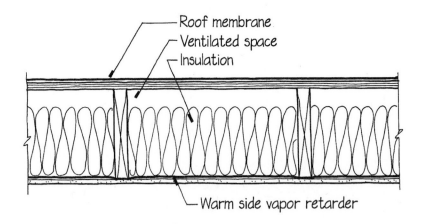

2. Vapor Retarder in Low-Slope Roof

3. In the most conventional type of low-slope roof construction, rigid board insulation is installed above the deck and beneath the waterproof membrane. In cool and cold climates, condensation of moisture is likely to occur in this type of roof, because a vapor retarder (the waterproof membrane) is placed on the cold side of the insulation, which is directly contrary to the logic of this detail pattern. If this type of detail must be used, a vapor retarder should be installed as close as possible to the warm side of the insulation, with at least two-thirds (⅔) of the insulation outside of the retarder. Additionally, the roofing manufacturer's literature should be consulted with regard to installing topside roof vents and a ventilating base sheet over the insulation to release any trapped moisture. The ventilating base sheet is generally a perforated sheet of asphalt-saturated felt that has been embossed or faced with granules in such a way that it provides tiny open channels along which water vapor can move laterally in both directions. This is especially important when a built-up or modified bitumen roof membrane is used because these membranes are vulnerable to blistering when vapor is trapped below them. If these precautions are not taken, vapor pressure can blister and rupture the roof membrane, and trapped moisture can destroy the insulation board and roof deck. See **Vapor Ventilation**, later in this chapter, for further information on ventilating insulated roof assemblies.

4. A preferable detail for a low-slope roof in a cool or cold climate is the inverted roof assembly, in which extruded polystyrene (XPS) foam insulation is installed on top of the roof membrane, allowing the membrane to serve both as a waterproofing membrane and a warm-side vapor retarder. The polystyrene foam absorbs very little water, so it retains its insulating effectiveness even when fully immersed. ▷

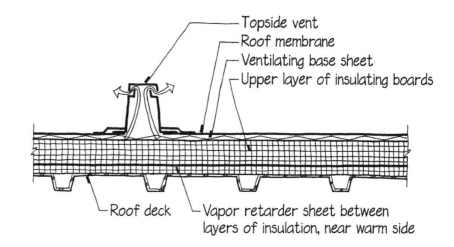

3. Topside Roof Vent

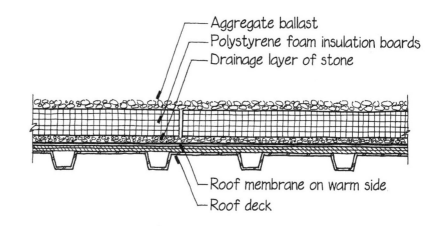

4. Inverted Roof Assembly

5. Spandrel glass for a curtain wall is often furnished by the manufacturer with insulation and vapor retarder already in place. Alternatively, insulated metal "back pans" may be installed using vapor-tight seals into the curtain wall frame. It is critical in this application that the vapor retarder be free of holes and well-sealed around the edges because the spandrel glass is vapor-tight and will not allow any trapped moisture to escape from the insulation.

6. Water vapor enters a wall or ceiling construction by two different means. One is air leakage through cracks and openings from the interior of the building into the wall or ceiling (see *Air Barrier System*, Chapter 2). The other is vapor diffusion, in which water vapor is forced through porous building materials by the difference in vapor pressure between the indoor and outdoor air. In most cases, air leakage transports far more water vapor than vapor diffusion. Working under this assumption, some builders and designers of houses do not install vapor retarders in their buildings. Instead, they take extreme care to seal all potential air leaks in and around the interior finish layer of construction. Sealants and gaskets are installed behind all the edges of the gypsum wallboard on exterior walls. Electrical boxes are carefully sealed to prevent air leakage. This strategy is called the airtight drywall approach. If this approach is used, the building owners must be vigilant to not puncture the airtight membrane for the life of the building – otherwise the strategy will fail. Code officials in the building's jurisdiction should be consulted in advance to verify acceptability.

7. Most vinyl wallcoverings are reasonably effective vapor retarders. Because they are installed on interior surfaces of buildings, they cause no problems in cold climates. But in air-conditioned buildings in humid, warm climates, they can become cold-side vapor retarders, causing moisture to condense on their exterior surfaces. This can result in mildew growth, unpleasant odors, and wall deterioration. Special vapor-permeable vinyl wallcoverings with integral mildewcides are available and should be specified for projects in hot, humid climates. ∎

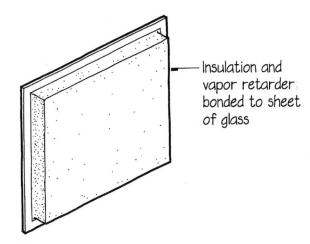

5. Insulated Spandrel Glass

Vapor Ventilation

Water vapor must be provided an easy escape route from the cold side of any vapor retarder. Do not place vapor-impermeable materials (Class I) on the cold side of insulation. This avoids trapping any small amounts of moisture that may get through the vapor retarder. It also allows stray moisture to be baked out of the insulation during periods of warm weather.

1. In the detail pattern *Warm-Side Vapor Retarder*, earlier in this chapter, two common examples of vapor-impermeable materials being placed on the cold side of insulation were illustrated. In one of these, a conventionally insulated low-slope roof, topside roof vents, and a ventilating base sheet are used to release trapped moisture. In the other example, insulated spandrel glass, defect-free fabrication, and installation of the glass units are required to avoid condensation problems, because no provision can be made for vapor ventilation through the glass to the outdoors. These are not optimal solutions.

2. In ordinary wood light frame construction, an air barrier sheet is used on the cold side of the wall, to reduce air infiltration (see *Air Barrier System*, Chapter 2). It is important that this air barrier sheet be permeable to water vapor so that it will not trap stray moisture in the wall but will allow it to diffuse to the outdoors in warm weather. Housewraps made of spun-bonded polyolefin (SBPO) fabric are effective barriers to the passage of air and liquid water but are semi-permeable (Class III) to the passage of water vapor. These qualities make them suitable for use on the cold side of a wall. Polyethylene sheeting and metal foil are impermeable to water vapor and should never be used on the outside of a wall in a cold climate.

3. Although common in residential construction, there is some controversy about the use of plywood sheathing on the outside of a wood frame wall. Because of its continuous internal surfaces of glue, plywood is not very permeable (Class II or III, depending on the humidity) to water vapor and, in theory, can trap moisture in the wall cavities and insulation.

Some detailers call for holes to be drilled a few inches apart in both directions all across the sheathing, to ventilate moisture. Others space the sheathing away from the insulation and provide screened ventilation openings to the outdoor air at the top and bottom of each wall cavity. Investigations of thousands of houses have failed to turn up very many examples of moisture trapped inside plywood-sheathed walls, however, especially when a warm-side vapor retarder has been carefully installed, so most detailers feel safe in continuing to use plywood sheathing in the conventional way.

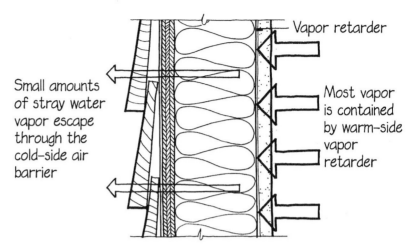

2. Cold-Weather Vapor Movement in a Wood Light Frame Wall

4. In wood-framed attics and roofs, cold-side ventilation is very important for several reasons. One is to prevent ice dams (see *Ventilated Cold Roof*, Chapter 1). Another is to reduce summertime overheating of the building. A third is to remove water vapor. The vapor problem can be much more acute in attics and roofs than in walls because convection transports moist air from indoors into the roof structure through such openings as lighting fixtures, ventilation fans, and attic hatchways. Attics are relatively easy to ventilate, using soffit vents and either a ridge vent or gable vents. Building codes generally require both high and low ventilation openings in an attic, with at least a 3 ft. (914 mm) difference in their elevation. They also specify the required minimum area of the openings, which is 1/150th of the area of the space ventilated.

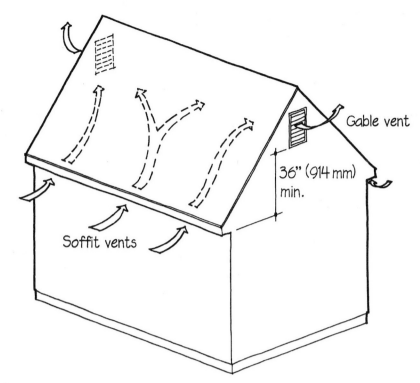

4. Vapor Ventilation from an Attic

5. Insulated rafters with the ceiling surface directly attached to their undersides can present a more difficult detailing problem than attics, because creating the necessary vents and air passages for code-mandated ventilation is challenging. A minimum 1 in. (25 mm) deep air passage beneath the sheathing and above batt or loose-fill insulation is required by building codes; this passage can be created easily and economically by using preformed vent spacer channels made of plastic foam or paper fiber. In cold climates, this usually leaves insufficient space for the code-mandated amount of thermal insulation, however. Sometimes this problem can be overcome merely by using deeper rafters than are structurally required, perhaps increasing their spacing from 16–24 in. (400–600 mm) for greater economy of material. If this leaves insufficient space for insulation, then the designer must replace some or all of the thickness of glass fiber batts with high-efficiency plastic foam insulation, add a layer of rigid plastic foam insulation below the rafters, or else furr above the rafters and add a second layer of roof sheathing to provide the required ventilation.

6. Several manufacturers market proprietary vented roof insulation assemblies that include thermal insulation, cold-side ventilation passages, and a nail-base top sheet to accept shingles. These are especially useful where the rafters themselves are to be exposed in the room below, as in heavy timber framing. The assemblies are quite thick and are attached to the roof with special long nails or screws that are driven through the insulation assembly into the roof decking. Some of these proprietary systems can also be applied over sloping metal roof decks and can be covered with metal or low-slope roofing membranes.

7. An air space or ventilation passage for water vapor is not always required in a roof deck assembly. Vapor permeable open-cell or low-density spray foam can be installed from below onto the underside of roof decking or sheathing. A structural insulated panel (SIP) or a cross-laminated timber (CLT) roof deck with rigid insulation above it has no cavity within the assembly.

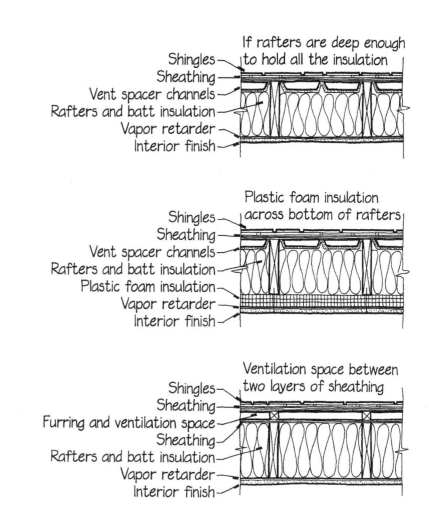

5. Roof Ventilation for Ceilings Attached Directly to Rafters

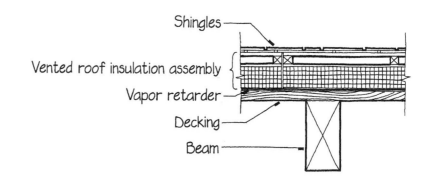

6. Vented Roof Insulation Assembly for Heavy Timber Roof

Condensate Drainage

Where condensation may occur within a building, provide channels and weep holes that allow gravity to remove the moisture without damage to the building.

1. Many proprietary designs for slope glazing systems and skylights are designed to catch and drain condensate that may run off the interior surface of the glass in cold weather. If this is not done, the condensate will drip into the room below. In this slope glazing purlin, condensate gutters are built into the lower flanges of the aluminum structural member. The gutter on the uphill side will catch moisture that runs off the glass above it. (The gutter on the downhill side is of no use, but having gutters on both sides makes it impossible for careless workers to install the purlin upside down.) Each purlin is supported at each end by an aluminum rafter. The rafter has a similar cross section to the purlin but is deeper. The connection between the two is made in such a way that water draining from the end of the purlin is caught in the gutter at the bottom of the rafter. Here it drains rapidly by gravity to the bottom of the rafter slope, where it escapes to the outside through weep holes.

2. Though condensation problems are generally much less severe in wall assemblies than in slope glazing systems, most proprietary metal curtain wall systems include channels, weep holes, and sometimes weep tubes to drain condensate and leakage from internal cavities (see also ***Drain and Weep***, Chapter 1). ∎

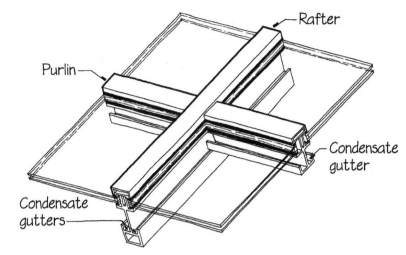

1. Condensate Drainage in a Slope Glazing System

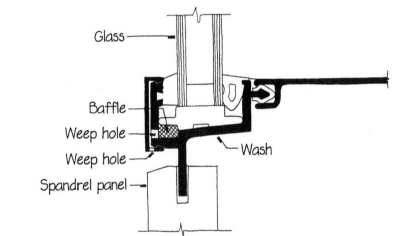

2. Condensate Drainage in an Aluminum Curtain Wall Horizontal Mullion

CHAPTER 5: Controlling Sound

Noise reduction, acoustic privacy, and good hearing conditions are qualities sought in almost every building. Controlling sound supports distraction free and functional hearing which, in turn, assists the quality of indoor environments. Interior acoustic issues are especially prominent for individuals who require calm, quiet living or working spaces. The details of a building contribute in important ways to achieving these qualities (see **Sensory Richness**, Chapter 14).

To reduce noise inside a building, exterior assemblies should be detailed to exclude outdoor noise. Much of an interior space's acoustic performance lies in its ceiling and wall design. Detail potentially noisy components of a building in such a way that they remain quiet. Use sound-absorbing materials within rooms to reduce noise levels from conversations and machinery. To achieve acoustic privacy, detail interior doors, partitions, floors, ceilings, and ductwork to reduce sound transmission between rooms.

Open interiors rely less on compartmentation; instead, design emphasis is placed on spatial configuration and surface treatments to achieve good acoustic performance. For good hearing conditions, reduce noise and provide an optimum combination and configuration of absorbing and reflecting surfaces within a room.

Controlling sound requires use of three basic acoustic strategies: absorbing; blocking; and covering. The detailer is well advised to work with a specialized consultant to achieve good acoustical qualities in a building, but many ordinary problems of noise, hearing, and privacy can be solved by means of four detail patterns (each pattern listed will be further explained later in this chapter):

> ***Airtight, Heavy, Limp Partition*** (p. 80)
> ***Cushioned Floor*** (p. 83)
> ***Quiet Attachments*** (p. 85)
> ***Sound-Absorbing Surfaces*** (p. 86)

Architectural Detailing: Function Constructability Aesthetics. Fourth Edition. Patrick Rand, Jason Miller, and Edward Allen.
© 2025 John Wiley & Sons, Inc. Published 2025 by John Wiley & Sons, Inc.

Airtight, Heavy, Limp Partition

The ideal soundproof partition is airtight, heavy, and limp. A thick, hanging sheet of soft lead sealed around the edges fulfills these requirements; however, it is an expensive, unattractive, and environmentally negative solution. Detailing partitions using a combination of standard materials incorporate the necessary qualities of airtightness, heaviness, and limpness.

1. The degree of airborne sound resistance of a partition to the transmission of sound is measured in units of decibels and is called its sound transmission class (STC). A higher number indicates greater sound transmission resistance. For a variety of partition construction details, STCs are tabulated in references such as the Gypsum Association's *Fire Resistance Design Manual* and the National Concrete Masonry Association's *TEK Manual for Concrete Masonry Design and Construction* (see **Appendix A, The Detailer's Reference Shelf**).

Codes require walls, partitions, and floors separating dwellings be at least STC 50. Tables 5-1 and 5-2 give recommended minimum STCs for walls and partitions in a variety of situations; higher values than these are desirable. Because background noise masks the intelligibility of sounds, partitions of lesser acoustical quality are considered acceptable in noisier neighborhoods.

TABLE 5-1: Selected Sound Isolation Criteria for Residential Walls and Partitions

	Quiet Neighborhood	Average Neighborhood	Noisy Neighborhood
Ambient Sound Level	Ave. 35–40 dB(A)	Ave. 40–45 dB(A)	Ave. 45–65 dB(A)
	Minimum STC	*Minimum STC*	*Minimum STC*
Between Dwelling Units			
Bedroom to bedroom	55	52	48
Living room to living room	55	52	48
Bathroom to bedroom	59	56	52
Kitchen, dining, or family room to bedroom	58	55	52
Within Dwelling Units			
Bedroom to bedroom	48	44	40
Living room to bedroom	50	46	42
Kitchen to bedroom	52	48	45
Bathroom to bedroom or living room	52	48	45

Federal Housing Administration/U.S. Department of Housing and Urban Development/Public Domain.

TABLE 5-2: Selected Sound Isolation Criteria for Nonresidential Walls and Partitions

Source-Room Occupancy	Receiver-Room Occupancy	Minimum STC
Executive offices, conference rooms, doctors' suites	Adjacent offices	50–55
Normal offices	Adjacent offices	45–50
Laboratory or manufacturing area	Adjacent offices	40–45
School classrooms	Adjacent classrooms	45
School classrooms	Corridor	50
School music or drama area	Adjacent music or drama area	55+
Mechanical equipment room	Any other room	60
Interior occupied room	Exterior	35–60

The American Institute of Architects/John Wiley & Sons.

2. This sampling of partition details illustrates the fundamentals of detailing a framed partition for acoustical privacy. The STCs of these partitions relate to the preceding tables. All of these constructions utilize readily available, inexpensive materials: gypsum wallboard and wood stud framing. Similar details have been developed for steel stud framing; the STC values are the same for wood and steel. Each partition is made airtight by using acoustical sealant around the edges, by avoiding electrical outlets or other services that pierce the wall, and by using heavy, tightly gasketed doors. The acoustic quality of a room is often determined by the weakest element of its enclosure. Elements that create voids in the enclosure system, such as windows and doors, can be the weakest link.

The lowest-rated partition illustrated (far left) uses gypsum board attached directly to the studs. In the next detail to the right, limpness is created by mounting the gypsum board on one side of the partition on resilient sheet metal channels that absorb vibrations. This results in a 10-decibel improvement in performance. A sound attenuation blanket of mineral fiber adds a further 10 decibels (second from right). The best performing acoustic partition shown (far right) is made heavy by applying additional layers of gypsum board and by making the two sides of the partition unequal in mass so that they will not vibrate at the same frequencies. The channels, sealants, and batts are all stock available items (see *Off-the-Shelf Parts*, Chapter 13). This mass / airspace / mass arrangement limits transmission of sound.

3. Masonry partitions generally have fairly high STCs. Masonry is a heavy material, and the STCs of unsurfaced masonry partitions are in direct proportion to their weight. Some types of concrete masonry are fairly porous, but airtightness can be achieved with paint or plaster. Limpness is a difficult quality to achieve in masonry itself, but it can be added by mounting resilient channels to a masonry wall and attaching a gypsum board finish layer to the channels. ▷

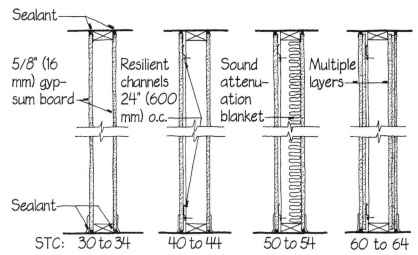

2. Sound Transmission Classes of Various Framed Partitions

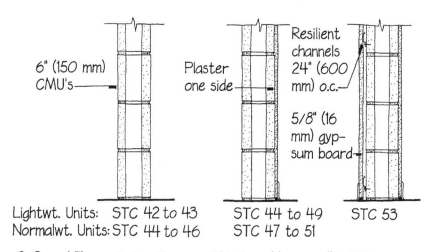

3. Sound Transmission Classes of Various Masonry Partitions

4. An opening in or around a door – a key-hole or ventilation grill, an undercut bottom edge, or a crack between the door and frame – can make an otherwise effective partition almost transparent to sound. Doors in privacy partitions should be avoided where possible. If a door is necessary, it should be solid-core wood or composite steel, designed and tested for acoustic isolation. These are typical acoustical gasketing details, using commercially available components, to seal the cracks around a door. Gaskets are detailed for easy replacement, as they deteriorate with use (see also **Weatherstripped Crack**, Chapter 2).

5. Ductwork should be laid out so that it does not furnish a path for sound to travel between one room and the next, rendering even the best of partitions acoustically worthless. If such ductwork is inevitable, it should be rectangular rather than round in cross section, because flat duct walls are less rigid, making them better at attenuating sound. They should also be lined with sound-absorbing material to prevent sound waves from propagating. The same principle applies to above-ceiling plenums and below-floor service chases.

6. Windows in buildings near airports, highways, and heavy industries often need to be as soundproof as possible. A single sheet of ordinary glass has an STC of only 28 to 36. Two layers of glass with air-space between, sealed carefully around the edges, provide a moderate amount of mass, airtightness, and some resiliency to achieve an STC ranging from 32 to 40. The same range of STCs can be accomplished with a single sheet of laminated glass, which consists of two layers of glass tightly sandwiching a soft plastic interlayer that imparts resiliency. In each of these examples, the lower STCs correspond to a glass thickness of ¼ in. (6.5 mm), and the upper STCs correspond to a glass thickness of ½ in. to ¾ in. (13 to 19 mm). Operable windows should be avoided in high-noise environments, because they are difficult to make airtight. ■

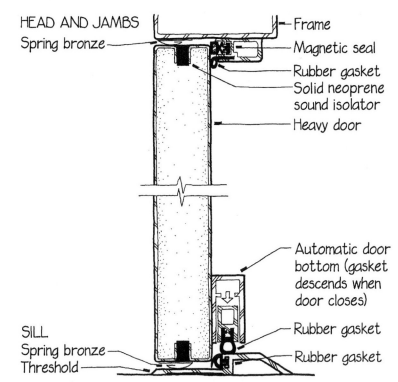

4. Acoustical Gaskets on a Door, STC 43 to 57

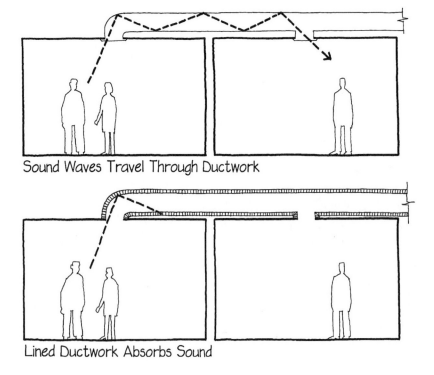

5. Sound Travel Through Ductwork

Cushioned Floor

The control of sound transmission through floors is often critical, especially in apartments, hotels, and dormitories, where people live above and below one another. In addition to blocking airborne sound, floors must also impede impact and vibration noises from heels and machinery. The criteria of airtightness, heaviness, and limpness that apply to partitions are joined by a fourth criterion when designing floors: cushioning.

1. The resistance to sound transmission of a floor assembly is measured in two ways. Resistance to the transmission of airborne sound is expressed in decibels as a sound transmission class (STC), the same as for partitions. Resistance to the transmission of impact noise is expressed in decibels as the impact insulation class (IIC). Both of these quantities need to be controlled through detailing to achieve the desired acoustical performance.

Generally, the IIC value for a construction assembly should be no lower than the STC criteria for that adjacency. Codes require assemblies separating dwellings be at least IIC 50. Table 5-3 gives recommended minimum STC and IIC values for residential floors in a variety of situations; higher values than these are desirable. Because background noise masks the intelligibility of sounds, floor and ceiling constructions of lesser acoustical quality are considered acceptable in noisier neighborhoods. ▷

TABLE 5-3: Selected Sound Isolation Criteria for Floor and Ceiling Constructions Between Dwelling Units

Ambient Sound Level	Quiet Neighborhood Ave. 35–40 dB(A)		Average Neighborhood Ave. 40–45 dB(A)		Noisy Neighborhood Ave. 45–65 dB(A)	
	Minimum STC	Minimum IIC	Minimum STC	Minimum IIC	Minimum STC	Minimum IIC
Bedroom above bedroom	55	55	52	52	48	48
Living room above bedroom	57	60	54	57	50	53
Kitchen above bedroom	58	65	55	62	52	58
Bedroom above living room	57	55	54	52	50	48
Living room above living room	55	55	52	52	48	48
Kitchen above living room	55	60	52	57	48	53
Bath above bath	52	52	50	50	48	48

Federal Housing Administration/U.S. Department of Housing and Urban Development/Public Domain.

2. Airtightness is easily achieved in a concrete or concrete-topped steel floor structure if openings for pipes, wires, and ducts are carefully sealed. Wood floor structures may be made airtight by adding a topping of poured concrete or gypsum, or by careful plaster or gypsum board work on the ceiling below. A concrete, steel, or wood floor is sufficiently heavy to attenuate airborne noise.

Impact noise can be reduced using limpness or resiliency in several ways. The most effective way in most situations is to install a heavy carpet – or other soft flooring material – and pad on top of the slab. This provides resiliency and also cushions heel impacts. Notice in the accompanying examples, however, that the carpet and pad do little to improve the STC of a floor. In the wood floor illustrated here, the increase in STC is achieved by mounting the gypsum board ceiling on resilient channels. Proprietary springy hangers can also be used to suspend the ceiling loosely, isolating vibrations between floor and ceiling. Structure-borne noise is not reduced by the use of loose sound-attenuation blankets between joists, because the structural framing bypasses these blankets.

3. Hard floor finishes such as ceramic tile, vinyl tile, sheet vinyl, or wood flooring and mass timber decks are generators and transmitters of impact noise. Sound-deadening board, resilient matting, or floating floor isolators installed between the top of the structural floor and the bottom of the finish floor can cushion these floors effectively. To be effective for the life of the building, these sound-deadening layers must resist compression and remain springy. ■

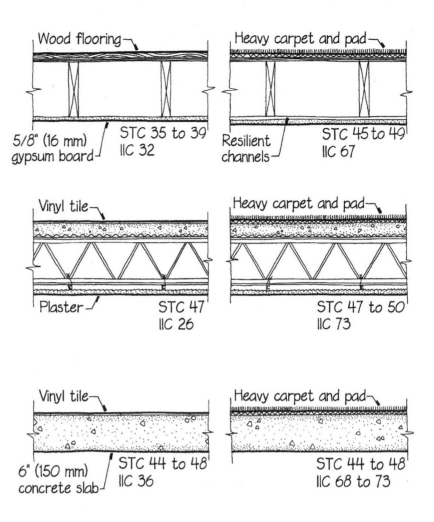

2. Effect of Carpet and Pad on Various Floor Constructions

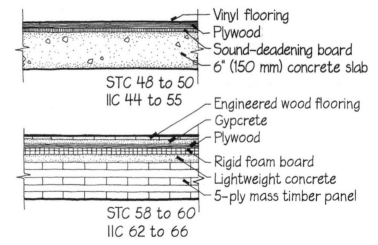

3. Cushioning a Hard Floor Finish

Quiet Attachments

1. Squeaks, bangs, rumbles, and other structural or mechanical noises in buildings can be reduced or prevented with careful detailing and proper maintenance. *Quiet attachments* are created by controlling the connections between materials, isolating details that absorb movement or vibration, and combining methods of connection – such as adhesive and mechanical – to reduce noise. A wood subfloor glued to the supporting joists and nailed is much less likely to loosen and squeak over time than a subfloor that is merely nailed. Screws or ring-shank nails are much less likely to loosen and squeak in a subfloor than common nails.

2. A prefabricated wood stair with housed stringers uses wedges and glue to create a tight unit highly resistant to loosening and creaking underfoot.

3. Doorstops, frame pads, and door closers dramatically reduce the amount of noise a door can generate as it opens and closes.

4. Motors, pumps, fans, and other machinery should be isolated acoustically from the structure of the building to reduce the transmission of structure-borne noise. Many types of resilient equipment mounts are available that use metal springs or rubber pads to isolate equipment vibrations from the structure. Flexible duct connectors should be used to join ductwork to fans. Vibrations from the source are dissipated by the flexible connectors and are not transmitted to the adjoining elements.

5. Hot water pipes and hydronic heating pipes expand and contract longitudinally when they heat and cool. This causes them to rub against their mounting brackets. A smooth plastic mounting bracket reduces friction against the pipe and virtually eliminates the ticking and scraping noises a metal bracket would generate. ■

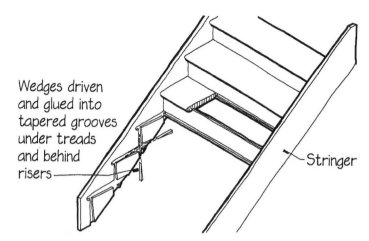

2. Prefabricated Wood Stair with Housed Stringers

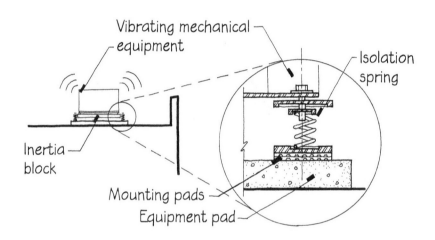

4. Vibration Isolating Equipment Mounts

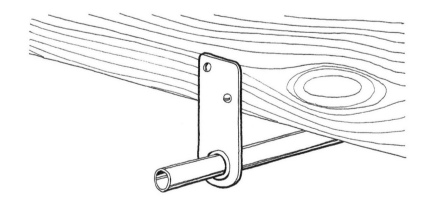

5. Plastic Bracket for Hydronic Piping

SECTION 1 ■ FUNCTION

Sound-Absorbing Surfaces

Soft, porous, thick finish materials absorb most airborne sound and reflect little. This makes them useful in achieving quiet conditions inside a building.

1. The accompanying table indicates the capacity of various surfaces to absorb airborne sound. The Sound Absorption Coefficient [which supersedes the Noise Reduction Coefficient (NRC)] indicates the average amount of sound energy absorbed by a material in the normal audible range (Table 5-4). A coefficient of 0.0 indicates the material is a perfect reflector of sound; 1.0 indicates it is a perfect absorber. A material with a coefficient of 0.80 absorbs 80 percent of the noise incident upon it.

2. A carpet and pad, upholstered furniture, and window draperies all absorb sound and are effective in reducing sound levels within a room. Unpadded carpet and thin upholstery and curtains absorb only very high frequencies of sound, however, leaving noise at middle and low frequencies as a continuing problem.

TABLE 5-4: Approximate Sound Absorption Coefficients of Common Materials

(Values measured across a frequency range of 250–2000 Hz)	Sound Absorption Coefficient
Brick, unpainted and unglazed	0.03–0.05
Brick, painted	0.01–0.02
Concrete, rough, unpainted	0.02–0.08
Concrete, smooth, painted	0.01–0.02
Concrete masonry unit, unpainted	0.29–0.44
Concrete masonry unit, painted	0.05–0.09
Cellulose fibers, sprayed	0.50–0.75
Polyurethane foam, rigid insulation board	0.30
Polyurethane foam, profiled acoustic panel	0.80
Carpet, on foam rubber pad	0.30–0.55
Wood tongue-and-groove floor	0.08–0.19
Plywood	0.10–0.18
Wood, perforated acoustic panel	0.75–0.90
Wood, perforated acoustic panel, with acoustic fiber in void	0.70–0.95
Mineral fiber acoustic ceiling panels, suspended, high noise reduction	0.75–0.90
Glass	0.02–0.10
Steel	0.07–0.10
Metal, perforated sheets, 13% open	0.64–0.97
Plaster or gypsum board, painted	0.01–0.07
Marble or glazed tile	0.01–0.02
Wood or metal seating (occupied)	0.80–0.85
Wood or metal seating (unoccupied)	0.19–0.38
Fabric upholstered seating (unoccupied)	0.37–0.60
Fabric curtains, varying weight	0.05–0.60
Water or ice	0.01–0.02

3. Ceiling-mounted acoustical tiles and panels are manufactured in a wide range of NRCs. Full ceilings of highly absorbent panels or tiles are useful in quieting noisy office or retail spaces. Partial ceiling coverage permits sound to enter voids between tiles or panels, to be absorbed by the ceiling cavity materials. The ability of an acoustical ceiling to absorb lower frequencies of sound can be enhanced by suspending it or furring it down from the structure above, and by installing sound attenuation batts on top of it. Acoustic plaster, even if properly installed, is an effective absorber only at higher frequencies.

4. Hard, acoustically reflective ceilings of wood, plaster, gypsum board, or prefabricated panels are appropriate in many types of spaces designed for good hearing of speech or music. Such spaces should be designed in collaboration with an acoustical consultant.

5. Proprietary acoustic panels made of fabric, perforated gypsum, or perforated wood can be selected to alter the sound absorption qualities of ceilings and walls. Manufacturers also provide acoustic design tools to aid the detailer in making appropriate selections for each surface of a room. For instance, a perforated cross-laminated wood panel may be chosen for a wall or ceiling surface to reflect voices in the room but absorb other frequencies. The perforations permit sound to pass through the surface to be absorbed by acoustically absorptive materials that are installed between furring strips. Other room surfaces may have similar wood panels that are grooved on the face but not perforated, and others that are smooth, each of which will reflect sound back into the room differently. ■

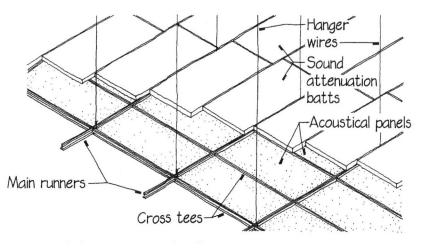

3. Suspended Acoustical Ceiling Seen from Above

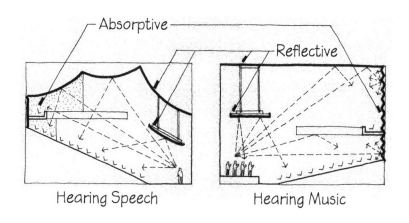

4. Locating Acoustically Reflective and Absorptive Surfaces

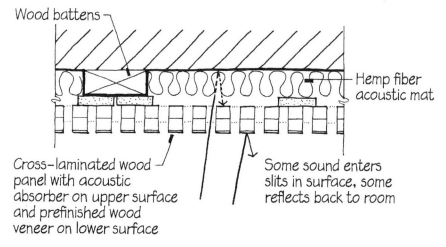

5. Acoustic Ceiling Assembly

CHAPTER 6: Accommodating Movement

A building is never at rest. Its movements, though seemingly small, are extremely powerful and can cause irreparable damage unless the building is detailed to accommodate them. The detailer must keep in mind a number of sources of movement in buildings:

- **Temperature movement** is caused by the expansion and contraction of building materials related to rising and falling temperatures. A material's temperature is chiefly affected by surrounding air temperature but is affected also by radiant energy as sunlight strikes a dark surface.
- **Moisture movement** occurs in porous, hygroscopic materials such as wood, plaster, masonry, concrete, and many polymers. These materials swell as they absorb moisture from water or humid air, and they shrink as they dry.
- **Phase-change movement** accompanies a change in the physical state of a material. The phase-change movement of primary interest to the detailer is the expansion of water as it freezes.
- **Chemical-change movement** takes place in certain construction materials as they cure or age. Gypsum plaster expands slightly as it changes from a slurry to a solid. Solvent-release coatings and sealants shrink as they cure. Reinforcing bars that rust expand and can crack the masonry or concrete in which they are embedded.
- **Structural deflections** always accompany changes in the loads on a building. Beams, slabs, trusses, and arches sag more as they are loaded more heavily, and sag less as their loads are reduced. Columns become shorter as loads are applied to them. Wind and seismic loads flex and rack exterior wall components; they move buildings laterally by substantial amounts.
- **Structural creep** is characteristic of wood and concrete, both of which sag permanently by a small amount during the first several years of a building's life and then stabilize.
- **Foundation settlement** occurs when the soil beneath a building deflects, creeps, or shifts laterally under loading. All foundations settle; if the settlement is small and is uniform across the entire building, little movement occurs within the components of the building itself. If settlement is nonuniform from one wall or column to another, considerable movement must be accommodated.

Table 6-1 associates typical causes of movement with various building materials. It shows that building materials constantly undergo small but inexorable amounts of movement in response to one or more causes.

We can predict, often with impressive accuracy, the magnitude of movement that will occur from each of these sources:

- Temperature movement can be quantified rather precisely using the expected range of temperature difference and the coefficient of thermal expansion of the material (see Chapter 1, Table 1-2).
- Moisture movement cannot be quantified with such precision, but we can predict it accurately enough to prevent it from causing damage to a building (see information later in this chapter). Phase-change and chemical-change movements can be estimated with varying degrees of accuracy.
- Structural deflections are computed very closely using standard engineering techniques, and structural creep can be quantified to within manageable limits. A geotechnical or foundation

TABLE 6-1: Causes of Movement in Building Materials and Their Results

Cause	Result	Concrete	Concrete masonry	Clay masonry	Stone	Wood	Steel	Polymers
Temperature change	Expansion/Contraction	Yes	Yes	Yes	Yes	Yes	Yes	Yes
Moisture content change	Expansion/Contraction	Yes	Yes	Yes	Yes	Yes	No	Yes
Initial moisture absorption	Permanent expansion	No	No	Yes	No	No	No	No
Water freezing (phase change)	Expansion	Yes	Yes	Yes	Yes	No	No	Yes
Cement hydration/Carbonation	Permanent shrinkage	Yes	Yes	No	No	No	No	No
Load application	Elastic deformation	Yes	Yes	Yes	Yes	Yes	Yes	Yes
Sustained load	Creep/Contraction	Yes	Yes	Yes	Yes	Yes	Yes	Yes

Architectural Detailing: Function Constructability Aesthetics. Fourth Edition. Patrick Rand, Jason Miller, and Edward Allen.
© 2025 John Wiley & Sons, Inc. Published 2025 by John Wiley & Sons, Inc.

engineer can provide enough data regarding expected levels of foundation movement to guide the detailer. During the life of a building, changes in the surrounding soil and water conditions, such as a deep excavation nearby, may call for further analyses.

In detailing a building, it should be acknowledged: Most movements are unpreventable and are caused by forces so large they cannot be restrained. Instead, movement joints between building components are provided, at such intervals and in such configurations that the movements can be absorbed without harm in these joints. Designers must be alert to where movement due to these unpreventable forces is most likely. For instance, thermal movement is likely to be more significant in dark wall or roof materials that are exposed to the sun on the sunny south or west elevations. Moisture movement is likely to be more radical on a window sill or base of a wall, where water is concentrated, than under an overhang. The curtain wall on the fortieth floor is different from the fourth floor in terms of anticipated movement because wind pressure is greater aloft; detailing must take that into consideration.

Without provision of movement joints, the forces that cause movement in a building would create their own joints by cracking and crushing components until the building's internal stresses were relieved. At best, the result would be unsightly; at worst, the result would be a leaky, unstable, and unsafe building.

The detail patterns that relate to accommodating movement in buildings are associated with several simple strategies. All of the patterns listed will be further explained later in this chapter.

The first of these is to manufacture and configure building materials in ways that minimize their tendency to move in undesirable ways.

Its associated patterns are:

Seasoning and Curing (p. 91)
Vertical-Grain Lumber (p. 94)
Equalizing Cross-Grain (p. 96)
Relieved Back (p. 98)
Foundation below Frost Line (p. 99)

A second strategy is to separate building elements that are likely to move at different rates and in different ways. Its patterns are:

Structure/Enclosure Joint (p. 100)
Abutment Joint (p. 102)

A third strategy is to divide large building surfaces that are likely to crack, crush, or buckle into smaller units of such a size that the likelihood of such failures is greatly reduced. This leads to the following patterns:

Expansion Joint (p. 103)
Control Joint (p. 106)
Sliding Joint (p. 109)

A fourth and final strategy is to divide a large building, especially one with a complex geometry, into two or more geometrically simple buildings, each of a size and compactness such that we can reasonably expect it to move as a unit in response to large forces, such as foundation settlement and seismic accelerations. This leads to the pattern:

Building Separation Joint (p. 111)

Seasoning and Curing

Many porous construction materials should be seasoned or cured for a period of time following their manufacture before they are incorporated into a building. This allows them to reach an equilibrium moisture content and to stabilize dimensionally before their movement is restrained by adjoining components of a building.

1. Wood is the building material most subject to dimensional change due to changes in moisture content. At the time it is cut, it is fully saturated with water. As it dries, it becomes stronger and stiffer. It also shrinks by very large amounts until it reaches its equilibrium moisture content, at which point it no longer gives off moisture to the air. Wood shrinkage and expansion in common species of softwoods can be quantified using industry references such as the Western Wood Products Association's "Dimensional Stability of Western Lumber Products" (see *Appendix A, The Detailer's Reference Shelf*). Also provided in *Appendix A* is a link to an online lumber shrinkage estimator. A shrinkage graph for a typical softwood is shown in drawing 4 in the following section, *Vertical-Grain Lumber*.

Shrinkage in wood varies, depending on grain direction and shape. Wavy grain and knots cause uneven shrinkage, resulting in distortion of the shape of the wood element (see the following section, *Vertical-Grain Lumber*). Wood is seasoned commercially either by stacking it in loose arrays for a period of many months to dry in the air or by drying it in a kiln over a period of a few hours or days, depending on its dimensions. Kiln drying generally produces a stable product, meeting the specified moisture content more quickly. Throughout its lifetime, however, a piece of wood seasoned by either method will absorb moisture and expand during humid periods and will give off moisture and shrink during dry periods. For these reasons, detailers cannot be certain how a given wood assembly will

Timber

Glue-laminated wood

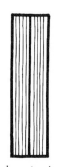
Laminated veneer lumber (LVL) (doubled)

Parallel strand lumber (PSL)

1. Timber and Engineered Wood Products

move for the life of the building. We cannot eliminate its movement, but we can employ techniques to moderate it.

Though made with the same porous materials, engineered wood products, such as glue-laminated beams, cross-laminated wood panels, laminated veneer lumber, and parallel strand lumber, tend to undergo much less drying, shrinkage, or distortion than solid timber. The wood used to make these products is kiln dried before being incorporated into the large wood elements. Distortion is minimized because wood grain direction varies in the members, with no prevailing direction of shrinkage. These products are manufactured and dressed to their final size after drying is complete.

2. Unseasoned ("green") lumber is sometimes used in construction, especially for framing. Special care should be taken in detailing the finish components of buildings framed with unseasoned lumber, because framing components will shrink by large amounts in the perpendicular-to-grain direction, which will apply severe stresses to finish components that are rigidly fixed to the frame. Fasteners such as nails and bolts may loosen as the wood shrinks.

Unseasoned lumber is also expected to distort by cupping, warping, and twisting as it dries to its equilibrium moisture content. See the following section, *Vertical-Grain Lumber*, to see how moisture affects the shape of a piece of wood. Unseasoned lumber should never be used for interior finish components. In fact, finish lumber should be the most carefully seasoned of all, dried to a moisture content that is in equilibrium with the air – usually about 11% by weight, but this varies from 4% to 14% for different climates and seasons.

3. Thermally modified timber (TMT) uses temperatures almost three times higher than normal kiln drying, to alter the chemistry of wood fibers, making them permanently resistant to biological attacks such as fungus and insects. TMT wood is harder and more brittle than kiln-dried wood and is more stable in shape and dimension. All species of wood can be treated in this manner, which typically darkens the wood; no surface finishes are required, but they can be applied if desired. TMT products are often used on building exteriors, where their durability and appearance qualities are valued. ▷

4. Concrete masonry units are manufactured with moisture content that has been controlled at the plant to reduce drying shrinkage after the units have been laid. Despite this, minor shrinkage is to be expected in concrete masonry units as a result of drying and carbonation, which is an unavoidable result of the curing process. Clay bricks, on the other hand, are devoid of moisture when they come from the kiln and expand very slightly over a period of weeks and months as they absorb small amounts of moisture from the air. It is wise to allow both types of masonry units to season for a time before using them in a wall; this has usually occurred before the units are purchased by the contractor. Seasoning may be abbreviated if specially made units are rush ordered. Masonry units can be monitored to verify that their equilibrium moisture content has been reached prior to use.

5. At the time concrete is poured, it contains more water than is needed for curing. This excess water evaporates slowly from the concrete, causing it to shrink slightly over an extended period. In addition, minor shrinkage is expected in concrete as a natural byproduct of the hydration process. An exception to this is concrete made with an expansive cement that offsets normal initial shrinkage. Concrete mix ratios and aggregates also affect the amount of curing shrinkage.

In most concrete walls and slabs on grade, it is possible to provide control joints to absorb the cracking that will be caused by this shrinkage (see **Control Joint**, later in this chapter). When pouring structural slabs that are very large in area and that cannot have control joints, minimize shrinkage distress by pouring each story of the building in smaller sections, separated by open shrinkage strips. After these sections have cured and dried long enough so that most shrinkage has occurred, the shrinkage strips are poured to complete the floor. Reinforcing bars should be spliced within the shrinkage strips so the separate areas of the floor can move independently while the strips are open. The concrete in the strips should be keyed mechanically to the slabs on either side. Supporting formwork must be left in place until the concrete in the shrinkage strips has cured. The locations of the shrinkage strips must be determined by the structural engineer.

Even "no slump" concrete used in concrete masonry units and some specialty concrete products will undergo shrinkage due to evaporation and hydration.

6. Moisture movement of cementitious materials and masonry can be approximated using Table 6-2.

Example 1 About how much will a monolithic concrete slab 210 ft. (64 m) long shrink during curing and drying? Use the average value within a range unless otherwise indicated.

(210 ft.)(12 in./ft.) = 2,520 in.
(2,520 in.)(0.00065 in./in.) = 1.64 in.
64 m = 64,000 mm
(64,000) (0.00065 mm/mm) = 41.6 mm

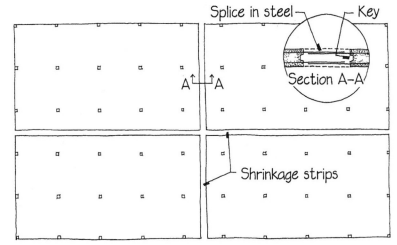

5. Plan of Large Concrete Slab with Shrinkage Strips

TABLE 6-2: Coefficients of Moisture Movement of Cementitious Materials and Masonry

	in./in. (mm/mm)
Curing and drying **shrinkage** of concrete	0.0005–0.0008
Curing and drying **shrinkage** of cement stucco	0.0008–0.0016
Curing and drying **shrinkage** of concrete masonry	0.0002–0.0004
Moisture **expansion** of brick masonry	0.0003–0.0005
Moisture **expansion** of gypsum wallboard	0.0004

Example 2 Approximately how much moisture expansion should be anticipated in a new utility-sized brick wall 175 ft. (53.3 m) long?

Brick units tend to expand initially, but the mortar binding them tends to shrink slightly as it cures. The overall amount of brick wall expansion tends to be greater when the brick sizes are large, because the brick units constitute a greater share of the wall volume. Large utility-sized units are used in this example wall, so the expected moisture movement will be at the upper end of the indicated range.

(175 ft.)(12 in./ft.) = 2,100 in.
(2,100 in.)(0.0005 in./in.) = 1.05 in.
53.3 m = 53,300 mm
(53,300) (0.0005 mm/mm) = 26.6 mm

7. When materials with different movement rates and directions are combined, joints must be detailed to provide needed flexibility. In the example shown, the coping on a parapet made of anchored brick veneer and concrete masonry is expected to rotate slightly as the materials reach equilibrium with the environment around them. In walls containing stone, brick, and concrete masonry, it is important to compare the properties of the particular materials and avoid interspersing materials that will move inconsistently. It is better to insert an entire course of concrete masonry into a brick wall than to insert isolated units at intervals. ■

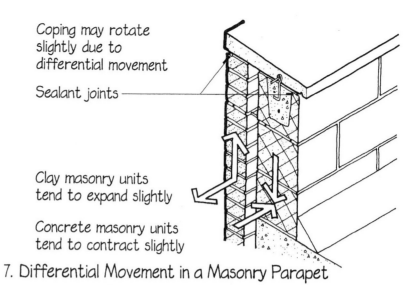

7. Differential Movement in a Masonry Parapet

Vertical-Grain Lumber

Boards and lumber used for flat finish components of a building should be sawn from the log in such a way that the growth rings of the wood run approximately perpendicular to the surface of the board.

1. When a log is seasoned, it shrinks very little along its length. It shrinks considerably in its radial direction (perpendicular to the growth rings), and it shrinks most of all in its tangential direction (along the growth rings). The amounts of shrinkage are very large, as the accompanying graph indicates. The amount of shrinkage depends on the difference between the moisture content when milled and when at equilibrium with its place in the building. Interior and exterior moisture contents will vary considerably, depending on the climate of the building location. Consult references by the American Wood Council and the Architectural Woodworking Institute in *Appendix A, The Detailer's Reference Shelf*, to find recommendations for a particular location.

When the natural grain is wavy or irregular along the length of a piece of wood, then seasoning distortion such as twisting and warping of the piece is more likely. Experienced carpenters order extra quantities so that they can cull out unacceptable pieces.

2. The larger shrinkage in the tangential direction causes a log to check (split along radial lines). It also causes pieces of lumber cut from different parts of the cross section of the log to distort during seasoning in a variety of ways. Checking is more likely if the wood is dried quickly.

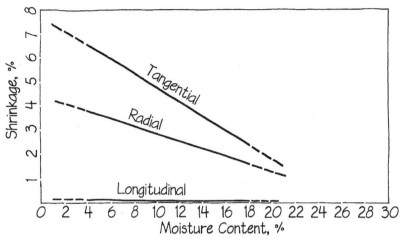

1. Shrinkage of Typical Softwood

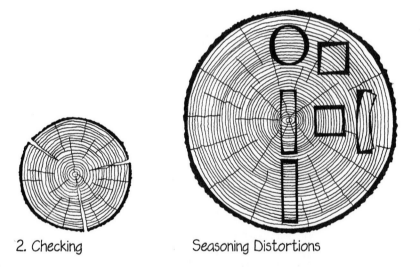

2. Checking

Seasoning Distortions

3. To avoid seasoning distortions as much as possible, boards and lumber can be cut from the log in such a way that the face of each piece is approximately perpendicular to the annual rings in the wood. This is referred to as rift sawing or quartersawing, and lumber cut in this way is often called vertical-grain lumber. Vertical-grain wood is best for flooring and for finish millwork that must remain flat – baseboards, window and door casings, and tabletops, for example. Vertical-grain lumber also wears better in furniture and flooring, because the harder summerwood bands occur very close together at the surface of each piece, protecting the soft springwood between from abrasion. Vertical-grain wood takes longer to saw than plainsawed lumber, however, and it wastes more of the log, so it generally costs more. For most uses, especially ordinary framing, plainsawed lumber is a satisfactory and economical choice, despite its tendency to distort. Boards and lumber cut from logs with many knots are more prone to distortion than "clear" pieces that are knot-free and have parallel grain patterns. Small-diameter logs are less likely to yield boards or lumber that have all of these desirable features.

4. Most outdoor decks are made of plainsawed decking. If the boards are laid with their bark side up, they will cup in a way that traps water during rainstorms. The proper way to lay decking is bark side down. The same principle applies to wood shingles on a roof. Shingles laid bark side down will have smaller openings at edges through which water may enter. To predict how a given piece of wood will change, remember that as it dries, the arcing annual rings on the end tend to become straighter. ∎

3. Most plainsawed boards are likely to cup

Quartersawing produces Vertical-grain lumber that distorts very little

Correct: Bark Side Down

Incorrect: Bark Side Up

4. Shrinkage Distortion of Plainsawed Decking

Equalizing Cross Grain

As its moisture content changes, wood shrinks and swells a great deal across its grain but very little along its grain. For purposes of detailing ordinary wood buildings, assume that the longitudinal shrinkage and expansion is essentially zero. Movement in the cross-grain direction is large in magnitude and difficult to quantify, because tangential movement (movement along the growth rings) is substantially larger than radial movement (movement perpendicular to the growth rings). In the plainsawed lumber used for framing, cross-grain shrinkage in a joist or a plate will take place at the radial rate, the tangential rate, or something between the two. The best thing to do is to assume the rate will be something between the two.

Cross-grain shrinkage is of greatest concern in dimension lumber. When engineered wood products such as glulam, I-joists, LVL, and wood trusses are used, the detailer must carefully accommodate their generally much smaller shrinkage rates. When engineered wood products are intermixed with dimension lumber in a floor assembly, special details must be used to control for their unequal shrinkage.

1. In platform framing, which is the most common way of structuring a light wood frame house, each level of floor framing interrupts the vertical studs that form the walls that support the upper floor and roof. The studs will shrink very little in the vertical direction of the building, but the floor framing, even if it consists of seasoned lumber, will shrink by a substantial amount, often ¼ to ⅜ in. per floor (6 to 9 mm). When detailing wood platform framing, it is important to provide equal amounts of cross grain wood at each level so that shrinkage will not cause tipping of floors or distress in interior finish materials. It is good practice to leave a space of about ½ in. (13 mm) in the sheathing panels at each floor platform, because the platform will shrink considerably and the panels will not.

The two-story studs shown in the balloon framing wall section on the far right will cause unequal shrinkage in the otherwise platform-framed building. When the wood is fully seasoned, the elevations of ceiling joists and roof rafters will be slightly higher where the two-story studs are used because the cross-grain shrinkage of the two floor assemblies will not take place.

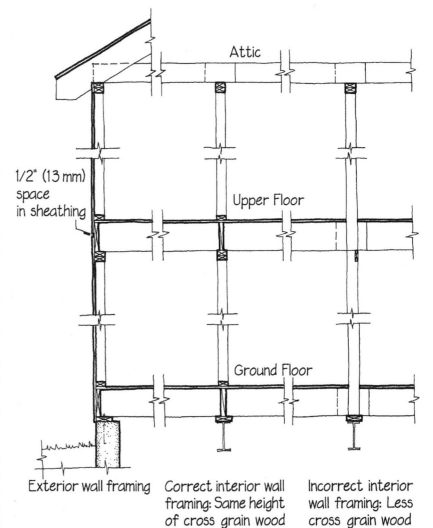

1. Equalizing Cross Grain Wood in House Framing

2. Masonry components of a wooden building, such as chimneys and exterior facings, do not shrink appreciably when compared with the wooden frame. Details of structural attachments and flashings that connect the wood and masonry must be designed to accommodate the differential movement. A sliding masonry tie will allow the frame to shrink without stressing the brick facing.

3. The flashings and counterflashings around a masonry chimney slip freely to allow the roof to drop a fraction of an inch in relation to the brickwork. ■

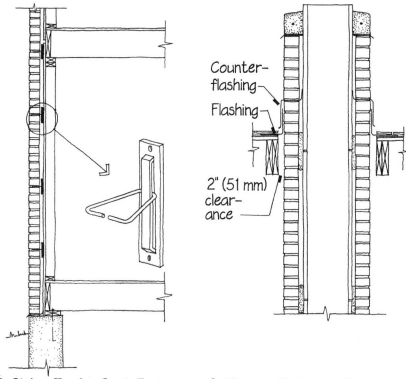

2. Sliding Tie for Brick Facing

3. Chimney Flashing at Roof

Relieved Back

Problems caused by cupping distortions in flat finish pieces of wood can be minimized by using a profile with a relieved back and by back priming each piece.

Cupping distortion is most evident in wide boards, especially if their grain is not straight and vertical (see **Vertical-Grain Lumber**, earlier in this chapter). Similarly sized manufactured wood products, such as medium-density fiberboard (MDF) and composites made of wood and resin, tend to be free of internal stresses that might cause cupping, but still may change in shape if not uniform in moisture content.

1. Cupping distortion of a wood board is caused by a difference in the amount of shrinkage experienced by the opposite sides of the board. The thinner the board, the less the force that can be exerted on it by this difference in shrinkage. It is common practice to relieve the backs of flat pieces of wood millwork by cutting one or more grooves, thus effectively reducing the thickness of the pieces and diminishing their tendency to cup. If a single, wide groove is cut, it also makes the piece easier to attach to a flat surface, because only the two edges need to touch.

In factory-produced millwork, the grooves are usually cut by shaping machinery. On the jobsite, it is usually more practical to cut multiple grooves using a portable table saw.

2. Back priming, the application of a coat of primer paint to the back side of a board, is also helpful in preventing cupping distortion of flat pieces of wood that will be painted. Siding boards, corner boards, exterior trim pieces, casings, and baseboards can all benefit from

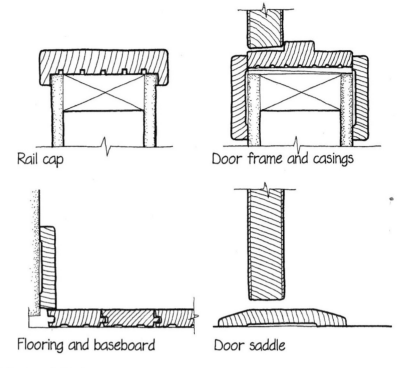

1. Relieved Backs

back priming. The effect of back priming is to cause both the front and back surfaces of the board to react to moisture at roughly the same rate. The back priming needs to be done at least a day in advance of installation, to give the primer time to dry. It should be noted in the millwork section of the specifications for the building and specified in detail under the painting section.

3. Closely related in principle to back priming is the practice of back facing a door or shelf that is surfaced with plastic laminate. The back facing prevents warping caused by unequal absorption of moisture by the two sides of the panel. Where it will not show, the back facing is usually made of a plain, low-cost laminate. Although it is virtually a necessity on shelves and doors, back facing is usually not required on surfaces that are tightly connected together in boxed assemblies, such as countertops and cabinet frames, because the bracing action of the box prevents severe warping. ∎

Foundation below Frost Line

One type of preventable building movement is frost heaving. Frost heaving is caused by water freezing in the soil beneath a building's foundations. Phase-change expansion of the water can cause the soil to expand up to 9%, lifting the building slightly. Under certain temperature and moisture conditions, larger amounts of lifting can occur as a result of the growth of long vertical crystals of ice under the foundation. It is impossible to eliminate groundwater, so foundations are placed on soils that will not freeze.

1. Building codes generally require the bottom of a foundation be placed at a level below the deepest level to which the ground freezes during a severe winter; consult the applicable building code for the location to determine the required depth. Exceptions to this general pattern are made only when there is no water below the foundation, such as when one is building on solid rock or permafrost, both of which are very rare situations. In locations not subject to freezing temperatures, building codes require that foundations must simply be at least 12 in. (305 mm) below finish grade.

2. Isolated pier foundations are economical and effective for decks, porches, and small wooden structures. A posthole digger or auger is used to excavate for each pier. The concrete should not be cast directly against the rough sides of the hole, however, because frost can heave upward against the rough sides of the pier. A smooth fiber tube form should be used to cast piers whose sides are smooth above the frost line. Similarly, a foundation wall should be cast in smooth forms, not directly against the walls of the trench.

3. The International Code Council (ICC) allows an innovative shallow foundation strategy that has been used successfully in cold northern European climates for decades. The frost-protected shallow foundation (FPSF) system uses an exterior layer of plastic foam insulation to contain heat that escapes from the building interior, to warm the soil beneath the foundation and keep it from freezing.

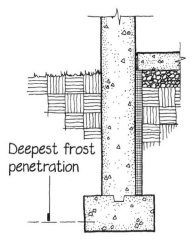

1. Foundation Below Frost Line

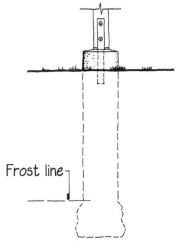

2. Smooth-Sided Foundation

3. Insulated Shallow Foundation

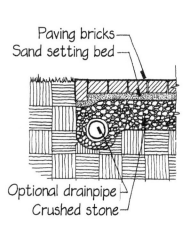

4. Brick Paving Laid in Sand

Owners must assure that the soil below the foundation is kept above freezing for the life of the building. This strategy should not be used for an unheated building, such as a barn or storage building, or for a building subject to interruption of its heating system in winter months. It is also not recommended where termites are found because they tend to burrow in the insulation. Building codes for relevant localities set forth minimum foundation depths and insulation requirements.

4. It is not practical to support outdoor pavings such as roads, patios, and walks, on foundations that go below the frost line; they must be supported at a much shallower level. Most frost heaving can be prevented, however, by placing the paving (concrete, asphalt, brick, or stone) on a thick, *well-drained* layer of crushed stone that is graded (sorted) so that it has no fine particles. The spaces between the stones drain water away from the underside of the paving and also furnish expansion space for water that freezes in the soil below. For brick and stone pavings, a sand setting bed above the crushed stone gives the mason a precise means of regulating the height of the masonry units.

The many small gaps in traditional mortarless, dry-stacked stone walls have a similar capacity to drain water and accommodate minor movement without cracking. ■

Structure/Enclosure Joint

The structural frame of a building and its infill components move in different ways and have different structural capabilities. They must be joined in ways that recognize these differences.

1. Interior partitions in buildings with steel or concrete frames are not strong enough to support the floors above and are not intended to do so. If a partition fits tightly against the underside of a floor slab, any deflection of the floor slab, no matter how small, will apply a load to the top of the partition. This may cause the building structure to behave in unanticipated and possibly dangerous ways, and it may cause the partition to buckle. To keep the partition from supporting a load, its structure should stop short of the underside of the floor slab. The size of the gap should be determined in collaboration with the structural engineer. The gap should be closed with an acoustical sealant or a soft rubber gasket, either of which will compress readily if the slab should deflect. In the steel stud partition illustrated here, the studs are cut short and are merely inserted into the upper runner track without fasteners, creating a slip joint to allow for floor movement.

2. A basement wall usually supports a portion of the weight of the building above. A basement floor slab does not. If the slab were rigidly connected to the wall, any slight settlement in the wall foundation would bend the slab and cause it to crack near the connection. A simple movement joint between the two isolates the slab from any movement in the structural wall. A similar joint should be detailed around interior columns, where they intersect the floor slab. This type of joint is often called an isolation joint.

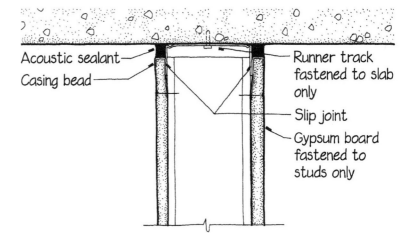

1. Structure/Enclosure Joint at Top of Partition

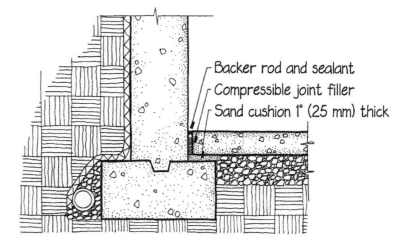

2. Structure/Enclosure Joint at Basement Wall

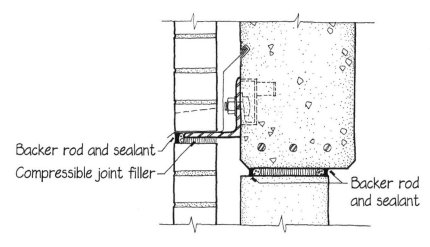

3. Soft Joint in Brick Veneer

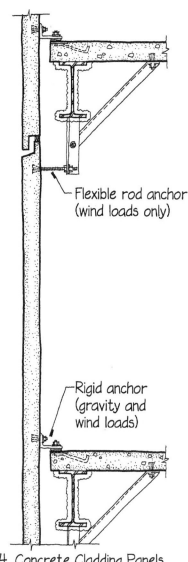

4. Concrete Cladding Panels

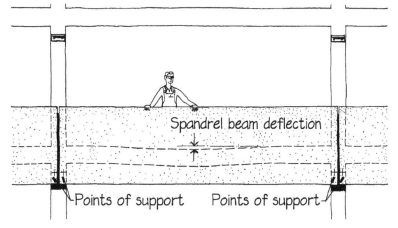

5. Bay-Width Spandrel Panel

3. A brick veneer curtain wall stands on a concealed steel shelf angle that is supported by the frame of the building at each story. The veneer is too slender to support any load except its own weight. If an ordinary mortar joint were used below the shelf angle, a slight deflection or creep in the structural frame or expansion of the veneer could cause the veneer to carry the weight of the building instead of the frame. This would be disastrous: The thin brick veneer would buckle and might even fracture suddenly and pop off the building. To keep this from happening, a soft joint of sealant is provided under each shelf angle. A similar soft joint is installed between the backup wall and the spandrel beam.

4. Story-high stone or precast concrete cladding panels are generally supported on the frame of the building near their lower edge. If a similarly rigid attachment were made to the frame near the upper edge, any deflection or creep in the frame would transfer the weight of the building to the cladding panel. A flexible rod anchor supports the panel against wind loads near its upper edge but does not permit the transfer of gravity loads between the frame and the panel. An alternative to the flexible rod anchor would be an angle clip with a vertically slotted bolt hole to allow free vertical motion in the anchor. Horizontal and vertical sealant joints isolate the panels from one another.

5. Bay-width spandrel panels should be supported at the column lines only; otherwise, they may be subjected to bending forces when the spandrel beam deflects under normal loadings.

The connections between frame and cladding are critical ones. Shelf angles and panel connections should always be designed in consultation with the building's structural engineer (see ***Small Structures***, Chapter 7). ∎

Abutment Joint

Abutment joints allow for movement between dissimilar materials or between old and new construction. Dissimilar materials tend to move at different rates and in different patterns. Old construction has already undergone foundation settlement, long-term structural movements, and initial moisture movements, while new construction has not. In either case, an abutment joint should be provided to allow for differential movement between the two parts of the construction.

1. This drawing shows an abutment joint between a masonry wall and a wood-frame wall. A small space separates the wood frame from the masonry, and a sealant joint of generous width allows for differential movement.

2. New and old masonry should not be interleaved but should be separated cleanly and connected by a flexible abutment joint. This is easier for masons to lay and avoids the cracking that might be caused by the shrinkage of the new mortar. For compositional considerations related to abutting materials in the same plane, see **Formal Transitions**, Chapter 14.

The same principles apply to the joints between new and old concrete assemblies. ■

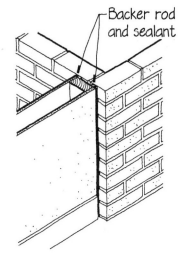

1. Brick Wall to Frame Wall

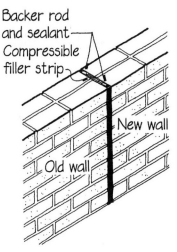

2. New Masonry to Old Masonry

Expansion Joint

Large surfaces of materials that tend to expand after installation should be divided into smaller surfaces by a regular pattern of expansion joints. Expansion joints also accommodate shrinkage and minor differential movement between structure and enclosure.

1. This expansion joint accessory for plaster allows for the slight expansion or contraction in the curing plaster, as well as for subsequent moisture or thermal movement, and movement in the underlying wall structure. The metal lath must be discontinuous along the line of the joint to allow for free movement. The expansion joint accessory is a simple metal or plastic bellows shape. At the time it is installed, it is closed with a plastic tape that prevents it from becoming clogged with plaster, which would be unsightly and would destroy its function. After the plaster has been applied, the tape is stripped away, creating a straight, clean, dark shadow line in the plaster surface. Similar details are used in gypsum wallboard and cement-based stucco applications. As with any joint, the pattern created by the expansion joints should be worked out and described to the builder in elevation view.

2. Long walls of brick masonry are subject to expansion as the bricks absorb moisture, and these walls require expansion joints at intervals to relieve the pressure this would cause. Dark brick walls on sunny exposures may require expansion joints at more frequent intervals to accommodate thermal expansion. Any reinforcing in the brickwork should be discontinued across the joint. In masonry expansion joints, it is often important that a spline or tongue-and-groove feature be provided that will maintain the alignment of the wall while allowing for the necessary in-plane movement.

3. Expansion joints in any material should be placed at locations of structural weakness in the surface, where cracking or crushing would tend to occur if no joints

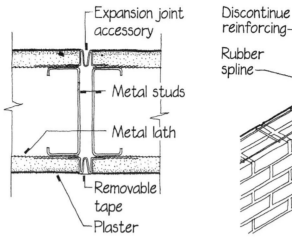

1. Expansion Joint in Plaster Wall

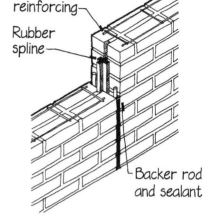

2. Expansion Joint in Brick Wall

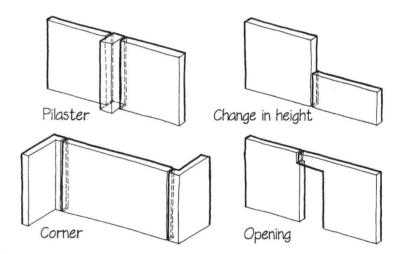

3. Locations for Expansion Joints in Masonry Walls

were provided. Window and door openings weaken a planar surface, so expansion joints are often placed to align with the edges of these elements, vertically, horizontally, or both.

Each expansion joint introduces a line of movement through a surface; it must continue without interruption to the extent of the surface. If it does not continue to the boundary of the surface, the portion without an expansion joint will likely crack roughly along the line of the interrupted expansion joint. ▷

4. Aluminum cladding components are subject to large amounts of expansion and contraction caused by daily and seasonal differences in air temperatures and by direct solar heating of the metal. Both horizontal and vertical expansion joints must be provided at appropriate intervals. Each joint must be designed to maintain the alignment of the components and to keep out weather while allowing for movement. In this example, vertical movement is accommodated by a sliding mullion connection at every other floor of the building and by the movement of the spandrel glass into and out of a deep recess in the horizontal mullions.

5. In aluminum cladding systems, horizontal movement may be taken up by vertical mullions that are split or have a bellows action. It can also be accommodated by sliding connections, where each horizontal mullion piece joins the verticals, and by glass movement in and out of the vertical mullions.

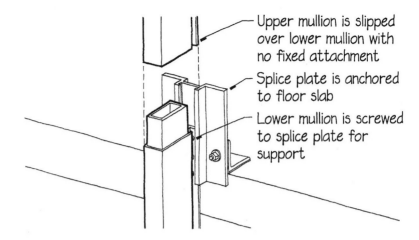

4. Expansion Joint in Aluminum Mullion: Vertical Movement

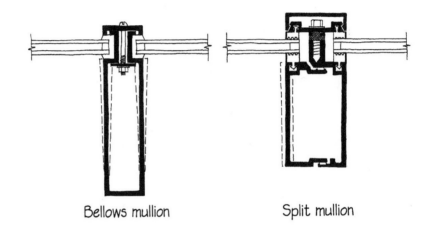

5. Expansion Joints in Aluminum Vertical Mullions: Horizontal Movement

6. Few building surfaces undergo more thermal movement than metal roofing, especially if dark in color. Sheet metals have high coefficients of thermal expansion, and roof surfaces receive more solar heat than other surfaces. Metal roofing is therefore made up of relatively small pans or panels, with many closely spaced joints, each of which is detailed to allow expansion of the metal without permitting water to enter. The keystone-shaped batten gives the metal pan plenty of room for movement, and the flat seam allows the pieces to slide.

The rate of thermal expansion of an area (or plane) of a given material is approximately twice its linear thermal expansion. Therefore, the copper pans in this roof will expand more than the linear copper caps on top of the battens. The folded seams in this detail are flexible enough to allow minor differences to occur.

7. Suggested maximum vertical expansion joint spacings are 30 ft. (9.1 m) for gypsum and gypsum/lime plaster, up to 125 ft. (38 m) intervals for solid brick masonry, and 25 ft. (7.6 m) for brick veneers. Vertical expansion joints in exterior insulation and finish systems should be at intervals up to 60 ft. (18.3 m), or less to match intervals of movement joints that are located in the substrate. Horizontal expansion joints are normally provided at story-height intervals in masonry veneers, stucco, and exterior insulation and finish systems. Expected movement of these materials can be quantified by using the procedure shown in the section "**Determining Widths of Sealant Joints**" in Chapter 1.

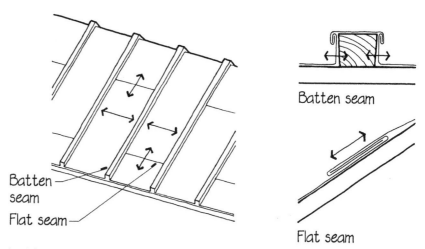

6. Movement Joints in Metal Roofing

Control Joint

A control joint is an intentional line of weakness created in the surface of a brittle material that tends to shrink or contract. Its role is to encourage any shrinkage cracking to occur within this joint to avoid random cracking of the surface around it. Unlike expansion joints, control joints are not compressible, so they only accommodate contraction of the surfaces around them. For this reason, they are sometimes called contraction joints.

1. A sidewalk crack is a control joint that is formed by tooling a deep groove into the wet concrete. When the sidewalk shrinks, cracking is channeled to the tooled groove. The sidewalk remains as a group of large, stable rectangular units, rather than as a weak array of irregular concrete fragments.

2. A concrete slab floor on grade should be divided by control joints into smaller rectangles that can be expected to stay crack-free. The joints can be created by tooling the wet concrete or by sawing it during the early stages of its curing. With either method, the depth of the joint should be at least 25% of the depth of the slab. Joints must be straight and, like expansion joints, they must continue to the boundary of each slab section — a task that may be difficult to achieve with circular saws typically used to cut the joint. Any reinforcing in the slab should be discontinued across the line of the joint. If it is important to maintain a level surface across the joint, smooth, greased steel dowels can be inserted. These allow for in-plane movement while preventing out-of-plane movement.

3. As seen in this plan view, ground slabs should be divided in a way that avoids slender or oddly shaped panels, because they are prone to cracking. A rectangular panel with a length greater than 1.5 times its width is likely to crack across its middle. Control joints are often used in conjunction with expansion joints and isolation joints, which are used to separate the slab from load-bearing walls and columns (see **Structure/Enclosure Joint**, earlier in this chapter). Isolation joints around columns and pilasters should be built or cut on a diagonal, as shown, to avoid inside corners that foster cracks.

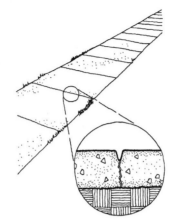

1. Control Joint in Sidewalk

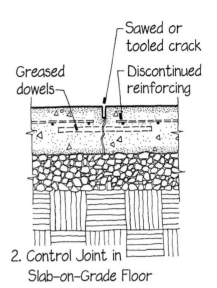

2. Control Joint in Slab-on-Grade Floor

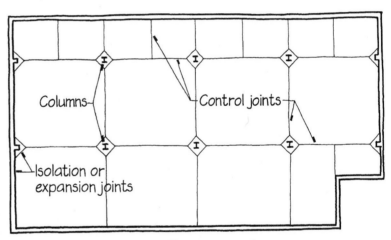

3. Plan of Joint Pattern in a Slab-on-Grade

4. Poured concrete walls are also subject to shrinkage cracking. Control joints are usually created by inserting strips into the formwork to create linear slots along which cracking will occur. The slots should reduce the wall thickness by at least 25%. Every second reinforcing bar should be discontinued to encourage cracking forces to concentrate at the line of the joint. Alternatively, all horizontal reinforcing bars may be discontinued, and a greased steel dowel may be used to align the walls and offer shear resistance. Review these details with your consulting engineer.

5. Concrete masonry walls need control joints, of which two examples are shown here. Both of these details interlock in a way that allows minor in-plane but not out-of-plane movement. As in concrete walls, a greased steel dowel can be placed in a bond beam unit to provide shear transfer between abutting masonry walls. ▷

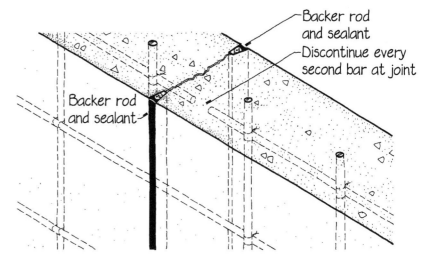

4. Control Joint in Sitecast Concrete Wall

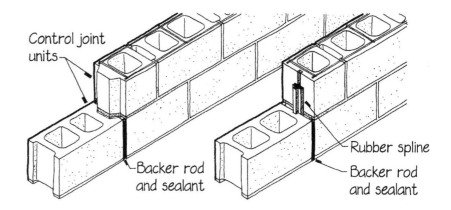

5. Control Joints in Concrete Masonry Walls

SECTION 1 ■ FUNCTION 107

6. Control joints in masonry or concrete walls should be located at locations of structural weakness, as seen in drawing 3 in the section *Expansion Joint*, earlier in this chapter.

7. In stucco construction, the term "control joint" is applied to a joint that also serves as an expansion joint. Stucco control joints are formed with an accessory that is similar to the expansion joint used in gypsum plaster walls. The lath should be cut completely along the line of the control joint to create a line of weakness.

8. When decorative surface treatments that are not intended to be control joints are cast or milled into brittle materials, they must be shallow (much less than 25% of the material thickness), or else they may result in cracks through the full thickness of the material. Poor appearance and a breach of the enclosure system can result. Detailers should consult with fabricators of stone, precast concrete, ceramic panels, and other brittle elements to establish safe limits for the depth of decorative surface treatments.

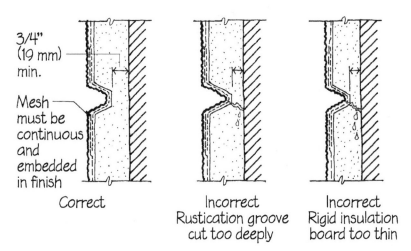

8. Horizontal Rustication Groove in EIFS Cladding

A decorative horizontal rustication groove created in an exterior insulation and finish system (EIFS) cladding creates an artificial plane of weakness in the cladding. Industry standards state that the thickness of the continuous layer of foam behind the reveal must be at least ¾ in. (19 mm) thick and free of seams or cuts. Reinforcing mesh and the finish coat thickness must be maintained following the profile of the groove. A half-round or trapezoidal profile shape is preferred over a simple V-groove, which concentrates movement stresses to one location, sometimes leading to unintended cracking.

9. Recommended control joint spacings for various materials are shown in Table 6-3.

TABLE 6-3: Recommended Control Joint Spacing for Various Cementitious Materials

Material	Maximum control joint spacing
Concrete slabs on grade	24–36 times slab thickness
Concrete exterior walls	2 times height of wall if <12 ft. (3.7 m) tall; equal to wall height if >12 ft. (3.7 m) tall
Concrete masonry veneers (joint reinforcing every second course)	24 ft. (7.3 m) or 1.5 times the height of the wall, whichever is less
Concrete masonry walls (reinforced and grouted)	40 ft. (12.2 m) or 3 times the height of the wall, whichever is less
Stucco walls	18 ft. (5.5 m), 144 sf in area (13.4 m^2), or 2.5 times the height of the wall, whichever is less

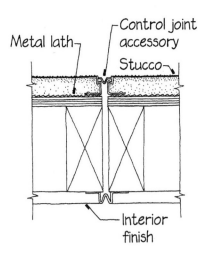

7. Control Joint in Stucco

Sliding Joint

Minor movement can often be accommodated by simply placing materials in separate planes and letting them slide past each other. Several traditional wood details rely on joints that allow components to slide past one another as they expand and contract with changing moisture content. The principles shown here for wood also apply to other hygroscopic building materials, which are materials that change in size as their moisture content changes.

Sliding joints also easily accommodate small differences in thermal or structural movement between various materials in an assembly. Some sliding joint details also make construction of the building easier or more forgiving (see **Sliding Fit**, Chapter 12).

1. Wood siding is subject to relatively large amounts of moisture movement because it is exposed to rain and snow, as well as to the drying effects of sunlight and wind. Overlapping horizontal siding should be nailed to the building in the pattern shown here, which allows each piece to slide beneath the piece above as it moves, thus relieving potential stresses.

2. Board-and-batten siding should be nailed in the pattern shown here in plan view; this provides sliding joints for moisture movement.

3. The entire width of a simple Z-brace door lies across the grain of its boards. The door is subject to so much moisture movement across its width that it is difficult to keep it fitted to its opening during both the dry and humid seasons of the year. The traditional panel door responds to this problem by minimizing the amount of cross-grain shrinkage across the width of the door, limiting it to the width of the two stiles, which totals only about 9 in. (230 mm). The narrow edges of the panels are recessed loosely into the grooves in the stiles and rails. This allows differences in moisture movement to be relieved within the structure of the door. ▷

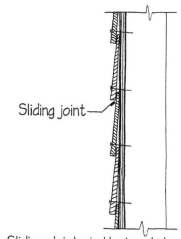

1. Sliding Joints in Horizontal Wood Siding

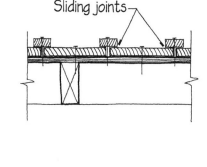

2. Sliding Joints in Board-and-Batten Siding

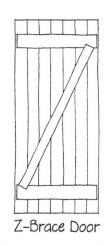

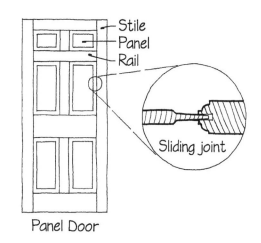

3. Sliding Joints in Panel Door

4. This manufactured storefront window head is specially designed to accommodate structural deflection or creep of concrete and differential thermal movement of concrete, aluminum, and glass. The concrete span above the window can deflect or creep up to ⅝ in. (16 mm) vertically without harmful consequence. The aluminum extrusion that holds the glass can slide vertically within the larger aluminum frame that is anchored to the concrete. Gaskets cushion the movement of the two aluminum elements while also sealing the gap. The smaller aluminum frame that holds the glass uses similar gaskets to permit differential vertical movement without sacrificing watertightness. ■

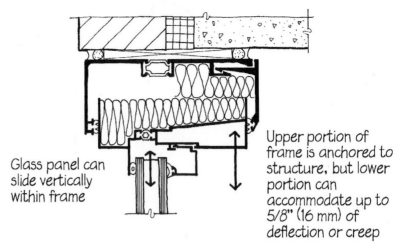

4. Deflection Head in Storefront Window Frame

Building Separation Joint

Complex building configurations should use building separation joints wherever there are significant horizontal or vertical discontinuities in the massing of the building. Buildings that are large in horizontal extent should be divided into separate structural entities, each of which is compact enough that it can react as a rigid unit to foundation settlement and other movements, thereby avoiding damage.

1. This drawing shows how building separation joints should be located at points of geometric weakness, where cracking would otherwise be likely to occur. Notice that the joints divide the building into compact rectilinear volumes. At each joint plane, the structure of the building is cut completely through, with independent structural support on each side of the joint. Building separation joints are often referred to as "expansion joints," but that understates their importance. They separate a large building into a set of smaller buildings so that the building can deal effectively with not only thermal expansion but also soil settlement, materials shrinkage, and seismic deflections. Building separation joint locations, spacing, detailing, structural support, and foundation should be designed in consultation with the structural and foundation engineers. Thermal and moisture movement, foundation settlement, and the relative seismic motions of the adjoining parts of the building all must be dealt with adequately. Consultants responsible for plumbing and mechanical systems must detail any service lines that cross these joints, to accommodate anticipated movement. As a general guide, spacings between building separation joints should not exceed 150 to 200 ft. (45 to 60 m).

2. Building separation joints must be covered to keep out the weather and to

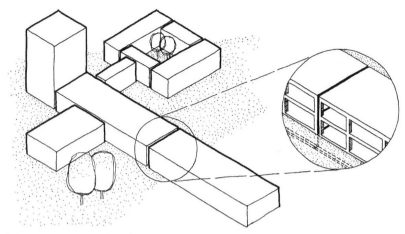

1. Locations for Building Separation Joints

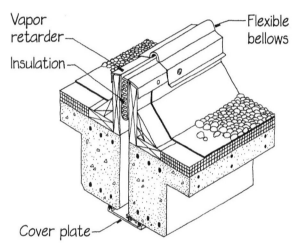

2. Building Separation Joint at Roof

provide continuity to interior surfaces. This is a typical design for a separation joint cover for a low-slope roof. A flexible bellows keeps water and air from leaking through the joint but adjusts readily to movement between the two sections of the building. A high curb on either side keeps the bellows from being submerged in water. The joint is filled with thermal insulation and a vapor retarder. The ceiling below is provided with a gasketed metal cover plate fastened to only one side of the movement joint, so that it can adjust to movement while retaining a reasonably attractive appearance. The bellows and the interior cover plate are common off-the-shelf components, typical of dozens of designs offered by a number of manufacturers. ▷

3. This building separation joint in a masonry exterior wall is closed with a flexible waterstop and sealant. The waterstop may be made of metal, plastic, or rubber. The interior wall surface is finished with the same cover plate used at the ceiling in drawing 2.

4. At the floor, a building separation joint cover must adjust to differential movements while supporting traffic loads and providing a smooth, nontripping transition between the floor planes on either side. Manufacturers offer many devices for achieving this. This example is based on two mirror-image aluminum extrusions that are cast into the edges of the two floor slabs. When the building is finished, two rubber bellows strips are snapped into the extrusions. Then a metal cover plate is fastened down to steel clips with spring-loaded bolts that hold it firmly in place despite any relative motion of the slabs on either side. ■

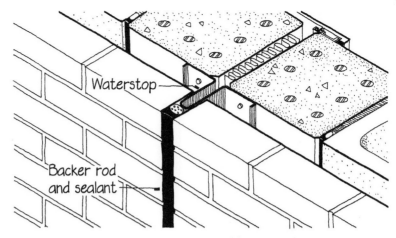

3. Building Separation Joint in Exterior Masonry Wall

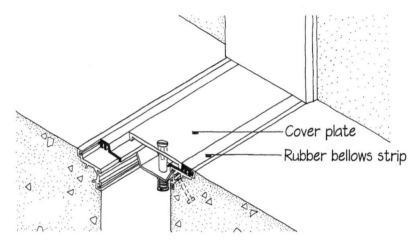

4. Building Separation Joint at Floor

CHAPTER 7
Providing Structural Support

That a building have a structural frame laid out, calculated, and detailed so that it is stable and will not deflect excessively is obviously important. Less obvious is the need to engineer smaller but still important structures that are component parts of the larger building. Even light structural loads should not be placed on interior and exterior enclosure materials without appropriate analysis.

Primary structural connections are normally detailed and constructed with the most stringent quality control of any part of the building. Secondary and tertiary structures are the connective tissues that hold the enclosure system to the frame and hold the finishes to the enclosure system.

Some of these small structures are within larger assemblies, such as metal ties within a masonry wall or lath below stucco. These elements are seldom tested in the field to verify their structural effectiveness, and many are not readily observable by anyone other than the crew installing them. Details need to be explicit and reliable to ensure installation will meet performance expectations.

Building surfaces in some cases become an armature for a variety of elements; examples follow in this chapter. Some of these elements may be unforeseen at the time the building is designed and constructed. Responsibility for the design of these elements may be initiated by a variety of design professionals, including the consulting engineers, architects, and manufacturers of building components, but it is best if the architect oversees their integration into the project. This becomes especially critical when the building is composed of many elements that are layered in complex assemblies.

The detail patterns that relate to providing structural support in buildings begin with recognition of the numerous structural elements the architect typically designs or coordinates. Each will be listed below and described more fully in this chapter.

Examples that are part of the primary, secondary, or tertiary (finish) system are described in:

Small Structures (p. 114)

Strategies for joining elements of different physical properties are described in the pattern:

Connecting Dissimilar Materials (p. 116)

Strategies for detailing structural connections so loads are not excessive are described in the pattern:

Distributing Loads (p. 118)

Architectural Detailing: Function Constructability Aesthetics. Fourth Edition. Patrick Rand, Jason Miller, and Edward Allen.
© 2025 John Wiley & Sons, Inc. Published 2025 by John Wiley & Sons, Inc.

Small Structures

There are many small and seemingly trivial structural problems the detailer must recognize and solve through standard engineering design procedures, working alone or with the help of a structural engineer. Manufactured building components are typically well detailed within their own system, but they require special attention where they meet other parts of the building. The architect must coordinate details from consultants, manufacturers' technical representatives, and other sources. In short, the architect details the larger relationships between smaller details. Optimal details address important structural agendas without sacrificing performance of the enclosure system or aesthetic features.

Examples of these challenges follow, listed according to the scale of their impact.

- Backup walls of concrete masonry need to be designed to carry wind loads and to transmit them to the building frame; this often requires steel reinforcing and special attachment details for the top of the wall. Steel stud backup walls must be engineered carefully to control lateral deflection so as to prevent cracking of exterior masonry veneers and brittle interior finishes.
- Masonry ties need to be checked for strength and rigidity to prevent deflection and cracking of the face veneer under wind or seismic loads.
- Attachments of cladding systems to the frame of the building – components such as shelf angles, mounting clips, and concrete embedments – must be engineered carefully for both strength and deflection.
- Entry canopies, awnings, and signage, which are sometimes added and replaced after the building is completed, need to be carefully engineered for varied dead and live loads (see drawing 1).
- Rainwater gutters and downspouts and their attachments to the building must be strong enough to resist worst-case snow and ice loadings.
- Fascias and soffits at the eaves of a wood-frame building often need special support details. These must resist wind uplift, bear the load of ladders, and provide a solid base for nailing.
- Any component of an exterior rainscreen wall that acts as an air barrier must be designed to resist full wind pressures and suctions, even if it is only a small weatherstrip gasket.
- Photo voltaic panels, sun-shading devices, light shelves, and vegetated screens are often incorporated into exterior envelopes as layered assemblies outside of the exterior wall or roof. These assemblies must be designed to endure dynamic loading from wind, snow, and ice. If they catch the wind, they may introduce live loads that are many times greater than their dead loads. The supporting building frame or exterior wall must be analyzed to verify that the integrity of the structural and enclosure systems is not jeopardized (see drawing 2).
- Projecting sashes need to have sufficiently rigid frames and attachments to resist loads from gusting winds. The larger the sash, the stiffer its frame must be.
- Flat metal spandrel panels need to be stiff enough so that they will not buckle under wind loads. They also need to be designed to appear flat under all conditions. Stone cladding panels must be strong enough so that they will not crack or deflect excessively. Extra panel

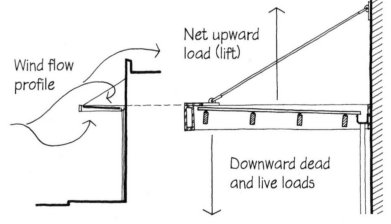

1. Building Canopy

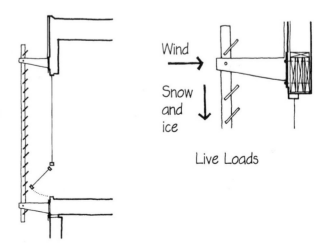

2. Cantilevered Sun Shading Device

thickness may be required to counteract the thermal warping potential of thin stone panels that are exposed to sunlight.

- A guardrail at the edge of a balcony, mezzanine, deck, or stair must meet building code requirements for resistance to lateral force. This requires a full-scale engineering analysis that includes meticulous attention to designing attachment details (see drawing 3).
- Grab bars must be designed to carry a 250-pound (1.11-kN) load applied at any point, in any direction. Towel bars, wall-mounted plumbing fixtures, and stair railings must be sufficiently rigid and must be fastened to the wall with sufficient strength.
- Pipe hangers, conduit hangers, duct hangers, and equipment mounts all need engineering attention.
- Large, heavy doors need frames, frame-to-wall attachments, hinges, latchsets, and closers with commensurate structural strength. Sometimes the wall itself must be strengthened around a heavy door.
- The selection of glass thickness, glass lamination, and mullion section requires engineering analysis. The depth of the mullion "bite" on the glass also needs to be carefully worked out. Too shallow a bite may allow the glass to pop out under wind load; too deep a bite may excessively restrict the wind-induced bending of the glass. Standard neoprene setting blocks are used to keep glass centered in the mullions. Literature from glass and mullion manufacturers usually offers guidance in these matters, based on the magnitudes of the expected wind pressures on the building (see drawing 4).
- Elaborate suspended plaster ceilings may require stronger support than the standard specifications for hanger wires and attachments.
- An ordinary bookshelf needs careful attention to the stiffness of the shelves.

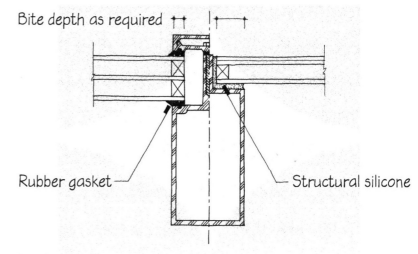

3. Loads on Handrails and Guards

4. Insulated Glass Units Bite and Setting

A nominal 1 in. (25 mm) board often is not stiff enough. A freestanding bookcase needs attention to lateral stability in both directions.

- Lighting fixtures, ceiling fans, and audiovisual equipment often require special attachments that are designed to bear their weight safely.

It is frequently left to the detailer to recognize smaller-scale structural problems such as these and to see they are fully engineered and detailed. When proprietary systems are selected, like a glass or metal curtain wall system, the detailer must verify the manufacturer's details are sufficiently strong for the particular project application.

Connecting Dissimilar Materials

When joining different elements of building systems, connections may be challenging to resolve. Structural systems may be made of concrete, masonry, steel, wood, and various composites. Enclosure systems may be made of these and many other materials that may not be as strong. Connections between them are critical, so the detailer must make transitions between elements efficient and reliable.

Connections in primary structural systems within a single material family are relatively simple to make. Steel frame elements are joined with bolts, pins, and welds; cast-in-place concrete has continuous steel reinforcement between columns, beams, and slabs; light wood elements are bolted, screwed, or nailed; and timber components are mortised, notched, pinned, or plated together. But how are connections between these different material families made?

1. Steel members are often connected to cast-in-place concrete using embedded fasteners, such as anchor bolts and special steel plates. The plasticity of fresh concrete is exploited to conform precisely to the shape of the metal connector, then harden permanently. A composite slab also utilizes the plasticity of concrete to create mechanical bonds between the concrete slabs, and profiled steel decks and shear studs mounted to the top flange of steel beams.

2. Wood and light gauge steel should not be embedded into fresh concrete, so they are typically fastened to cured concrete. Fasteners such as anchor bolts can be embedded in the wet concrete, or fasteners can be anchored into the hardened concrete. Lag and shield connections can be created by drilling a hole into the concrete, then inserting a sleeve in the hole to receive a metal fastener that holds the wood, light-gauge steel, or other element in place. In some cases, a powder-actuated fastener can be used, reducing the time needed for installation.

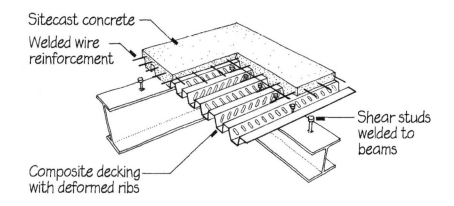

1. Composite Deck: Concrete Bonds to Profiled Steel Elements

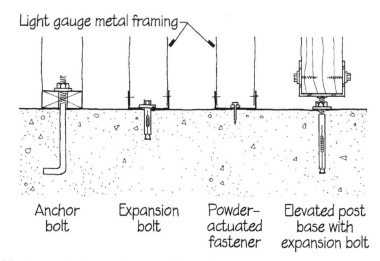

2. Mechanical Connections to Concrete

3. Light wood frames sometimes incorporate steel beams and other shapes within them to carry concentrated loads. Nails and screws commonly used by carpentry crews will not penetrate the steel members. Wood ledgers and nailers can be bolted to the steel flanges and webs, so that the carpenter's nails can easily connect joists, rafters, and studs to the steel members.

4. Exterior finishes are often installed using many small fasteners to minimize the visual presence of each fastener. In contemporary construction, these finishes are seldom connected directly to the building's primary structural system, because water, air, and thermal control layers are between the enclosure and primary structure. Exterior finishes are often connected to intermediate armatures – such as furring strips, concealed aluminum frames, and other devices, which are installed over the control layers – with relatively few connections through the control layers to the structural substrate. Intermediate armatures collect many small connections from finishes, and transfer loads to primary structure using only a few connections.

5. Roof-mounted mechanical equipment, photovoltaic arrays, satellite communication devices, and other equipment are often located above vulnerable waterproof membrane and insulation layers. They are typically elevated on intermediate armatures, such as short posts and frames, which carry their loads through the vulnerable layers to the structural deck below. The relatively few posts can be carefully designed and installed to minimize disruption of the important control layers while providing firm anchorage for the equipment, sometimes with the addition of a vibration-dampening feature. (See *Quiet Attachments*, Chapter 5) They also permit maintenance of the equipment and of the roof surface, which are substantially independent of one another. ■

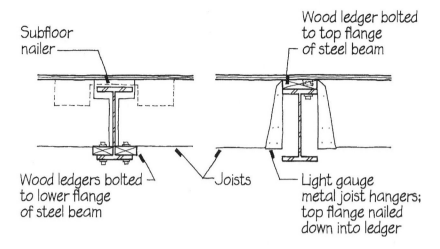

3. Connecting Light Wood Framing to Steel Beam

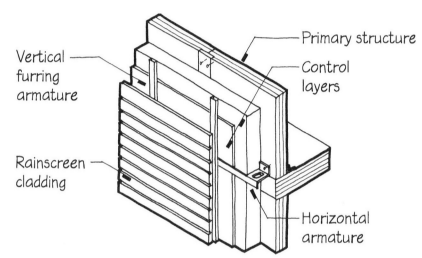

4. Intermediate Armatures in a Rainscreen Assembly

Distributing Loads

Connections transfer stress from one element to another using fasteners and other devices. When the strengths of the elements or the fasteners are unequal, it is important that the limits of each material be recognized in the design of the detail.

1. Even small structures can produce concentrated loads that may exceed the bearing capacity of a material. A light-wood-frame residence may use a truss, LVL, or flitch beam for a large or heavily loaded span, but the supporting structure must be analyzed to be sure the slender wood studs below it will not be overloaded. A built-up column can be made by bundling multiple studs, or a steel tube section can be incorporated into the wall thickness to carry the concentrated load down to the foundation.

Conventional light frame trusses are made of 2 in. (50 mm) nominal lumber, which results in concentrated stresses at the connections. Nails or screws could split the wood pieces or exceed the fiber stress capacity of the wood. Truss fabricators therefore use toothed plates at these intersections; the numerous small, nail-like teeth collect the stresses from one member and transfer it through the plate to the adjoining members, without causing splitting or crushing of the wood pieces.

2. When wood framing members bypass one another, split rings or toothed washers can be used at the interface of the members to transfer stress. When steel bolts tighten the assembled members, the steel rings or toothed washers engage enough volume of wood to stay below its compressive strength limits. The steel ring is split to accommodate small volume changes in the wood due to moisture and temperature fluctuations.

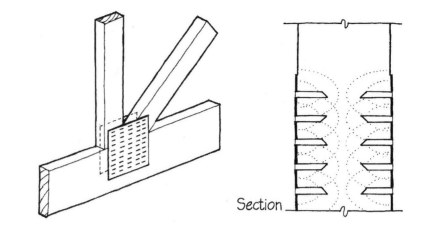

1. Toothed Plate

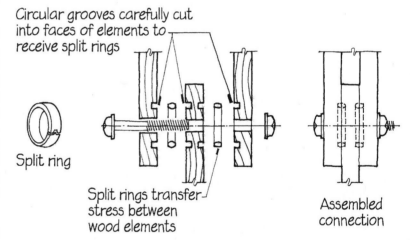

2. Split Rings in Wood Framing Connection

3. Unlike traditional wood joinery, with its interlocking mortise and tenon connections, a contemporary wood frame made of heavy timber or glue-laminated wood typically uses steel plates and angles at the connections, held together with multiple bolts. The steel interface results in a connection whose strength is more certain, and it also requires less labor or specialized skills to execute. The sizes of wood members may also be reduced, because the details do not require that up to half of the wood material be subtracted to make an interlocking connection. The much greater loads at the beam-to-column connection call for steel connections, whereas the minor loads between each layer of the glue-laminated beam can be transferred using structural adhesive.

4. If preferred, the steel plates used to connect wood members can be concealed within the members and secured using many small self-tapping steel dowels. To be accurate, the wood members are typically fabricated off-site, using CNC (computer numeric controlled) equipment to produce accurate kerfs. Steel plates are then inserted into the kerfs in the field, and multiple self-tapping steel dowels are driven through the wood and steel plates. Since wood is dimensionally unstable across its grain, it is recommended that the width of the array of dowels not exceed 8 in. (203 mm), to avoid the possibility of cracking due to shrinkage of the wood.

Steel fasteners are the most common type we use because they are very strong, but if overtightened they can crush or distort the wood. Steel fasteners securing nonstructural elements to the structural substrate can crush rigid plastic foam or rubber gaskets they are meant to secure. ▷

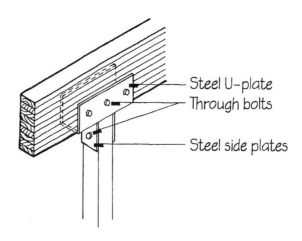

3. Steel Plate Connection Between Wood Structural Elements

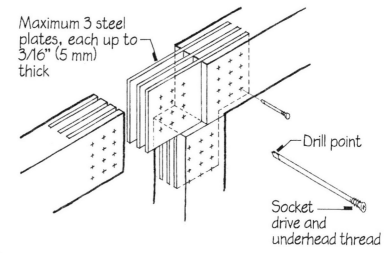

4. Concealed Steel Plates and Self-Tapping Steel Dowels

5. Steel framing members are typically joined with high-strength steel bolts that are carefully tightened so that the friction between the tightly squeezed faces results in stress transfer directly from member to member. This creates what is known as a slip-critical or friction-type connection. The steel members are not harmed because their compressive strength is extremely high, much higher than that of most other materials in the building.

Cedar roofing shingles are typically secured with annular ring shank nails through their thin upper ends. The heads of the nails are to be driven so that the underside of the nail head is against the upper face of the wood, but not so far as to embed the nail head into the wood. If nails are driven too far into the wood, the shingle would likely split sooner or later, and the wood element would be constrained from minor swelling as its moisture content increased. A slate shingle is also held with nails at the upper end, which are driven through prepunched holes in the shingles. The shingles are "hung" loosely on these nails to the roof sheathing. If the nails were driven hard against the brittle slate, the shingles would almost certainly crack.

6. Composite exterior cladding panels are often made of thick low-density foam wrapped with thin sheet metal. If a screw or bolt went through this composite and was tightened, the concentrated stress at the head of the fastener would dimple or even pierce the metal facing and would crush the soft foam. Composite panels of this sort are therefore often secured at their edges, where the sheet metal can be shaped to interlock and to be secured to the concealed frame that holds them. The sheet metal flanges distribute the load of the connection to the whole edge of the panel.

Masonry walls bring together stone, brick, and concrete masonry products of

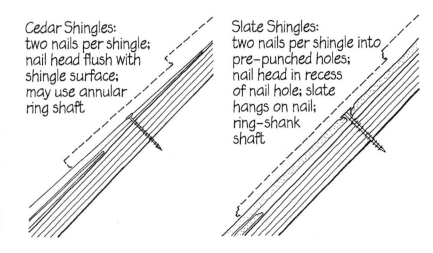

5. Hand-Driven Nails in Shingle Roofing

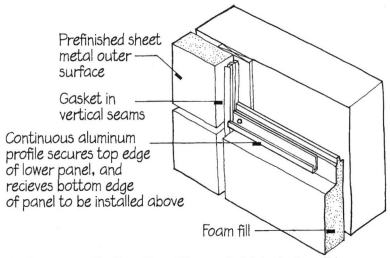

6. Composite Cladding Panel Secured at Interlocking Edges

varying strengths; they are held together with mortar of a strength that the designer can specify. Optimal results occur when the strengths of the elements of the masonry assembly are not abruptly different from one another. When repairing a historic masonry wall made with relatively weak brick fired in a traditional periodic kiln, it is best that any new brick be of approximately the same strength and bonded using mortar that matches the compressive strength of the masonry units. If contemporary high-strength mortar were used in such a project, it is likely that it would transfer excessive stress to the brick units, causing them to crack. ∎

CHAPTER 8

Providing Passages for Building Services

Every building is laced with a three-dimensional web of distribution lines for mechanical and electrical services – ductwork, piping, and wiring for heating, cooling, ventilating, hot and cold water, sewage, fire suppression, electrical energy, illumination, telephones, temperature controls, computer networks, intercommunication systems, antennas, and alarm systems. Nearly all existing buildings have been retrofitted with distribution lines for which they were not originally designed, making it safe to assume that every building on the boards today will be called upon in the future to house services not yet imagined.

In detailing a building, it is important to work with the designers of the mechanical, plumbing, electrical, and communications systems to furnish passages for service distribution lines that will run through the building, both now and in the future. In most cases, these lines should be comfortably concealed; if they are exposed to view, it should be by design, not by default. Generous spaces should be provided for the lines, with sufficient worker access points and workable interconnections from one plane of distribution to another. This allows economical installation, sustainable maintenance, and future change of the services (See *Maintenance Access*, Chapter 10). It will also avoid having the appearance of the building and its details spoiled by the improvised installation of service systems unanticipated by the designer and detailer.

As services in buildings become increasingly dense, complex, and interconnected from the standpoint of building operations and maintenance, design professionals must collaborate closely to provide an efficient arrangement of compatible services. Water pipes are typically kept distant from power distribution rooms, and telecommunication wires must be isolated by distance or shielded from power distribution wires, to avoid interference. Protocols based on the technical requirements of each system should guide the initial design and the ongoing maintenance of these services.

Not all electrical services are visible. Unseen networks such as wireless fidelity (WiFi) and cellular networks work best in wide-open settings. Massive wall, floor, and roof constructions can interfere with these networks. Radiant foils used as facings on rigid insulation can also interfere with some networks. Placement of networks within the particular fabric of the building determines network efficiency. A coordinated effort by engineers, architects, and network service providers can result in the optimal performance of wireless networks.

To provide a fully three-dimensional network of passages, two detail patterns must be combined (see the corresponding sections later in this chapter):

> *Vertical Chase* (p. 122)
> *Horizontal Plenum* (p. 125)

At each point of intersection between chase and plenum, the various services must have space to make the transition from vertical to horizontal.

Ductwork, piping, and conduits may be exposed in a building rather than concealed in chases and plenums, but this functional and, in some aspect, aesthetic decision does not necessarily lead to more economical construction (See *Nonconflicting Systems*, Chapter 11). Vertical and horizontal spaces still need to be reserved for these services, and funds must be allocated for additional design time to lay out neat arrangements of lines, additional installation time to permit a high standard of workmanship, and the cost of painting and finishing the lines.

Architectural Detailing: Function Constructability Aesthetics. Fourth Edition. Patrick Rand, Jason Miller, and Edward Allen.
© 2025 John Wiley & Sons, Inc. Published 2025 by John Wiley & Sons, Inc.

Vertical Chase

A vertical chase is a concealed passage in which services can run from ground to roof and floor to floor. A hollow wall that serves as a vertical chase can often perform some horizontal distribution functions as well.

1. The hollow vertical spaces between wood or steel studs in a wall or partition furnish convenient passages for small-diameter services, usually without further attention from the detailer. Vertical runs of electrical wiring or water supply piping fit easily into these spaces, provided they can penetrate the bottom and top plates where the wall meets the floor and ceiling. Steel studs with their pre-punched holes also make horizontal runs of wiring easy. Horizontal runs of wiring through wood studs require that the studs be drilled, which is easy and acceptable if the holes are not too large. Long horizontal runs of piping are generally difficult to thread through holes in studs. Waste and vent piping, with their larger diameters, often require deeper studs, a double row of studs, generous horizontal furring, or a dedicated chase. Deep horizontal furring over studs offers chases both ways, minimizing interference between studs and service lines.

2. In an exterior wall or any wall adjoining unheated space, water piping must be kept on the interior side of all thermal insulation, to prevent freezing in cold weather, even if the pipes themselves are jacketed with insulation. It is safest to lay

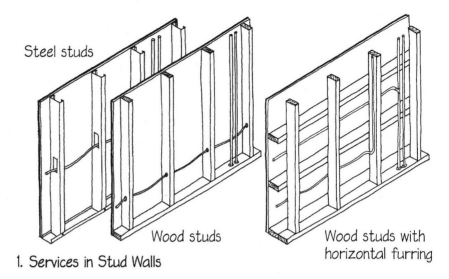

1. Services in Stud Walls

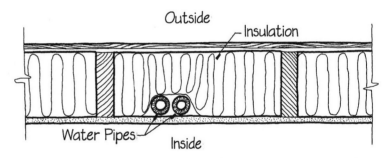

2. Water Pipes in Exterior Walls

out a building so that all water piping is contained in interior partitions, avoiding exterior walls entirely. If water piping must be installed in an exterior wall, be sure the insulation detail is noted in the section of the specifications relating to thermal insulation. Make a note to inspect the wall after it has been insulated and before it is closed up, to be sure the pipes are fully inside the insulation.

3. A masonry wall, even one composed of hollow concrete blocks, does not offer easy routes for piping and wiring. A typical solution for small-diameter service lines is to furr the interior face of the wall with metal or wood strips. The service lines pass through or between the strips and are concealed by a finish layer on the inside. Thermal insulation may also be added between the furring strips. For larger-diameter service lines, the furring may take the form of a stud wall spaced away from the masonry by the required distance. This strategy is equally applicable to cast-in-place or precast concrete walls.

4. Plumbing waste and vent lines generally will not fit within a standard-thickness stud partition. In some cases, larger studs can be used to create sufficient space for the pipes. In most cases, it is preferable to frame a double wall with enough clear space between so the pipes can run freely in both horizontal and vertical directions. It is not enough to allow a space a little larger than the diameter of the largest pipe in the wall; there must also be space enough for supply piping to cross in front of the waste and vent risers and, in many cases, for smaller-diameter horizontal waste and vent pipes to cross the larger-diameter vertical runs (see **Installation Clearance**, Chapter 11).

5. Certain sizes of flat and oval ducts are designed to fit between wall studs, but they have limited air-handling capacity. Additional thickness is often required for thermal insulation around the ducts, especially in exterior walls. Even if a duct fits between studs, it may require the removal of so much of the top and bottom plates of the wall that remedial strengthening of these elements is required. Larger ducts often require special framing. ▷

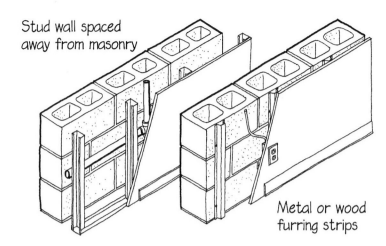
3. Furring of Masonry Walls

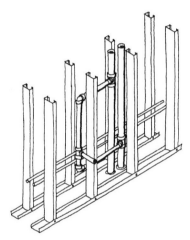
4. Double Wall for Plumbing

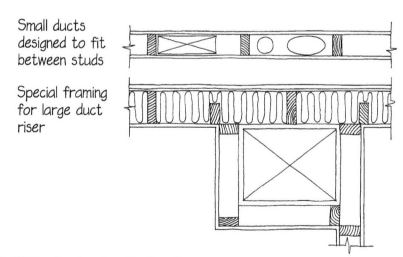
5. Fitting Ducts into Stud Walls

6. Most larger buildings require dedicated chases or shafts for major vertical runs of mechanical and electrical distribution lines. These must be located and sized through extensive consultation with the professionals who design each system. A vertical electrical shaft generally adjoins an electrical closet at each floor where transitions are made to horizontal lines of distribution. A vertical shaft for ductwork sometimes connects to a fan room at each story, but more often it connects directly to the horizontal runs of ductwork at the ceiling or floor. If a ductwork shaft is hemmed in by stair towers, elevator shafts, and plumbing walls, these connections may be difficult or impossible. Check with consultants regarding separation of power and communication lines, to avoid electrical interference.

7. Vertical pipes and electrical conduits are sometimes housed in interior or exterior column covers. The interior location is usually preferable, both for protection from freezing and for ease of connection at each story. Care must be taken to avoid interference with floor beams. Air ducts, if they are small enough, can also be routed through these passages.

8. There are some general precautions to consider relative to any type of vertical chase or shaft. These vertical passages must line up accurately from one story to the next, avoiding horizontal zigs and zags that are costly and troublesome. Access panels must be provided at points specified by the designers of the various systems. Remember that new service lines will likely occupy these spaces in the future (see **Accessible Connections**, Chapter 11). The passages must be fully enclosed with materials that meet the fire-resistance requirements of the applicable building code.

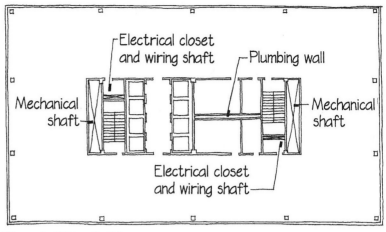

6. Plan of Office Building

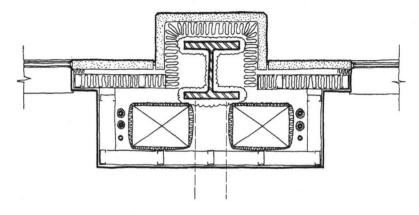

7. Plan of Vertical Services In Column Cover

The spaces where piping, conduits, or ductwork go through each fire-rated floor and wall must be fire-stopped to the same level of protection as the assembly being penetrated. Specific requirements vary according to the size and quantity of penetrations, but generally details must utilize tested products that will prevent the passage of flames and hot gasses. At minimum, this will involve using mineral batt or putty materials that have been designed and tested for this purpose. Ductwork passing through fire-rated walls must be equipped with heat and smoke sensors that automatically close dampers inside the ducts when there is an emergency. The sensors must be accessible for periodic inspection and maintenance. Concealed service chases in combustible construction are required to have fire blocking where vertical and horizontal cavities meet, and at intervals of 10 ft. (3 m) in vertical stud and furred cavities. ■

Horizontal Plenum

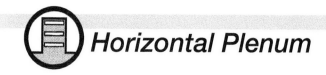

A horizontal plenum is a space that permits each service to be routed to any point on a floor.

1. Most floor and ceiling constructions structured with wood or steel joists afford considerable space for ducts, wires, and pipes. Open-web joists allow easy distribution in both directions, provided that ductwork of the required sizes fits their triangular openings. Holes have to be created in wood or sheet metal joists to allow services to run in a perpendicular direction. The sizes and locations of these holes must conform to specific code limitations, or they must be cleared with the structural consultant. Steel castellated beams and cellular beams have hexagonal or circular holes at their neutral axis to similarly permit services to run laterally.

2. A furred-down ceiling creates lateral passages for electrical wiring, but not enough height for piping or ductwork.

3. A suspended ceiling creates a horizontal plenum within which every type of service can run. The plenum space must be high enough to accommodate all the planned services, but its height should be minimized to avoid excessive overall building height. Horizontal zones must be reserved within the plenum for each of the major services. Generally, the lowest stratum is reserved for lighting fixtures and sprinkler pipes, the next higher stratum for ductwork, and the highest for structure and fireproofing. The height of each of these strata must be agreed upon in advance, and the plenum plan of each bay of the building must be designed so that columns, fire separation walls, air diffusers, lighting fixtures, speakers, sensors, and sprinkler heads all have reserved zones in which to descend through the ceiling without encountering other systems. This requires full cooperation among all of the professionals involved in the integrated design of the building. Establishing clear protocols to coordinate placement of these services will determine the order for initial construction, and for the future as services are updated.

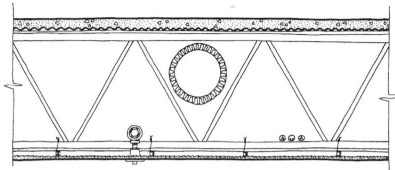

1. Plenum in Open-Web Joists

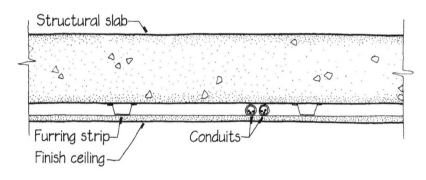

2. Furred-Down Ceiling

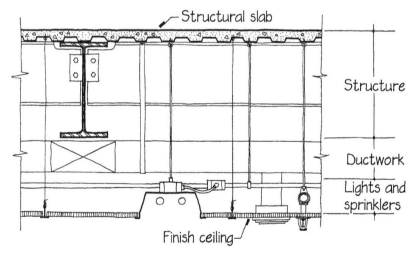

3. Plenum Above Suspended Ceiling

Finish ceiling surfaces are not required but may be used to achieve desired spatial qualities or to conceal overhead services. If ceiling surfaces are installed, they must provide service access at all required points, either through removable tiles or panels or through special access doors. ▷

4. Access doors, air diffusers and grills, sprinkler heads, speakers, fire and smoke sensors, and lighting fixtures can create visual chaos in a ceiling. Reflected ceiling plans should be designed cooperatively by the entire design team to create an orderly and well-coordinated overhead landscape.

5. An alternative to the suspended ceiling plenum is an underfloor plenum created by an access floor raised 3 to 18 in. (75 to 460 mm) above the structural floor. This permits the floor structure of a building to be left exposed beneath, as a finish ceiling. This is a particular advantage in such situations as converting an old building with heavy timber or monolithic concrete floors to a new use. It may also be well suited to buildings with dense computing networks, especially if they are rearranged frequently. Easier access to power and communication lines makes changes simpler and less costly. Ducts and small mechanical boxes can be placed in this underfloor chase, or it can become a continuous air supply plenum. An underfloor plenum or duct can supply air closer to occupants; it provides them with an opportunity to control airflow locally.

6. In some laboratory and hospital buildings with unusually elaborate services that must be serviced and altered frequently, standing-height plenums called interstitial ceilings are constructed to facilitate maintenance access, thus minimizing disruption or contamination by maintenance operations of the spaces served. These are usually created by means of a modular steel ceiling grid suspended on steel rods from the floor above. Gratings on the grid can support workers and tools, or the ceiling panels themselves may be designed to safely support them.

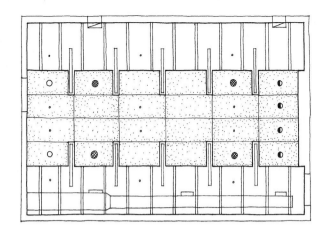

4. Coordinated Reflected Ceiling Plan

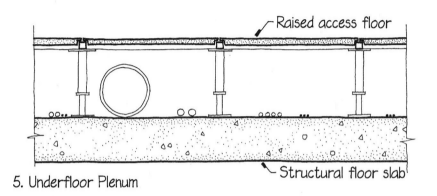

5. Underfloor Plenum

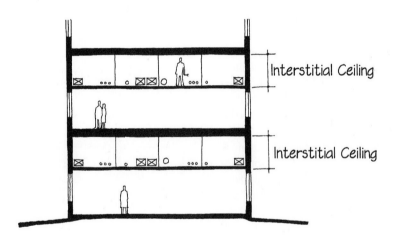

6. Interstitial Ceilings

7. There are various systems for creating hollow passages for electrical and communications wiring within the structure of a floor. These include cellular steel decking and cellular raceways that are cast into concrete floor structures. Any such system must be designed in collaboration with the mechanical and electrical consultants, the structural designer, and the manufacturer of the raceway components. Shielded compartments control electromagnetic interference between power and communication networks. Note that these passages, which are generously sized for wiring, are too small to be used for pipes or ducts.

8. In buildings with relatively modest requirements for mechanical services, horizontal distribution may take place primarily above a central corridor or above a strip of dropped ceiling that runs around the perimeter of the building. This is an economical approach that can work well in hotels, dormitories, apartment buildings, and classroom buildings.

9. In general, any horizontal plenum space must connect generously with the vertical passages that feed it. Where it meets a fire wall or a fire separation wall, the wall must penetrate up through the plenum to close tightly against the structural floor above. Any ducts that cross this fire separation must be provided with fire dampers, and any other penetrations must be sealed with fire-rated construction. Care should be taken to avoid creating acoustical flanking paths through a plenum space (see *Airtight, Heavy, Limp Partition*, Chapter 5). ■

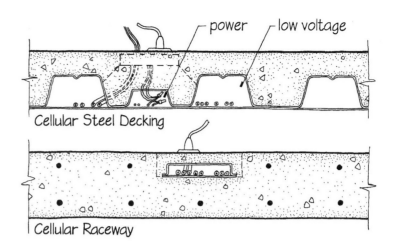

7. Wiring Within the Floor Structure

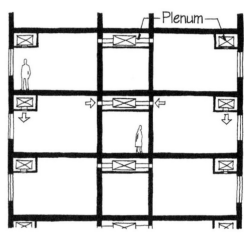

8. Plenum Above Dropped Ceiling

CHAPTER 9 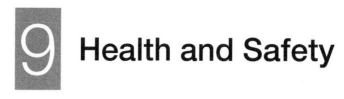 Health and Safety

Millions of people are injured needlessly each year in unsafe buildings, and millions more become ill because of unhealthy buildings. People trip and fall on unsafe floors and stairs. They cut, scrape, or gouge themselves on rough surfaces, sharp edges, and broken glass. They are poisoned by off-gassing fumes from various adhesives and plastics, and by smoke from building fires. People who are ill, aged, or otherwise disabled may find themselves unable to reach whole areas of a building because of physical barriers that have been incorporated into the architecture. Most health and safety issues in detailing are regulated by building codes; others are merely based on common sense.

When particular materials or construction assemblies are found to be fundamentally unsafe, building codes or other regulations are often revised to exclude them. Ongoing improvements and innovations in construction materials and details must include consideration for public health and safety. Detailers are expected to assess a new material or a new detail to thoroughly investigate its health and safety implications. Manufacturers will often provide needed information about materials and proprietary assemblies, and may assist in further testing if needed.

Detailers rely on many organizations that produce and disseminate information about materials and methods of construction. Designers are not responsible for the methods of construction used, but should nonetheless design details that do not present unusual risks for builders. National codes and standards organizations, professional and trade associations, master specifications, and manufacturers are parts of this information base. References that appear in *Appendix A, The Detailer's Reference Shelf*, and internet searches are used by detailers to remain current with best practices.

Chapter 9: **Health and Safety** and Chapter 10: **Providing for the Aging of the Building** address issues about the health, safety, and welfare of people over the building's entire life cycle, from construction to at least its end of use. Designers and detailers have a professional responsibility to safeguard buildings in order to protect people.

Designed details in buildings must meet changing performance requirements and regulations. They must demonstrate understanding of the behavior of occupants. Building occupants are affected by building details and the decisions of their designer. Detailers learn about the consequences of how people interact with building details through formal post-occupancy evaluations (POE) or other informal feedback channels. These channels provide important information fueling the ongoing improvement of building details.

Detail patterns relating to health and safety are the following (see the corresponding sections later in this chapter):

Safe Footing (p. 130)
Fall Protection (p. 132)
Safe Edges (p. 134)
Safe Glazing (p. 135)
Nontoxic Materials (p. 136)
Fire-Safe Materials (p. 137)
Fire-Resistant Assemblies (p. 138)
Barrier-Free Design (p. 140)
Universal Design (p. 141)

Architectural Detailing: Function Constructability Aesthetics. Fourth Edition. Patrick Rand, Jason Miller, and Edward Allen.
© 2025 John Wiley & Sons, Inc. Published 2025 by John Wiley & Sons, Inc.

Safe Footing

Tripping and slipping are two occurrences the detailer must guard against in floor and stair details.

1. Tripping on floors can be caused by any abrupt change in floor level, such as floor-mounted doorstops, unusually high thresholds, and/or changes in floor material. Thresholds in existing buildings are permitted by building codes to be up to ¾ in. (19 mm) high; in new construction they may be up to ½ in. high (13 mm). Floor level changes may not exceed ¼ in. (6 mm). All thresholds and transitions greater than ¼ in. in height must have beveled edges with a slope not greater than 1:2 (a 50% slope). Ideally, all finish flooring surfaces are at the same elevation, avoiding even minor transitions that may be unnoticed. Finish flooring materials may vary within a building and may be of varying thicknesses. The substrates that support the finish flooring may need to vary or adjust so that finish flooring surfaces are aligned.

2. Tripping on stairs can be avoided by careful compliance with building code provisions. A lifetime of using commonly proportioned stairs equips most people to navigate new stairs with ease. There should be a very good reason for choosing to make stairs steeper than the standard rule of thumb of 2 risers + 1 tread = 27 in. (686 mm). Proportion treads and risers as the codes require, and take care when inspecting construction that excessive variations do not creep into tread and riser dimensions. Do not design stairs with only one or two risers; people tend not to see them until they have fallen on them. Always comply precisely with building code handrail requirements.

3. Egress stairs may not have open risers, and stairs not considered to be egress stairs are limited to riser openings that will not allow a 4 in. (102 mm) sphere to pass through.

4. Use abrasive tread inserts to prevent slipping on stairs that are made of polished materials, such as marble or metal. Use contrasting colors at tread nosings to enhance visibility and safety.

5. Pay particular attention to flooring materials likely to become wet. In public entries and lobbies with stone or tile floors, use a slightly rough or textured surface finish, rather than a highly polished one. In kitchens, bathrooms, and showers, avoid smoothly glazed floor tiles.

Approaches to public entries may be sheltered with a canopy to keep them dry and may be equipped with gratings or mats to remove most water and snow from footwear before people enter the building.

6. Although there are no legal guidelines for the coefficients of friction of floor materials, such coefficients are published by many flooring manufacturers. In general, avoid flooring materials with a coefficient of friction less than 0.50. Use higher values for ramps and for floors or stairs that may become wet.

It is recommended that routes to be used by persons with disabilities have a static coefficient of friction of at least 0.60, and at least 0.80 for ramps.

The static coefficient of friction between rubber soles and dry troweled concrete is 0.60–0.85, but it is only 0.45–0.75 when the concrete is wet. For rubber soles on an icy concrete surface, it is only 0.15.

7. Wood floors and stair treads are common in residences but are not suitable in high-traffic public buildings, because even hardwood species will wear with so much use. Tread nosings are particularly susceptible to splintering and will become dangerously rounded with use. A worn nosing may exceed the maximum ½ in. (13 mm) radius set by building codes. Wood in exterior settings is also vulnerable to algae and plant growth, which can reduce its static coefficient of friction from 0.50 to an unsafe 0.15.

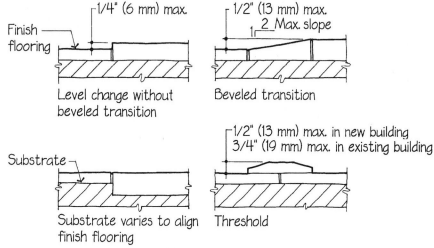

1. Acceptable Flooring Transitions

8. Thick, loose carpet is difficult to traverse in a wheelchair. Carpet in accessible routes and in accessible rooms must be securely attached with either a firm cushion or no cushion. Maximum pile thickness in non-residential buildings is ½ in. (13 mm); check with the manufacturer to make sure that the pile type and length conform to accessibility provisions of the building code.

9. Metal gratings give good traction underfoot, but openings must be small to allow passage of people with strollers, in wheelchairs, using canes, or wearing shoes with small or pointed heels. Gratings should have spaces no wider than ½ in. (13 mm) in one direction, and elongated openings must be oriented perpendicular to the dominant direction of travel.

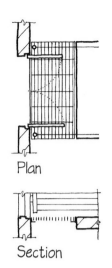
Plan
Section

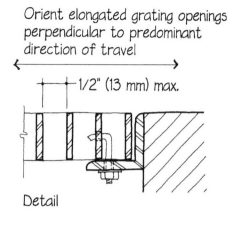
Orient elongated grating openings perpendicular to predominant direction of travel
1/2" (13 mm) max.
Detail

9. Acceptable Gratings

10. Passenger transit platforms without guards, such as train and subway platforms, are required to have a 24 in. (610 mm) wide detectable warning at the edge. This tactile signal is made using a specific pattern of raised truncated domes that are recognized by people who are visually impaired. Use of a contrasting color would also enhance perception of the edge. This code provision does not apply to bus stops that abut a normal-height street curb.

11. Ramps and landings for use by persons with disabilities must have edge protections wherever the vertical drop-off is greater than ½ in. (13 mm). Allowable edge protections include extending the floor surface at least 12 in. (305 mm) beyond the inside face of the railing, or providing a minimum 4 in. (102 mm) tall curb or barrier at the edge of the floor surface.

12. It is difficult to look up and look down at the same time. A person is likely either to trip or bump his or her head on stairs with insufficient headroom. Always draw large-scale sections of stairways to be sure that code requirements for headroom are met. Given the general increase in height of the population, it may be advisable to provide more than the required minimum headroom wherever possible.

Fall Protection

Handrails are gripping surfaces required by code to help prevent falls by people on stairs and ramps. Guards are required at open edges of floors, balconies, mezzanines, decks, ramps, stairs, and landings.

1. Building codes and accessibility standards are explicit in their requirements for detailing handrails and guards. Stairs, except in certain residential buildings, are required to have handrails on each side, except on aisle stairs where a center rail is provided. Ramps with a vertical drop of 6 in. (152 mm) or more are required to have handrails on both sides. If the vertical drop of a ramp, landing, or floor level is 30 in. (762 mm) or more, guards are required.

2. Handrails are provided on stairs and ramps to help steady and prevent people from falling. Such handrails must be of such size and shape in cross section that an adult hand can grip at least three-quarters of the perimeter of the rail. Generally, an uninterrupted round piece of metal pipe or wood is best. Noncircular cross sections must have a thickness of 1–2¼ in. (25–57 mm) and must have a perimeter dimension of 4–6¼ in. (100–160 mm). Rectangular pieces of wood are hard to grip and are illegal under most codes. Every handrail must be set away from the wall by at least 1½ in. (38 mm) and must be mounted a specified distance above the floor, stair, or ramp. The wall behind the handrail must be smooth to prevent scraping of knuckles, and the edges of the handrail must have a minimum radius of ⅛ in. (3 mm).

3. At the top and bottom of each flight of stairs, a handrail mounted on the wall must run out horizontally at least 12 in. (305 mm)

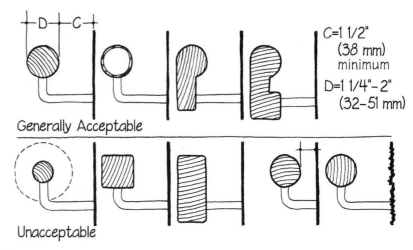

2. Handrail Profiles

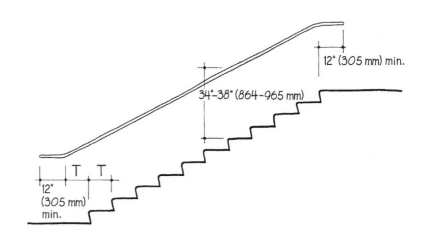

3. Stair Handrail

beyond the end of the stair, and it must be turned in toward the wall so that it will not snag clothing. Handrail mountings must be engineered carefully to keep the rail rigid and to hold it tightly to the wall against any expected push or pull. The center handrail in a switchback stairway must be continuous from one flight to the next. If there is no center wall in a switchback stairway, the center handrail is also a guard and must be provided with balusters, as described in the following paragraphs.

4. Guards must be provided to prevent people from falling over the edge of any abrupt change of 30 in. (762 mm) or more in floor level. Exceptions are permitted at edges of stages, service pits, or loading docks. Minimum guard heights are specified in the building codes, but it is often desirable to make the guard higher, to avoid unpleasant psychological feelings of danger. A guard around a court or an atrium should be at a height that is comfortable to lean on with the elbows.

The balusters, safety glazing panels, mesh, cables, or other infill between the guard and the edge of the floor must be spaced such that an unsupervised small child cannot slip through. Research has shown the maximum clear opening within a guard should not pass a ball more than 4 in. (102 mm) in diameter. Building codes use this figure for guards up to 36 in. (914 mm) above the floor; above that height the pattern can be slightly more open, allowing a sphere of up to 4⅜ in. (111 mm) in diameter to pass. Even if the applicable code allows for some openings larger than 4 in. (102 mm), it would be wise to stick to the smaller figure, because larger dimensions are demonstrably less safe. Horizontal balusters are generally legal, but if balusters are vertical, it is more difficult for a child to climb over the guard.

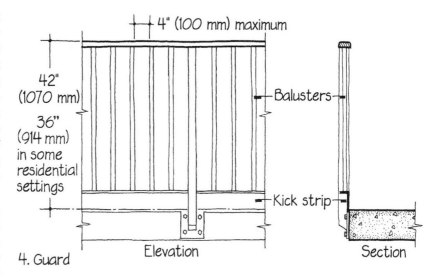

4. Guard

Building codes often require a solid kick strip or curb several inches high at the base of a guard. Its function is to prevent debris on the floor from accidentally being kicked through the guard and onto people below.

5. Building codes specify structural requirements for guards, handrails, and grab bars to prevent them from collapsing under the forces that people apply to them. This means that rails, posts, and particularly the attachments of the posts to the floor edges must be engineered with great care to resist large lateral loadings. They must be designed to carry a concentrated load of 200 lb. (91 kg) pushing or pulling, horizontally or vertically, *and* a distributed load of 50 lb. per sq. ft. (2.39 kPa) (see *Small Structures*, Chapter 7). ∎

Safe Edges

Although not generally covered by building codes, an important safety concern of the detailer is to provide safe edges and surfaces wherever people come in contact with a building.

1. Avoid splinters from wooden interior components by using vertical-grain wood and chamfering or rounding all corners.

2. Do not place rough surfaces of masonry, plaster, stucco, or concrete along stairs, hallways, and entrance areas where people are likely to brush against them. Avoid sharp edges and corners, especially in common contact points like handrails, guards, and door and window hardware.

3. Use round columns or column wraps rather than square ones in corridors and lobbies.

4. Be sure doorknobs, locks, and handles are set back sufficiently from the frame of the door so that knuckles will not be skinned accidentally.

5. Non-pinching aluminum doors are available for use in entrances to schools and commercial buildings. These are designed so that they are unlikely to injure a child's hand. The hinge stile is cylindrical and is hinged at the centerline of the cylinder so that it cannot draw in and pinch a hand or a finger. The lock stile has a generous clearance between the door and the frame that is closed with a large, soft rubber gasket.

6. Edges of sheet metal flashing, exterior cladding, and rainscreens should be folded back to form a hem or fabricated to turn sharp edges away from people. ∎

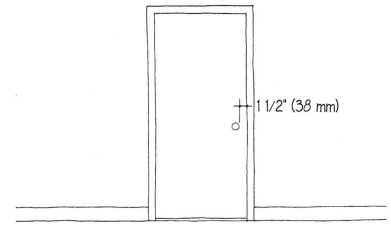

4. Doorknob Clearance

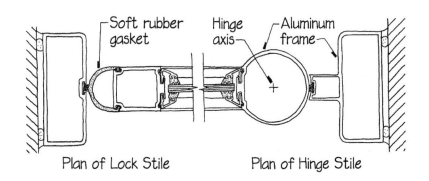

5. Nonpinching Door

Safe Glazing

Glass usage in buildings is code regulated to prevent several types of glass-related injuries.

1. Avoid using glass in such a way that it does not seem to be there. Many early buildings in the modern style featured sheets of glass that ran from floor to ceiling and were purposely detailed to be virtually invisible. People tended to run into these transparent walls, sometimes shattering the glass and injuring themselves badly, even fatally, on the sharp spikes of glass. Using safety glazing alone does not solve the safety problem with floor-to-ceiling glass. People can be injured just by the impact of running into a large, invisible, unbreakable sheet of glass. It is wise to install a horizontal mullion or a handrail across the glass to warn of its presence, or to use glass that is etched, printed, or tinted to make it more visible.

2. Building codes require that any glass in or near doors must be safety glazing. The same requirement applies to glass walls and to large areas of glass near the floor. Glass within 60 in. (1524 mm) above adjacent walking surfaces of stairs, landings, and ramps must be safety glazing. Glass within 60 in. (1524 mm) of the water's edge in a pool, spa, or bathtub must also be safety glass. All-glass doors, guards, or balcony fronts must be made of safety glass.

3. Safety glazing is made of tempered glass, laminated glass, wired glass, or impact-resistant plastic. Check appropriate building codes to determine which of these products is permitted for a specific location in a building. These products are much stronger than ordinary annealed glass and are much less likely to break. If tempered glass does break, it disintegrates into small, blunt granules rather than large, sharp spears.

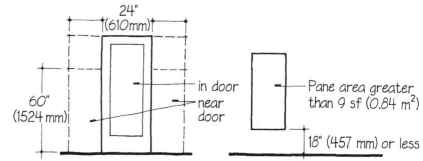

- Glass in exterior or interior doors
- Glass within 24" (610 mm) of vertical edges of door, unless lower edge is at least 60" (1524 mm) above floor
- Glass panes greater in area than 9 sf (0.84 m²) and lower edge is 18" (457 mm) or less above floor

2. Locations Usually Requiring Safety Glazing

4. Overhead glass, such as in skylights or curtain walls inclined more than 15 degrees from the vertical, can cause injury if broken by a windblown or falling object and falls on people below. Building code requirements for the glass in skylights and sloped glazing systems are complex, but the most common code-conforming solution is simple: Use laminated glass in any overhead glazing. If broken, the laminated glass, with its soft plastic interlayer, tends to hang together and to remain in its frame. In multiple-layer overhead glazing systems, only the layer facing the interior needs to be laminated glass. If glass other than laminated glass is used overhead, then a noncombustible screen with a mesh not larger than 1 × 1 in. (25 × 25 mm) must be installed within 4 in. (102 mm) of the glazing. This screen is intended to protect people below from falling glass fragments.

5. Safety glazing is dependent upon firm support in a frame. Excessive deflection of the glass, or gradual lateral movement of the glass in its frame, may cause the edge of the glass to come free of its frame. The detailer should provide support for glass at all edges and limit glass deflection to less than $1/175$ of the glass edge length, or ¾ in. (19 mm), whichever is less. See **Sealant Joints and Gaskets** (Chapter 1) for typical glazing details.

6. Light-transmitting plastics, such as polycarbonate and acrylic, are impact resistant, lightweight, and often less costly than glass. They are unfortunately less resistant to combustion and may give off toxic gases when burned. Codes usually prohibit their use in large assembly buildings, institutional buildings, and exit passageways, unless the building is fully sprinklered. Refer to relevant codes for additional detailing factors associated with plastic glazing.

7. Glazing products in fire-rated doors and walls are highly restricted by building codes. See **Fire-Resistant Assemblies**, later in this chapter. ∎

Nontoxic Materials

Buildings can make people ill unless great care is taken to select and detail materials to avoid toxic effects.

1. The toxicity of materials used in construction is under ongoing scrutiny and increasing regulation, and it is a significant concern of any sustainable design initiative. A variety of "red lists" identify and designate as harmful those chemicals, elements, and materials known to pose risks to humans and other living creatures or the environment. For years, specific laws and industry regulations have mostly eliminated the following from new construction: lead paint; asbestos; toxic preservatives such as creosote, pentachlorophenol, and copper arsenate; formaldehyde emissions from insulating foam and wood panel products; and hydrocarbon solvents that evaporate from coatings, sealants, and adhesives.

Construction material producers are increasingly using Environmental Product Declarations (EPDs), prepared according to Product Category Rules (PCRs), to quantitatively disclose in a standardized format the environmental impact associated with each product. This transparency will make the material selection process better informed. The primary responsibility for avoiding toxic substances in construction rests with the specifier; however, the detailer should also take care to avoid designing details reliant on toxic materials or harmful processes. For instance, avoid using wood panel products, textiles, and adhesives that emit formaldehyde gas. Plywood, oriented-strand board, and particle-board products often give off formaldehyde in interior applications, especially when new. Either formaldehyde-free products may be specified or these products can be manufactured in a manner that encases harmful compounds so that they do not exceed allowable formaldehyde emission standards. Some paints, preservatives, solvents, and plastics also give off irritating gasses and volatile organic compounds (VOCs) that can cause allergic reactions in many people. Search for products that reduce formaldehyde and VOC emissions in buildings, or use alternative finishes, such as powder coatings on metal, that do not produce harmful emissions.

2. Some toxic substances, such as mold spores and pollen, are airborne contaminants that can be effectively addressed using the building's filtration and ventilation systems. Interior temperature and humidity can also be effective in controlling biological organisms. Consider the inside of the ductwork to be an interior space, even if ducts are in an attic or crawl space, since occupants breathe whatever passes through them. Duct interiors should be detailed with smooth surfaces and joints. Routine building maintenance should monitor ducts to be sure they are dry and free of contaminants.

3. Certain external elements of buildings need to be kept distant from open windows and from any area where people might be walking or standing. These include cooling towers, air exhaust louvers, and plumbing vents. Cooling towers may harbor several kinds of pathogenic microorganisms that can cause Legionnaires' disease and other respiratory illnesses. Air exhaust louvers discharge stale air from a building, with its moisture, smoke, odors, and bacteria. Plumbing vents (the open top ends of vertical runs of waste and vent plumbing) smell very bad and carry disease organisms.

4. Indoor air quality can also be harmed by infiltration of toxic compounds from outside sources, such as radon gas, auto exhaust, and lawn and pest control chemicals. The normal metabolism of building occupants affects indoor air temperature and humidity. Occupants' use of tobacco products, cleaning solutions, and personal care products can also affect indoor air quality.

5. Monitoring interior air quality is more important in buildings that have reduced air infiltration or that have reduced fresh air entering the mechanical systems. In such well-sealed buildings, even low levels of off-gassing may accumulate to harmful levels. Architects and building owners can control indoor air quality by eliminating sources of toxins, separating occupants from them, and ventilating interiors to discharge toxins.

6. Materials that are safe in the finished building may be unsafe during manufacturing, construction, or repair processes. Airborne mineral and glass fibers may result from the installation or cutting of some construction materials and can irritate the skin, eyes, and mucous membranes of workers. Excavation, renovation, and demolition processes may cause workers to contact many harmful materials or to inhale unhealthy airborne substances. Existing building materials now recognized as unsafe should be identified in advance of the work, and appropriate precautions should be taken, including provisions for worker safety and for containment and safe removal of harmful materials. ∎

Fire-Safe Materials

Select structural and interior finish materials in buildings to minimize danger from fire.

1. Fire safety is the basis on which building codes regulate the finish materials that may be used inside buildings. Several factors are considered. A Flame-Spread Index indicates how fast a flame will spread across a surface of a given material. A Smoke-Developed Index indicates how much smoke the burning material will give off. And a Fuel-Contributed Index indicates how much fuel the material will contribute to the blaze. These factors are measured by laboratory tests and are expressed in clear terms for each material.

2. The detailer should become familiar with the way in which the building code applies these ratings to interior finish materials. The safest materials are Flame Spread Index Class A and include inorganic materials such as concrete, masonry, metal, and gypsum products. Class B materials include some plastics, such as vinyl laminate and wall coverings. Class C materials include most wood products and some plastics. For all three classes, the Smoke Developed Index cannot exceed specific limits. Generally, the taller and larger a building, the less the amount of combustible material that may be used in its construction. A single-family dwelling may be made entirely of combustible materials. In a very tall or very large building, the structural members must be noncombustible, be encased in noncombustible protection, be fully protected by an active fire-suppression system, or must comply with prescriptive Heavy Timber code stipulations. A single building may use more than one of these strategies (see *Fire-Resistant Assemblies*, later in this chapter). Combustible finish materials may be permitted only in limited quantities.

3. Within a building of any use or occupancy, highest fire ratings are called for in vertical exits and passageways, followed by horizontal exits, followed by rooms and enclosed spaces. Buildings without fire-suppression sprinklers generally are required to have higher fire ratings than fully sprinklered buildings.

4. Some building codes also regulate the density and toxicity of the combustion products that a material may give off. Many building materials produce highly toxic gasses when they burn. Among these materials are wood, asphalt, some synthetic carpets and fabrics, and many rubber and plastic materials. Foam plastic insulation inside a building must be covered with a fire-resistant finish, such as plaster or gypsum wallboard. Carpets, draperies, and upholstery should be chosen to avoid highly combustible materials and toxic combustion products. ■

Fire-Resistant Assemblies

Prescriptive building codes set forth the designer's choices of structural systems and building components according to the occupancy, height, and floor area of the building that is being designed. Building codes place a priority on public health and safety, and especially on fire safety. These priorities affect building design and building construction at all scales, including details.

It is important to note that these priorities should also be considered during the safe construction of a building. A fire-resistant assembly that relies on encasement of vulnerable materials is often not fire resistant until it is nearly complete. Active systems like building sprinklers are not effectively fire-suppressive until the building is finished. During construction, a building is vulnerable because there may be no completed fire management systems. Although not responsible for the means and methods of construction, the detailer must be familiar with the applicable building codes and the sequence of construction to help minimize this vulnerability. The owner, architect, and contractor would all be well advised to include a discussion in a preconstruction meeting about fire-resistant strategies that can be employed during the construction process.

1. Building codes such as the International Building Code (IBC) center on two comprehensive tables: One designates the height and area limitations for buildings of different uses, according to the type of construction that is used. The other defines each construction type in terms of the fire-resistance rating required for each of its major components (structural frame, bearing walls, nonbearing walls and partitions, floor construction, and roof construction). Using these two tables, the detailer can quickly establish the range of construction materials and systems from which the building may be built.

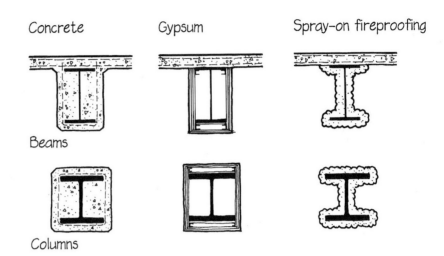

3. Prescriptive Fire Resistance Strategies

2. Additional tables in each building code give required fire-resistance ratings for fire barriers, fire walls, and fire doors.

3. Passive fire-resistance ratings for building components or assemblies such as structural elements, walls, floors, roofs, and doors are determined through standardized testing procedures carried out by impartial laboratories. These ratings are measured in hours, generally indicating their durability in a building fire. Ratings are tabulated both in the publications of those laboratories and in literature that is available from relevant trade associations and individual manufacturers. The detailer should assemble an up-to-date collection of websites and publications for use in selecting appropriately fire-resistant building components. A good start on this collection would be to acquire the Underwriters Laboratories' *Fire Resistance Design Directory* and the Gypsum Association's *Fire Resistance Design Manual*. See **Appendix A, The Detailer's Reference Shelf** in this book for sources of these publications.

138 PART I DETAIL PATTERNS

4. Penetrations of fire-rated assemblies, such as floors, fire walls, and fire separation walls, must be sealed or otherwise protected by code-approved means against the passage of fire, smoke, and hot gasses. Small holes through floors, such as pipe and conduit penetrations, are usually closed with fire-rated sealant systems marketed by a number of manufacturers. Gaps between exterior cladding and the edges of floors are sealed with safing, which usually consists of high-temperature mineral fiber batts supported by simple metal hooks or clips. Doors and door frames in fire walls and fire separation walls must have fire-resistance ratings, as specified by the relevant building code. Building codes restrict glass areas in fire doors and in fire-rated walls (see Safe Glazing, earlier in this chapter). They must be made of wired glass, which holds together even after it has been broken by fire, or clear fire-rated glass ceramic, which is typically thicker and more costly. At the point where a duct passes through a fire-rated wall, it must be fitted with a metal fire damper, a flap that closes automatically by means of a fusible link if the temperature in the duct rises above a set level. Vertical chases and shafts that pass through floors must be enclosed by walls of specified fire resistances.

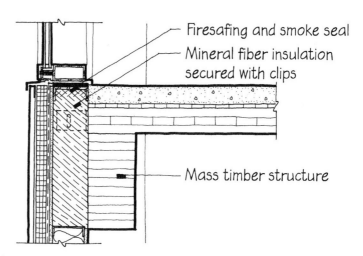

4. Sealing the Gap Between Cladding and Floors

5. Building codes recognize that safety can be enhanced by supplementing passive fire-resistant assemblies with active fire-suppression methods, such as fully automatic sprinkler systems and smoke-control systems. Rather than encasing vulnerable elements in a noncombustible layer, active methods typically use water or fire-extinguishing inert gas to suppress fire. These methods are effective but are vulnerable to interruption of pressurized water throughout the extensive plumbing network. Many designers use a combination of passive and active fire-resisting strategies to provide maximum protection. Because it is difficult for firefighters to reach upper floors of buildings, codes require all new buildings more than 55 ft. (16.76 m) above ground level to be equipped with automatic sprinklers.

Building codes permit fully sprinklered buildings of a given use and construction type – including combustible materials such as wood – to increase their height and area. Maximum egress corridor lengths and many other design elements are also affected in sprinklered buildings. Early in the design process, the architect must determine whether the building will be sprinklered so that building design and detailing decisions are based on clear assumptions.

Sprinkler systems typically call for a regular grid of overhead valves that should be coordinated with lighting, sensors, and other networks in the overhead zone.

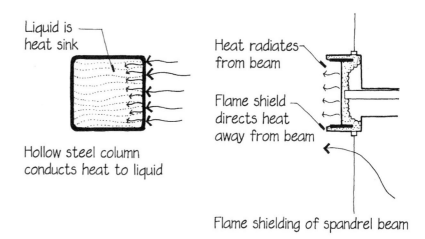

6. Performance-Based Fire Resistance Strategies

6. Building codes address most typical situations by prescribing minimum acceptable conditions. But in unique and complex buildings, there is often a need to find alternative solutions to achieve the intent of the code. Codes therefore contain a provision allowing designs and products to be used that differ from the specific code provisions, but that can be proven to fulfill the intentions of the code.

> An alternative material, design, or method of construction shall be approved where the code official finds that the proposed design is satisfactory and complies with the intent of the provisions of this code, and that the material, method, or work offered is, for the purpose intended, not less than the equivalent of that prescribed in this code in quality, strength, effectiveness, fire resistance, durability, and safety (IBC 2018, 104.11).

Alternative strategies to achieve fire resistance can therefore be used, provided they are first approved by the relevant officials. Proven fire-resistant strategies, such as liquid-filled steel frames and flame shields that direct heat away from vulnerable steel framing, are not included in the normal prescriptive building codes; however, they can be permitted through the performance code process. The architect may need to use sophisticated analytical software programs, full-scale testing, or other means to demonstrate the merits of the alternative proposal. Doing so requires time and funding, but it may yield superior building performance and occupant safety and may introduce new materials or assemblies to the array of known solutions.

Barrier-Free Design

Buildings open to the public must be planned and detailed in specified ways that make them accessible to all members of the population, including those who may use wheelchairs or crutches; the aged, blind, or deaf; and those in ill health. Nearly everyone experiences a disability at some point in life. Wherever possible, buildings should be designed to be universally accessible. Barrier-free design underscores the inclusive design effort required to remove physical barriers from the built environment for people with disabilities.

In multifamily housing projects, a small percentage of the dwelling units must conform to barrier-free standards so they may be occupied by people with disabilities. The legal requirements for barrier-free design of buildings are detailed in the Americans with Disabilities Act, or ADA; in various building codes and state laws; and in the American National Standards Institute (ANSI) ICC A117.1, *Accessible and Usable Buildings and Facilities*. *Architectural Graphic Standards* also gives extensive information on barrier-free design.

In a given jurisdiction, building codes may not include all provisions of ANSI ICC A117.1 or of the ADA Accessibility Guidelines. Designers and detailers should not rely solely on building codes to determine compliance with all accessibility requirements. This detail pattern can list only a few of the ways in which provisions of these documents affect the detailing of a building:

1. The most prominently visible result of barrier-free regulations is that there must be accessible routes into and through the building. Outdoors this can involve nearby accessible parking spaces, curb ramps, and specified types of ground surfaces. Accessible doors and entrances are ensured by regulations that relate to signage, clear widths, types of floor surfaces, wheelchair maneuvering clearances, vestibule size and configuration, door hardware, door closers, door opening force, and automatic doors. Ramps or elevators may be required to reach all floors of public buildings. The dimensions and inclination of ramps, the provision of landings, and the details of ramp handrails are all closely specified, as are elevator dimensions and controls (see **Geometry and Proportion**, Chapter 14).

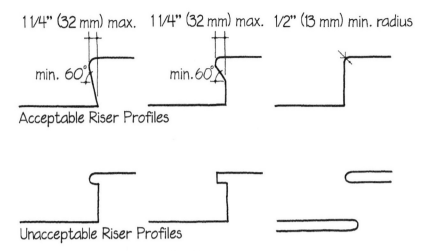

2. Barrier-Free Stair Riser Profiles

2. Stairs must be profiled so people on crutches can climb them easily. This eliminates abruptly projecting nosings that can catch the toes of a person on crutches as they slide up a riser. Open-riser stairs are also prohibited for accessible stairs. Instead, a smoothly profiled riser is required.

3. Accessibility regulations furnish minimum dimensions and details for wheelchair maneuverability in interior doorways, vestibules, corridors, and toilet rooms. Specified numbers of wheelchair-accessible toilet compartments and lavatories are required. Grab bars are required in toilet compartments to allow disabled occupants to move on and off toilets, and generous compartment dimensions are necessary to allow for wheelchair access. A percentage of the lavatory basins must be designed to allow a wheelchair to move in underneath; hot or sharp objects under lavatories must be insulated or shielded to prevent contact. Lavatory fittings must be of a type that can be operated by persons with impaired hand and arm dexterity. Showers and bathtubs require grab bars and access dimensions for wheelchairs.

Reception and sales counters must be designed with lower sections for use by people in wheelchairs.

4. Drinking fountains must be of specified types that allow a wheelchair occupant access to the stream of water, and the valve must be operable by persons with impaired hand and arm dexterity. Public telephones must meet accessibility requirements.

5. Dwelling units designed for occupancy by disabled persons generally must feature easy access from ground level, wide doorways and generous vestibules, accessible toilet and bathing facilities, and kitchen cabinets, appliances, and storage facilities that are designed to be accessible from a wheelchair.

6. Building codes specify minimum numbers and dispersed locations of wheelchair spaces in assembly facilities, such as athletic arenas, auditoriums, concert halls, opera houses, and theaters. Accessibility and space requirements are spelled out in considerable detail.

7. To aid persons with visual disabilities, surface materials and colors of important building features may be differentiated from their surroundings, using contrast. This is especially important for avoiding danger, such as at stair nosings, vehicular crossings, transit platforms, or pool edges. ■

Universal Design

Building designs should recognize that people vary widely in sizes, abilities, preferences, and communication skills. Everyone is at some point young, old, ill, injured, or otherwise challenged. The design of buildings, products, and details should be as inclusive as possible – that is, easy for the greatest number of people to understand and use. Universal design advocates for solutions that are good for everyone, instead of specialized design solutions for some people that are separate or different from the solutions for others.

Table 9-1 outlines seven key principles of universal design and gives a brief description and design guidelines for each.

These principles go beyond barrier-free design and such regulations as the Americans with Disabilities Act. They may be used to evaluate existing designs and to guide the design process of broadly usable products and built environments.

TABLE 9-1: Principles of Universal Design

Principle	Guidelines: Key elements that should be present in a design that adheres to the principle
1. Equitable use The design is useful to people with diverse abilities.	a. Provide the same means of use for all users: identical whenever possible, equivalent when not. b. Avoid segregating or stigmatizing any users. c. Provide privacy, security, and safety equally to all users. d. Make the design appealing to all users.
2. Flexibility in use The design accommodates a wide range of individual preferences and abilities.	a. Provide choice in methods of use. b. Accommodate right- or left-handed access and use. c. Facilitate the user's accuracy and precision. d. Provide adaptability to the user's pace.
3. Simple and intuitive use Use of the design is easy to understand, regardless of the user's experience, knowledge, language skills, or current concentration level.	a. Eliminate unnecessary complexity. b. Be consistent with user expectations and intuition. c. Accommodate a wide range of literacy and language skills. d. Arrange information according to its importance. e. Provide effective prompting and feedback during and after task completion.
4. Perceptible information The design communicates necessary information effectively to the user, regardless of ambient conditions or the user's sensory abilities.	a. Use different modes (pictorial, verbal, tactile) for redundant presentation of essential information. b. Provide adequate contrast between essential information and its surroundings. c. Maximize "legibility" of essential information. d. Give clear instructions or directions. e. Provide compatibility with a variety of techniques or devices used by people with sensory limitations.
5. Tolerance for error The design minimizes hazards and the adverse consequences of accidental or unintended actions.	a. Arrange elements to minimize hazards and errors: Make the most used elements the most accessible; hazardous elements should be eliminated, isolated, or shielded. b. Provide warnings of hazards. c. Provide fail-safe features. d. Encourage attention in tasks that require vigilance.
6. Low physical effort The design can be used efficiently and comfortably, with a minimum of fatigue.	a. Allow users to maintain a neutral body position. b. Use reasonable operating forces. c. Minimize repetitive actions. d. Minimize sustained physical effort.

continued

TABLE 9-1: *(continued)*

Principle	Guidelines: Key elements that should be present in a design that adheres to the principle
7. Size and space for approach and use Provide appropriate size and space for approach, reach, manipulation, and use, regardless of the user's body size, posture, or mobility.	a. Provide a clear line of sight to important elements for any seated or standing user. b. Make reach to important components comfortable for any seated or standing user. c. Accommodate variations in hand and grip size. d. Provide adequate space for the use of assistive devices or personal assistance.

Adapted from: "The Principles of Universal Design" by The Center for Universal Design, NC State University.

1. Landings along ramps and stairs provide a space to rest when people are moving from floor to floor of a building. For a ramp, landings are required for every 30 ft. (9.1 m) of horizontal distance traveled. A stair landing is necessary if the floor-to-floor height is greater than 12 ft. (3.7 m). The opportunity to stop and rest is essential for people who are carrying a heavy load or who are unable to endure long periods of exertion as a result of a physical condition or ailment.

1. Design for Efficient Use and Minimum Fatigue

2. Swinging and sliding doors can be a potential hazard if too much force is required to open them or to stop them from closing. In the event of a fire, it is essential that people of all sizes and capabilities be able to open a door. It is also important that everyone be capable of stopping a door so that it does not close too swiftly and cause injury.

2. Design for People of All Sizes and Capabilities

3. Doors, appliances, and plumbing fixtures should employ hardware that is designed to be operated by all people, whether or not they are physically able to firmly grasp an object. Levers should be chosen in lieu of knobs where possible so that a simple application of pressure can set the hardware in motion, thus activating the mechanism with greater ease.

4. All people, regardless of stature or ability, have optimal ranges of reach for performing different tasks. According to the Occupational Safety and Health Administration, the zone closest to the body is the preferred work zone, with optimum performance often being diminished the greater the reach. It is also important to consider that different tasks may occur at different distances from the body. For example, fine motor skills and accuracy must occur close to the body and eyes for optimum control, while larger movements that may require more leverage – or that are dangerous – should occur a little farther from the body, but close enough to maintain control.

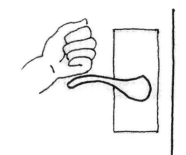

3. Select Hardware That is Easy to Use

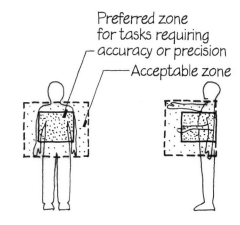

4. Design Facilities in Which Critical Tasks Can Be Carried Out in Optimum Work Zones

CHAPTER 10

Providing for the Aging of the Building

When designing and constructing a building, the hope is that it will last a very long time. Most buildings do. And, as discussed in the preceding chapter, most buildings do a remarkable job protecting the health, safety, and welfare of its occupants. But as the months and years pass, buildings change, or the environment changes around them. The act of making buildings and the decision of how and where they are made have consequences. Their surfaces wear, they weather, and they gather dirt or biological growth. They undergo chemical changes such as fading and corrosion. Components of the building fail and are replaced. The building is remodeled or renovated from time to time. Often a beautiful building grows less so as these changes take place. In some cases, a building may grow more beautiful and take on added character as changes take place. Some buildings last only a short time; others last for centuries. Some buildings intended for short-term use survive for decades because of their quality and merit. There are many reasons for these differences in service life. Most have to do with materials and detailing.

Many of the detail patterns throughout this book have a profound effect on the rapidity with which a particular building ages, but there are three categories of detail patterns that relate specifically to managing the life cycle of a building. Each of these detail patterns are listed below and described more fully later in this chapter.

The first category contains patterns about designing a building with a perspective toward its entire lifetime:

> *Life Cycle* (p. 146)
> *Expected Life* (p. 148)
> *Surfaces That Age Gracefully* (p. 150)

The second category relates to the need to maintain a building:

> *Repairable Surfaces* (p. 152)
> *Cleanable Surfaces* (p. 153)
> *Maintenance Access* (p. 154)

The third category includes six patterns that have to do with building deterioration:

> *Dry Wood* (p. 156)
> *Protected and Similar Metals* (p. 158)
> *Less Absorbent Materials* (p. 161)
> *Robust Assemblies* (p. 163)
> *Building Armor* (p. 164)
> *Extreme Event Protection* (p. 166)

Architectural Detailing: Function Constructability Aesthetics. Fourth Edition. Patrick Rand, Jason Miller, and Edward Allen.
© 2025 John Wiley & Sons, Inc. Published 2025 by John Wiley & Sons, Inc.

Life Cycle

Architects understandably focus chiefly on the initial conditions of the building, while also considering the impact on conditions "upstream" and "downstream" of the building itself. Building materials come from someplace, they are used in the building, and then they go someplace else. The building's distant and long-term impacts on the environment must be considered if advances in building design and construction are to be sustainable.

1. Construction transforms raw natural materials into useful building elements, each of which has its own life cycle. These materials expire physically at varying rates, or they become functionally obsolete as improved products become available.

2. Owners and regulatory bodies may require that specific environmental impact objectives be met in order for a project to be built. Life Cycle Assessment (LCA) addresses the qualitative influences, and Life Cycle Cost (LCC) analyses address the economic implications. No single aspect of LCA dominates all others, but a given project may give priority to one aspect over others. The detailer should look creatively at various options to find the strategy most appropriate for a particular project. Many digital LCA and LCC modeling tools are available to examine options and document results. Technical references and rating systems are also available to aid in this process.

LIFE CYCLE OF A BUILDING MATERIAL
(with associated environmental impact at each stage)

1. Source of material; *Impact*: Extraction of renewable or nonrenewable material from nature, material recycled from previous use, or some combination

2. Transport of material to site; *Impact*: Means, distance, and type of fuel

3. Industrial processes: refinement of raw material, fabrication of finished product; *Impact*: Energy types and quantities consumed, generation of by-products

4. Construction processes and maintenance or repair during service life; *Impact*: Energy types and quantities consumed, generation of by-products

5. Building operation; *Impact*: Energy types and quantities consumed for illumination, heating, and cooling; influence of materials on indoor air quality; impact on outdoor air and water quality, etc.

6. Deconstruction or demolition; *Impact*: Energy types and quantities consumed, generation of by-products

7. Reuse of serviceable components and recycling of salvageable materials; *Impact*: Energy types and quantities consumed, generation of by-products

8. Disposal of waste; *Impact*: Air and water quality impact, transport means, distance and type of fuel

3. The priorities for some building elements may be different from others because of differences in their service lives. For instance, use of recyclable materials is a higher priority for carpet and roofing membranes that must be replaced periodically during the life of the building. Durability is the highest priority when designing the foundation and primary structural system of a building. Recyclability is of greatest concern when the service life of the element is short, and it is less important when the service life is very long.

4. Renewable resources such as wood should be used at rates lower than the rate at which they are replenished by nature.

5. Nonrenewable resources should be used efficiently and durably, and they should be reused or recycled at the end of the service life.

6. Many manufacturers offer information about the origins of their products, making it easier for designers to choose low impact products. Labels on materials and certificates of authenticity document the claims. The increasing use of international Environmental Product Declarations (EPDs) based on accepted Product Category Rules (PCRs) provide designers with a robust factual indication of a material's

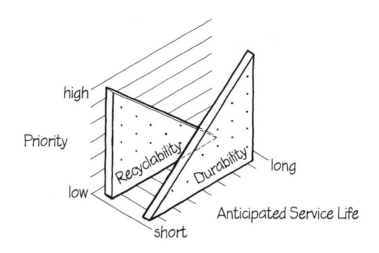

3. Priorities Vary Depending upon Anticipated Service Life

initial environmental impact. Accessibility to objective environmental data regarding materials and processes empowers detailers to make informed decisions.

7. Embodied energy is the energy needed to extract, refine, process, transport, install, and reuse or dispose of a material. It is very difficult to measure, but generally materials that (1) require a great deal of energy to extract or manufacture, (2) are transported a great distance, or (3) require greater maintenance while in service will have the highest embodied energy. Materials of local origin that are not energy intensive in their manufacturing process will likely have the lowest embodied energy. Embodied energy constitutes only about 2% of all energy consumed in the life of the building, a tiny fraction compared to the energy used to operate the building. Despite this, it is an important constituent of LCA and LCC analyses, because energy use often correlates with economic costs and environmental costs, such as harmful carbon dioxide and pollutant emissions.

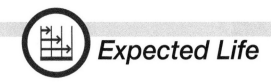

Expected Life

Question: How long should a material or detail last? Answer: The durability of a specific building material or detail must be proportional to its intended useful life.

1. The useful life of a material or an assembly is determined by how its intrinsic physical properties resist deterioration caused by conditions of its environment, use patterns, workmanship at the time of installation, and maintenance while in service. This life span is also affected by nonphysical factors such as economic forces, aesthetics, and functional obsolescence, but these issues exist beyond the scope of this book.

2. Decisions regarding materials and details are based on a premise about the anticipated life span of the building. Buildings should always be built well; however, materials and details appropriate in a building meant to serve for a few years may be different from those for a building meant to serve for 100 years or more. To illustrate this point, consider the critical role flashing plays in the patterns for controlling water (see **Drain and Weep, Moisture Break**, Chapter 1) against the expected life of the material selected for the purpose. Stainless steel flashing is less appropriate for a temporary structure like an exposition building that will be used for a few months or years, compared to a state capitol building with an unlimited life expectancy. Conversely, it is not appropriate for the stone-clad statehouse walls to use PVC flashing, which has a reliable service life of only about 10 years. Balancing the initial costs of a project against the life cycle costs of a building, including operational and maintenance expenses, is a significant aspect of design detailing. An element of risk exists in the value engineering process of any project to match required performance, quality, and safety with the lowest possible LCC.

The premature failure of a building material may result in damage to adjoining materials, requiring costly and disruptive repairs. Premature failure is especially regrettable when an otherwise durable assembly fails because of a weak link – whether that failure is one of the specified material or the detailing and assembly sequence. Ideally, the detailer should anticipate the forces acting on an assembly and design the details so that the components expire uniformly or in manageable segments.

Predicting the service life of a detail or an assembly is difficult because there is often insufficient knowledge about the actual performance of specific materials and details in specific environments. Therefore, detailers and owners should construct durability criteria for materials and details on the basis of previous experience. Direct observation of existing buildings is one way to increase practical knowledge about how materials and assemblies perform. For new products, manufacturers can arrange for independent parties to perform accelerated weathering tests and relevant ASTM tests to gauge how the new products hold up in particular service environments.

3. Establish a premise about the service life of the building in general, for instance, for 25 years, 60 years, 100 years, or more. There are no legal standards for this, but precedents for the type of building are a good indication. Available evidence suggests that the service life of buildings is approximately twice the 30–50 years used in some of the common LCA and LCC models. Recognize that it is not necessary that all elements of an entire building expire at the same time. Establish service life tiers, within which the elements should last about the same length of time.

TABLE 10-1: Service Life Tiers

1	**Permanent:** Should last as long as the intended life of the building; priority placed on durability	Primary structure and primary enclosure system	Major load-bearing elements and building envelope
2	**Long Life:** Should last 20 years minimum	Major building service systems	Elevators, furnaces, boilers, chillers, major fans, plumbing and electrical systems
3	**Medium Life:** Should last up to 20 years or with change in occupancy	Interior enclosure systems	Partitions, flooring, ceilings
4	**Temporary:** Should last up to 10 years; priority placed on recyclable or rapidly renewable materials	Furnishings, interior and exterior finishes	Surface finishes, sealants

Adapted from "Guideline on Durability in Buildings," Canadian Standards Association, S478.

4. To lower initial construction costs, elements of a detail are sometimes eliminated, or less durable alternative elements are chosen, often with disastrous results. Many expensive recladding projects are the result of hastily made cost-trimming decisions that save less than 1% of the future needed repair costs. Lower-quality execution during initial construction often results in higher maintenance costs or shorter service life. Knowledgeable detailers should play a central role in making optimum choices regarding substitutions of materials and details.

5. Just as we have an operating manual for our automobile, architects may offer to provide building owners or managers with a guide summarizing the maintenance and replacement cycles anticipated for each tier of the building systems. Owners and maintenance staff are collaborators in determining the building's life span; maintenance procedures need to be followed if the actual service life is going to meet the predicted service life.

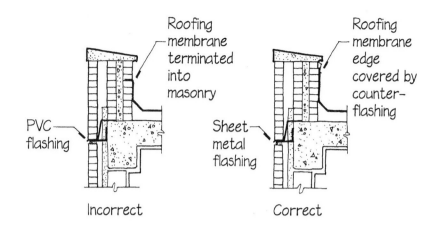

6. Anticipating Service Life--Two Versions

6. Details for all building elements should be designed to be accessible in proportion to their longevity. Building elements that are scheduled for replacement at the most frequent intervals, such as lighting tubes and air filters, should be detailed to make routine maintenance easy. Low-slope roof membranes should be detailed so that the membrane can be replaced without requiring that the parapet be reconstructed. Furnaces and boilers are not replaced frequently, but when they are replaced, the bulky, heavy equipment must be accessed without removing walls or other durable assemblies.

Surfaces That Age Gracefully

Choose materials that assume added visual character as they age, rather than those that look progressively worse due to weathering or use with the passing years. Designers should select materials and develop details that evolve without degrading.

Even perfectly crafted building surfaces begin to change the instant they are finished. Nothing shows a blemish or a speck of dirt more readily than a smooth, uniform surface. To keep it looking brand-new requires a substantial and questionable, not to mention unsustainable, maintenance obligation.

1. Most species of wood deteriorate rapidly outdoors unless they are stained or painted. A few species are naturally resistant to decay, however. If left uncoated, in some settings they weather gradually to attractive shades of brown and gray. These species include Cypress, Redwood, White and Red Cedars, Teak, Ipe, and various tropical hardwoods. Heartwood is inherently more resistant to deterioration than sapwood. Weather will slowly erode the surfaces of these woods, requiring eventual replacement.

2. Clear coatings, such as most types of spar, urethane, and marine varnish, are vulnerable to sunlight. It makes them become brittle and weakens their bond to the wood beneath, causing them to peel off in a year or two. Clear coatings containing ultraviolet (UV) filters are much more durable and are slow to yellow.

Stains carry pigment into the pores of the wood but do not form a film on the surface; they permit the wood grain to remain visible. Paint is an opaque film over the surface of wood or other substrates. Outdoors, bright paint colors fade quickly and unevenly. White paint, through an intentional chalking process, renews itself continually and tends to remain attractive. Earth-color pigments and soft grays tend to hold their colors longer in sunlight than do brighter hues. All exterior varnish, stains, and paints require regular maintenance. The interval is shorter if exposures to sunlight, water, and heat are severe.

3. Among metals, ordinary steel rusts away, unless it has been painted. Stainless steel, especially in a brushed finish, retains its good looks indefinitely without painting. Mill-finished aluminum forms a self-protecting oxide coating and does not corrode further, but this coating is thin, easily damaged, and splotchy-looking. Through the process of anodizing, aluminum can be manufactured with a thick, durable coating of oxide that contains an integral color of the designer's choice, and it will look good for decades. Copper forms a self-protecting oxide coating that is usually an attractive blue-green or dark brown in color, depending on the pollutants in the atmosphere; it is a traditional choice for a metal that ages gracefully outdoors. Copper can be chemically pre-patinated at the factory to create an aged appearance, even though new. This might be useful when replacing a portion of a weathered surface. This chemical treatment alters the surface of copper, sometimes making it weather differently than natural copper. Lead protects itself with a white oxide coating. Zinc is naturally corrosion-resistant, even in marine settings. It has a matte medium-gray color and is very stable if not exposed to acids or alkalis. A copper-steel alloy called "weathering steel" forms a tenacious, self-protecting coating of red-brown oxide on its exposed surface and needs no painting. Weathering steel is not corrosion resistant; its surface oxidizes intentionally and rapidly, acting as a passive barrier against further corrosion. Because oxidation is a type of corrosion, the outer surface of this product is sacrificed to preserve the underlying layer. Weathering steel, lead, and copper tend to shed some of their oxide coatings, staining surfaces below. Care should be exercised in detailing assemblies with these materials to catch and drain all rainwater that has flowed over them before it can run onto such stainable surfaces as stone, concrete, wood, and glass.

4. In general, matte surfaces age more gracefully than glossy surfaces, which tend to weather rapidly to a matte finish on most materials. A mirror-finish stainless steel panel, for example, soon grows dirty, obscuring its luster, whereas a matte-finish stainless steel surface changes relatively little in appearance as it accumulates the same amount of dirt. Glossy paints lose their luster quickly in sunlight, chalking to a matte texture. Exceptions include glass and glazed ceramic tiles. These lose some of their sheen as they grow dirty, but when washed they regain their lustrous surfaces and bright colors.

5. Smooth concrete surfaces – those formed against steel, plastic, or overlaid plywood – tend to reveal every small flaw resulting from the form surface, the mix, or the placement method. They also change appearance rapidly as they weather, becoming rougher and attracting more grime. The concrete surfaces that are more tolerant of flaws and that weather more gracefully are those formed with heavy textures, such as exposed aggregate, sandblasted, bush-hammered, board-formed, or ribbed surfaces.

6. Countless historic buildings attest to the capacity of stone, brick, and other masonry surfaces to age gracefully. Like different species of wood, different types of stone and manufactured masonry products vary in their response to environmental forces and use patterns. These materials have been chosen for harsh exposures because they are inert. They generally perform quite well despite having no coatings or surface treatments, and require little maintenance. Even in challenging urban or industrial environments, exterior surfaces made of granite, limestone, sandstone, brick, terra-cotta, and concrete masonry generally perform well. Contemporary products are available in an unprecedented range of colors and textures, whose qualities can be matched with project needs.

7. Glass is one of the few materials that is not altered significantly by exposure. However, films and coatings applied to glass, such as low-E coatings, are vulnerable and must be applied to interior surfaces of glazing assemblies so that routine weathering and cleaning will not harm them.

8. Plastics such as polycarbonate and acrylic are sometimes used in glazing applications. They are lighter in weight and may be less costly than glass; however, their surfaces are much less hard, so they may become scratched or dulled or discolored more readily than glass. Such materials should not be used in high-traffic applications, such as glazed panels in an entry door.

9. Sealants are available in a wide variety of colors, making it possible to select initial colors that match surrounding materials. It is likely they will weather differently than adjoining materials, causing the sealants to become more prominent over time. Chemicals in adjoining materials or used in building maintenance may also cause sealant colors to change. Detailers are urged to review manufacturers' technical information to select the best products.

10. How water will flow over all exterior surfaces of a building is another important consideration. Not only can water itself harm materials and assemblies, but it can also carry atmospheric debris and water-soluble chemicals that will stain or otherwise harm materials in their path. Be especially thorough in addressing water flow at transitions (see Chapter 1). Always orient edges of materials in the same direction as the descending water, like shingles on a roof. Areas of greatest concentrated water flow will be scoured clean and may even be eroded as the water removes material in its path. Where flow is less rapid, particles and chemicals will be deposited onto surfaces, often darkening them. When these two conditions are in close proximity, as they often are, a contrast of clean and soiled surfaces may result. This chiaroscuro effect may be attractive and add visual depth to a carved stone capital of a classical building but may be less appreciated on other building surfaces.

11. Textured exterior wall surfaces will darken over time, especially where they are most exposed to airborne particles or where minor biological growth can occur. Surfaces of a building become more orientation- and place-specific as this happens. The change is a subtle index of what and where the surface is, and it may not threaten the integrity of the assembly.

12. Indoors, smooth, shiny, plain-colored surfaces age badly when compared to surfaces that are physically or visually textured. A stylish, shiny black plastic end table shows every grain of dust, every scratch, and every water spot or ring, whereas an oak end table with a transparent finish calls attention to its grain figure, distracting the eye effectively from dust, scratches, and stains. A pure white polished marble floor would be a maintenance nightmare, while a rough slate floor will absorb lots of dirt and damage before it requires attention. A plain-colored sheet vinyl flooring shows each scuff mark and spill, while a patterned flooring conceals them. A white-painted wall in a public school corridor will need to be washed frequently, while a dark, durable, textured wall surface can go months without cleaning. Bright chromium and brass surfaces need constant polishing for their quality to be sustained, while matte-varnished or oil-finished wood and brushed bronze almost never need it, even growing more beautiful with age, patina, and use.

13. Porous materials that people touch will generally darken over time, as the oil from fingertips wearing on the surface lends color and sheen to that surface. An oak newel post at the base of a stair is not harmed by this change; the change is a record of the usefulness of the detail.

Repairable Surfaces

Detailers cannot prevent wear. They can assemble materials and details so that building surfaces wear evenly and slowly. It is important to anticipate the inevitable need to repair the surfaces of a building and to utilize materials that may be repaired easily and inconspicuously.

1. Some materials are monolithic or seamlessly whole once installed; examples include sitecast concrete, stucco, and plaster. Others are discrete pieces embedded in a monolithic base, such as masonry or tile. A third category includes discrete pieces that are fastened or anchored to a structural substrate, such as precast concrete or rainscreen panels. The appropriate method of repair varies according to these categories.

2. Blemishes in monolithic surfaces are generally patched or repaired to blend with the surrounding surface. Patches or repairs to unpainted surfaces will stand out if they do not match the varied textures and colors present in the surrounding surface. A wall surface of painted gypsum board or gypsum plaster is only moderately resistant to damage, but if it is gouged or scratched, it is easily and invisibly repaired using materials that can be purchased at any hardware store. The unifying paint layer is superficial and inexpensive and is expected to be reapplied with some frequency anyway. Surfaces such as varnished wood paneling, marble wainscoting, or wallpaper are far more difficult to repair if damaged, because their inherent pattern cannot be duplicated easily.

3. Damaged pieces embedded in a monolithic base must be carefully extracted, then replaced. A floor or wall of polished stone or ceramic tile, while inherently durable and attractive, can be very difficult to repair if a unit of material is damaged. The individual stone or tile can be troublesome to remove, and replacement materials often do not match the surrounding material in color or pattern. The matching problem can be minimized by using a more variegated pattern in the original installation: a mix of several colors of tiles, for example, or a highly variegated blend of stone, in which a slight color mismatch created by a later repair will not be noticeable.

4. Discrete pieces that are individually fastened may each be replaced with a matching item. A surface made up of a large number of small, individually attached units, such as a roof of shingles or slates, does not tend to look bad if one or two units are damaged. It is easily and unobtrusively repaired by replacing the damaged units. Initial discrepancies in appearance between new pieces and nearby weathered ones will moderate with time.

5. If a very large sheet of glass is chipped or cracked, it becomes unattractive and dangerous, and it must be replaced. This requires the services of a crew of professional glaziers, a glass truck, and sometimes a crane. But if a small lite of glass in a many-paned window cracks or chips, it can safely be left in place until it becomes more badly damaged, and its eventual replacement is easy work for individual maintenance personnel.

6. Some curtain wall cladding systems made of metal, glass, or thin stone panels are "stick systems" that are detailed to permit easy replacement of an isolated piece within a broad wall surface. When selecting these systems, investigate the manufacturer's details regarding incremental replacement. Sheets of glass can usually be replaced using standard gaskets or metal hardware. Metal and stone cladding panels vary regarding anchoring details; in general, anchors at panel edges are more easily accessed for replacement than those concealed behind panels. Cladding pieces secured with adhesives and welds may be much more difficult to remove, especially if the bonds are out of reach (see *Detailing for Disassembly*, Chapter 11).

7. In sustainable design and construction, exterior assemblies are increasingly made up of additive layers of products, each performing a specific function or set of functions. In such assemblies, the exterior finish layer can often be replaced in its entirety, or damaged pieces can be replaced, with very little harm to the underlying layers.

8. Future availability of a specific color, texture, or shape is not ensured, especially if a product is unique or custom-made for the project. In those cases, the owner may be well advised to acquire and stock a small quantity of the special items for future use. Alternatively, portions of the building that are most vulnerable to deterioration may be made of common materials and standard assemblies, anticipating availability in future years.

9. An alternative strategy to reduce the effort and expense of surface repair is to use surface materials resistant to noticeable blemishes. Vegetated building surfaces such as green roofs and walls can present seasonal variation without ever appearing broken or flawed. A dry-stacked rubble stone wall has a similar forgiving visual quality. Acceptance of the naturally varied appearance rather than a crisp uniform aesthetic means that repairs only need to be undertaken when functional performance fails, not because of superficial features. ■

Cleanable Surfaces

Detailing decisions affect the ease and expense of keeping a building clean.

1. Surface finishes need to be matched carefully to the areas in which they are used. Kitchens, bathrooms, shower rooms, laundries, and wet industrial areas should be finished in materials that can be cleaned by washing in place. Water-resistant materials with smooth, dense surfaces are best: stainless steel, plastic laminates, glazed ceramic tiles, glazed concrete masonry, terrazzo, sheet rubber or vinyl flooring, and porcelain. The best detailing of these materials features rounded, crack-free junctions, such as integral cove interior corners and bullnose exterior corners. Junctions in wall and floor surfaces in commercial kitchens must be coved and closed to no larger than 1/32 in. (1 mm). Jointless surfaces can be made of welded thermoplastics. Self-cleaning and antibacterial nanotechnology coatings can be integrated into some surfaces and manufactured products. These are especially useful in clinical areas requiring a high standard of hygiene.

2. Thin-film technology has been incorporated into some proprietary glass cladding and skylight products to make the glass self-cleaning. The special coating is applied to the exterior surface (#1 surface), where ultraviolet light causes a chemical reaction that breaks down organic dirt particles and detaches them from the glass. Normal precipitation or water from a hose then carries the particles away. Manufacturers state that the coating does not need to be reapplied for the life of the glass unit. A similar photocatalytic coating has been applied to exterior concrete surfaces to make them self-cleaning, even in industrial and urban settings. In addition to keeping the concrete clean, this white titanium dioxide-based coating also removes pollutants from the air. This proprietary cement technology can also be incorporated into cement-based stucco and concrete masonry units.

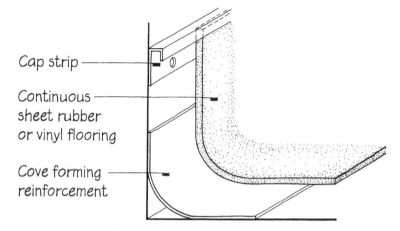

1. Integral Cove at Floor to Wall Transition

3. Avoid installations that complicate the cleaning process. Multi-stall toilet rooms with wall-mounted fixtures and ceiling-hung partitions can be cleaned much more quickly and satisfactorily than rooms in which everything is mounted to the floor. Assembly seating and commercial kitchen equipment represent two other areas in which well-chosen equipment with seamless, smooth surfaces can make this task easier.

4. Materials susceptible to water damage, such as gypsum products and wood, should be avoided in wet areas. At the very least, they should be finished with gloss or semi-gloss, water-resistant coatings so that they can be washed. It is better to adopt more durable, washable materials, such as smooth-finished rubber sheets, plastic laminate, resin panels, or fiberglass.

Structural elements in wet areas should be made of materials that can endure an episode of water exposure, such as light gauge steel, steel, masonry, or concrete. Experience shows that wood products that are exposed to water in floods only one time remain vulnerable to biological attack by mold and fungus.

5. Absorbent materials such as carpet and upholstery are totally inappropriate in wet areas. Even indoor-outdoor carpet absorbs food spills, soap, and urine, and it cannot be cleaned adequately. Wood floors, even with polyurethane finishes, are not resistant to water. Cracks open between the pieces of flooring because of normal seasonal changes in the moisture content of the wood, allowing water to penetrate and lift the varnish from beneath, resulting in an unattractive surface that cannot be washed properly.

6. In dry areas of a building, a much wider selection of materials is both possible and appropriate. Carpeting can be cleaned economically with regular vacuuming and occasional shampooing. Wood floors can be kept clean, attractive, and resilient with dust mopping, occasional scrubbing, and periodic sanding and refinishing. Gypsum surfaces finished with either paint or wallpaper require only sporadic cleaning and infrequent renewal. Details with cracks and sharp inside corners will attract and hold unacceptable amounts of dirt in most dry areas of a building. ■

Maintenance Access

Many components need to be detailed to allow for maintenance and inspection access throughout the life of the building.

1. Metal and glass curtain wall systems are available in both internally glazed and externally glazed systems, referring to whether the glass can be replaced by workers standing inside the building or only by workers on outside scaffolding. In buildings greater than a story or two in height, there is an obvious maintenance advantage in adopting an internally glazed system.

2. The glass on buildings that are more than three stories tall cannot be washed by workers on ladders. Special provisions must be made for window washer access. This can be in the form of operable windows that bring all exterior glass surfaces within an arm's reach, but they are not always practical in very tall buildings because of high wind velocities at upper levels. A design for a tall building should include provisions for movable window-washing scaffolding and safety attachments.

3. Building components that may require adjustment or replacement during the life of the building should be attached with screws or bolts so that they can be removed and replaced rather than welded, glued, or nailed permanently in place. This is why we use screws rather than nails to attach hardware to doors, lighting fixtures to walls and ceilings, and shading device hardware to windows. It is simpler to install and maintain short segments of flexible, threaded plumbing supply lines to fixtures than it would be to solder rigid copper pipe.

4. Concealed plumbing, mechanical, and electrical components that require inspection and maintenance should be placed behind snap-off covers, hinged access panels, manholes, handholes, or access ports of appropriate sizes and shapes. Never permanently seal off any component of a building that moves, that connects electrical wires, that may need cleaning, or that may deteriorate or go out of adjustment prematurely. Examples include pipe valves, ductwork dampers, electric motors, pumps, plumbing cleanouts, electric junction boxes, lighting ballasts, transformers, heating and cooling coils, and telephone wiring junctions. Work continually with plumbing, electrical, mechanical, and structural consultants to see that all necessary access devices are provided (see *Horizontal Plenum*, Chapter 8).

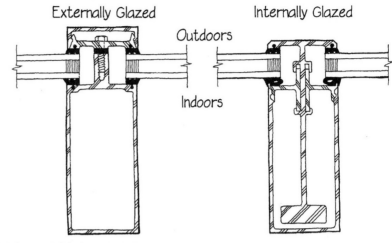

1. Vertical Mullion Details

4. Access for Inspection and Maintenance

5. Horizontal and vertical mullions in most storefront and curtain wall systems do not accommodate electrical lines within them. However, some manufacturers have produced special mullions that can contain small power and communication lines, which can be easily accessed through snap-fit covers. These can serve nearby office workstations or can connect to active electrochromic glazing panels or photovoltaic panels held in place by the mullions.

6. Maintenance access generally requires floor space. A residential oil or gas burner needs a clear space about 3 ft. (900 mm) square for servicing. A horizontal boiler needs considerable free space for cleaning and replacing tubes. Electrical and communications switchgear needs free frontal access and sufficient space to remove and replace components. Large boilers, chillers, fans, motors, and pumps that will not fit through normal doors, corridors, and elevators may need to be replaced someday and may require industrial doors or removable access panels for that eventuality.

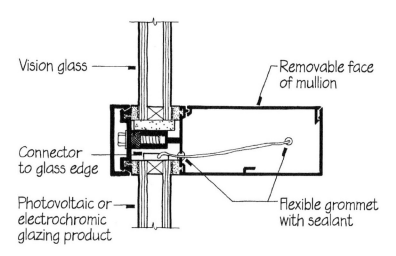

5. Horizontal Curtain Wall Mullion with Integrated Electrical Access

Lay out spaces for mechanical, plumbing, electrical, and communications equipment in close cooperation with engineering consultants, to be sure these concerns are accommodated.

7. Maintenance access is most important in service-intensive buildings, such as hospitals and laboratories. Offices with ever-changing workstation configurations need convenient access to power and communication networks. Interior room surfaces in workplaces may expose service networks to view or may contain them behind access panels that are easily removed.

Dry Wood

Wood must be detailed to stay dry; otherwise, it will decay in only a few years. Even decay-resistant species and chemically treated wood will last longer if kept dry.

1. A traditional covered bridge is durable because it is covered to keep water off the joints in the wood trusses. Joints between pieces of wood that are exposed to the weather absorb and hold moisture by capillary action. This encourages decay. In most climates, uncovered constructions made of ordinary wood seldom last as long as a decade before their joints rot beyond repair. Exposed exterior wood constructions with many joints, such as fences, decks, sunshades, railings, benches, gates, and doors, should be made of decay-resistant wood. Painting does not offer sufficient protection; normal seasonal moisture movement in the wood causes the paint to crack at the joints, allowing water to enter.

2. Wood must be kept well away from the ground to stay dry and free from decay. In the sill detail of a wood-frame building, all wood is kept at least 6 in. (152 mm) above the surface of the soil. As a further precaution, it is required to use pressure-treated or naturally decay-resistant wood for the sill plate that rests on a concrete or masonry foundation, because moisture may rise from the ground through the porous material of the foundation and wet the underside of the sill. In a crawl space, only treated wood or wood that has high resistance to decay should be within 18 in. (460 mm) of soil. On wet sites or in very damp climates, a continuous flashing should be installed between the sill and the foundation, as a barrier against capillary moisture rising from the soil.

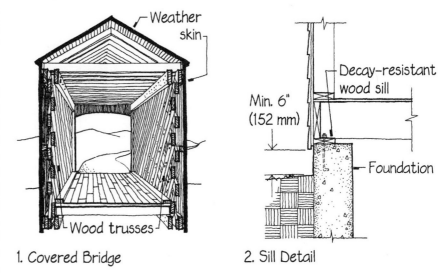

1. Covered Bridge

2. Sill Detail

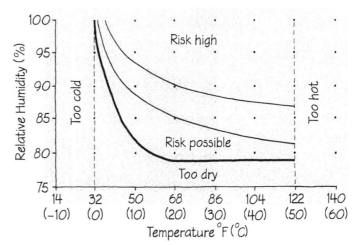

3. Risk of Mold Growth in Wood

3. The microorganisms that cause decay in wood need three things to survive: air (oxygen), food (cellulose), and small amounts of moisture. Natural wood is often the source of both food and moisture. Usually, decay is discouraged either by treating the wood with chemicals to make it unfit as food, by selecting a wood species that is unappetizing to the microorganisms (see Table 10-2), or by keeping wood dry, which is generally below 20% moisture content. Wood buildings in Nordic countries survive for hundreds of years without paint or preservatives because the conditions for mold growth seldom exist.

TABLE 10-2: Natural Decay Resistance of Wood Species (heartwood durability shown)

Very resistant	Resistant	Moderately resistant	Nonresistant	Nonresistant
Western juniper	Cedar	Western larch	True fir	Spruce
Bald cypress	Cypress	Douglas fir	Hemlock	Birch
Chestnut oak	Redwood	Red oak	Maple	Aspen
Ipe	Hickory	Elm	Sweetgum	Walnut
	White oak	Green ash	Poplar	Balsa
		Longleaf pine and Eastern white pine	Pines (other than Longleaf and Eastern white)	Basswood
		Mahogany, teak		

4. Paradoxically, wood that is completely and permanently submerged in water will not decay. This is because water does not allow the organisms in the wood access to air. Thus, untreated wood is sometimes used for foundation pilings in soils that are completely saturated with water. This works well if the water level in the soil does not drop. In cases where the water level has fallen, piles have rotted at the level where the saturated soil joins the drier soil above, the one location where air, water, and wood are all available to the decay organisms.

5. All wood-destroying insects require moisture to survive. Many species can live only in damp wood and are easily discouraged by details that keep wood dry. The most common species of termites are subterranean, but they can attack dry wood if they have access to damp soil. These species are dealt with by keeping wood at least 6 in. (152 mm) above the soil line and by installing a continuous flashing with projecting edges between the sill and the foundation. Alternatively, a foundation made of sitecast concrete or fully grouted concrete masonry units may be used. Both will require that the tubes built by these termites to contact the ground can be easily spotted and destroyed. Soil poisons can also be used against this type of termite to create a chemical barrier, but the safety of these poisons must be monitored carefully to minimize environmental damage and prevent illness to occupants. To avoid chemicals, a fine stainless steel mesh can be installed, prior to construction, across the soil below the building. A few species of termites that thrive only in very warm, damp climates can live in dry wood without soil contact, taking their moisture from the air or the wood itself; these are dealt with by poisoning them through fumigation. Treatment with very hot or cold temperatures is also possible.

Wood-framed buildings in locations where termites exist should not have rigid insulation or EIFS (exterior insulation and finish systems) reaching vertically across the 6 in. (152 mm) margin that separates the wood from the ground, because termites will easily tunnel through it undetected to reach the wood above.

Protected and Similar Metals

Many architectural metals are vulnerable to atmospheric corrosion due to oxidation and to bimetallic corrosion due to contact with incompatible metals. Protect vulnerable metals from oxidation and avoid exterior details in which two different metals are attached directly to one another.

1. Simple atmospheric corrosion is oxidation that occurs when air and moisture are present simultaneously on the surface of a metal. Most nonferrous metals (such as aluminum, zinc, brass, bronze, lead, and copper) quickly form stable, self-protecting oxide coatings that prevent further corrosion. Stainless steels and certain weathering steels are also self-protecting.

2. Ordinary steel (carbon steel), wrought iron, and cast iron need protective coatings to avoid destruction by oxidation (rusting) if they are used outdoors or in wet interior environments. These may take the form of paint, various factory-applied organic coatings, or metallic coatings.

3. The most common metal used for protective coating of steel and other ferrous metals is zinc. Zinc coating is known as galvanizing. Galvanizing works because the zinc slowly sacrifices itself through oxidation to protect the underlying steel, even healing small scratches in the coating with its oxide. Eventually, the zinc weathers away, leaving the steel to rust. This can take from as few as 5 years to a longer period of 40 years, depending on the thickness of the coating and the presence of salt and industrial/urban pollutants in the air. For the longest possible life, use the heaviest available zinc coating. This coating is usually applied by means of traditional hot-dip galvanizing. There are many other methods of galvanizing, some of which result in only thin coatings that have a short life. Careful research is needed during the detailing process to determine the degree of protection required in a given situation, and to specify the galvanizing process, thickness of coating, and bond strength that will best satisfy this need.

4. Bimetallic corrosion is an electrochemical reaction that can occur when dissimilar metals are either in direct contact or linked by an electrolyte that can conduct electrically charged ions from anode to cathode metals. Because of contaminants that are always present, both rainwater and groundwater are electrolytes. When rainwater or groundwater comes in contact with a building assembly that includes two different metals, a galvanic reaction can occur, generating an electrical current that will corrode one of the metals with astonishing rapidity. The safest approach in detailing to avoid bimetallic corrosion is to use the same metal in all of the components of an exterior detail: aluminum nails with aluminum roofing sheet, aluminum screws and bolts in aluminum cladding components, copper nails with copper roofing, and steel bolts in steel structural shapes.

5. It is often necessary, however, to resolve potential problems like attaching aluminum cladding sheets to a steel supporting frame or an aluminum antenna mast to a copper roof. To solve these problems requires looking deeply into the nature of the galvanic reaction between dissimilar metals. Metal manufacturers should be asked to provide to the detailer technical data about their particular alloys and multi-layered metal products so that compatibility can be understood.

Metals vary in their chemical activity. When two different metals are brought together and bathed with an electrolyte such as rainwater, an exchange of electrons takes place that protects the less active metal (the cathode) while corroding the more active one (the anode). The greater the difference is between the activities of the two metals, the greater the potential for corrosion.

6. In Table 10-3, the common architectural metals are ranked with respect to their relative activities: The most active metals are at the top, and the least active are at the bottom. Metals with similar levels of activity are grouped together. In general, it is safe to combine metals that are in the same group.

TABLE 10-3: Galvanic Series of Unweathered Metals

Most Active (Anode)	Magnesium and its alloys
	Zinc
	Galvanized steel and iron
	Aluminum
	Steel
	Wrought iron
	Cast iron
	Active stainless steel[a]
	Lead-tin solder
	Lead
	Tin
	Brass
	Bronze
	Copper
	Silver solder
	Nickel
	Passive stainless steel[a]
	Titanium
Least Active (Cathode)	Silver
	Gold

[a] Whether stainless steel is considered "active" or "passive" depends on its surface finish. Stainless steel normally forms a self-protecting coating of chromium oxide and is considered passive. The electropolished surfaces used on some architectural hardware and trim are also passive. But if the coating of chromium oxide is disturbed by grinding, machining, or wire brushing, the finish becomes active. Most stainless steel fasteners are active. Active stainless steel can be made passive by treatment with acids. The detailer should work closely with the manufacturer of the stainless steel product if these distinctions become important in preparing a detail.

Staining and corrosion by electrolysis can result when the rainwater washing from one metal flows onto a dissimilar metal. This is especially problematic when run-off from a less active metal flows onto a more active metal. Run-off from copper and zinc will attack steel, galvanized steel, and aluminum, so should be directed away.

7. If a metal from one group is in direct contact with a metal from another group, the potential for galvanic corrosion is roughly proportional to the distance between the two groups in the galvanic series. For example, an exterior detail that used zinc or galvanized nails in copper roofing sheets would combine a metal from the most active group with one from the next-to-least active group; the zinc nail heads would be consumed by corrosion after only a few rainfalls.

8. The rate of corrosion is also affected by the relative surface areas of the two metals. If the area of the less active metal is very large in relation to the area of the more active one, corrosion will be very rapid. This would be the case with zinc nails in a copper roof. If copper nails were used in a zinc roof, however, the area of the less active metal would be very small when compared with the area of the more active one, and corrosion would be very slow. Nevertheless, one would be foolish to detail a zinc roof with copper nails because of the extreme difference in activity between the two metals. However, this area effect is useful in combining metals that lie more closely together on the galvanic series, such as stainless steel screws (which have an "active" finish) in an aluminum window. Aluminum screws in a stainless steel window, on the other hand, would be at great risk because of the very large surface area of the less active metal compared with the more active one.

9. The rate of bimetallic corrosion is minimal when there is no electrical conduction between metals, when the metals have the same electrode potentials, or when the area of the less active metal (cathode) is tiny compared to the area of the more active metal (anode).

10. Taking all these factors into account, and relying also on data from actual installations, the American Architectural Manufacturers Association has developed Table 10-4, which suggests the best fasteners to use with different combinations of metals. ▷

TABLE 10-4: Fastener Metals for Joining Various Metal Combinations

Fastener metals are listed in order of preference:

- *Aluminum to Aluminum*
  - Aluminum
  - Stainless steel
  - Zinc-plated steel
  - Cadmium-plated steel

- *Aluminum to Stainless Steel or Carbon Steel*
  - Stainless steel
  - Zinc-plated steel
  - Cadmium-plated steel

- *Copper Alloys to Copper Alloys*
  - Bronze
  - Brass
  - Nickel-silver
  - Stainless steel

- *Copper Alloys to Aluminum (Note: joining of these metals is not recommended.)*
  - Stainless steel

- *Copper Alloys to Stainless Steel*
  - Stainless steel
  - Bronze
  - Brass

- *Copper Alloys to Carbon Steel*
  - Bronze
  - Brass

- *Carbon Steel to Carbon Steel*
  - Stainless steel
  - Zinc-plated steel
  - Cadmium-plated steel
  - Nickel-plated steel
  - Chromium-plated steel
  - Carbon steel

- *Stainless Steel to Stainless Steel*
  - Stainless steel

Adapted from the *Metal Curtain Wall Design Guide Manual:* Reproduced by permission of the American Architectural Manufacturers Association.

11. Mitigating opportunities for corrosion is important in both mechanical and welded joints. Welded joints, a durable and irreversible molecular bond made by fusion, are at once more rigid and more susceptible to fatigue than fastened joints. When welding connections, ensure that the welding rods match the chemical composition of the metal being welded. Selection factors to identify the correct welding rod include the chemical composition and tensile strength of the base metal, the welding process used, and the welding position. This is especially important where welds should match the color of the surrounding metal. Mockups and simulated weathering tests are the best way to verify that the desired appearance will result.

12. In many cases, it is possible to avoid corrosion between dissimilar metals by separating the metals with an electrical insulating material. The insulation might take the form of a plastic or synthetic rubber washer, gasket, shim, sleeve, or bushing that is placed between the materials. It might be a nonconductive coating on one of the materials. It might be a plastic or plastic-headed screw or bolt. A municipal water supply pipe made of steel can be safely joined to copper pipes inside the building using a plastic coupler that isolates the two metals electrically. Obviously, the insulating material should be durable, because if it disintegrates, the metals will come into contact and corrode. Insulating washers made of plastics and rubber are often vulnerable to ultraviolet light, so they should be capped with a metal washer to prevent exposure to sunlight. Insulating materials would be the best answer to attaching an aluminum mast to a copper roof, because the two metals are too reactive with one another to join in any other way.

13. There are also damaging chemical reactions that can occur between metals and certain nonmetallic materials. Steel will not corrode in concrete that is free of acidic admixtures, as long as it is completely surrounded by concrete, and outside water cannot penetrate. Aluminum, however, is chemically incompatible with concrete, especially when the concrete is fresh. Aluminum should never be used in direct contact with concrete, mortar, stucco, and other cement-based materials. Lead flashings tend to corrode in mortar and are not recommended for use with masonry. Naturally decay-resistant woods contain acids that can react chemically to cause corrosion of some metals, and some chemicals used in pressure treating of wood can cause similar problems. Consulting literature from the trade organizations and manufacturers that promote these woods for recommendations on fasteners and flashings is strongly recommended.

14. In this example detail for anchoring stone facing panels to a building, stainless steel is chosen for the anchor because it will not rust. This avoids staining of the stone and corrosion failure of the anchor which, in turn, avoids the spalling of the stone that could occur from the expansion of steel as it rusts. Stainless steel is also resistant to the acid chemistry of such stones as granite. The stainless steel anchor is fastened to its support angle with a stainless steel bolt, nut, and washer. A plastic shim and sleeve are used to isolate the stainless steel components from the galvanized steel support angle. A galvanized steel washer is used against the back of the galvanized angle, isolated from the stainless steel bolt head by a plastic washer. While the whole detail could be executed in stainless steel, the support angles would be much more expensive in this material. ∎

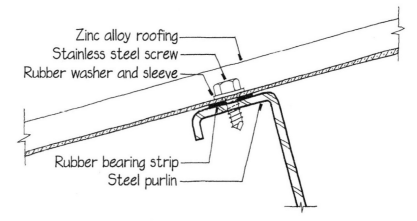

12. Attachment of Zinc Alloy Roofing to a Steel Purlin

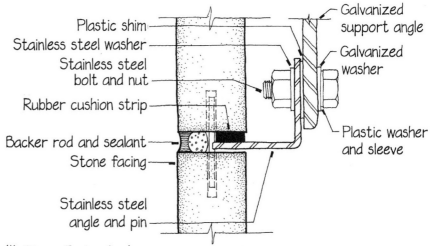

14. Stone Facing Anchor

Less Absorbent Materials

Exterior building surfaces should be made of materials that absorb as little water as possible. This applies to both the outer surfaces of waterproof barrier walls and other elements in the path of water, such as the cavity behind rainscreens.

1. Unless building walls are protected by a generous overhang or are in a very dry climate, they should be faced with materials of very low absorbency. Even vertical surfaces get wet from precipitation. Building cleaning activities and landscape irrigation may also wet walls periodically. Impermeable materials such as glass, metals, and most plastics are intrinsically resistant to water. Porous materials are often vulnerable to water., Such materials may also convey moisture to vulnerable adjoining materials.

2. In climates with cold, wet winters, hard materials such as concrete, stone, and brick are subject to spalling and flaking of the surface, caused by water soaking into the material and then freezing. The expansion of the freezing water exerts pressure from within the material and forces flakes to fracture from the surface. This effect can be minimized by using materials that absorb as little water as possible.

In all climates, wet materials under foot can become dangerously slippery. Water absorption in a paving material reduces friction, can lead to icing of the surface, and encourages mossy biological growth (see **Safe Footing**, Chapter 9).

3. Concrete formulated with a low water-cement ratio has fewer pores created by the escape of excess water and is less susceptible to freeze-thaw damage than more watery concretes. Concrete that will be exposed to cold winter weather should also be formulated with an air-entraining admixture. During the mixing process, this admixture causes the formation of microscopic air bubbles that make up 2–8% of the volume of the concrete. The resulting voids in the concrete reduce freeze-thaw damage by acting as expansion chambers for the freezing water.

4. Denser stones, such as granite, are less water absorptive and hold up better in wet locations in cold climates than more porous stones, such as limestone and sandstone. Traditional stone buildings often have granite foundations and then change to limestone or marble above ground level.

5. Clay bricks for exterior use in cold, wet climates should be Grade SW (severe weathering, ASTM C62), which comprises bricks that do not absorb very much water. Even Grade SW bricks must absorb some water; otherwise they would not bond to mortar.

Bricks for paving are especially vulnerable to freeze-thaw deterioration; in severe climates, only Class SX clay bricks, as defined by ASTM C902, should be used, and concrete paving bricks should have a water absorption of 5% or less, as called for in ASTM C140. Precast concrete grid pavements should meet the standards of ASTM C1319 regarding compressive strength and a maximum water absorption rate of 10 pounds per cubic foot (160 kg/cu. m).

6. Glazed masonry products such as terracotta, clay bricks, and concrete masonry have much lower surface absorbency than unglazed units. However, moisture may enter the wall through other avenues, such as mortar joints, and then enter the masonry units through unglazed surfaces that are in contact with the mortar. This sometimes causes the glazed surface to spall. When using glazed masonry units on building exteriors, check with the manufacturers for mortar joint specifications; a chemical may be added to the mortar mix to reduce water absorption.

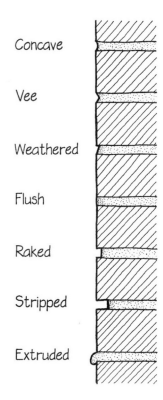

7. Mortar Joint Profiles

7. Mortar joints in masonry are tooled to create a finished profile. The tooling is more than cosmetic: Tooled profiles help the mortar joint shed water by compressing the mortar at the face of the joint, making it denser and less absorptive of water, and sealing it more tightly against the masonry units on either side. In climates with cold winters, noncompressed joints – such as flush, raked, stripped, and extruded joints – should be avoided, because they are too absorptive. Raked and stripped joints are also undesirable because they tend to trap water on the shallow horizontal brick surface. The concave and vee profiles are the best from the standpoint of weathering. ▷

8. Like the mortar joints shown in drawing 7, walls built using porous materials, such as wood, masonry, concrete, and stucco, should have profiles that shed water quickly. Corbels and reveals add visual interest; however, they introduce small shelves on which water can puddle to be absorbed into mortar or other wall materials. Fractured surfaces of concrete or masonry will be much more porous and profiled than unfractured versions of the same material.

9. The more absorbent the material, the steeper the **Wash** (Chapter 1) should be, to shed water quickly. Even small surfaces that face skyward should be impermeable, very steeply sloped, or detailed for easy replacement as they deteriorate. This principle applies to parapet copings, window sills, chimney caps, and many other building elements.

10. Less absorbent materials are also more resistant to graffiti or environmental staining, and are generally more tolerant of aggressive cleaning methods, making them good choices where graffiti and environmental staining are expected.

11. The useful life of absorbent materials can be extended by reducing their absorbency. Porous wood becomes less absorbent when painted or stained. Concrete masonry units can be manufactured with an additive in the mix that reduces their absorption rate. After construction, walls made of concrete, masonry, and stucco can be treated with various clear penetrating compounds to reduce their absorbency, while still allowing vapor to escape. These compounds need to be reapplied periodically during the life of the building.

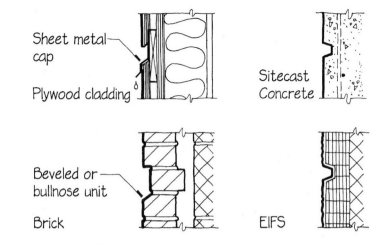

8. Horizontal Reveals

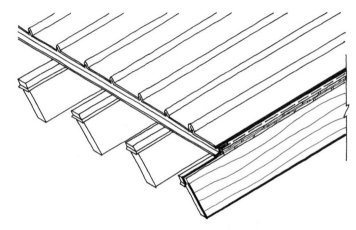

12. Caps on Exposed Rafter Tails

12. Some materials have a microscopic grain or pore structure that makes some surfaces more absorbent than others. The end grain of a piece of wood siding, for instance, is much more porous than its broad face. Exposed strata edges of sedimentary sandstone are more porous than the surfaces parallel to those layers. Detailers should cap exposed end grain on wood rafter tails, or they should cut the rafter back at an angle, to minimize exposure of the end grain to the weather. ■

Robust Assemblies

The rate of aging of a building is often determined by redundancy of the multipart assemblies used to resist deterioration in appearance and performance. Unlike traditional monolithic barrier walls, contemporary exterior envelopes are often layered assemblies in which each element performs a distinct or specialized function. Critical functions may be addressed by more than one element, to increase certainty that this function will be performed.

Separating and layering elements may reduce premature aging of the building in two ways. Overall deterioration can be reduced by detailing assemblies with primary and secondary functional strategies. Permitting functionally obsolete elements to be upgraded or replaced to keep up with changing performance expectations offers a different path to the same goal. Structural support, waterproofing, thermal insulation, air and vapor control, ventilation, service distribution, and other functions occur in discrete layers that may be detailed with long-term performance as a priority.

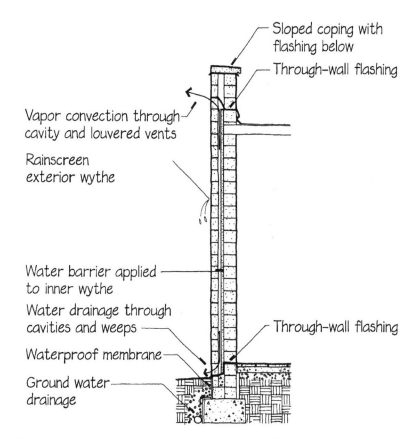

1. Water and Moisture Resistance in Masonry Cavity Walls

1. For maximum life, a properly detailed masonry cavity wall has a well-crafted veneer to repel most water and a clear cavity with flashing and weeps to direct water out. Metal ties between the veneer and the backup wythe of masonry should be made of stainless steel to avoid corrosion. Two-part adjustable ties or ties with drips built into them are advantageous because they release water before it can bridge across the cavity to the inner wythe. The cavity can be compartmented to use pressure equalization to resist wind-driven rain penetration. By allowing air to convect through it, the cavity can carry water vapor out of the assembly. The inner wythe of masonry should be coated with a fluid-applied air and water barrier to reduce the chances of moisture passing toward the interior. This wall is durable and robust because it has redundant layers and multiple strategies to resist water, the chief agent of deterioration in this case.

2. Materials may not be perfect. Workmanship during installation may not be perfect. Maintenance may not be perfect. The building assembly can still work if it incorporates tolerance for imperfection in its details. Assemblies or details that are thin, one-layer barriers lack redundancy. If these are used, extreme care must be taken to be sure they are detailed, installed, and maintained flawlessly and on a regular schedule.

3. Well-detailed buildings have a better chance of being well maintained. They often outlive their initial program many times over, and new functions or technical improvements are more likely to be introduced in them with care, not as violent intrusions. A building made with consideration to fundamental principles of design and crafted of materials appropriate for the task will offer value to its future stewards. A poorly detailed building is more likely to become unsightly as surfaces and joints deteriorate, discouraging building occupants and provoking owners to make – or avoid making – difficult or costly repairs. Architects enhance a building's useful life through competent technical detailing and with deliberate thought regarding future maintenance.

Building Armor

A building needs to be armored where it is likely to get kicked or scuffed, pushed or punched, bumped into, or splashed.

1. A busy door in a public building may need several kinds of armor: an escutcheon plate around the knob and lock, where hands and keys rub and scratch; a push plate where people shove against the door to open it; and a kick plate across the bottom.

2. An ordinary wall base detail uses a baseboard as armor against scrub mops, vacuum cleaner nozzles, legs of furniture, and flying feet. A traditional dining room adds a wood chair rail molding around the walls at the line where the backs of chairs can gouge the plaster or paneling.

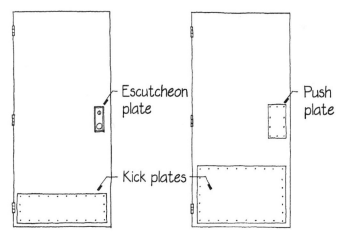

1. Door Armor

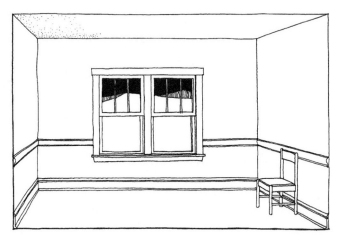

2. Baseboard and Chair Rail

3. Most contemporary wainscoting is a form of armor. It may be made of vinyl wallcovering, tile, concrete masonry, or stone. Often its purpose is to make the wall tough and washable in the zone where it will be rubbed against, poked, kicked, and run into. Sometimes it is intended to make the wall water-resistant in wet areas of a building.

4. Hospitals and nursing homes use corner guards and wall guards to armor walls against wheelchairs, gurneys, pushcarts, and cleaning equipment.

5. Outdoor forms of building armor include curbs and bollards to confine vehicles to roads and drives, and corner guards, protective posts, and dock bumpers where vehicles are allowed to come close to the building.

6. Avoid superficial colors and finishes in high-traffic areas where surfaces are likely to be damaged. Worn and chipped surfaces will reveal inner colors or textures that are different from those on the outside, making the blemish even more apparent. Sand-finished brick, surface-pigmented concrete, and EIFS are all materials that are superficially coated; they should be avoided in high-traffic areas.

7. Skateboards and roller blades can damage outdoor stairs, walls, and landscape features, unless surfaces are made unsuitable for damaging activities. Durable elements can be embedded into construction materials or secured to surfaces to discourage abuse. The edges most susceptible to abuse can be detailed with integral ribs, grooves, ridges, or premanufactured guards to eliminate long, continuous slides. ■

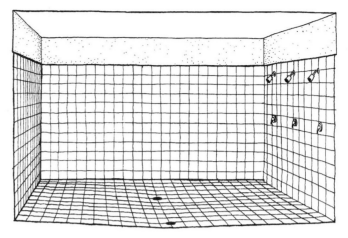

3. Tile Wainscot in Shower Room

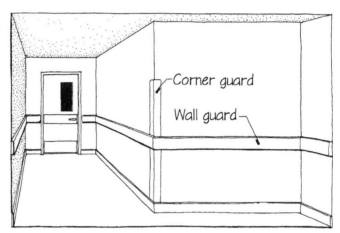

4. Corner Guards and Wall Guards

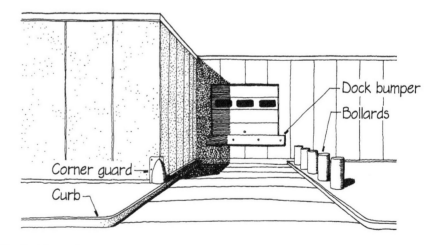

5. Outdoor Armor

Extreme Event Protection

Building massing, surfaces, and details are often shaped by unusual environmental or human-made conditions that occur infrequently, perhaps only a few times during the service life of the building. While building designers address the ordinary conditions, they must also make buildings that have a chance of surviving extraordinary but plausible conditions. The best way to avoid damage due to extreme events is to build far away from them; however, many building locations are subject to some threat of at least one extreme event, so designers must try to prepare for them at all scales of a project.

Many extreme events are so rare that it is impractical to direct resources toward them. Buildings designed and built also should not be expected to resist natural or human-made events whose destructive forces are so extreme that preventive measures would be unreasonable or would disproportionately skew the qualities of the building away from its normative needs. Alternatively, for a given location, threats of winter storms, hurricane-force winds and rain, and storm flooding can be reasonably estimated on the basis of history and experience. Building designs in such settings should strive to meet expected challenges.

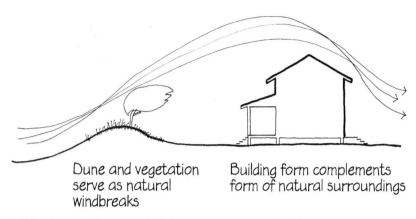

1. Windbreak Slows and Redirects Wind over Building

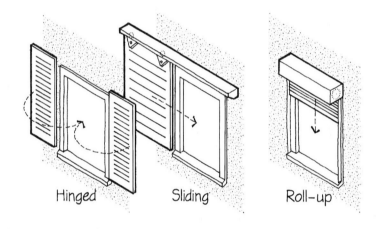

2. Shutters Protect Vulnerable Window Materials

1. Wind can damage buildings directly and indirectly through airborne debris. Several detail design strategies can help mitigate extreme wind forces and protect vulnerable parts of a building.

Windbreaks located upwind from the building can direct the main current of air over and around the building, while slowing the air that passes through the windbreak. Windbreaks can be either natural or constructed. Natural elements that can serve as a windbreak include dense vegetation, such as trees and shrubs, or earth dunes, mounds, or berms. Constructed elements could include walls, fences, or screens. For maximum effectiveness, windbreaks can be configured in coordination with a building's roof or wall shapes to deflect air over or around the building.

2. Exterior glazing is particularly vulnerable to airborne debris carried by high winds. Broken windows can lead to pressurization of building interiors, which can cause other portions of the building envelope, such as sheathing, to come loose. Traditional methods of window protection, such as shutters, have been used for centuries to protect glazing from wind and airborne debris. Contemporary solutions to accomplish this include louvers, sliding panels, roll-up shutters, or other more complex elements. The basic strategy is to temporarily shield a vulnerable material with a stronger material.

3. When designing in areas prone to high winds, select roof and wall materials that will not detach and become harmful airborne debris under strong winds. Sheet materials can exhibit sail-like qualities and must be reliably secured to the structure. Individualized elements such as wood shingle siding and roofing reduce the force of each piece of debris and can be replaced more easily on a piecemeal basis. Membrane roofs should be fully adhered or mechanically fastened, rather than secured with rock ballast, which high winds can easily lift up and turn into projectiles.

4. In flood-prone areas, breakaway panels and skirting may be used near ground level to permit floodwaters to flow beneath the building without transferring lateral loads to the building structure. Breakaway panels are sacrificed to avoid causing failure of the primary structure. In high-hazard zones (designated on FEMA maps as V or VE zones, indicating that they are in the 100-year floodplain), building owners are permitted to enclose portions of the building that reside within the floodplain, provided the spaces are unconditioned storage or parking spaces and are enclosed with breakaway assemblies. Breakaway walls, lattice, or insect screening in these locations must become detached from the primary structure when loaded between 10 and 20 pounds per square foot (479–958 Pa). Although not required, it would be advisable for these elements to be hinged or tethered to something stable so that they are not carried downstream to cause damage elsewhere.

5. Floodwater turbulence often causes scouring or erosion around pilings or columns that support elevated floors. The base of these elements must be deep enough to withstand scouring. Ground slabs are permitted in the floodplain, provided they are not attached to the primary building structure. Erosion of soil at the edges of fixed ground slabs is to be expected, so the slab should be reinforced to span such voids.

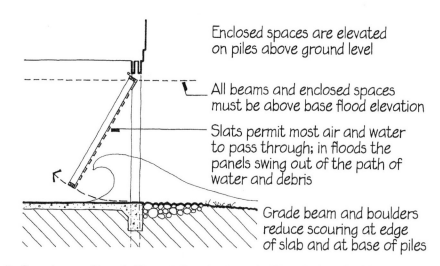

4. Breakaway Panels Permit Floodwaters to Pass below Building

SECTION 2
CONSTRUCTABILITY

A detail may work perfectly to prevent water or air leakage, optimize thermal efficiency, manage expansion and contraction, and perform every other functional requirement, but if it proves troublesome or unnecessarily expensive to make: The detail is not a good detail. The owner of a building has a right to expect construction to proceed smoothly, swiftly, and economically. The contractor and workers who construct the building have a right to expect it to go together with no more than the normal degree of difficulty. For the designer, a smooth construction process generally produces a building with fewer performance defects and fewer problematic disputes among project stakeholders. Constructable details are essential to a smooth construction process.

The effort to design constructable details can lead the designer into explorations of building craft that may yield substantial aesthetic or performance benefits: Much of what we admire and enjoy most about great buildings can be traced to a deep understanding of the craft evident in their details. Consider the beauty of Gothic vaulting, whose form sprang from the craft of stone masonry. Think of the interiors of German and Austrian Rococo churches, which owe much of their beauty to their full exposition of the plasterer's craft, or think of the satisfying forms of Arts and Crafts woodwork, which grew from a thorough understanding of the joiner's craft.

Many contemporary buildings derive visual impact from steel connections, concrete forms, or panelized assemblies that make knowledgeable use of the craft disciplines of these modern technologies. A contemporary construction site combines handcrafting and machine production side by side.

Construction tools today are guided by the hand, eye, and brain of a skilled craftsperson, but also by the tireless robotic arm and CNC (computer numeric controlled) program of a computer application. Optimizing use of an unprecedented array of materials and production options has become a catalyst for new architectural solutions.

Constructability can be summarized in three general guidelines:

1. A detail should be easy to assemble.
2. A detail should be forgiving of small inaccuracies and minor mistakes.
3. A detail should be based on the efficient use of construction facilities, tools, and labor.

The logic of these three guidelines organize the detail patterns found in this section of the book and may be summarized in a single sentence: A building needs to go together easily and efficiently, and it should do so even though many things can be expected to go wrong during the construction process.

Architectural Detailing: Function Constructability Aesthetics. Fourth Edition. Patrick Rand, Jason Miller, and Edward Allen.
© 2025 John Wiley & Sons, Inc. Published 2025 by John Wiley & Sons, Inc.

CHAPTER 11  Ease of Assembly

Ease of assembly is very important. A detail that is difficult to build is almost certain to be expensive and will often be executed poorly. A detail that goes together simply is economical with regard to labor and will generally be done well. There are 10 detail patterns that concern ease of assembly. Their names are almost self-explanatory, because these patterns deal with commonsense issues: keep it simple; reduce effort; and provide sufficient space for workers to do their work.

It is generally easier to assemble elements that share common features. Choose a family of materials or components that share similar physical properties, like brick and concrete block, or are designed to be joined readily, such as glass and aluminum cladding components. These are compatible because they come from common sources or have been refined through use in previous projects.

The scale of the project and the type of construction process selected may affect the application of these patterns. In a small project such as a house, the builder may possess many diverse skills and may install everything from rough to finished elements in the building. In such projects, custom features executed by a broadly skilled craftsperson may be more feasible. In a larger project, it is more likely each system and subsystem will be installed by a different crew of specialized workers. In a project that relies on prefabricated panels or volumetric units, careful coordination and considerable skill are needed at their connection both in the detail drawing and on the construction site.

No matter the building scale or the uniqueness of its features, effective details should describe the optimal way to achieve the intended finish condition. The patterns in this group will help the detailer anticipate and address the challenges faced by those who build the project. Each pattern will be described later in this chapter.

> ***Uncut Units*** (p. 172)
> ***Minimum Number of Parts*** (p. 174)
> ***Parts That Are Easy to Handle*** (p. 176)
> ***Repetitious Assembly*** (p. 179)
> ***Simulated Assemblies*** (p. 181)
> ***Observable Assemblies*** (p. 183)
> ***Accessible Connections*** (p. 184)
> ***Detailing for Disassembly*** (p. 186)
> ***Installation Clearance*** (p. 188)
> ***Nonconflicting Systems*** (p. 189)

Architectural Detailing: Function Constructability Aesthetics. Fourth Edition. Patrick Rand, Jason Miller, and Edward Allen.
© 2025 John Wiley & Sons, Inc. Published 2025 by John Wiley & Sons, Inc.

Uncut Units

With certain materials, it saves time and money to detail so that few, if any, units of material need to be cut.

1. Off-the-shelf products, such as dimensional and engineered lumber, gypsum board, plywood, and clay or concrete masonry units, are all manufactured to standard dimensions that designers and detailers must take into account. Other products, such as precast concrete hollow-core floor decks, sitecast concrete formwork, and corrugated metal roofing panels, also have industry standard dimensions that the detailer should respect. Working with the standard dimensions of building materials minimizes the need to cut them.

The standard shapes of manufactured products should also be respected. Rectangular concrete masonry units can easily make T and L intersections but have difficulty making odd-angled intersections or short-radius curves. Structural bays of precast concrete double-tees are simplest to construct if they are rectangular in plan and have a dimension that is a multiple of the precast element's width.

2. When materials of varying sizes are to be combined in an assembly, choose products that share a common dimensional module. The dimensions of the various materials should be whole number multiples of this module, or they should yield whole numbers when divided into the module. Often the module of the coarsest (largest) material governs building dimensions. For instance, in a wall made of brick and concrete masonry, the governing module is the concrete block, which is larger than the brick.

3. Brick masonry and concrete masonry should be dimensioned and detailed with little need to cut bricks and blocks. This often involves slight adjustments in the dimensions of the building, as well as in the sizes and spacing of openings such as doors and windows.

4. Concrete masonry should be dimensioned in multiples of 8 in. (203 mm), making small corrections for the thickness of a mortar joint where required. Over its entire length, outside corner to outside corner, a concrete block wall has one fewer mortar joints than it does blocks, so ⅜ in. (9 mm) should be deducted from the nominal length of the wall to arrive at the actual dimension.

5. Between an outside corner and an inside corner, a concrete masonry wall has the same number of mortar joints as blocks, so the actual length of the wall is the same as the nominal length. In other words, the length will be an exact multiple of 8 in. (203 mm).

6. An opening in a concrete masonry wall has one more mortar joint than it does blocks. Therefore, the nominal dimension must be increased by ⅜ in. (9 mm) to find the actual dimension. The same principle applies to an inside dimension between masonry walls.

7. The general dimensioning principles that have just been described also apply

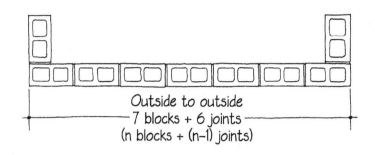

4. Outside-to-Outside Masonry Dimension

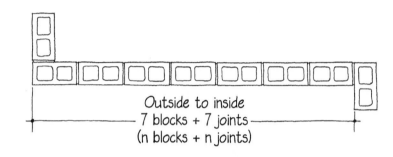

5. Outside-to-Inside Masonry Dimension

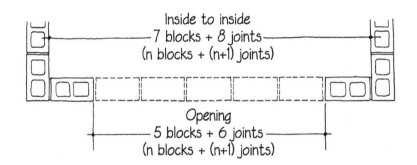

6. Inside-to-Inside Masonry Dimension

to brickwork, stonework, and other types of masonry. They also apply to terra-cotta, or other ceramic products that are used in a ventilated rainscreen. In this application, an open reveal is used instead of a mortar joint, but it plays the same role as the residual dimension between uncut manufactured elements. The labor required to cut these materials may increase the in-place cost of the unit as much as tenfold.

Before preparing a detail, determine what type of masonry units you will be using and what their dimensions will be. Decide on the dimension of a standard mortar joint or reveal. Then note each dimension on the drawing, both as numbers of masonry units and as feet and inches (or millimeters). This makes the work easier for the masons, and increases the likelihood that the wall will be built as intended.

8. Even for easily cut materials, such as gypsum board, it is economical to work with uncut units as much as possible. A wall that is 8 ft. (2440 mm) high is easily boarded with two uncut horizontal sheets of gypsum board. An 8 ft. 6 in. (2591 mm) wall requires the addition of a narrow strip of board that takes time to cut and is not sufficiently stiff. Additionally, because of the need to use the tapered edges of the board at all butt joints, only two 6 in. (152 mm) edge strips can be cut from a board, and 75% of the board would have to be thrown away. A wall that is 10 ft. (3 m) high can be built without waste and with a minimum of cutting, because a sheet split lengthwise can be fully utilized to cover the extra 2 ft. (610 mm) of height, covering two portions of the wall.

9. If the floor plan of a wood-frame building can be dimensioned in 4 ft. multiples (1220 mm), few sheets of subflooring will need to be cut, and there will be little waste. This dimensioning strategy also minimizes waste of joist material, which is furnished only in lengths that are multiples of 2 ft. (610 mm).

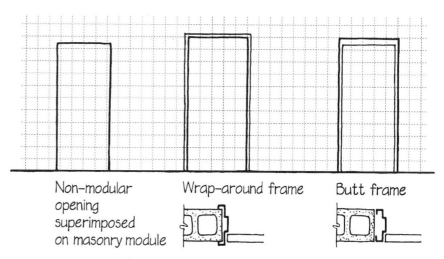

13. Modular Coordination

10. It is almost impossible to completely eliminate cutting in all the different materials used in a building. It is difficult to make the floor of a room come out to even dimensions for ceramic tile units, for example. Tile setters are accustomed to having to cut all the tiles around the edge of a room. The same is true for vinyl composition tile, ceiling tiles, wallpaper, baseboards, and many other interior finish materials (***Dimensional Tolerance***, Chapter 12).

11. In projects designed to use mass timber panels, precast concrete cladding, unitized curtain wall panels, or glue-laminated arches, the dimensional module is not preordained by the manufacturer. Instead, a module is created by the designer for the project and then is used repeatedly in the project to achieve economies of scale. Once established, the production runs should yield elements that require little or no cutting.

12. Cut edges and surfaces may not be suitable for exposure to view or to weather. Cut edges are often raw and have a different surface quality than the factory-produced condition, and they may not weather well. As a result, they may need to be placed in a protected or concealed position in the assembly.

13. Materials or products from different sources may have limited commonality regarding product dimensions. If compatible dimensions cannot be found, consider altering the design slightly to match a modular dimension. For instance, a 3 × 7 ft. (914 × 2134 mm) door and frame unit in a concrete masonry wall may be increased to 3 ft. 4 in. × 7 ft. 4 in. (1016 × 2235 mm) to agree with the module of concrete masonry. In this case, a wraparound door frame that matches the masonry opening is used. Alternatively, a butt-type door frame could be used to make the necessary adjustment to fill the space between the original door size and the masonry module. In this case, the frame could be 2 in. (51 mm) thick at both jambs and 4 in. (102 mm) at the head. Both of these solutions are significantly better than cutting all of the masonry units surrounding the opening.

14. Ventilated rainscreens do not require watertight closure of facing materials at openings or corners. Uncut elements can bypass one another at a corner and use reveals (see ***Reveal***, Chapter 12) to separate them from one another. Rectangular acoustic ceiling panels may be suspended above noisy portions of an irregularly shaped room, not touching the bounding walls. This eliminates the need to cut pieces that would have otherwise intersected the walls. ■

Minimum Number of Parts

The fewer the number of different parts a detail requires, the more efficient and productive the construction process is likely to be.

1. A construction worker assembling a connection in a building needs to have all the required parts close at hand. The fewer the number of different parts, the less time will be spent looking for misplaced items or restocking depleted supplies, and, generally, the fewer tools will be required. A framing carpenter needs to always have at least three sizes of common nails available, as well as a nail gun, a hammer, a tape measure, a square, and a pencil. These items are carried on a tool belt for ease of access and use. This works out reasonably well, because the carpenter executes a standardized set of operations and can rely on the tool belt as an organizer suited for that workflow. But if a special framing detail requires several sizes of screws as well as nails, the tool belt no longer has sufficient pouches, and the carpenter's efficiency is reduced. Reduced efficiency results in increased costs of labor and time.

2. In an operation such as installing aluminum curtain wall mullions, the installer may need one or more wrenches, one or more screwdrivers, a rubber mallet, a tool for inserting rubber gasketing, a level, a tape measure, and a large variety of parts: mullion sections, connecting angles, shims, bolts, screws, and gasketing. The number of these different parts and tools should be kept to a minimum. It is especially important to avoid parts that differ so little from one another that they can be confused easily, such as 1 in. long and 1⅛ in. long (25 and 29 mm) screws of the same diameter and head style.

3. A masonry wall pattern that requires three different kinds of brick and two colors of mortar would tax a mason's patience. There would not be sufficient space at the mason's workstation to keep the five different types of materials within reach, and such an elaborate pattern would present a great number of opportunities for errors to occur – errors that would be difficult and costly to correct. Reducing the number of parts to two brick types and one mortar color does not greatly reduce the pattern solutions available. Using different coursing patterns and introducing relief on the surface adds levels of depth, texture, subtlety, and craft to the mason's work.

4. When precast concrete panels are used to clad a building, it is better to fabricate fewer panels of a larger size than to use a greater number of small panels. Large panel sizes reduce the amount of handling and coordination; the number of connections to the building frame is also reduced. To avoid a monotonous appearance in elevation, large panels can be designed with a variety of patterns or surface treatments, or may incorporate fenestration systems.

5. A corollary to this pattern is that if there are fewer parts in the building, then each part should perform a greater number of functions. Elements that only perform one function, unless essential, are often edited out of the design, especially when economic constraints are prominent.

6. To improve overall building performance, contemporary exterior walls tend to be composed of many more layers than their monolithic barrier-wall predecessors of a century ago. Today's higher performance expectations are often achieved using several specialized products, rather than using a smaller number of lower-performing products. However, when two or three functional tasks can be achieved by one product, the designer should seize upon the detail opportunity. For instance, air and water control can often be achieved using a single synthetic membrane. If it consists of a large sheet or a continuous fluid-applied membrane, rather than many small pieces that must be meticulously spliced and overlapped to perform as a continuous control layer, that is even better.

7. One strategy to reduce the number of parts in a building is to use prefabricated subassemblies. Building construction is evolving toward greater use of preassembled components that are made up of smaller elements. Use of these unitized building assemblies is intended to speed building completion without increasing cost or compromising quality. With this approach, the more technically complex parts of a building may be preassembled in a factory, using techniques that are more specialized or precise than in the field. These parts are then transported to the site for installation. Story-height wall panels or three-dimensional building volumes of windows, exterior cladding, insulation, and wiring may be erected in a single, rapid step. The number of parts is reduced, but each part is equipped to perform a greater range of functions (see *Factory and Site,* Chapter 13).

8. Every building will have some details that are challenging to design or are difficult or costly to construct. It is best to minimize the number of occurrences of these details in the building, to reduce the chance of failure. For instance, water leakage is more likely on flat roofs with perimeters, penetrations, and drainage details that are difficult to execute perfectly. So it follows that having many small roofs above each protruding window in a tall building would be more risky than grouping a stack of windows into one protruding form, with a single roof at the top. Simplifying details and simplifying the overall building configuration go hand in hand. Performance is improved without sacrificing the basic design intent. ■

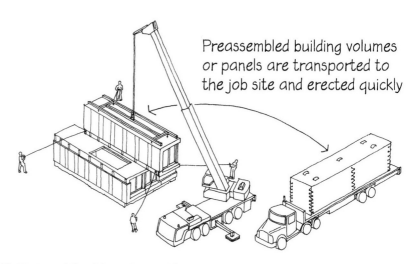

7. Unitized Building Assemblies

Parts That Are Easy to Handle

The detailer should always be conscious of the size and weight of components used in a particular building assembly, and conscientious of what will be required of workers on the jobsite to handle and install them.

1. A standard brick takes its size, shape, and weight from the dimensions and capabilities of the human hand. A bricklayer works efficiently and comfortably by holding the masonry trowel in one hand while lifting and placing bricks repeatedly with the other. If a substantially larger brick is specified, the bricklayer may fatigue more quickly or suffer potential injury, and may have difficulty maintaining proper alignment of bricks in the wall.

A construction element of moderate weight may be hard to handle if outside the ergonomic "power zone," which is close to the body between mid-thigh to mid-torso (see *Universal Design*, Chapter 9). If workers must lift normal concrete blocks high overhead to thread vertical conduit or rebar through the cells before placing the unit into mortar at waist level, their shoulders and back will suffer, as will the quality of their work.

The Occupational Safety and Health Administration (OSHA) does not set an absolute limit on weight of lifted objects but observes that lifting loads heavier than 50 lbs. (22.7 kg) will increase the risk of injury. It recommends that heavier loads be lifted by two or more workers, and that tasks be rotated among members of the crew. Many trade unions have work rules concerning maximum weights of various kinds of materials and tools, and these must be taken into account.

A- or H-shaped concrete masonry units could have been specified

1. Heavy Loads and Awkward Postures Lead to Injury and Poor Work

2. Very small parts should be avoided, especially where the worksite might be dark, wet, or cold, making it difficult to see and handle the parts. Tweezer-size parts should be avoided altogether. Finger-size parts, such as nails, screws, bolts, and nuts, are easy to handle in warm to moderate temperatures and in adequate light. Hand-size components, such as wood shingles, bricks, and tiles, are ideal for the worker to handle. A concrete block, wood stud, clapboard, or plywood panel requires the use of both hands, which is acceptable but less desirable, because it necessitates laying down tools to lift the component.

Some components take two people to handle: a jumbo concrete block, a full-thickness wall panel, a frame for a wall or partition, or a large sheet of glass. This is reasonable in most situations. To build a simple, large plane of concrete masonry, a mechanical assisting device such as a material unit lift enhancer (MULE) may be appropriate. These devices can lift heavy double-sized units and require only slight movement by the mason to lift and place it.

Very large sheets of glass are challenging because of their weight and fragility. They may require special equipment to move safely. Components that require three or more workers are awkward and waste time while introducing added risk in the installation process. Unitized curtain wall panels require special equipment and skill to install but may take less labor and time in comparison to the large wall area of each panel.

3. Hoists and cranes come in many configurations, reaches, lifting capacities, and maneuverabilities. Components requiring the use of a crane should be avoided unless there will be a crane on the site to lift many other components as well. Sometimes, of course, it is economical or unavoidable to rent a crane to hoist a single large component into place, but such situations should be studied carefully, because crane time is expensive.

4. Cranes and hoists must be selected and located on the site so that they are able to lift the required components and to place them where they are wanted. This is largely the business of the contractor, but the detailer should be sure that all details that require crane lifts lie within reach of likely crane locations. Lifting materials over a lower portion of a building to reach a higher portion is a typical problem. Overhead power and telephone lines can also inhibit the work of a crane. Materials hoisted by crane cannot be delivered below elevated assemblies, such as a metal roof deck on a steel frame. They may need to be delivered to the lower floors before the upper floors are framed and covered with metal decking. (See **Rehearsing the Construction Sequence**, Chapter 13)

5. Building components must be sized to fit available transportation modes. Highway widths and clearances govern the sizes and weights of trucks, which in turn determine the maximum sizes of most building components. Check local jurisdictions for these parameters. A given state may have different limitations, but in the United States, the general dimensions permitted on interstate and primary highways are 8 ft. wide, 13.5 ft. tall, 75 ft. overall length, and 48 ft. trailer length (2.4 m wide, 4.1 m tall, 22.9 m overall length, and 14.6 m trailer length). Oversize loads can be trucked in some situations, with accompanying fees and permits; additional cost penalties are

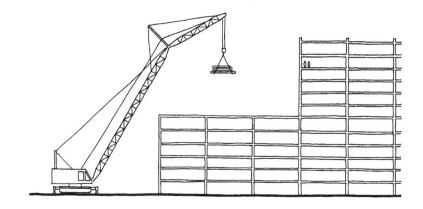

4. Crane Reach

charged for off-hour deliveries and special police escorts. Streets and bridges serving construction sites sometimes limit the length and weight of construction components, so these too must be checked. Barges or railroad cars can be used to carry oversize components to some waterfront and railside construction sites.

6. Building openings have a lot to do with sizes of components. Even in a typical house, a temporary opening must be left in the exterior wall of each floor to allow a delivery truck to hoist bundles of gypsum board to the interior of the building; this can be a large window or door opening, or it may be necessary to leave a portion of the wall unframed and unsheathed. A standard, one-piece, tub-and-shower unit can be used only if it is installed before the interior framing is completed. Once the partitions are framed and the wallboard is on, the one-piece tub can no longer be brought in, and a three-piece unit must be used instead.

Installation of some large-building equipment such as boilers and fans, or large furnishings such as pianos or conference tables, can require that wall cladding and partitions be omitted temporarily from certain areas. Also remember that large furnishings and pieces of equipment often need to be changed during the life of the building. Paired doors without a fixed astragal provide a wide and useful opening to address those needs. Strategic placement of large windows or grouping several smaller windows into a movable set may be considered. ▷

7. Ease of handling includes consideration of the possibility that parts can be inadvertently installed backward or upside down. Wedge anchor inserts installed in formwork before concrete is poured are useless and impossible to replace if they are installed upside down. They should be manufactured with prominent *UP* indications, and the detailer should make note to the construction supervisor to check the installation of these components very carefully before concrete is poured.

8. Reglet components are also susceptible to inverted installation.

9. Where possible, detail components so that they are either symmetrical and can be installed in either direction, or so that they are asymmetrical in a way that only permits them to be installed correctly. This curtain wall anchor tee cannot be installed upside down, because it is symmetrical: Either way will work. If the vertical spacing between bolt holes is different from the horizontal spacing, it will also be impossible to err by installing it sideways. ■

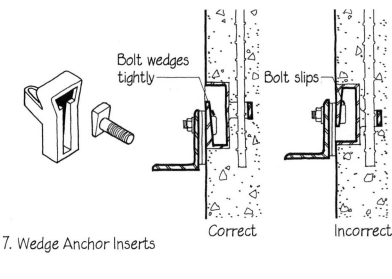

7. Wedge Anchor Inserts

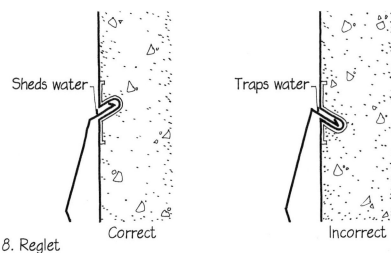

8. Reglet

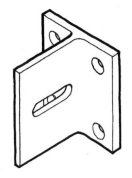

9. Anchor Tee

Repetitious Assembly

All other considerations being equal, details that construction workers repeat again and again are more economical and less error-prone than nonrepeating details.

1. Special conditions often lead to errors in construction. A steel floor frame in which all of the filler beams are the same size, with one exception, is likely to end up with the special beam in the wrong place, unless the connection details for that one beam are special enough to prevent a mix-up. For this reason, filler beams are usually engineered to be all the same size, even if this means a slight diseconomy in weight of steel. The same principle applies to reinforcing bar patterns in repetitive beams and slabs. In both cases, the labor efficiency is more important, from a project cost standpoint, than the material inefficiency.

2. It is easiest – and least error-prone – for bricklayers to lay continuous facings of running bond, and this is all that most buildings require them to do. Unfortunately, running bond offers little aesthetic character, and masons often enjoy a challenge to their craftsmanship more than the boredom of unrelieved repetition. When designing brickwork patterns that use corbelled, recessed, or different-colored bricks, try to design patterns that are repetitious within their variety, so that the bricklayer can easily learn the pattern and keep track of what is going on. Highly intricate or irregular patterns require that the mason refer constantly to the drawings. This takes time and can lead to errors that are difficult and expensive to correct. ▷

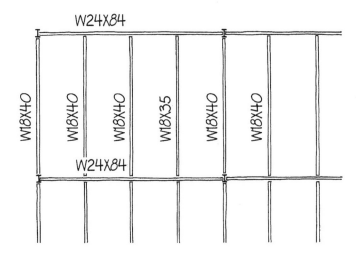

1. Plan of Steel Floor Framing

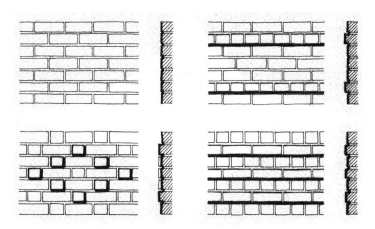

2. Repetitious Variety in Brick Masonry Patterns

3. Formwork construction accounts for a significant portion of the costs associated with site-cast concrete structures. The easiest and least expensive forms to build are level, continuous, uninterrupted surfaces of formwork. This is why flat plate structures are usually the most economical system for light loads and short spans. It is also why joist bands, which use more concrete and steel but are extremely easy to form, often cost less overall than beams that are proportioned optimally for material economy but require more complicated formwork. Where deeper beams are used in any concrete structure, it is usually more economical to make all the beams the same depth so that their formwork will be repetitive, even if loads vary somewhat from beam to beam. Within the repetitive concrete shape, the amount of steel reinforcement may vary in response to loads.

4. This pattern is especially important when the project schedule or budget is constrained. It may be less important in a very small project, where almost everything is uniquely made, and where efficiency of means is not a high priority. If a project calls for very high priority on reducing construction-related CO_2 emissions, then the added labor needed to fabricate elaborate formwork may be justified because it reduces the amount of concrete needed. Repetitious assembly might also be less critical in the case of the use of mass-customization techniques, in which digitally controlled mechanisms in a shop or factory quickly and accurately produce many slightly varied products. ■

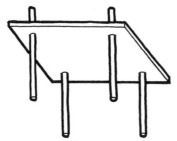
Flat plate: Flat formwork

Joist bands: Flat formwork plus pans

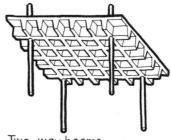
Two-way beams: Pan formwork

Deeper beams: Elaborate formwork

3. Repetition in Formwork

Simulated Assemblies

Build representative samples of challenging or unusual details, to simulate the construction processes and to reveal the qualities of the finished product. The sample is the "dress rehearsal" of the intended building assembly.

1. Simulating the construction of unusual building assemblies helps to avoid costly and difficult removal of unsatisfactory work, and establishes acceptable standards of appearance and workmanship. This is especially important when materials or construction techniques are innovative, unfamiliar to the builder, or dependent on a particular quality of workmanship.

2. Much of the flow of information in a project is from the architect to the builder. The simulated assembly allows the builder to demonstrate explicitly what the result will be, at minimal cost. It is an excellent vehicle to bring expectations of architects, builders, and owners into convergence. Once accepted, the simulated assembly sets the standard for quality of work and appearance. It should be left safely on the site for the duration of the project, serving as a record of many qualitative features that are difficult to describe through drawings or specifications.

3. Changes in a detail are easiest and least expensive to make early in the design process, and they are most difficult and costly when the detail is part of the finished building. Costs of changes escalate steeply at each stage in the design and construction process. Erasing a sketch is much easier than jackhammering concrete. Simulated assemblies help identify areas where changes are needed before they become part of the finished building.

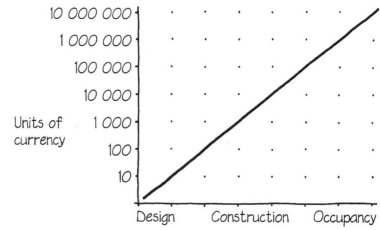

3. Cost to Change a Feature During a Building Project

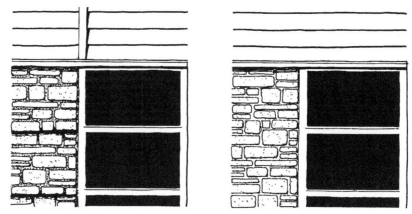

Various materials, colors, textures and details are compared.

4. Sample Panels and Mockup Panels

4. A sample panel may be used to demonstrate the exposed appearance and workmanship of the detail or assembly. The materials, colors, textures, joints, and accessories intended for the building are used in the sample panel. It may be freestanding, apart from the building, or may be the first portion of the actual building. Sometimes multiple freestanding samples can be prepared, each revealing a variation in material or finish, to give the best possible basis for final selection. ▷

5. A mockup assembly may be used for more complex details or assemblies. Like a sample panel, the mockup demonstrates appearance and workmanship, but it also shows critical features within the assembly. In layered wall assemblies, the ties, drainage cavities, rainscreen features, insulation, or air barriers can be demonstrated. These features can be observed and potential technical performance can be assessed, using experimental testing if necessary. For instance, a mockup wall cladding assembly can be tested under simulated storm conditions to evaluate its resistance to wind-driven rain. Although more expensive than a sample panel, a mockup assembly often leads to savings during construction because discrepancies and problems are greatly reduced.

6. Mockup assemblies may consolidate key details from many parts of the building into a smaller composite assembly. Although less useful for assessments of the aesthetics and proportions of the project, this approach is an economical means to demonstrate the technical execution of many challenging features.

7. The sample panel or mockup assembly usually includes intended finishes, such as

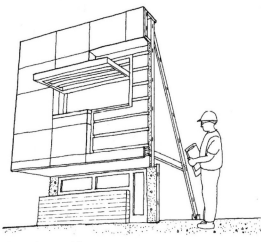

6. Consolidated Mockup Assembly

Key materials and details of a multi-story building are combined in a mockup that is only 20' (6m) tall

paint, caulk, and mortar tooling profiles. These finishes should also be cleaned or powerwashed, just as the actual building will be, because these processes sometimes alter the final appearance of the finishes. For building additions or adaptive reuse projects, the simulated assembly allows for accurate comparisons of new and existing conditions.

8. In most projects, crews composed of several tradespeople, each with different experience and skills, carry out the installation of materials. The simulated assembly establishes a common standard of workmanship; it is a useful and durable reference for the workers, allowing them to minimize variation due to differences in techniques. This is especially important when freehand finishing techniques are used, such as brick or stone masonry, stucco, or a textured concrete slab. ∎

Observable Assemblies

Critical details in an assembly should be observable when built.

1. The detailer should design assemblies that can be built from their structural substrate toward the exposed faces of the assembly so that the materials and their connections are visible at each stage of completion. A builder can better control the quality of the work if it can be seen while being installed. This is not a problem in most construction processes, but in others it is very difficult to achieve.

A plumber has difficulty seeing all sides of a copper pipe connection that is to be soldered beneath a sink. Even threaded fittings are more likely to be stripped if the installer cannot see whether the elements are aligned correctly. Flawed details are often those that cannot be clearly observed at critical steps during construction.

2. It is difficult to observe fluid materials when they are incorporated into rigid assemblies. Examples include casting concrete into formwork, grouting cells in concrete masonry, or blowing insulation into stud cavities. Is the fluid material located where it was meant to be, and not elsewhere? Small openings or inspection ports in the rigid assembly could make those critical areas observable to the builder during installation. The port may be a small hole in the facing material or a void made by omitting one of the facing elements, such as a masonry unit. After the assembly is substantially complete and inspection reveals no problems, the inspection port can be closed to match surrounding surfaces, or it may be fitted with a cover to allow for future inspection.

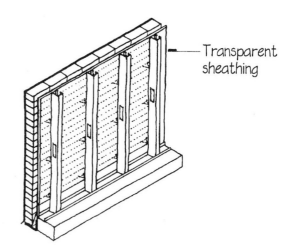

4. Sample Panel with Observable Cavity

3. Critical details sometimes become concealed soon after they are installed, and they may be vulnerable to harm by subsequent construction activities. For example, cavities within masonry walls must be clear so that water can drain, but they may become clogged by falling mortar crumbs as the wall is built higher. Inspection ports near the bottom of the cavity would permit observation and, if large enough, would permit debris to be removed.

4. Sample or mockup assemblies (see the preceding section, *Simulated Assemblies*) can be made using transparent or perforated materials in the place of opaque materials, in some locations, permitting observation inside the assembly. For instance, transparent sheathing over studs in masonry veneer walls would permit the critical cavity between the sheathing and the veneer to be observable. When this is done, masons will naturally take greater care to keep the cavity clear of mortar droppings and other debris, yielding a built work of better functionality, greater durability, and lower maintenance costs. The techniques that produced good results in the sample panel can then be applied to the actual building.

5. Sophisticated nondestructive tools exist to make conditions inside an assembly observable. These tools include a borescope for optical investigation through small openings, infrared thermography and electromagnetic (radar) scans, impact-echo testing, and others. Each tool has a particular capability, but most should be used by a trained operator. Unfortunately, these tools are seldom available to the builder while the work is taking place, and they therefore rarely enhance the quality of initial construction. These techniques can, however, be employed after initial construction to detect features that are hidden from view.

Accessible Connections

It is important to design details in such a way that workers can reach the work easily.

1. For maximum comfort and productivity, a worker should be standing on a level, secure surface, working between waist height and shoulder height, within a couple of feet (about 60 cm) of the front of the body. This ideal is achieved readily in a factory setting, but it is more difficult to achieve on a construction site. Overhead work is fatiguing, as is work that requires stooping or squatting. Excessive reaches put the worker dangerously off balance. These positions are also likely to result in less-than-perfect workmanship because critical features of the detail may be hard to see or difficult to execute in awkward postures.

2. Cladding that is designed to be installed from inside the building saves money on scaffolding and generally results in high worker productivity and optimal workmanship.

3. Continuously adjustable scaffolding or staging with guardrails is the next best thing to standing on a level floor. A hydraulic bucket or a short stepladder would be nearly as safe and comfortable as scaffolding. A straight ladder or a very tall stepladder is more precarious than any of the foregoing means of support and also leads to lower productivity because of the difficulty of moving the ladder and the time it consumes. The least desirable means of worker support is a seat harness suspended on ropes – it is relatively dangerous, productivity is low, and good workmanship is hard to achieve. Detailing can sometimes take these differences into account by avoiding finicky work in awkward places, prefabricating assemblies that would be difficult to fabricate in place because of precarious access, and placing fasteners in locations that are easy to reach.

4. Avoid creating apparently logical details that cannot be assembled because of accessibility problems. This innocent-looking detail for attaching cladding panels to a masonry backup wall will not work,

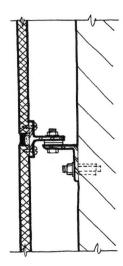

4. Inaccessible Connection

because there is no way for a worker to insert the screws into the lower edge of a panel. Develop details with a step-by-step review of the likely construction sequence to avoid problems (See ***Rehearsing the Construction Sequence***, Chapter 13)

5. Avoid connections that lie behind columns and spandrel beams, in sharp inside corners, or in re-entrant corners. These positions are difficult to reach, if they can be reached at all. In tight locations such as these, be sure that the worker can not only reach the connection but also has space for the hammer, wrench, or screwdriver that must be used to make the connection. The worker should also be able to see the connection rather than have to work by "feel" alone.

The best location for a cladding connection to the spandrel of a building is on top of the edge of a floor slab, where full access is easy. A connection in this location will have to be covered by interior finish surfaces, such as convector covers, but the connection will be much easier to make than connections at the ceiling or in the cramped gap between the spandrel beam and the cladding.

6. Connections may also need to be accessible for building maintenance, renovation, or deconstruction at the end of the element's useful life. This is especially important for elements expected to have a useful life shorter than that of the building as a whole, such as mechanical systems, finishes, and roofing. At the end of the entire building's life cycle, deconstruction and demolition will progress more safely and will yield resources of greater salvage value if connections can be dismantled without damaging the elements. ■

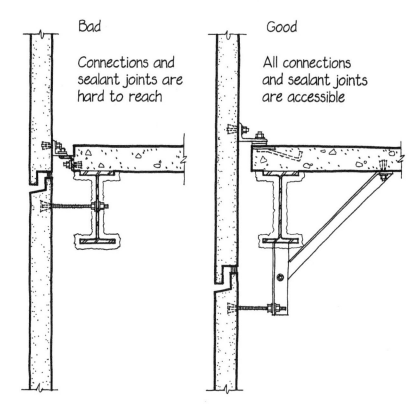

5. Cladding Panel Connections

Detailing for Disassembly

Details built with reversible connections make deconstruction easier and will increase the salvage value of elements removed from the building. The "cradle to cradle" concept advocates that, among other things, designers minimize environmental impact at the end of a building component's service life. Rather than performing demolition and disposal, the preferred outcome is salvaging useful products for reuse, recycling most others, and sending minimal amounts of waste to landfills (see **Expected Life**, Chapter 10).

1. Not all building projects are intended to be permanent. Temporary structures are an increasingly common building type; they may provide a normal range of architectural qualities, but for limited time frames. Examples include expositions, pavilions used for summer months, annual gatherings for cultural or religious events, and structures that support periodic sporting or performance events. Interior installations in office and retail spaces are often temporary, changing every few years. Temporary assemblies may be made of materials that exceed the building's service life, so a deliberate strategy to reuse materials and components has merit.

Detailing for disassembly is most appropriate when the building material or assembly is a candidate for reuse without substantial processing. Examples may be steel framing elements, doors and windows, cabinetry, and plumbing fixtures. In many cities, building material exchanges exist to economically market salvaged materials. Salvaged slate or clay tile roofing, thin stone cladding elements, stained glass, fireplace mantles, and many other items are often prized in specialty salvage markets. In some cases, sustainability rating systems will also reward use of salvaged materials and assemblies.

2. Disassembly is simplest when connections that can be undone easily are used,

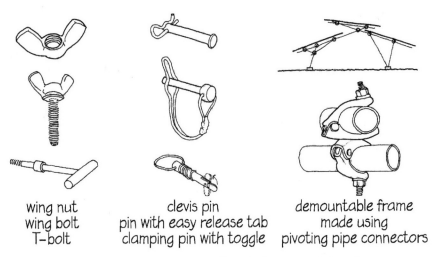

2. Fasteners for Easy Disassembly (labeled top to bottom)

wing nut
wing bolt
T-bolt

clevis pin
pin with easy release tab
clamping pin with toggle

demountable frame made using pivoting pipe connectors

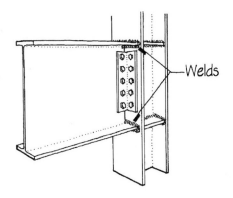

3. Welded Moment Connection Between Beam and Column

such as bolts or screws, and some nailed and snap-fit connections. Connections that rely on rivets, welds, cements, adhesives, and structural sealants often require excessive labor to dismantle, making their disassembly uneconomical. For simple connections that are undone frequently, wing nuts, spring-type clevis pins, and snap-fit interlocking connectors can be considered. They do not require tools and are quick to use, facilitating efficient erection and reconfiguration of simple assemblies.

3. Steel frames often use bolted connections, which can be removed without harming the valuable steel elements. However, if the connection is also welded to make it a moment connection, the removal may result in the steel member being recycled rather than reused. To be reused, the steel elements must be handled as carefully as they were when being shipped and installed, when new. They must not be bent or cold-worked during disassembly; otherwise, engineers will be unsure of their physical properties.

4. Structural precast concrete elements are more easily disassembled than a monolithic sitecast concrete frame. However, unlike steel members, the precast elements may have physical properties that are unknown to a structural engineer; they are typically custom-made for the project, and many key features, such as their reinforcement, are not observable. For this reason, they are seldom reused.

5. Avoid creating assemblies with inaccessible or hidden fasteners. For example, when finishing interior spaces, secure wood panels or tack surfaces with accessible screws, not with countersunk nails that are filled to conceal their locations. On the building exterior, prefinished rainscreen panels can be secured with exposed stainless steel screws, rather than with recessed screws that are spackled and painted over. If laid out in an orderly pattern, the screws can add a nice visual detail to the building, while also allowing for quick disassembly of the panel when called for replacement or dismantling.

6. Prefabricated proprietary systems are common for interior office partitions and furnishings. Configurations can be changed with little effort or waste because of the modular design and connections that are easily done and undone. Some modular housing systems apply the same principles to the building envelope, permitting the size of the building to be altered, and permitting window, door, and solid wall panels to be interchangeable. These systems keep component sizes reasonably small so that shipping and installation processes need only commonly available equipment, and alterations are made quickly. ■

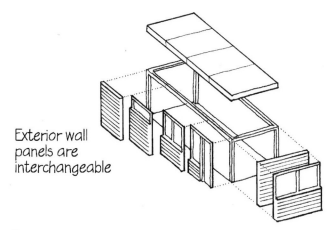

Tamper resistant fasteners such as torx screws impede disassembly

low-profile head, torx drive
button head, square drive
round head, phillips drive

5. Accessible Fasteners

Exterior wall panels are interchangeable

6. Prefabricated Kit of Parts

Installation Clearance

Every component of a building needs a little extra space in addition to its own dimensions.

1. Any component that has to be installed between two other components needs a small amount of additional room so that it can be maneuvered into place. A steel beam is always cut slightly shorter than the space between columns; if it were not, it would bind during insertion and would be almost impossible to install.

2. Similarly, a window or door unit is mounted in a rough opening that is slightly larger than the unit. This gives space to guide the unit into its final position, and it also allows adjustment for inaccuracies in both the wall and the window unit. The window unit is mounted in the rough opening with wedge-shaped shims that allow very precise adjustments for dimension and plumb. Follow manufacturer recommendations in sizing the rough opening for each window or door.

3. A bathtub or a kitchen base cabinet can be difficult to insert into the end of a room unless the room is slightly larger than the unit, to provide a clearance for installation. The gaps at the ends of a cabinet are closed with filler strips provided by the cabinetmaker and cut to size on the construction site. The gaps around the tub are filled with wall finish materials (such as ceramic tile or a plastic tub surround) and a sealant.

Installation clearances are relatively small dimensions that make it easier to put pieces together; however, they are not intended to provide the much larger construction tolerances needed in building assemblies (see **Dimensional Tolerance**, Chapter 12). ■

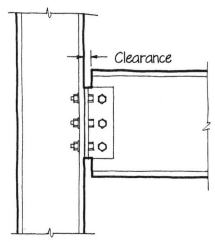

1. Elevation of Steel Beam-to-Column Connection

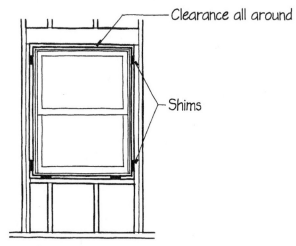

2. Installation of Window in Rough Opening

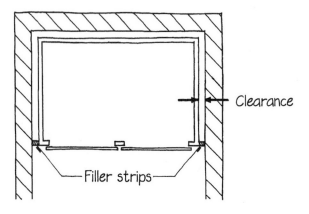

3. Plan of Cabinet in End of Room

Nonconflicting Systems

A building should be detailed so its various parts and systems mesh smoothly in three dimensions. This requires the detailer to create zones reserved for each of the systems to avoid costly clashes during construction and to make operational maintenance easier.

1. In the typical project organization – in which the structural frame of a building is designed by one professional, the mechanical and electrical systems by others, and the enclosure and finishes by still others – coordination is necessary to avoid a situation in which a beam, a duct, a conduit, a sprinkler pipe, and a cladding attachment are all detailed to occupy the same space in the building. Separate zones need to be reserved throughout a building for vertical structure, horizontal structure, cladding, plumbing risers, and vertical and horizontal runs of the various mechanical, electrical, and communications services (see *Vertical Chase* and *Horizontal Plenum*, Chapter 8).

2. Suspended ceilings are so common because they avoid conflict by hanging in their own unobstructed zone beneath all the complex geometry of the building frame and building services. This makes them easy to install and consequently inexpensive. Raised access flooring provides a similar zone between the floor surface and the structural deck, through which power and information networks can be easily distributed. Both zones are readily accessible as the networks are updated, as is often needed in offices.

3. Cladding that runs in its own zone outside the columns and spandrel beams is much easier to detail and to install than cladding that is interrupted by framing members. It has other advantages as well: The frame is protected from temperature extremes and moisture; thermal bridging of the frame is avoided; and there tend to be fewer problems with leaking and differential thermal movement.

4. A section of steel column is connected to the next higher section at waist height rather than at the floor line. This is not only convenient for ironworkers to reach, but more importantly, it avoids conflict with the beam and girder connections that lie just below. The edge of the floor slab is usually cantilevered a short distance past the face of the columns and spandrel beams, to avoid conflict between the framing and the cladding. Reinforcing steel in a concrete column is also spliced just above each floor level, rather than in the congested area just below, where the steel from the slabs, beams, and girders intersects the steel in the column. ▷

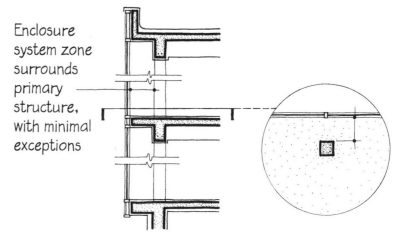

3. Zoning of Structure and Enclosure

Enclosure system zone surrounds primary structure, with minimal exceptions

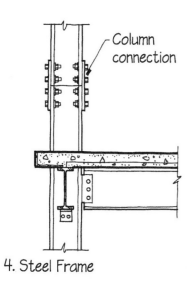

4. Steel Frame

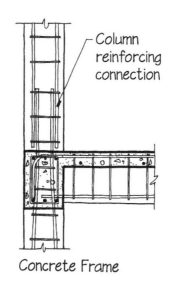

Concrete Frame

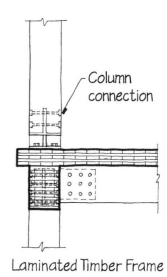

Laminated Timber Frame

SECTION 2 ■ CONSTRUCTABILITY   189

5. Avoid embedding electrical conduit or plumbing lines in sitecast concrete or masonry load-bearing components. If embedments are unavoidable, make them minimal to avoid weakening the structural components. Never locate a major switchbox or distribution spine within major structural walls, because the related service lines may displace substantial amounts of structural materials. Coordinate consultants' plans for each subsystem with the structural engineer to be sure that the structure is not undermined by services.

6. Establish a clear strategy regarding how the various subsystems in a building will relate to one another. Highly integrated subsystems, where elements are interdependently arranged in a tight-fitting array, may achieve greater efficiencies, such as reduced vertical dimension for services between ceiling and floor deck. But this approach is often found to be costly, time-consuming, and impractical, both during initial construction and when services are modified during the life of the building. Rather than a tight-fitting, integrated, glovelike strategy, a loose-fitting, additive, mittenlike strategy is usually better for building durability and performance over time. It is more accommodating of changes in the physical makeup of the building, and it allows the various workers to install their subsystems more independently.

7. Building information modeling tools confidently and accurately show the size, shape, and positions of all building systems. This allows designers, consultants, and builders to forecast precisely where conflicts are likely, and to address them during the integrated design process, long before they are installed in the building. These modeling tools can also be used by workers in the field to visualize exactly where each element is to be installed. However, be aware that tight-fitting assemblies may be challenging to install and difficult to update during the life of the building.

8. Detailed modeling of such systems follows a general diagram setting forth the layers or strata for competing services.

The generic diagram shown illustrates a strategic zoning of space for each system in a typical overhead plane and can be adapted to accommodate specific needs for each project. Buildings equipped with under-floor plenums, interstitial service floors, and other special features may have a different set of services in the overhead plane.

Structure is at the top, where the floor or roof decks require support. Below that is one of two layers for plumbing lines, which may include main lines for sprinklers, and roof storm drains and waste lines from plumbing fixtures above; both of these are relatively large, and both need to gradually slope so gravity keeps their contents moving. Below that is a zone for ducts, which are large and function best if straight and their shape doesn't hinder airflow. Next is a second layer for plumbing, containing insulated hydronic plumbing lines and smaller supply lines, whose contents are under pressure; these can change in elevation if needed. Sloping pipes that cannot fit above the ducts could be placed in this lower plumbing layer also. Closest to the ceiling are the small but numerous electrical and telecommunications lines. These often engage sensors, alarms, Wi-Fi devices, and lighting in the ceiling plane; here they are easily accessed as they are updated or rerouted most frequently. Smaller ducts can pass through this layer to reach mechanical diffusers in the ceiling plane, which is usually suspended from the structural deck above. ∎

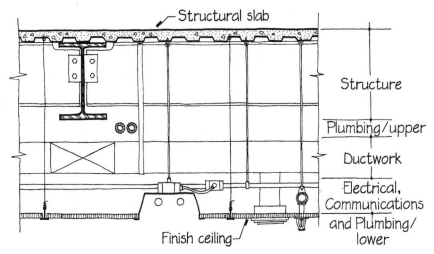

7. Zoning of Overhead Space for Building Services

CHAPTER 12  Forgiving Details

The ability to create forgiving details is among the most important and rewarding skills of the detailer. A forgiving detail is one that provides a way for a worker to deal easily with inaccuracies or mistakes. Most traditional details are very forgiving of inaccuracies and mistakes; because they evolved over a period of many years, these details gradually incorporated features that made them easier and more convenient for workers. Worker convenience should never come at the cost of critical functional performance. The designer optimizes these dual objectives in the details.

When inventing new details, the designer should pay particular attention to avoiding features or conditions that would "trap" the worker if they are not done perfectly. The history of modern architecture includes many stories of architects who designed unforgiving details. Historical accounts generally depict the architect as struggling heroically to force factories, contractors, and workers to achieve new standards of precision and fit in their work, in order to make new kinds of details possible. Unfortunately, many of these stories ended badly, with the project stakeholders estranged and construction schedules – not to mention costs – out of control.

Remember: Even highly skilled craftspeople do not work with machine-like accuracy. If a detailer forces a design on builders who they know are not sufficiently skilled or trained to do that job, then the detailer is the one responsible for the poor result. No one should expect A+ results from workers whose skill level is C–.

The same principle applies to use of industrial processes; the detailer must know their limits and work within them.

Details should be attractive and functional; however, details should also be practical within the material and labor reality of the project's construction processes. Digital drawing and modeling tools work to extraordinarily close tolerances, much closer than highly skilled craftspeople; they even work to closer tolerances than CNC (computer numeric controlled) machines. But even the best parametric fabrication tools require recalibration periodically. There is no reason to design details to tolerances that exceed the tolerances of the means of execution. To illustrate, there is no value in drawing footings to tolerances of 0.1 in. (2.5 mm) when they are being excavated from previously undisturbed soil with a 24 in. (610 mm) wide backhoe.

Understanding the principles and applying a handful of patterns for designing forgiving details can help the designer avoid these mistakes. Each will be discussed in this chapter. They are as follows:

> ***Dimensional Tolerance*** (p. 192)
> ***Sliding Fit*** (p. 197)
> ***Adjustable Fit*** (p. 201)
> ***Reveal*** (p. 204)
> ***Butt Joint*** (p. 206)
> ***Clean Edge*** (p. 209)
> ***Progressive Finish*** (p. 211)
> ***Forgiving Surface*** (p. 213)

Architectural Detailing: Function Constructability Aesthetics. Fourth Edition. Patrick Rand, Jason Miller, and Edward Allen.
© 2025 John Wiley & Sons, Inc. Published 2025 by John Wiley & Sons, Inc.

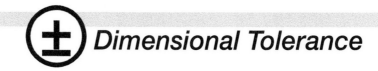

Dimensional Tolerance

A dimensional tolerance is a maximum amount of variation expected from an intended measurement because of normal inaccuracies in manufacture and installation. In building construction, dimensional tolerance parameters generally become more rigorous and increase with the level of fit and finish.

TABLE 12-1: Dimensional Tolerances of Common Measuring Devices

Device	Tolerances at 50 ft. (15 m)	Tolerances at 100 ft. (30 m)
Sonic measuring device	±3 in. (76.2 mm)	not recommended
Steel measuring tape	±1/8 in. (3.2 mm)	±1/4 in. (6.4 mm)
Laser range finder	±1/16 in. (1.6 mm)	±1/16 in. (1.6 mm)
Construction laser	±1/32 in. (0.8 mm)	±1/16 in. (1.6 mm)
Laser 3D scanner	±1/1000 in. (0.03 mm)	±1/1000 in. (0.03 mm)

1. There is a tolerance associated implicitly with every dimension on a set of drawings for a building. These tolerances have a direct effect on how details are designed. Establishing acceptable variations from perfection simply recognizes the nature of a particular material, type of construction, or human limitation. We state the allowable tolerances explicitly, and built works within these tolerances are not considered defective. Tolerances are needed because of thermal and moisture movement, structural settlement and deflection, workmanship, and other factors. This pattern is especially important in large buildings composed of prefabricated components, where "cut to fit" methods are not used.

Tolerances are based on material properties and construction methods, not on the capacity to measure accurately. Laser 3D scanners and global positioning system (GPS) surveying instruments are far more accurate than most construction methods. Tolerances cannot accommodate careless measurement, nor can they be eliminated by measuring very accurately. Tolerances associated with various measuring devices are compared in Table 12-1.

2. This base plate for a steel column is not attached directly to the top of a site cast concrete footing or pile cap. While the footing cannot be perfectly flat or perfectly located, the column location must

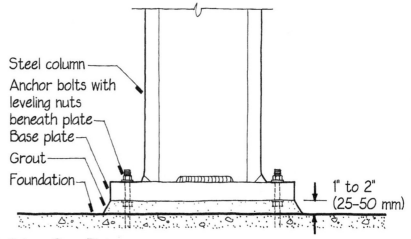

2. Column Base Plate

be very precise. To manage this potential conflict of material systems, the base plate is located and leveled on shims or leveling screws above the top of the footing, and the space between is filled with grout. This solution provides a tolerance vertically for the expected imprecision of the footing and also a full bearing surface between the base plate and the footing.

For function and constructability, it is important that the top of the footing not be higher than the bottom of the base plate. At least 1 in. (25 mm) of clearance must be provided for the insertion of grout. To accommodate this, the top of the footing might be dimensioned to lie between 1 and 2 in. (25 and 51 mm) lower than the bottom of the base plate. Providing a vertical dimensional tolerance of 1 in. within which the footing installers can work is reasonable for this type of material system.

To avoid problems in the horizontal plane, a plywood template is used to position the column's anchor bolts in the concrete footing. This template is often made from the same shop drawing used by the steel fabricator to make the column base, virtually ensuring a match.

3. Every trade and craft has its standard level of precision. Precision of pieces inside a door lock is very high; precision in pouring a concrete footing or driving a pile into the earth is very low. Good detailing accounts for the normal tolerances for dimensional inaccuracy in each phase of construction. Primary structure assemblies generally require greater tolerances than finishes, which are often handmade to fit, and use finer tools to achieve greater quality control. Finish elements also can be "rejected" in small increments if not suitable. Replacing structural elements would be more costly and more difficult, so tolerances are more accommodating.

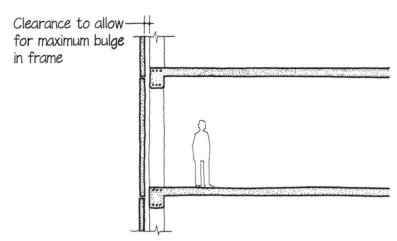

3A. Clearance Between Frame and Cladding

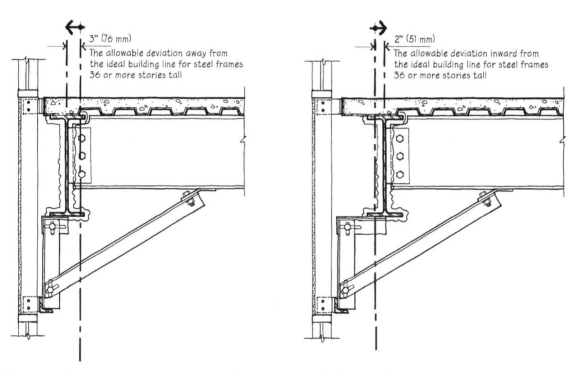

3B. Allowable Deviation from Ideal Plumb Line in Tall Steel Frames

The accompanying Table 12-2 gives a small sampling of accepted industry standard tolerances for different materials and building systems. Every detail of a building should respect the tolerances associated with the material and element.

This table and the assembly tolerances shown in Chart 12-1 reveal it is considered acceptable, if not normal, for a steel building frame to be out of plumb by as much as 3 in. (76 mm), and a concrete frame may be even farther out of plumb. When different systems of construction are combined, the varied tolerances must be carefully accounted for. When systems of differing tolerances are combined, the one with the roughest tolerances (furthest from the ideal) drives the design.

4. A cladding system cannot be designed to attach tightly to the spandrel beams of a building. The cladding for a building with a concrete frame should be installed in a plane that lies at least 1 in. (25 mm) outside the face of the spandrel beams, and a more generous distance than this would be prudent, considering that building frames are not always built to accepted tolerances. In practice, a cladding installer measures the faces of a building frame with great precision before beginning work and establishes planes for the cladding that will clear the largest bulges on each face. The cladding attachment details must provide for a range of dimensional adjustment, using devices such as shims, slotted fastener holes, and threaded fasteners, which allow for these tolerance dimensions (see *Adjustable Fit*, later in this chapter) without compromising performance integrity. ▷

TABLE 12-2: A Sampling of Accepted Dimensional Tolerances in US Construction[a]

Concrete

Dimension of footing in plan	–½ in., +2 in.	–13 mm, +51 mm
Squareness of residential foundation	½ in. for 20 ft.	1:500
Plumbness of outside corner of exposed wall or column	Up to 83.33 ft.: lesser of 0.20% of height or ±½ in.; above 83.33 ft.: lesser of 0.05% of height or ±3 in.	1:500 up to 25.4 m height; 1:200 over 25.4 m height
Plumbness of wall or column other than at outside corner and exposed	Up to 83.33 ft.: lesser of 0.30% of height or ±1 in.; above 83.33 ft.: lesser of 0.10% of height or ±6 in.	Up to 25.4 m: lesser of 0.30% of height or ±25 mm; above 25.4 m: lesser of 0.10% of height or ±152 mm
Variation of wall from building line in plan	±1 in.	±25 mm
Variation in wall thickness, up to 12 in. (25 mm) thick	–¼ in., +⅜ in.	–6.35 mm, +10 mm
Variation in level of beam or flat slab	±½ in. for 10 ft.; ±¾ in. for entire length	±6.35 mm for 3.05 m; ±9.5 mm in any bay; ±19 mm for entire length

Precast Concrete

Plumbness of wall or column	±¼ in. for 10 ft.; ±1 in. for 100 ft.	±6.35 mm for 3.05 m; ±25 mm for 30 m
Joint width between architectural wall panels	±¼ in.	±6.35 mm

Structural Steel

Plumbness of column	1 in. toward or 2 in. away from building line in first 20 stories; max. slope 1/16 in. per story; 2 in. toward and 3 in. away above 36 stories	25 mm toward or 51 mm away from building line in first 20 stories; max. slope 2 mm per story; 51 mm toward and 76 mm away above 36 stories
Column length	±1/32 in. up to 70 ft.	±1 mm up to 21 m
Beam length	±⅜ in. for depths of 24 in. and less; ±½ in. for greater depths	±10 mm for depths of 610 mm and less; ±13 mm for greater depths

Marble, Limestone, Granite

Deviation from square in any one stone	±1/16 in.	±1.6 mm
Length and width of panels	±1/16 in.	±1.6 mm
Thickness of panels	±1/32 in. up to ½ in. thick; ±⅛ in. from ½–1⅝ in. thick; ±¼ in. over 1⅝ in. thick	±1 mm up to 13 mm thick; ±3 mm from 13–116 mm thick; ±6.4 mm over 116 mm thick

Masonry Wall

Deviation from plan location and plumbness of wall	±¼ in. for 10 ft.; ±⅜ in. for 20 ft.; ±½ in. for entire length	1:500
Thickness of multi-wythe wall	–¼ in., +½ in.	–6.35 mm, +13 mm

Prefabricated Wood Structural Frame

There are no industry standards for the placement of prefabricated engineered-wood products, such as glue-laminated timber, I-joists, LVLs, PSLs, and wood trusses. Consult with manufacturer for recommended tolerances.

Wood Light Frame

Floor evenness	±¼ in. for 32 in. parallel to joists; ±¼ in. for 10 ft. perpendicular to joists	1:125 parallel; 1:500 perpendicular
Wall plumbness	±¼ in. for 10 ft.	1:500
Prefabricated truss, I-joist, LVL element length	±¼ in.	±6 mm

Exterior Cladding

Aluminum curtain wall mullions deviation from location in drawings	±⅛ in., or manufacturer's standard	±3 mm, or manufacturer's standard
All-glass curtain wall deviation from location in drawings	±1/16 in. for 3 ft.; ±½ in. for 100 ft.; or manufacturer's standard	1:500
Aluminum cladding panels (CNC-fabricated)[b]	±1/64 in. for 15 ft.	1:10,000

Interior Finishes

Plumbness of steel stud framing	±½ in. for 10 ft.	±12.7 mm for 3.05 m
Flatness of suspended acoustical ceiling	±⅛ in. for 10 ft.	±3.17 mm for 3.05 m

[a] These values are excerpted from a number of standard industry sources. A full summary of construction industry tolerances can be found in *Handbook of Construction Tolerances*, David Kent Ballast, John Wiley & Sons, 2007. Consult publications of individual industry associations for tolerances for each material.
[b] Not an industry standard; this is data for a specific project (Experience Music Project, Seattle, Washington, Gehry Partners).

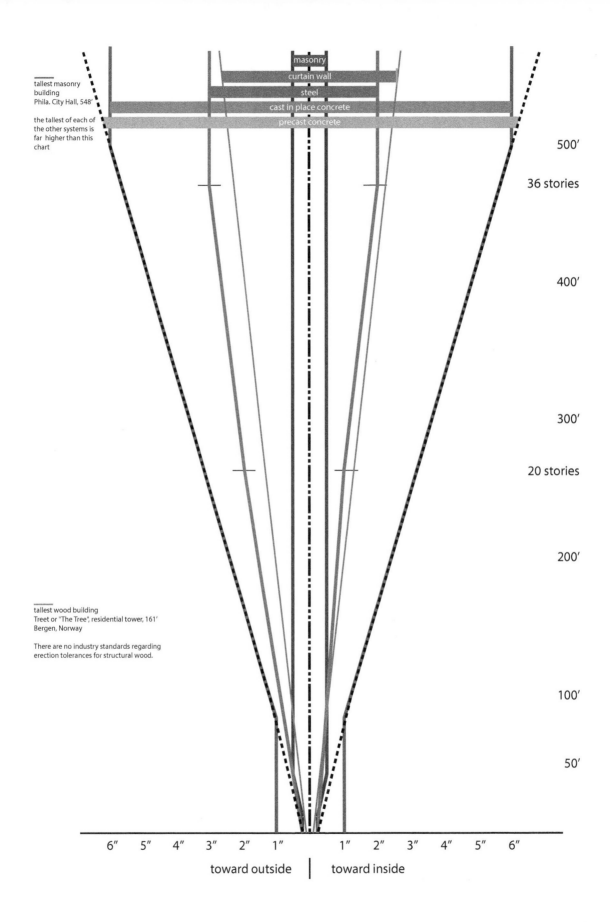

CHART 12-1: Graphic Comparison of Erection Tolerances for Various Construction Assemblies

5. Deflections and creep in beams and slabs complicate the picture. It is unwise to detail prefabricated partitions or cladding panels to fit closely under beams or slabs. Even a generous sealant joint between the two is often insufficient to accommodate normal deflections. It is better to locate cladding panels entirely outside the structure and to mount them in such a way that they are isolated as much as possible from deflections and creep in the frame. Good communication and collaboration among the detailer, the structural engineer, and the cladding manufacturer is critical to limit spandrel beam deflections and to provide sufficient horizontal movement joints in the cladding.

Non-load-bearing partitions should be separated from the floor structure above by sealant beads or gaskets whose height is determined by the structural engineer (see **Structure/Enclosure Joint**, Chapter 6). A vertically slotted light gauge steel slip track at the head of a partition can accommodate up to 1.7 in. (43 mm) of deflection of the beam or deck above, while maintaining alignment of the attachment.

6. Where dimensional tolerances accumulate from a set of assembled components, each with its own individual tolerance, an overall tolerance can be calculated by taking the square root of the sum of the squares of the individual tolerances.

If, for example, a building bay is clad with three precast concrete panels, with each panel having a tolerance of ±⅛ in. (3 mm), and a window unit with a tolerance of ±¹⁄₁₆ in. (1.5 mm), the overall dimensional tolerance for one bay is figured as follows:

Overall tolerance:

$$= \pm\sqrt{\left(\frac{1}{8}\right)^2 + \left(\frac{1}{16}\right)^2 + \left(\frac{1}{8}\right)^2 + \left(\frac{1}{8}\right)^2}$$
$$= \pm 0.23''$$

Overall tolerance:

$$= \pm\sqrt{(3)^2 + (1.5)^2 + (3)^2 + (3)^2}$$
$$= \pm 5.4 \text{ mm}$$

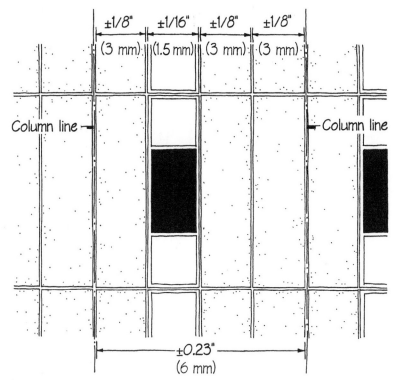

6. Cumulative Tolerance in Cladding Panels

7. Large building components require greater tolerances, especially if they are difficult to alter at the construction site. For example, a tall steel frame requires significantly larger tolerances for plumbness than a masonry wall. This is because the masonry wall, though handmade, is composed of very small pieces; each course presents an opportunity for correcting the alignment so as to come close to the ideal. Multistory steel columns have fewer opportunities to correct alignment.

8. Calling for closer tolerances than standard trade practices will likely increase project costs and extend the project timeline. Extraordinarily close tolerances will also result in more elements being discarded or being removed from installed work.

9. To integrate project design with project delivery, design detailers and builders should collaborate to review acceptable tolerances for all stages of construction. Potential conflicts should be identified prior to construction. Digital and building information modeling can help do this; however, to do so, those models must represent the relevant construction tolerances. Remember: Workers cannot work to the same tolerances as the digital model. When conflicts occur or when tolerances are exceeded, designers and builders should again collaborate to find a solution. It is not acceptable to quietly disregard functional features of a detail, such as an expansion joint that is too wide or too narrow, thinking that it is sufficient if it has an acceptable finish appearance. ■

Sliding Fit

The easiest, most forgiving dimensional relationship between two components of a building is a sliding fit, in which one component overlaps another and can be positioned merely by sliding.

1. Overlapping shingles on a roof or a wall exemplify a sliding fit. Many wood trim details use a sliding fit to avoid difficult alignment problems. This wood eave soffit could be made from a single piece of wood; however, this would be difficult and time consuming, because two opposite edges of the same piece would have to be fitted at the same time. Because the dimension between the back of the fascia board and the siding tends to vary somewhat, and because neither the fascia board nor the siding tends to be perfectly straight, it is much easier to install the soffit board to fit the fascia as tightly as possible while staying well clear of the siding. Then the gap at the siding is closed with a smaller trim piece or molding. To account for waviness of the fascia board, a small, flexible molding might be placed into the corner between the fascia and the soffit. The soffit and the two trim pieces are all examples of sliding fit.

2. A wood baseboard is installed to cover the uneven gap between finish wall and floor surfaces. A single-piece baseboard works well if the floor and wall surfaces are perfectly flat, but this is seldom the case. The baseboard is simply too stiff to bend into the low spots of the wall and floor. A traditional three-piece baseboard addresses this problem by adding two thin, flexible moldings: a cap to hug the contours of the wall and a shoe to mold itself to the floor. The cap and shoe combine, using a sliding fit against the baseboard, to provide the flexibility to adjust to undulating contours. ▷

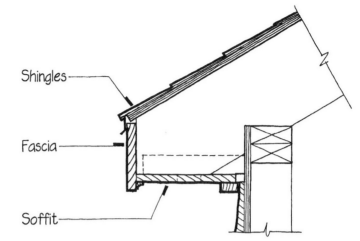

1. Wood Eave Detail

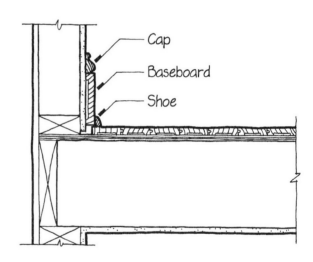

2. Baseboard

3. In general, a sliding fit involves a component that is free to move in at least one direction and whose face is against the face of another component. Sliding fit also involves aligning a component to two adjacent, perpendicular planes. The shingle is aligned to the surface plane of the next lower course of shingles and to an imaginary perpendicular plane that intersects the course line of the shingle. The soffit board is aligned to the horizontal plane of the level cuts on the rafter ends and to the vertical plane of the back of the fascia board. The baseboard aligns to the vertical plane of the wall and the horizontal plane of the floor. A kitchen base cabinet also aligns to the floor and wall planes. These are all easy fits.

When a third adjacent plane of alignment is added, the problem of fitting becomes more difficult. If the three planes are accurately perpendicular to one another and if the component to be fitted is perfectly square, the fit is easy. However, if there is inaccuracy anywhere in the relationship, the component will have to be trimmed to fit without a gap.

If the third plane of alignment is opposite to one of the other planes rather than adjacent, the fitting problem is even more difficult.

When fourth and fifth planes of alignment are added, the fitting problem becomes acute. These situations should be avoided.

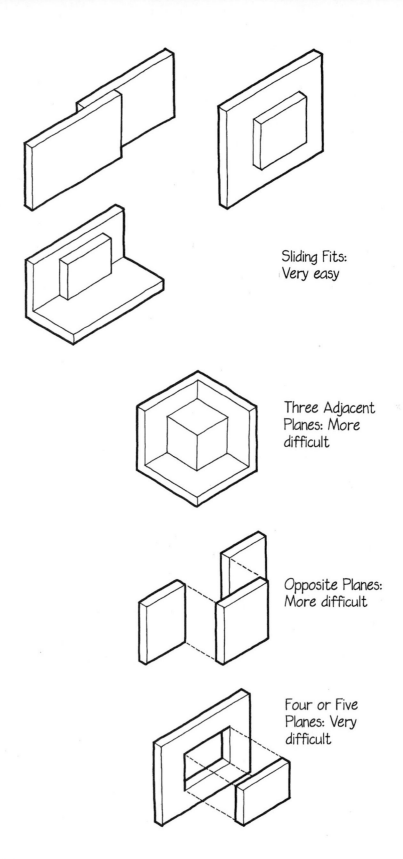

3. Planes of Fit

4. Most prefabricated residential window units avoid five-plane fitting problems by specifying a rough opening in the wall that is considerably larger than the window unit. This generous clearance reduces the problem to fitting against the wall plane only. The flange on the window unit aligns to the plane of the wall sheathing, and the unit is leveled and plumbed as it "floats" in the rough opening, supported by pairs of wedges on all four edges that are adjusted easily and precisely to fill the gap between the framing and the window unit.

5. The more difficult part of window installation is fitting the interior casings. Because of normal tolerances in wall thickness caused by variations in framing lumber dimensions and plaster thickness, the frame depth of the window unit may not match the thickness of the wall exactly. The usual practice is to install wooden extension jambs that make up the difference between the depth of the window unit and the thickness of the wall. These extension jambs are laborious to fit because they must align to two parallel planes: the inside face of the window unit and the face of the plaster. An easier fit is provided by a detail that returns the plaster onto the jambs of the window unit. The plaster return must be shimmed out from the rough jamb to align with the jamb of the window unit. A small trim piece is usually required to cover the groove in the edge of the jamb of the window unit. ▷

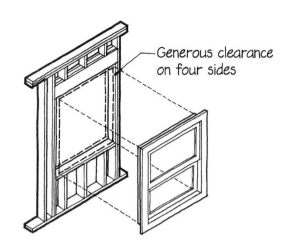

4. Window Installation

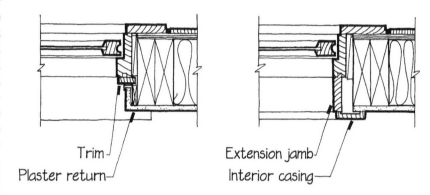

5. Interior Finish at Window Jamb

6. Butt-jointed cladding panels such as composite metal enclosure systems represent a potentially difficult five-plane fit. It is extremely important that the panels be manufactured to dimension, be square, and be flat within very narrow tolerances. This is generally feasible, because they are made in a factory using precision fixtures and machines.

In attaching the panels to the building, freedom of alignment in all three axes (x, y, and z) must be provided by the connectors (see the following section, *Adjustable Fit*). This allows the panels to be aligned easily to the same plane, to level, to plumb, and to horizontal and vertical dimension. The width of the joint that surrounds each panel and separates it from its neighbors must be sufficient to allow for any expected deviation in dimension and alignment (see *Sealant Joints and Gaskets*, Chapter 1).

Details vary, depending on the particular cladding system, but most incorporate a sliding fit feature into what appears to be a butt-jointed detail. The plan detail of the vertical joint shows two examples of sliding fit. They make this detail easier to install, and they accommodate minor in-plane movement. On one side, the clip is screwed to the continuous extrusion that is secured to the wall assembly, but the clip on the other side has a tongue-in-groove sliding fit with the continuous extrusion. The second example of sliding fit is the composite metal strip that is placed in the reveal, which slips into grooves in the mounting clips. Both permit a small range of movement in the plane of the panel and accept minor errors in measuring, cutting, or installing the pieces.

7. The common method of mounting large lites of glass makes them much easier to fit than cladding panels, because, in reality, they align only to one plane – the plane of the gaskets against which they are placed. The four edges of each lite have a sliding fit into the mullions and against the gaskets, allowing for fairly large tolerances in dimension and squareness. ■

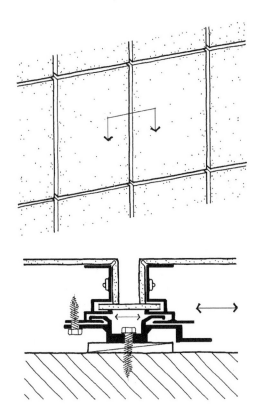

6. Butt-Jointed Cladding Panels

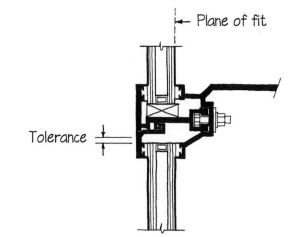

7. Mounting of Glass in Aluminum Frame

Adjustable Fit

Because maintaining perfect dimensional accuracy in construction is impossible, every building component that must be positioned accurately should be detailed so its alignment can be adjusted during and after assembly.

1. This manufactured bracket for a precut glass shelf must be aligned precisely to a vertical line on the wall so that the shelf will fit snugly into the closed pocket in the bracket. To allow for a normal tolerance in measuring and drilling the screw holes in the wall, the matching holes in the bracket are slotted. The slots are horizontal so that the weight of the bracket will bear directly against the shank of the screw, regardless of where in the slot the screw is located. This detail does not provide for vertical adjustment of the bracket or for correction of any waviness in the plane of the wall; it provides for adjustment only in one axis.

While basic shelf brackets, such as the ones used to mount rough shelves in a basement or a garage, might be nailed to the wall, a nail does not make any provision for precise adjustment or readjustment of the bracket position. Adjustable connections generally use threaded fasteners, either screws or bolts, to provide greater control during assembly and to allow for later readjustment or removal and replacement, if necessary.

2. Anchor bolts in concrete are difficult to place with precision and are often out of alignment in two axes. This manufactured metal post base responds to the problem by providing a very large hole, together with an even larger washer in which the bolt hole is off center (eccentric). This allows for adjustment in two axes. If the height of the top of the concrete (the third axis) is inaccurate, steel shims or grout can be used beneath the post base. The post itself can also be cut a bit shorter or longer, as required. ▷

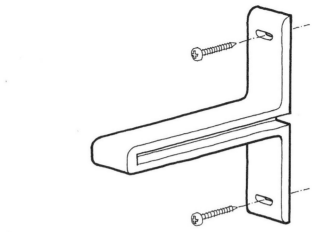

1. Bracket for Glass Shelf

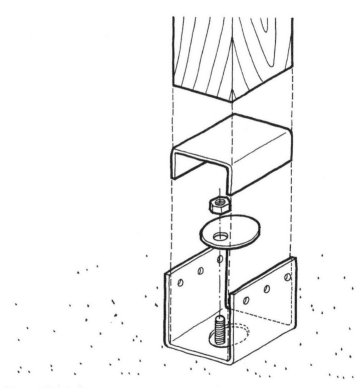

2. Metal Post Base

3. This wedge insert and askew-head bolt allow vertical adjustment for the location of a steel shelf angle used to support a masonry facing on a concrete building frame. The inner face of the outer wall of the insert and the head of the bolt create an opposing pair of wedges that lock securely together against a downward load in any vertical position.

In case the wedge insert does not align exactly in the horizontal plane with the prepunched hole in the shelf angle, the hole is punched as a horizontal slot. The horizontal orientation of the slot allows the shelf angle to transfer gravity loads directly to the bolt shank without slipping, regardless of the exact position of the bolt in the slot.

A third axis of adjustment is provided by the insertion of steel or high-impact plastic shims of various thicknesses between the shelf angle and the face of the concrete spandrel beam. The shims are horseshoe-shaped so that they will stay in place until the bolt is tightened.

By combining the wedge insert, the slotted hole, and the shims, a connection detail with triaxial adjustment has been created to reconcile the relatively large dimensional tolerances of a concrete frame with the close tolerances of building cladding systems. Similar connection details are used to attach shelf angles to steel framing.

4. This is a simple triaxial detail for fastening a stone or concrete cladding panel to the face of a building. Shims between the slab and the angle clip allow for vertical adjustment. In-and-out adjustment comes from the slotted hole in the base of the clip.

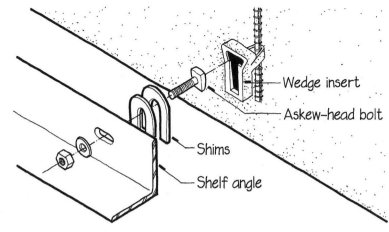

3. Adjustable Support for Shelf Angle

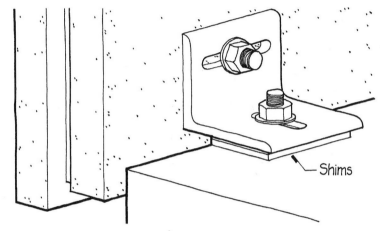

4. Adjustable Panel Anchor

Lateral adjustment in the plane of the cladding is provided by the horizontally slotted hole in the vertical leg of the clip. The slots are oriented so they do not compromise the load-carrying security of the connection: It would be a detailing mistake to provide for vertical adjustment by using a smooth-edged vertically slotted hole in the vertical leg of the clip, because this might allow the bolt to slip under gravity loading.

5. When vertical adjustment is needed, the vertical slotted hole can be made in a steel anchor that has a serrated vertical leg. Once the anchor is set to the correct height, then a serrated washer with a matching profile is installed so that the teeth engage the face of the anchor as the bolt is tightened. This anchor makes it possible to precisely position the height of the supports for stone cladding panels, and will not move vertically under loading. Serrated plates can be used to increase friction wherever a slotted hole is in the same axis as the forces.

6. A steel angle frame supporting a brick veneer wall over a long window opening needs to be adjusted precisely to place the shelf angle in the correct position. Pairs of slotted holes in opposing orientations make this easy, but they are not secure against slipping under load. This problem is avoided by welding all the connections once the proper alignment has been verified with surveying instruments prior to installation of the brick veneer cladding. ■

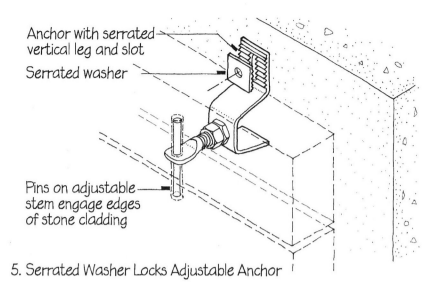

5. Serrated Washer Locks Adjustable Anchor

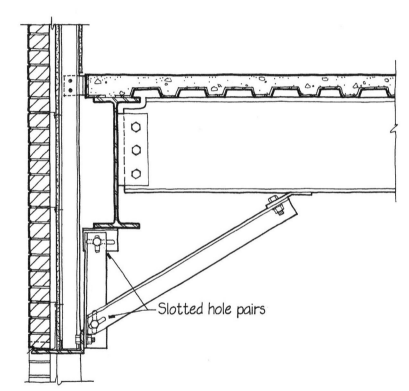

6. Support Frame for Brick Curtain Wall

SECTION 2 ■ CONSTRUCTABILITY   203

Reveal

A reveal is a recess or offset between two pieces of material where they come together. Functionally and aesthetically, reveals can be used to avoid having to make an exact alignment or meet an exact dimension, to cast a shadow line for compositional purposes, or to cast a shadow line that hides minor defects in workmanship.

1. Finish carpenters work against heavy odds to create attractive, well-crafted trim: The surfaces being trimmed are often out of plumb, out of level, out of dimension, and wavy. The lumber with which they work is often slightly crooked or warped, even out of dimension, and it will change dimension constantly during the life of the building, in response to changes in humidity. These factors make it inadvisable to ask the finish carpenter to create a flush edge where two planes of trim come together at the jamb of a window or a door. If a small but significant reveal is included in the detail, slight misalignments, crooks, and moisture movements will seldom be noticed, because they will merely change the dimension of the reveal slightly, but not the presence of the basic feature. Slender reveals demand more consistent materials and installation than wider reveals. If a flush detail is insisted upon, it will be more expensive to make, and it will be perfectly and reliably flush only at the instant that it is completed, before moisture expansion and contraction begin to take effect.

A reveal of this type also multiplies the parallel lines that surround the window or door – an effect that is aesthetically pleasing to the eye.

2. A reveal of another type can be used to create a shadow line to conceal imperfections in a joint. In this example, the rabbeted edge of the cap forms a reveal and becomes the apparent joint.

3. Reveals also work well at joints and exterior corners of stone and concrete facings, both to create shadow lines for compositional purposes and to disguise connections that may be less than perfect. For another kind of reveal often used in this type of situation, see the quirk miter illustrated in drawing 5, in the section ***Butt Joint***, later in this chapter.

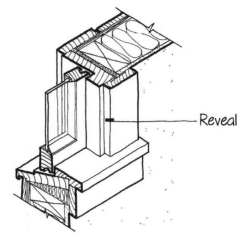
1. Reveal on Window Casing

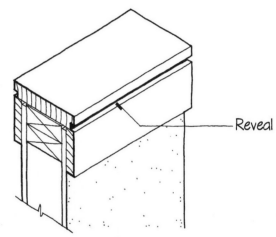
2. Reveal on Railing Cap

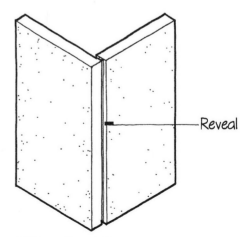
3. Reveal at Corner of Stone Panel Facing

4. Rustication strips attached to concrete formwork create shadow lines to conceal irregularities that occur where one pour of concrete joins another, or where one panel of formwork butts another.

5. Reveals in composite metal cladding systems subdivide a large surface into manageable pieces and accommodate minor thermal movement. ∎

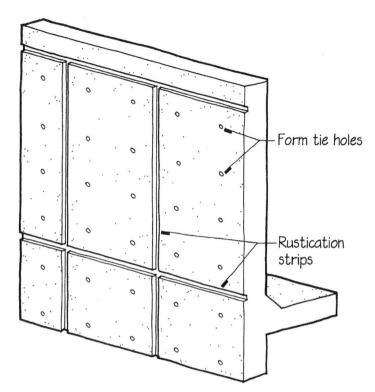

4. Concrete Wall and Parapet with Rustication Strips

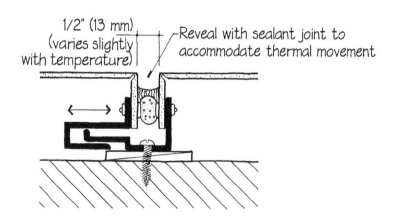

5. Composite Metal Cladding Joint

Butt Joint

A butt joint is the simplest way of assembling two components. It is also the most desirable way of doing so under most circumstances.

1. Mitered corners are an attractive type of butt joint, but they present several significant performance problems. One is that they create a sharp edge on each piece of material at the corner, and sharp edges are both fragile and potentially dangerous. Another problem is that to realize its aesthetic potential, a miter must be fitted very closely and precisely. This is often difficult to do when the pieces being mitered are long, wide, or warped. A miter between pieces of wood presents a third problem: Because wood shrinks a great deal perpendicular to its grain and very little along its grain, a 45-degree cut across a board will no longer be 45 degrees after the board has shrunk or expanded. Miters in wood tend to open up unattractively after construction as the building is heated and the wood dries out. Snug miters must be cut and joined when the wood is at equilibrium moisture content with a stable surrounding environment (see *Equalizing Cross Grain*, Chapter 6).

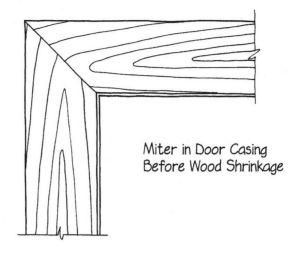

Miter in Door Casing Before Wood Shrinkage

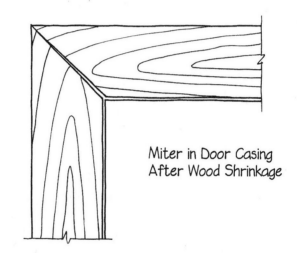

Miter in Door Casing After Wood Shrinkage

1. Effect of Wood Shrinkage on Miter Joint.

2. A simple butt joint avoids most of these problems. It has no sharp edges. It is easy to fit. And if it does open slightly when the wood dries, it does so evenly. A butt joint is especially forgiving if it includes a reveal (see **Reveal**, earlier in this chapter). In this example, the reveal is created by simply cutting the top piece of casing a bit longer than it needs to be.

3. Another effective approach to this same connection is to use a corner block that is both thicker and wider than the casing pieces it joins, creating a total of four reveals and two butt joints. ▷

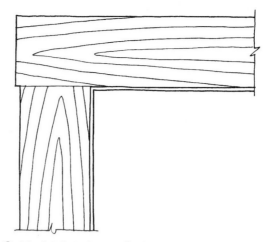

2. Butt Joint in Door Casing

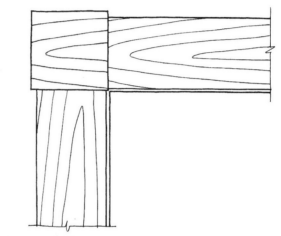

3. Corner Block in Door Casing

4. It is also possible to butt wood moldings at inside corners to avoid the unattractive opening up that might occur in a miter joint. This special type of butt joint is called a coped joint. It is produced in several steps. The first piece of molding is butted at right angles into the corner and nailed. The second piece of molding is mitered to establish the line of the cope. Finally, a coping saw is used to cut the second piece of molding at an angle of 90 degrees or slightly less, following the edge of the miter as a guide. The coped end of the second piece butts tightly to the contoured side of the first piece. The coped connection looks the same as a mitered connection but retains its tight fit even if the moldings shrink slightly.

5. Sometimes a good solution for joining long edges is the quirk miter. It has no sharp edges and is fairly forgiving of fitting problems because of its built-in reveal, but it retains the satisfying visual symmetry of a miter.

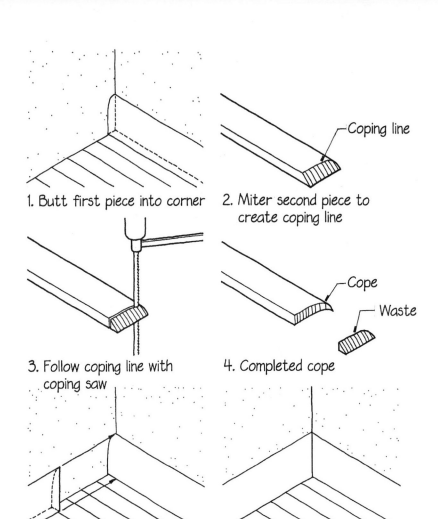

4. Coping a Joint in a Molding

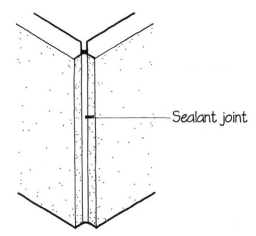

5. Quirk Miter Between Precast Concrete Panels

Clean Edge

Where a material or a surface ends, it should do so neatly and decisively. Clean edges reflect understanding of functional material properties and construction processes to ensure a durable and attractive result.

1. Two kinds of edges that are unforgiving are sharp edges and feather edges. Sharp edges are dangerous and are very susceptible to damage before, during, and after construction. If damaged, they are almost impossible to repair. Feather edges are created when we try to smooth one material into another, as in joining a plaster wall to a masonry wall that lies in the same plane, by smoothing the edge of the wet plaster onto the face of the masonry. A feather edge looks unattractive and is so fragile that it often cracks apart in a short period of time. The feathered edge has so much surface area compared to its volume that it is vulnerable to moisture and thermal movement. It is also impossible to make a smoothly feathered edge in anything but very fine-grained plaster or drywall finishing compound. It does not work, for example, to try to create a feathered wash with mortar on top of a masonry chimney: The sand in the mortar is too coarse to feather, and the thin, insubstantial wash will soon crack and detach itself from the masonry. Instead, a chimney should be terminated with a reinforced concrete cap that has a clean, thick edge and a wash on the top (see **Wash**, Chapter 1).

2. Venture to make sharp edges on concrete only when the construction crew's control of concrete placement is of the highest caliber. Sharp edges in formwork often do not fill properly with concrete during pouring and are likely to be damaged when the formwork is stripped – an operation that takes place while the concrete is still weak and very brittle. Use chamfer or fillet inserts in the corners of formwork to eliminate sharp corners on concrete; even 90 degree corners are dangerous, unattractive, and difficult to execute well. They are also much more susceptible to damage during construction and occupancy. If sharp corners are required, then the concrete specification and placement methods must be adjusted to be sure that the concrete fills the tight corners. Coarse aggregate, low-workability concrete, and under-vibration can all result in voids rather than filled corners. Formwork removal must also be done cautiously to avoid damaging the vulnerable corners. Some damage is virtually certain, and even the best of repairs will be obvious to the eye.

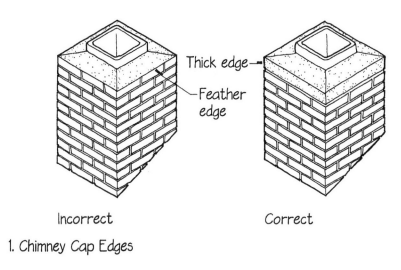

Incorrect — Correct

1. Chimney Cap Edges

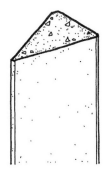
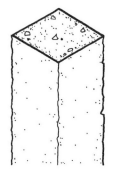
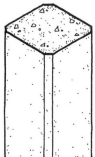

Incorrect: Sharp Edges — Correct: Chamfered Edges

2. Edge Details for Concrete

SECTION 2 ■ CONSTRUCTABILITY 209

3. Sharp angles on stonework and masonry are also unforgiving of minor construction mishaps and are very difficult to repair. Chamfered edges, rounded edges, quirk miters, and reveals are clean, forgiving edge details for sharp masonry corners. To create these types of corners in brickwork, specify specially molded or extruded brick shapes. Acute-angle corners that are woven of rectangular bricks have water-catching recesses that lead to premature deterioration. Bricks cut to an angle with a chisel or a saw have an unattractive and porous finish on the cut surface. Cut surfaces do not match the appearance of the uncut brick next to them in the wall, and are prone to spalling later.

4. Exposed edges of plaster, stucco, and gypsum board must always be bounded by appropriate casing beads and corner beads. These help the plasterer to maintain a constant thickness of wall and to create clean edges that join neatly to surrounding materials. There are many accessory strips manufactured in metal and plastic that the detailer can use to create crisp, cleanly finished reveals and joints in plaster surfaces. ■

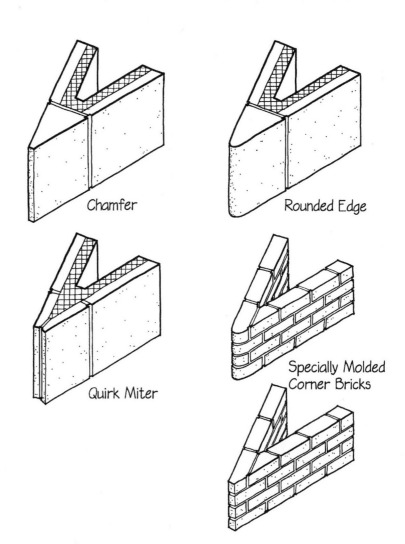

3. Clean Edges on Sharp Corners of Masonry

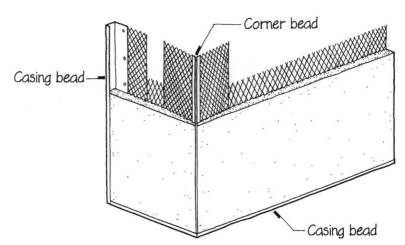

4. Clean Edges on Plaster and Stucco Surfaces

Progressive Finish

As a construction process progresses, each stage of work should be more finished than the stages that preceded it, and the installation of fine finishes should be delayed until as late in the construction process as possible.

1. Imagine two different ways of finishing the interior side of a wall of poured-in-place architectural concrete. One way is simply to form and pour the concrete very carefully and leave it exposed. The other is to form and pour the concrete somewhat less carefully and then, late in construction, furr its interior surface and add a finish layer of gypsum wallboard and paint.

The exposed concrete surface would seem to be the more direct, simple, secure, and economical option to choose, because it involves less material, fewer steps, and fewer trades. It is, however, a very unforgiving finish. Any defects in the formwork and ties, any inconsistencies in vibrating the concrete, any cold joints or slight differences in color between batches of concrete, and any staining or damage to the wall during subsequent stages of construction will be painfully obvious in the finished surface.

Using furring and gypsum wallboard, the concrete work can be done in a much less exacting way, and any subsequent construction damage to the concrete surface appearance will be of little consequence. After most construction operations are done and the wall is completely sheltered from the weather, the furring strips are mounted to the concrete, shimming if necessary to produce a plumb, flat surface. The wallboard is mounted, taped, spackled, sanded, and painted. Its junction with the floor is concealed behind a baseboard. Any last-minute damage to the gypsum wall, even if someone puts a wrench or a foot through it, can be repaired quickly and invisibly with drywall compound and paint. The overall cost of the concrete wall plus painted gypsum finish may be less than the overall cost of simply exposing the concrete wall. This is because the wall with a painted gypsum finish has been finished progressively rather than in a single, irrevocable step. The progression is from rough, crude structural surfaces to finer gypsum surfaces to very fine surfaces of paint, with the rough edge at the bottom covered by a baseboard.

Progressive finish involves successively better approximations of the degree of finish ultimately desired, and it delays the finer degrees of finish until as late as possible in the construction process, to avoid their being spoiled by rougher operations.

Of course, a painted gypsum surface does not possess the satisfying solidity and character of a well-made concrete wall. The client and the designer may prefer the concrete, and in that case they should have it, but they must recognize it is an unforgiving finish, expensive and risky to produce, and difficult to repair. It must be detailed, specified, supervised, and budgeted accordingly. ▷

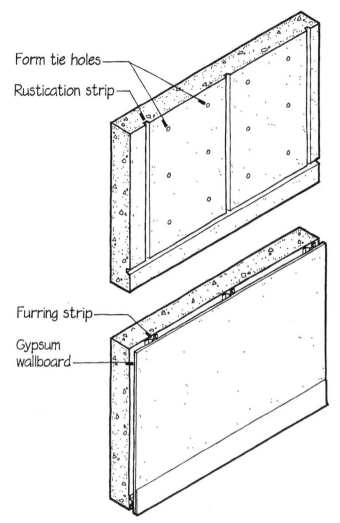

1. Exposed Concrete Versus Furred Gypsum Finish

2. Similarly, an exposed concrete slab is an unforgiving floor finish – one that should be used only if the designer is sure the contractor will have experienced, reliable, highly skilled concrete finishers to produce it. Even under these conditions, the slab is exposed to a considerable risk of damage or staining throughout the construction process. More forgiving and often less expensive overall is to cover the slab at the very end of the construction sequence with a material such as carpet, plastic tile, or ceramic tile.

3. Exposed ductwork, piping, and conduits can be attractive in their sculptural complexity, but they are not necessarily cheaper or easier overall than services concealed above a suspended ceiling. Additional expenses associated with exposed services include increased design time (to lay out attractive arrangements of the lines), increased fabrication and erection time (to allow for a higher standard of workmanship), durable covers for pipe and duct insulation, and painting. These extra expenses often add up to more than the total cost of a suspended ceiling. Fortunately, in many buildings, the extra money is available, and the blandness of the suspended ceiling can be avoided.

Some clients may tolerate or even prefer the informality and visual complexity of exposed building services. This also makes it easier to repair services or install new ones in the future. (see ***Maintenance Access***, Chapter 10)

4. Light frame construction in wood or metal is based on the idea of progressive finish. The rough, unattractive structure is erected first; then the exterior is finished; then the mechanical, electrical, and insulating work is done. The interior finishes come late in the process, covering the messiness of the frame and mechanical work and culminating in trim, flooring, paint, and wallpaper that cover all the preceding work in successive layers.

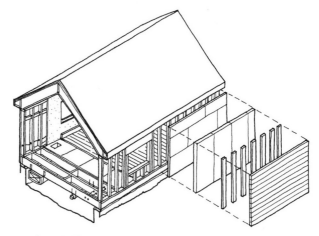

4. Layers in Light Frame Construction

5. Many contemporary buildings are made using conventional, inexpensive underlying materials, with much more refined and technically advanced materials covering them. A sleek metal rainscreen over a sitecast concrete wall, or a crisp glass and aluminum curtain wall over a fireproofed steel frame, are examples of this practice. In some cases, there is little similarity between the underlying materials and the outer surfaces. Independent of the aesthetic challenges this presents, the detailer needs to be vigilant to avoid potential conflicts in the physical properties of dissimilar materials and systems of construction. It is also important to anticipate the needs of various tradespeople, all layering their work over the work of those who came before them.

6. A potential disadvantage of using progressive finish is that initial stages of work may be executed casually and may contain flaws, and these flaws may be excused because later steps will cover them up. Standards of workmanship should be established and followed for all segments of construction, based upon objective criteria. For instance, spackling compound installed in a very large gap between adjoining sheets of gypsum board will likely shrink and crack noticeably as it dries, not fully correcting the underlying problem. Similarly, a rough and unsanded spackled wall surface should not be excused because it will later be painted. The painted surface will still be rough and irregular, and it will look unfinished.

7. Problems can occur when rough work comes after finished work. A mason laying the upper courses of brick in a wall can spill mortar into the cavity, permanently clogging the weeps that had been so well executed just an hour before. Changes in the owner's program partway through building construction may lead to a change order that calls for installed partitions to be removed and new ones configured. Moving a large and heavy conference table into office space can lead to damage of doorways and interior finishes. Identify tasks that are not progressing toward more refined conditions, and try to minimize their harm to completed work. ■

Forgiving Surface

Some types of finish surfaces make things easier for construction workers, because they conceal or camouflage small inaccuracies and blemishes.

1. Because of problems associated with working in the tiring, awkward overhead position, gypsum board workers and plasterers find it difficult to make a ceiling surface completely smooth and planar. There are almost always some slight flaws in the joints of gypsum board ceilings and minor blemishes in overhead plaster work. A textured finish on a ceiling can keep these imperfections from being detected, making the prior operations easier and more economical. A smooth-surfaced ceiling, especially one with a gloss paint on it, accentuates every defect.

2. Avoid lighting a smooth plaster surface with a window or a light fixture that casts light across it at a very sharp angle, because such light casts long shadows from otherwise insignificant flaws, making the surface look much worse than it really is. The same surface lit from an angle approaching 90 degrees will appear to be of perfect workmanship. Alternatively, a very rough-textured surface can be attractive when lit at an acute angle.

3. Concrete cast in formwork made of individual boards looks good, even if there are many flaws in the boards or bubbles in the concrete, because such defects become lost in the overall texture. Concrete

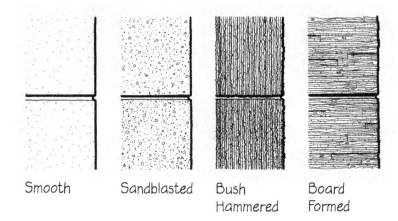

Smooth   Sandblasted   Bush Hammered   Board Formed

3. Different Concrete Finishes

cast against a smooth steel or plastic surface shows any defects prominently, and an attempt to patch them will only make them more blatant. Smooth, flat, uniform concrete is unforgiving and does not come easily. It is the result of extra efforts by designers, detailers, and craftspeople.

Almost any type of texture will work to hide defects in concrete: sandblasted, bush hammered, corrugated, or ribbed. Integral pigments in the concrete mix can conceal minor color variations when the wall is new and later as it weathers.

4. In a wall constructed of very precisely made bricks in a stack bond pattern, each brick must be laid with extreme care, because any slight dimensional misalignment of a brick will stand out from the rest of the pattern. Running bond or other bond patterns are more forgiving for the brickmason. Traditionally, bricks vary somewhat in size, color, and shape, and a wall made of such bricks is a richly textured tapestry in which minor misalignments only add to the visual interest. Minor variations in the wall are less apparent when the mortar color is similar to masonry unit colors.

5. A sheet of solid-color plastic laminate that has a small flaw in it may have to be discarded in the shop before being installed. A patterned laminate will camouflage many small scratches, spots, and dents. Forgiving surfaces of this sort are easier to maintain and may not need to be replaced as frequently. ■

CHAPTER  # Efficient Use of Construction Resources

Efficient use of construction resources often corresponds directly with a building's details. If not thoroughly considered from this point of view, a seemingly simple, straightforward detail can conceal endless problems in materials procurement, tool and machine utilization, construction scheduling, and even labor relations. Problems add time and cost money.

In this chapter, the focus is on utilization of *construction* resources, but this focus is within the larger imperative to use all resources efficiently. In many countries, the construction sector is the greatest source of landfill waste, and building operations are responsible for much of the energy consumption and carbon dioxide released to the atmosphere. Building design and detailing can contribute substantially to lowering these and other adverse by-products. Efficient use of construction resources will help address larger environmental, societal, and economic goals.

The detail patterns associated with efficient use of construction resources include the following:

> *Factory and Site* (p. 216)
> *Repetitious Fabrication* (p. 218)
> *Rehearsing the Construction Sequence* (p. 220)
> *Off-the-Shelf Parts* (p. 223)
> *Local Skills and Resources* (p. 224)
> *Aligning Forms with Forces* (p. 226)
> *Refining the Detail* (p. 229)
> *All-Weather Construction* (p. 230)
> *Pride of Craftsmanship* (p. 232)
> *Accepted Standards* (p. 233)

Architectural Detailing: Function Constructability Aesthetics. Fourth Edition. Patrick Rand, Jason Miller, and Edward Allen.
© 2025 John Wiley & Sons, Inc. Published 2025 by John Wiley & Sons, Inc.

Factory and Site

In-factory work and on-site work each has associated advantages and disadvantages. An important task of the detailer is to allocate the work of making a building thoughtfully between the two for optimum construction speed, quality, and cost.

1. In the factory, the weather is always dry, and temperatures are always comfortable. Lighting is good, large machines and tools with impressive capabilities and extreme accuracy can be utilized, and workers can work in comfortable and safer postures. Hourly wages for factory workers are substantially lower than for on-site workers, and worker productivity is higher, because of the factors mentioned earlier in this paragraph. Elements and subassemblies can be checked for quality before they become part of the building. But the sizes and weights of the components created by the factory are restricted by the dimensions and capacities of trucks or other transport methods, as well as the particular condition or location of the project site.

On the jobsite, the weather and available light vary greatly in quality. Tools and infrastructure resources are not as sophisticated. Access to the work is not always ideal. Hourly wages are higher, and productivity ranges from high to low, depending on weather, light, tools, and access. Very large assemblies can be created onsite, unconstrained by transport limitations. Local sourcing often reduces environmental impact and may help earn credits in sustainable design rating systems. Assemblies can be monolithic and built to actual required size and shape, which is a particular advantage in renovation work.

2. At the relatively small scale of a custom-designed house, the optimum mix of factory and site operations is well established. Building form and layout operations, such as foundations, framing, roofing, siding, and insulating are done on the site, using simple factory-produced components, such as formwork panels, masonry blocks, dimension lumber, wood panel products, shingles, and insulation batts. Windows and doors, which require high precision and exacting finishes,

3. Factory-Made Wall Assemblies

are not made on-site but are ordered as prefabricated units from factories. Electrical wiring, plumbing, and heating and cooling networks are installed on-site, but such exacting components as light fixtures, faucets, ductwork, furnaces, boilers, convectors, and registers are factory made. Finish surfaces for ceilings, walls, and floors are installed on-site, using factory-produced panel products in many cases. Interior doors and cabinetry are made as units in factories and simply nailed or screwed into the house. In general, the smaller, highly precise, highly finished components are made in the factory and installed, while the larger elements of the building are created on-site from simple, easily fitted pieces of factory-made materials.

3. In many larger buildings, the choices may not be so obvious. Should a concrete frame be precast or sitecast? Should a building be clad with brickwork or stonework that is assembled on the site, or should it be clad with factory-made panels? Should partitions be constructed on-site, or should they be interchangeable prefabricated panels? These are complex choices that involve the entire building design team. In projects using an integrated design and delivery model, the construction team can provide valuable insight on these choices based on current market costs, product availabilities, and logistics strategies for the specific jobsite.

4. At one time, only truly mass-produced items were manufactured at a factory. Now there are at least three categories of factory production (see Table 13-1). One is the familiar mass-production using traditional analog mechanisms to produce thousands or even millions of identical artifacts, which are cataloged and warehoused for later use in an unspecified project. Rolled steel shapes, aluminum extrusions, and dimension lumber are common examples of this method.

A second manufacturing method exploits computer-aided manufacturing (CAM) to produce customized variations of the same basic artifact quickly and economically. Examples include CNC (computer numeric controlled) mechanisms, which can be subtractive, such as laser, water-jet, and plasma cutters; routers; drills; punches; robotic mills, and so forth. CNC mechanisms may also be additive, such as 3D printers, selective laser sintering, and welders. Or they can be transformative tools, which are those that reshape a material, such as wire benders and sheet metal rollers and stampers. CNC processes can be economical because, once programmed with the digital design, they can produce multiple unique artifacts without loss of speed.

TABLE 13-1: Factory Production Methods

	Mass Production	Computer-Aided Manufacturing (CAM)/mass customization	Customized Repetitive Manufacturing (CRM)
Mechanism or tools	Traditional analog	Digital CNC; can be subtractive, additive, or transformative	Either analog or digital CNC; may use CNC to produce forms for analog processes
Relation between mechanism and artifacts	Mechanism directly produces artifacts	CNC mechanism directly produces artifacts	CNC mechanism produces intermediate tool used to produce artifacts
Durability of machinery/ Durability of tools	High/medium	High/low; same machinery and tools used to make many different artifacts	Varies; sufficient durability for given project
Cost of machinery/ Cost of tools	Medium/low	Medium to high/low	Low to medium/low to medium
Volume of same items in run	Large volume; may be unlimited (at least 1000s)	Very small volume (1 to 1000)	Low to mid volume (10s to 1000s)
Relation between design and making	Intermediate steps required (shop drawings, prototypes, etc.)	Can be direct (digital file sent to CNC machine)	Varies depending on whether analog or digital or both are used
Relation between manufacturing and specific building project	Indirect	Direct; made for specific project	Direct; made for specific project
Repeatability of artifact produced	High	None to low	Medium to high

A third manufacturing method is customized repetitive manufacturing (CRM), which makes optimal use of both traditional analog and digital methods to produce repetitive artifacts of limited runs, typically for a single building project. CRM methods may use a CNC machine to produce a custom mold, which is used to produce a few hundred wall cladding panels or ceiling coffers for a single building, after which the mold is recycled. Compared to mass-production processes, CRM methods can use less durable and less costly means of production because the volume of manufactured artifacts is relatively small.

5. Some projects involve a high degree of integration of factory and site production, calling for increased collaborations among architects, contractors, and product engineers. New materials or products may be developed for use in a particular building, such as a novel metal cladding system or a glass skin that uses an innovative braced frame to hold it in place. Technically sophisticated, factory-made assemblies such as these may be delivered to the site for installation by specialized crews trained by the wall system manufacturer.

6. In-factory work generally involves greater capacity for precision, speed, and replication than on-site work. However, exceptions exist: advanced technology is sometimes present at the construction site, and work at factories is sometimes carried out using archaic yet still optimal means. For instance, at the construction site, building elements may be guided into place to within millimeters of their intended location using global positioning system (GPS) surveying. At the factory, specially shaped bricks are still made by placing freshly formed, unfired "green" bricks into a wooden box the shape of the intended brick, then having a worker manually pull a piece of piano wire through the clay to cut off any portion protruding from the box. Both of these are appropriate levels of technology, meeting the specific criteria for accuracy, speed, volume, and cost unique to each task. ∎

Repetitious Fabrication

Buildings are made of countless components, each of which is produced using processes intended to balance product qualities with fabrication efficiency. Repetitive fabrication processes generally increase both quality and efficiency, because greater investment can be made in the fabrication process and its required infrastructure; this economy of scale investment is prorated over many products to reduce the per-unit cost.

1. When physical properties of a component must consistently meet a high standard – for example, a piece of structural steel or an optically perfect piece of laminated glass – considerable investment is made in a manufacturing process that is used over and over again, yielding products that are consistent in almost every way. Regulatory and pre-installation performance standards for many construction materials and assemblies are met because the manufacturing and fabrication processes used to produce them are controlled and repetitive. When fabricated to the same sizes, the pieces are uniform in appearance, interchangeable, and easy to fit into assemblies with standardized details (see *Repetitious Assembly*, Chapter 11).

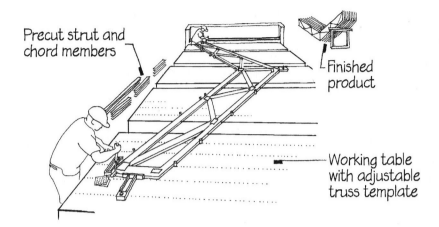

2. Limited Run of Wood Truss Fabrication

2. Mass-production manufacturing facilities have long used repetitive fabrication methods to boost quality and reduce per-unit costs. Off-site fabricators of wood trusses adapt repetitive fabrication concepts to limited runs of trusses for a given project. Pre-cut strut and chord elements making up a truss are stored next to a template/jig that guides the positioning of each piece prior to joining them all together with toothed plates. When one run of trusses is completed, the program for cutting struts and chords is changed, and the template is configured for the next design. Glue-laminated timber manufacturers similarly carry out limited runs for a particular project.

Aluminum composite cladding panels, stenciled precast concrete wall panels, and custom-fitted glazing products are fabricated off-site according to the requirements for each particular project. Pieces for a given project are typically produced from stock supplies in limited runs for which the fabricator uses templates or mechanical aids to guide the making of each piece.

3. Concrete masonry units are mass-produced by the thousands in almost identical units; after curing, these units are split into two or more pieces. The split faces vary in appearance and shape, but the process used to produce them is highly repetitive. The manufacturer may repeat the use of the mold box to make thousands more units of the same shape with a different color or texture simply by altering the concrete mix.

4. On-site processes also gain efficiency by making fabrication processes repetitive. Cages of steel reinforcing bars for cast-in-place concrete columns are typically laid out and wire-tied on a jig at ground level; then, the cage is moved into place and wrapped by formwork. Flying formwork for a cast-in-place concrete waffle slab are also often repetitively laid out at ground level, then lifted by crane into place for the next pour. Used formwork is lowered back to ground level for quick cleaning and repair, in preparation for the next use. Work is more productive and safer when steps are repeated in a familiar, predictable, and controlled workplace.

Complex wiring and plumbing assemblies designed for dozens of hospital rooms are sometimes repetitively preassembled at the construction site on a template, then moved into place as the headwall in each patient room.

Stick-built curtain wall assemblies are sometimes fabricated into panels on-site, using precut aluminum extrusions, glass panels, gaskets, and connecting hardware shipped there by the various manufacturers. The "kit of parts" pieces are assembled in a routine manner to yield components that are standardized for the project, meet close tolerances, and are produced with lower transportation costs than if unitized methods had been used. Component fabrication can take place at the jobsite under cover on bad-weather days, giving the construction team an alternative way to be productive. ∎

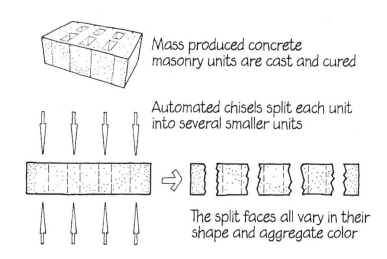

3. Repetitive Manufacturing Process to make Varied Products

Rehearsing the Construction Sequence

The act of designing and drawing a detail should be based on a mental process that rehearses the sequence in which the detail will be assembled on the building site. Building a detail drawing step by step in accordance with the order of construction helps identify and solve problems before they become problems in the field. This approach is equally applicable to assembling large prefabricated panels or crafting small connections between different materials.

1. In the mind of a construction manager or worker, a detail drawing should create a vivid, dynamic picture of actual materials, fasteners, tools, and operations. From the detail drawing, the builder should be able to visualize a logical and workable process for assembling that part of the building. A good habit for the detailer to develop is to design and draw each detail in the order in which its pieces are assembled, thinking simultaneously of the actual construction operations that are represented by each new element of the drawing and trying to see the detail not as an object but as a process, which is how the builder will see it. This creates the opportunity for the detailer to rehearse the construction sequence mentally, searching for better ways of doing things, identifying potential challenges, and looking for components that will not go together easily on the construction jobsite. For important details and elaborate assemblies, the detailer might sketch out, for their own enlightenment and scrutiny, a series of drawings that show the assembly sequence step by step. If the detailer is using digital drawing or modeling methods, each step could be a different layer of the drawing or component in the model. In cases where an entirely new and unfamiliar construction sequence is required, these sequential illustrations should be cleaned up and used as part of the construction drawings.

To a beginning detailer, a detail drawing may appear almost as an abstraction possessing little meaning in terms of the actual materials,

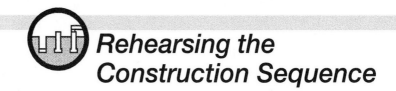

Step 1
Wall frame is erected

Step 2
Upper floor is framed

Step 3
Upper floor wall frame is erected, sheathing and siding are applied

(sequence continues on next page)

1. Rehearsing the Construction Sequence of a Wood-Frame Dwelling: Steps 1–3

tools, and processes required. Through office experience, reading, and jobsite visits, the beginner should acquire as quickly as possible a critical base of knowledge of what details really mean in the assembly of a building and what their impact on a builder will be.

This knowledge base is never complete and will grow throughout the detailer's career; the hardest part is to get a strong enough start in this learning process to become a fully effective designer of realistic details. Rehearsing the construction sequence mentally when drawing each detail can help materially in this education.

2. When rehearsing the construction sequence, look for signs of inefficiency, such as excessive numbers of separate trades, repeated visits by the same trade, and connections that workers and their tools cannot get to (*Accessible Connections*, Chapter 11). Also look for lack of temporary support for components, lack of alignment references, fitting problems (see *Sliding Fit*, Chapter 12), and risks of damage to previously completed work by gouging, scratching, or staining (see *Progressive Finish*, Chapter 12).

Strive for a detail that requires a minimum number of trades and visits per trade, uses sliding fits only, needs little or no temporary support, requires no special tools, and has a minimal need for ladders or scaffolding – in short, a detail that will go together like clockwork. ▷

Step 4
Wiring, insulation, and vapor retarder are added; walls are plastered

Step 5
Flooring is installed

Step 6
Detail is completed with baseboard

1. Rehearsing the Construction Sequence of a Wood-Frame Dwelling: Steps 4-6

3. Rehearsal of a construction sequence can often reveal hidden problems with a detail that initially appeared satisfactory. Consider this detail for a recessed wood baseboard. It looks like a clean, contemporary detail that will be easy to build using standard components. But rehearse the construction sequence: Normally, the gypsum wallboard and its casing bead are installed first. Then the flooring is laid, and lastly the baseboard is installed. This means that the baseboard must be fitted precisely between two parallel planes, which is difficult (see *Sliding Fit*, Chapter 12). If the surface of the hardwood floor is at all wavy (which is likely; see *Dimensional Tolerance*, Chapter 12) or if the casing bead of the wallboard is not perfectly straight and level (also likely), fitting the baseboard between them will be a nightmare – costly in terms of time and worker morale. Changing the construction sequence to install the flooring and baseboard before the wallboard risks damage to the flooring and makes the floor sanding and varnishing more difficult. Precisely dimensioned wood blocks could be used as temporary gauges to locate the casing bead at the proper height above the subfloor, but this would not prevent difficulties arising from waviness of the subfloor or finish floor. This is fundamentally a bad detail – one that will be expensive and troublesome. It may not even look very good when finished because of varying crack dimensions between the baseboard and the edge bead, and because of deviations from the intended perfect alignment of the faces of the gypsum and baseboard.

4. The recessed baseboard detail could be improved somewhat by adding a deep reveal to the upper edge of the baseboard, to create a dark shadow that would conceal a variable crack width at that location.

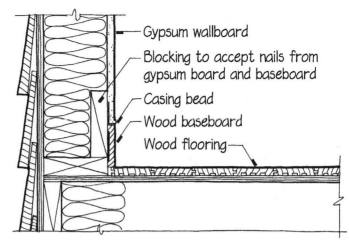

3. Recessed Baseboard: Original Version

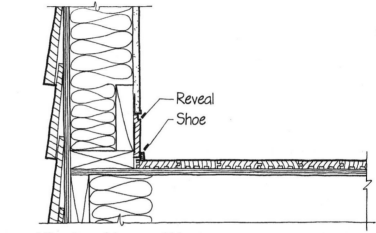

4. Recessed Baseboard: Improved Version

The addition of a shoe molding would conform easily to the contours of the floor and allow a generous installation clearance for the baseboard.

5. Drawing the construction sequence in this manner represents clearly the materials, tools, and processes used to make the building initially. The reality is that this is just the *beginning* of the building's service life (see *Life Cycle* and *Expected Life*, Chapter 10). Additional drawings could rehearse the processes of maintaining and renovating the building. Finally, the last drawing in the series would be the deconstruction process, with salvageable and recyclable materials easily separated from waste materials (see *Detailing for Disassembly*, Chapter 11). ■

Off-the-Shelf Parts

Using readily available materials and components makes construction easier. Construction project scheduling is more difficult when materials or components are not off-the-shelf products.

1. Certain building components are commonly available almost everywhere. The builder of a tract house can make a single telephone call to a materials supplier, and the next morning a truck will arrive at the construction site and leave behind every component needed to construct and sheathe the frame: lumber, wood panels, nails, air and water barriers, and even shingles, siding, windows, and doors. Interior finish components are equally available. But sometimes just one special component can cause the whole process to break down. Suppose the design details and specifications call for a new, improved kind of air-barrier paper that has just come on the market. Suppose further that no one verified if the new product was locally available, and it is not. Because the specification is prescriptive rather than performance-based, the builder orders the paper from a distant supplier, and it takes several weeks to arrive. Meanwhile, the construction process has to stop, because the siding cannot be applied until the air-barrier paper is there. This causes unnecessary and costly delays.

The moral of this not-so-hypothetical story is simple: If speed and ease of construction are the highest priorities, do not use anything but standard, off-the-shelf products. Regional differences may exist regarding which components are commonly available in a given market, so it is prudent to check *local* suppliers or provide flexibility in product selection by specifying performance requirements.

2. If there is a strong reason to do otherwise, make a preliminary phone call or two to establish availability of the nonstandard product. If necessary, work directly with the builder or contractor to be sure the product is ordered well in advance of need, and be ready to specify an acceptable alternative product if supply problems persist and construction delays loom. Do not be afraid to use new products but be aware of potential supply problems. A good detailer does their part to solve potential supply problems before they occur. And a voice of experience: Do not try too many new products on the same project, or these logistical problems may multiply.

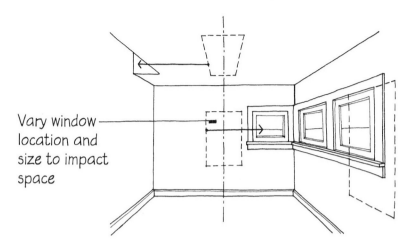

Vary window location and size to impact space

3. Conventionally Detailed Products Used in Novel Ways

3. Some architects use off-the-shelf parts in novel or unusual ways, gaining the advantages of stock products without sacrificing aesthetics and functionality. Simply placing an industrial lighting fixture or stair tread into a residential setting can meet function and budget objectives with an interesting solution. Excessive heat gain through a skylight may be addressed by mounting above the glass a stock piece of perforated corrugated metal, rather than fabricating a custom louver system. Even a conventionally detailed window can have a noticeable and positive impact on a space if it is twice or half the size of conventional usage.

4. A stock item can sometimes be customized on the construction site to create a fresh aesthetic effect without altering its functionality or complicating the installation process. It is easy, for example, to saw wood trim pieces to different widths, treating the eye to a new proportion, or to use a router to give the trim pieces new edge profiles.

5. Many important building elements are not actually stock items; that is, they are not made in advance, waiting for purchase. Steel and precast structural elements, wood trusses, glass and aluminum curtain wall systems, and large mechanical units are not produced until the order is received. It is wise to contact fabricators and find out what lead times will be, and ask about the availability of particular materials the project will need. Asking these types of questions in the earliest stages of an integrated design process can have a tremendous impact on the project's design direction and constructed solution. In a global marketplace, demand for certain materials may spike, spurring higher costs and longer lead times. For instance, a steel column made using a wide-flange section may require more lead time for a fabricator than one made of a tube section, simply because the basic wide-flange sections are on back order from the manufacturer.

Small orders of steel elements may take a surprisingly long time to be fulfilled by a fabricator, because small, less profitable orders are vulnerable to being bumped in the sequence by large, more profitable orders.

Local Skills and Resources

Building details should reflect knowledge of the labor force and material resources used to construct the building.

1. Know what kind of contractors and workforce will be executing a building's details. When asked a few years ago to design a new building and pavilions for a school in a remote forest in the Pacific Northwest, the architect developed details in such a way that it could be framed with logs and heavy timbers by a crew of loggers using chain saws and axes. The details were worked out from the beginning with this in mind, and the constructed buildings are not only handsome but also have a unique character that is created in large part by the unusual details. This may be an extreme example, but the premise remains sound whether the building is being detailed for do-it-yourself homeowners, volunteer laborers, or small contractors who have only rudimentary tools and equipment. Sometimes the jobsite will be remote from power lines, so the building's details should not require so many electrically driven tools that they will overload a portable generator. Conversely, if the project will likely bring together a pool of creative, skilled craftspeople, consider including in the design features that will display their talents. Drawings and specifications assume all builders are equally capable of executing the project, but this is seldom true. Many architects and builders work together on successive projects because they form a productive, complementary, and understanding team.

2. Sometimes the project location presents constraints. For instance, if potable water will not be available on the jobsite until construction is well along, then the early stages of construction must be designed to require as little clean water as possible.

Sometimes the project location presents special opportunities. For example, if there are local sources of relatively inexpensive stone, brick, glue-laminated wood, precast concrete, or perforated stainless steel cladding, perhaps the design should include them to take advantage of that proximity. The local labor force is likely to be familiar with local materials, so the necessary skills will also be available at a reasonable cost. Be prepared to adapt the design to constraints and opportunities associated with the location.

3. It is important to be familiar in advance with local labor practices. Are the building trades unionized, and, if so, what are the union rules regarding jurisdictions and work practices? Does a particular mason's union, for example, specify the maximum weight of masonry unit that a mason can handle alone? Which union has jurisdiction over installing stone cladding panels on a steel truss backing – the ironworkers or the masons? If the trades are not unionized, what are their usual ways of going about things? Try to detail in such a way that the labor force will have no trouble dividing the work among the trades and can follow their usual practices.

4. Builders in various regions have their own customary ways of doing things. In some areas of North America, most residential foundation walls are made of poured concrete, and, in other areas, they are made of concrete blocks. The predominant material in any one area is usually cheaper, and a larger group of competing subcontractors is familiar with its use. Steel fabricators in some areas prefer to bolt even their shop-fabricated connections, while others like to weld them. Certain regions have excellent stucco contractors, whereas others do not. The same is true of tile roofing installers, wood shake installers, and several other trades. Do not restrict a project or its details to these customs in every instance, but exploit them whenever feasible and practical. Conversely, when the design runs counter to the prevailing labor customs, be prepared to do the additional work necessary to help line up subcontractors and materials.

5. Local wisdom is not always correct. Common practice in a given location may simply be the residue of countless ad hoc episodes over many years and may not actually constitute good practice. The saying, "What is good is not always popular, and what is popular is not always good," may apply here. The construction industry changes constantly as new knowledge, materials, and regulations alter the way buildings are designed, constructed, and maintained. Many practices once permitted by the building codes are not permitted now. Standards of acceptable practice evolve because manufacturers change product features, and technical improvements result from recent research. Tolerances and standards of workmanship in the construction trades may evolve in step with these changes.

The detailer is expected to incorporate relevant current conditions into the design. Part of every built project is the give and take between architect and builder regarding what each believes to be the best practice. The architect initiates this dialogue and ultimately is responsible for concluding it after considering a wide array of sources.

6. Not only are there differences in the relevant codes and ordinances from one city to another, but there are also slight differences in how they are enforced. Do not assume that a code interpretation granted in one jurisdiction will be honored in another. When uncertain whether a detail is going to be acceptable, look for precedents in the area and contact the appropriate officials.

7. If unfamiliar with customary practices in the area, invest some time in visiting construction sites or recently completed buildings comparable to the one you are designing. Architects may also collaborate professionally with local counterparts to tap into this kind of local wisdom.

8. Local builders may be hired as consultants during the design development phase of the architect's work, in an effort to fully integrate local skills and customs into the construction documents. The cost of this consultant is often offset by reduced construction bid prices. Builders inflate their bids if they are uncertain about the materials or methods to be used. Drawings and specifications that present the project in terms the builders understand will generally be rewarded with lower costs – and better quality.

9. Sustainable design objectives can be addressed by using local construction materials and assemblies. The environmental impact of building construction can be reduced when transport distances are reduced. Common rating system credits can be earned when materials are extracted and manufactured from within a prescribed distance from the construction site. In some rating systems, the allowable travel distances vary depending on the means of transportation used to convey the materials, allowing a greater distance if the means of transport has a lower environmental impact.

If a project is intended to earn such credits, it is important for the designer to follow the particular rating system's methods of calculation, because they are sometimes complicated. The most effective strategy to earn the credit is to place a priority on locally sourcing a few "big ticket" (high percentage of construction costs) materials and assemblies, making up the building and to verify that these sources are within the radius called for by the rating system. Some manufacturers assist designers in preparing documentation regarding extraction and manufacturing distances needed to earn these credits. ■

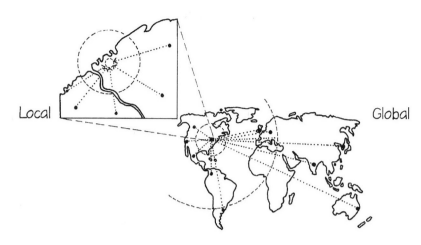

9. Local Sourcing of Materials Can Reduce Environmental Impact

Aligning Forms with Forces

The most efficient way for forces to be transferred is to flow directly through forms. Aligning elements with the forces they bear can reduce the size and mass of the assembly. This principle applies at all scales, not only to a building's primary structural systems, but to all parts of its assemblies. Even minor elements such as a stair, a cabinet, or a chair should embody this principle to support themselves and their imposed loads.

1. The trajectory of forces through a form can shape structural elements and guide material selection, resulting in a building that uses materials wisely and expresses the way those materials work. A thorough discussion of architectural structures is beyond the scope of this book; however, it is useful to address the substantial amounts of construction resources that make up the structural system of a building. Rational awareness of force paths can reduce material quantities, which reduces costs and environmental impact.

For the same reason the smallest and the largest spans of a building are not constructed to the same depth. A combination of intuition and rational analysis can be used to create forms that deploy material resources to meet – but not substantially exceed – what is needed.

2. Surface-active structural systems such as folded plates, vaults, domes, and shells are most efficient when shaped to match the trajectory of forces. These structural forms redirect external forces to a path that aligns with the shape of the surface. Any openings in these surfaces are shaped and positioned to allow forces to flow around them without abrupt changes in direction.

3. A concrete joist slab and waffle slab are more efficient than a solid flat plate because they channel forces through ribs and reduce material where it is not needed. The articulated slabs place more material farther from the neutral axis, improving their strength to self-weight ratio.

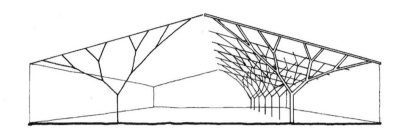

1. Efficient Structural Forms Align Materials with Forces

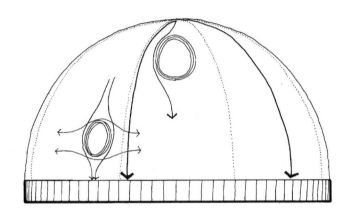

2. Forces Align with Dome Surfaces and Flow Around Openings

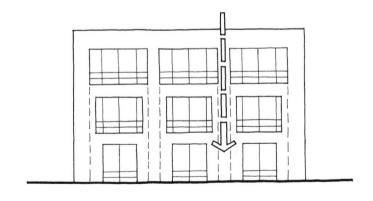

3. Forces Align and Taper in Load-Bearing Walls

Cantilevered beams and slabs can taper like a tree branch toward the extent of their reach, where the loads are less. Similarly, the thickness of reinforced concrete or masonry walls and columns can diminish with height in a multistory building, expressing lesser loads and conserving materials.

4. When forces are aligned with the structural line or plane (column or wall) that supports them, the element is simpler to design and is less massive than when forces are eccentric or out of plane. A multistory orthogonal structure will be lighter and more efficient if its columns or walls are aligned vertically, because deep transfer beams will not be needed. Construction of the building will be simpler, and details between structure and enclosure can be standardized.

Where vertical forces through continuous columns are interrupted, trusses or inclined columns will likely transfer loads more efficiently than a horizontal beam. Trusses are composed of elements bearing only axial loads in tension and compression vectors. Trusses are typically less bulky than beams and perform the structural span with less self-weight. This principle is also applied to space frames, geodesic domes, diagrids, lattice, and tensile structures. Doing more with less remains a vital objective in design at all scales.

5. Frames typically carry given loads with less mass and volume of material than a load-bearing wall system. But columns that are inclined off the plumb line lose their efficiency the more they deviate from the vertical. The weight of steel in a simple braced frame almost doubles if the columns are 20 degrees from vertical. Columns of precast or cast-in-place concrete are even less efficient when inclined, because their self-weight (dead load) is even more substantial than that of steel. Heroic cantilevers and gratuitous inclined frames may seem to express structure, but if they do so irrationally, they waste materials and resources. Deflection and creep of these frames may also result in long-term movement, which may harm adjoining assemblies and materials. Architectural expression need not waste resources. Quite to the contrary, the insightful display of efficiency, structurally or otherwise, may be a genuine source of architectural expression. ▷

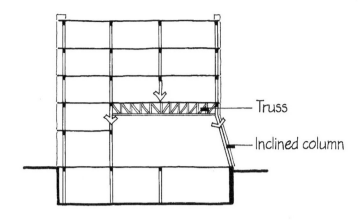

4. Transfer of Forces in a Conventional Structural Frame

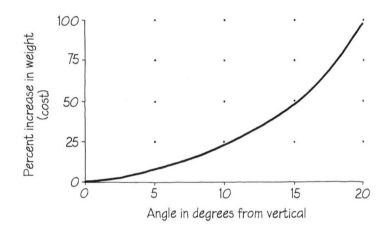

5. Inclined Steel Frame Increases Cost

6. A platform-framed residence can be built using only 15% of the wood volume needed to build the same-size house using traditional log construction. The volume of materials is reduced significantly by milling logs into lumber and by putting materials where forces exist and not elsewhere. The advanced framing technique (also called "optimum value engineering") goes a step further. In this system, studs, joists, rafters, and trusses all share a 24 in. (610 mm) spacing, and, more importantly, all are aligned vertically. This eliminates the need for double top plates, which serve as small transfer beams in unaligned frames. Eliminating deep headers above windows and doors in non–load-bearing walls, and swapping metal clips and hangers for jack studs and some studs at corners, also reduce lumber needs. The reduced volume of wood in outer envelopes leaves more space for thermal insulation, decreasing heat train through lumber and increasing overall thermal performance. Careful planning and coordination of the frame is needed, but reductions in labor and lumber of up to 25% can result.

7. Awareness of the trajectory of forces through an assembly cues the designer to place materials of sufficient strength and volume in proportion to stress concentrations. Correspondingly, where stresses are low or nonexistent, materials can be thin, weak, or even omitted. Understanding forces will

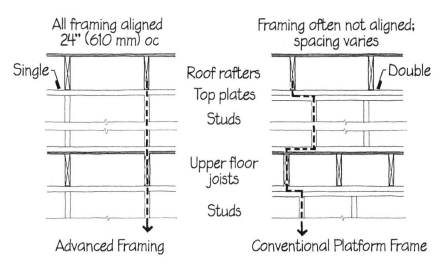

6. Alternative Light Wood Frames: Gravity Forces Compared

inform the design of structural systems, will help determine where interior spaces can be large, and where openings in walls can be located with minimal harm.

8. Aligning forms with forces is a means of reducing the mass of a building, which may help reach several sustainability objectives. All building materials come with an embodied energy "cost," which varies with each material, but by reducing the volume or mass of materials used to make the building, one can address this important environmental measure. Buildings designed with tectonic frames are typically rather open spatially, which may be advantageous regarding daylighting and ventilation. Skeletal frames may also be more adaptable to future changes in the building's functional program, which may result in a longer building life with reduced renovation burdens.

Designers must inform themselves in order to make appropriate choices for a project. Countless solutions exist between construction systems that are composed of fewer, leaner, high-tech, high-performance materials versus those that are denser, more solid but perhaps lower in environmental or economic cost. ∎

Refining the Detail

Even good details can be improved and refined. Familiar or stock solutions have limits, and limited value, especially when addressing new circumstances. The concept "Truth through making" (*verum ipsum factum*, Latin) recognizes that even a well-conceived detail is not fully understood until it is made.

1. Details are where the architect's and the builder's shared interests in quality converge. Craftspeople are excellent resources for the detailer. Their knowledge of construction materials and processes is intimate, and they often have insights about the detail that benefit the architect. Observe them as they work, make note of what things they do easily and well, and what things give them problems. Speak to builders to see if they have any suggestions about how a detail could be improved or more easily built. In short: Curiosity and communication contribute to the development of effective details.

2. In some offices, the designer and detailer may never visit the construction site, resulting in an unfortunate disconnect between design intent and construction reality. It is important to establish a routine process through which comments about details can be conveyed from the construction site back to the office, providing a needed feedback loop through which the details can be improved. The person from the office who is responsible for construction administration should prepare specific notes regarding materials, details, and specifications that were found especially successful or unsuccessful during the construction phase. These notes should be reviewed by designers, detailers, and specifications writers as a point of reference for future projects.

3. Like design in general, detailing is an iterative process. Whether in the office, at the fabricator's shop, or at the construction site, look actively for opportunities to make the detail better. Refinement through sample panels and mockups, even refinement as parts of the building are constructed, should be encouraged as the natural completion of the design and construction process. Changes to a planned detail must advance the detail's basic architectural intentions. Changes detrimental to the architectural intentions are not refinements, no matter how beneficial they may be to the project schedule or costs.

4. Never hastily discard a carefully thought-out detail because a builder or supplier thinks an alternative is better. Listen to the alternative, but also take the time to thoroughly consider its implications for and influences on other aspects of the project. Substitutions sometimes have secondary effects on adjoining elements, functional aspects, or finished appearance that are not obvious initially.

5. Each completed building offers a learning laboratory for the detailer. It is often gratifying and enlightening to revisit projects years after occupancy, to observe the performance of materials and details. Some owners may even be willing to invest in a formal post-occupancy evaluation, or POE, of construction systems at intervals as part of their maintenance program. The owner may incorporate these evaluations into the maintenance schedule and projected service life tiers for the building (see ***Expected Life***, Chapter 10). The detailer can assemble a manual of successful details that have been refined through use, ready for further improvement in the next project.

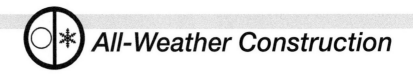

All-Weather Construction

TABLE 13-2: Weather Conditions Suitable for the Application of Selected Materials.

Masonry products shown on left / Paint products shown on right

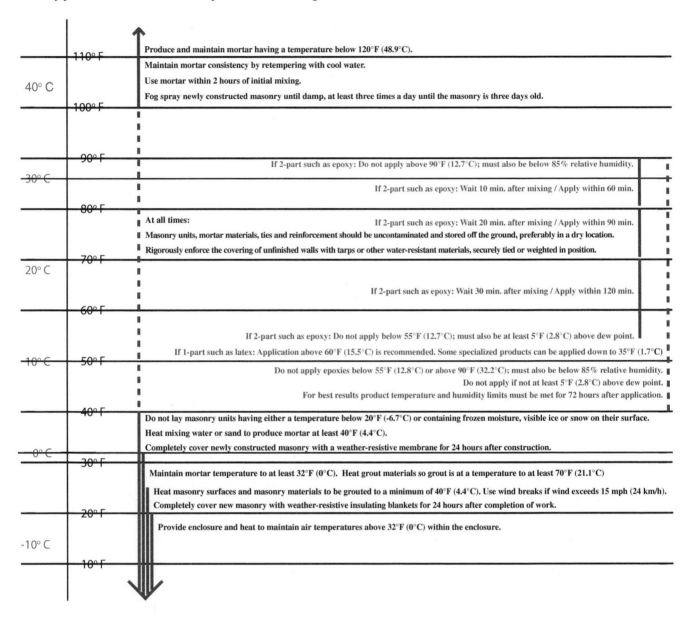

Based on Brick Industry Association TECHNICAL NOTES on Brick Construction:
#1 "Cold and Hot Weather Construction"; June 2018
#7b "Water Penetration Resistance - Construction and Workmanship"; November 2017

Based on multiple sources, including Sherwin-Williams:
"Exterior: Product Application FAQs"; January 2024
"Epoxy Coatings Guide"; January 2024

Details should be designed with due consideration to the weather sensitivities of the various construction operations and the time of year when those operations are likely to occur.

1. Certain construction operations are very weather sensitive. Low-slope membrane roofing cannot be installed over a wet roof deck, but a low-slope standing seam metal roof can be. Exterior painting should not take place under rainy conditions, hot windy conditions, or cold conditions; this may indicate that prefinished exterior materials are preferable for certain projects. Concrete and masonry work can

be problematic in very hot or very cold weather, which might lead the designer to select a precast concrete, steel, or heavy timber system if extreme temperatures are anticipated during construction. Stucco work cannot be done in very low temperatures, but precast concrete panels can still be placed.

2. Carefully review the manufacturer's application instructions for all materials; call upon product representatives to assist in specifying the best product for the circumstances anticipated.

Table 13-2 provides examples of the ways weather conditions relate to two common material applications. On the left side is a summary of instructions from the clay masonry industry about brick construction in various weather conditions. These instructions are driven by the conditions needed for cement-based mortar in the masonry assemblies to cure properly and for the finished construction to be free of unwanted biological or chemical threats.

On the right in the table is a summary of parameters from paint manufacturers about the application of one- and two-part paint coatings. Paint is ideally applied to clean, dry surfaces in moderate temperatures and low humidity. But these conditions are not common on many construction sites and in some locations may not exist outdoors for many months of the year. Keep in mind that the temperature parameters apply not only to the ambient air temperature but also to the temperature of surfaces to which the paint is applied, and to the paint in the bucket. If these conditions are not met, the paint may be impossible to apply, it may vary in color or sheen, it may peel or blister, and it may have a very short service life.

Early in the morning, building surfaces may still be too cool or damp with dew. Paint applied late in the afternoon may be fouled by condensation after dusk. Experienced painters "follow the sun" to avoid applying paint in direct sunlight or on surfaces that the sun will strike soon after application; this avoids the heating and premature drying that sunlight would cause. Some of the parameters shown here for paint may also be applicable to other surface finishes that take time to mature.

3. Fluid-applied compounds, peel-and-stick sheets, and adhesive tapes are increasingly relied upon in air and water barriers, vapor retardant layers, flashing, and many other applications (see **Air Barrier System**, Chapter 2). Installation of these products must be to surfaces that are clean and free of grease, dirt, and other contaminants; otherwise, the products will not bond properly, which they must do for the life of the building. Many products also require that surfaces be within a specified temperature range and must be dry. Most note that they must be kept dry for some specified time after application. When products are layered over one another, installers must allow time for full drying, curing, or solvent release in underlying layers before applying the next layer. Warranties are void if manufacturer's instructions are not followed. Repairs of control layers are almost impossible to carry out because finishes conceal the critical details.

4. Few field-applied materials are mature immediately upon application. For many materials, several hours, days, or sometimes weeks are required in order for the product to reach full performance criteria. Lower temperatures often slow the curing or drying time needed. Until that time, it is vulnerable to harm. Exterior applications are most vulnerable because they are most exposed, but even interior finishes are sometimes applied before the building is fully enclosed with controlled temperature and humidity. Interior grade plywood for a subfloor of a house may be exposed to heavy rains before the roof or windows are installed, resulting in delamination of the plywood as the glue fails.

5. Some building materials are more vulnerable to sunlight than they are to rain or freezing temperatures. Roofing and cladding materials are typically resistant to ultraviolet light, but the layers below them are often synthetic materials that are quite vulnerable. In the completed building, the underlying layers are sheltered from UV exposure by the cladding, but they may be harmed during construction before the cladding is installed. Contractors may install the air and water barriers over the substrate and think that the rainscreen crew can come months later to install the cladding, but many fluid-applied air and water barriers have only a 30-day tolerance for UV exposure. Other synthetic barriers and flashings may be effective for 60, 90, or 180 days. If these limits are exceeded, the product may need to be replaced or reapplied, and warranties may be void. Product selection and construction scheduling must be coordinated closely so the finished building does not contain degraded products.

6. The dimensions of large, prefabricated components, such as steel, precast concrete, and glue-laminated beams, are established inside factories where temperatures are moderate. When moved outdoors, they will change in size, especially in very hot or very cold weather. Surveyors may have to factor this into their calculations when these members are erected.

7. Select materials and components for each project with an eye to the time of year and the temperatures and precipitation expected when it will be built. Anticipate potential problems with weather-sensitive operations, and eliminate the problems in advance by selecting appropriate systems and components, if possible. In any case, be prepared to propose alternative ways of doing things if weather problems develop.

Pride of Craftsmanship

Remember: Construction is more than an act of assembly. Construction is a craft. Rare is the construction worker who does not have a love of good work and a pride of craftsmanship that can be brought out by an inspired detail.

1. Most bricklayers spend months or years at a stretch laying nothing but running bond facings and are delighted (if sometimes tentative at first) to have an opportunity to create a more decorative pattern bond, a corbelled ornament, a curving wall, or an arch. Finish carpenters respond readily to the opportunity to work with fine hardwoods and delicate moldings. Certain plasterers still know how to do decorative texturing and even plaster ornament. Painters can be easily persuaded to do masking, striping, and stenciling to create colorful patterns. Most heavy timber framers readily apply chamfers, quirks, and lamb's tongues to their beams and columns.

Proceed cautiously and judiciously into these areas. Some traditional expressions of craftsmanship can be exceedingly expensive if they are misused or overused; however, it is often possible, within even a modest construction budget, to add a few small touches to the project in key locations that will lift it above the ordinary level of craftsmanship.

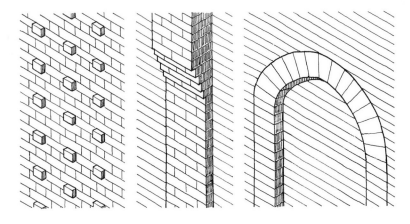

1. Expressing Craftsmanship in Masonry

2. Even where overt expressions of pride of craftsmanship are not used, workers appreciate intelligent details that make the best possible use of their skills. By contrast, they dislike arbitrary, uninformed details that force them to do things that are awkward or difficult to do well. Learn what workers in each trade can do best and most economically; detail accordingly. This will result in a lower contract price, and, just as importantly, it will motivate the construction team, helping to make the building the best that it can be.

3. Workers thrive when they can confidently and efficiently meet goals. Clear communication, clear detail drawings, and clear performance specifications set an important foundation to a successful construction product. Never set the construction team up for disappointment by being ambiguous about what is expected. This applies to both the configuration of elements in the assembly and to the standards of workmanship. Excellent craftsmanship depends on all the parties in the project sharing a common vision of what is expected.

Accepted Standards

Details should conform to norms that are known, understood, accepted, and applied throughout the construction industry. These norms are embodied in the published standards of a number of building construction-related organizations. By conforming to these norms and referencing them in the written specifications for each project, the detailer eliminates many ambiguities and potential sources of misunderstanding from the construction documents. The standards identified in this pattern are common in the United States. Check in other jurisdictions to find what the relevant standards are.

1. Suppose, for example, that the detailer specifies a paving brick simply as "suitable for use as pedestrian paving in the Chicago climate." This leaves considerable uncertainty as to what is "suitable." The masonry contractor may have had good experiences with a particular brick on previous jobs, but the bricks of the same type that are purchased for the current job may be defectively manufactured and may deteriorate rapidly in winter weather. The detailer could remedy this situation by specifying the maximum water absorption that the brick may have, but this leaves the contractor with the task of requesting absorption test results from the manufacturer. Without resorting to a prescriptive or proprietary solution, the entire dilemma could be avoided by merely specifying that the paving bricks must be Class SX pavers, as defined by ASTM C 902. ASTM C 902 is a standard specification for pedestrian and light-traffic paving bricks that is promulgated by ASTM International (formerly the American Society for Testing and Materials), a major standards-setting organization in the construction industry. ASTM C 902 is known and understood throughout the masonry industry, and bricks that conform to it are so designated in manufacturers' literature. It includes standards for strength, water absorption, saturation, abrasion resistance, warpage, chippage, dimensional tolerances, efflorescence, and other criteria, as measured by standard laboratory tests. By citing ASTM C 902, the detailer not only avoids potential communication problems and misunderstandings but also adds to the construction contract a very powerful, well-considered set of requirements that avoid a number of potential disasters.

2. Voluntary consensus standards are set by various organizations, which then carry out conformity assessment and safeguard the integrity of the standards in manufacturing and construction.

ASTM is a major source of accepted standards in the United States, with considerable adoption internationally. It publishes standards for many construction materials to establish consistency in how competing products will perform. Objective standards represent a level playing field for the global construction materials marketplace.

Many other organizations have also established standards for other materials and assemblies that have become widely accepted. These include the American National Standards Institute (ANSI), a private, not-for-profit organization that develops standards and accredited testing procedures for many construction materials and industrial products used in buildings. Agencies within the US Department of Commerce also produce standards, as do many nongovernmental organizations (NGOs) that are affiliated with particular industries.

In Canada, standards corresponding to those by ASTM are set by the CSA Group (formerly the Canadian Standards Association). The Swiss-based ISO (International Organization for Standardization) is the world's largest developer of technical standards. It has representatives from many countries and seeks to build consensus between governmental and commercial interests globally.

Standards organizations increasingly collaborate to lower barriers to international free trade, while enhancing product integrity and quality. In many sectors, equivalent product data is presented using the nomenclature that ASTM, ANSI, CSA Group, ISO, and others call for. Some standards are even written with the names of two or more standards organizations in their titles, meaning that the standards are identical.

3. Standards underlie much of an architect's work and are essential to the construction of buildings. If there were no standards, it would soon be apparent that materials or products were of poor quality, incompatible with available equipment, unreliable, or dangerous, or that they simply did not fit. It is taken for granted when products meet expectations. When detailing and writing specifications, the role played by standards in raising levels of quality, safety, reliability, efficiency, and interchangeability of building elements becomes apparent. Standards are used to establish that building products and assemblies originating from foreign sources conform to established norms, thereby allowing companies to compete globally.

The publications of some of the more prominent standards-setting organizations are included in the reference list at the end of this book. Detailers should become familiar with the accepted standards for all construction materials and assemblies, and they should use these standards as much as possible in specifying and detailing. ■

SECTION 3
AESTHETICS

A building should perform well. A good building should go together easily and efficiently. A great building should please the senses. A great building should go beyond function and constructability to engage the mind and the heart. Details play a large role in meeting this important goal for a building. Every truly great building has great details: details that contribute to the aesthetic themes of the building, that harmonize with one another, and that create beauty out of the ordinary materials and necessities of construction. A building with a splendid thematic idea can fail as architecture if its details are poorly matched to its primary aesthetic, if its details do not relate strongly to one another, and if its details fail to lift their materials above the ordinary.

The detail patterns relating to aesthetics are few, but each is powerful and expansive. They require greater effort and insight to implement than any of the patterns relating to function and constructability. For the following detail patterns, see the corresponding sections in Chapter 14.

The primary aesthetic requirement for detailing is that all the details of a building should contribute to its formal and spatial theme. Aesthetic features of details should be as effective and meaningful in future years as when they were built. These requirements are developed in the detail patterns:

> ***Contributive Details*** (p. 237)
> ***Timeless Features*** (p. 240)
> ***Geometry and Proportion*** (p. 241)

Details may be elaborated to feature certain inherent characteristics or they may be decorative for purely visual or experiential effect:

> ***Hierarchy of Refinement*** (p. 243)
> ***Intensification and Ornamentation*** (p. 245)
> ***Sensory Richness*** (p. 247)

Details may be developed whose role is to unify and give order to the visual composition of building elements that otherwise might seem disjointed or unrelated. This role is introduced in the patterns:

> ***Formal Transitions*** (p. 248)
> ***Didactic Assemblies*** (p. 251)
> ***Composing the Detail*** (p. 252)

These nine patterns serve to focus the detailer's attention on some important aesthetic issues that arise in detailing. They constitute a small part of a much larger field of study—architectural composition—that will amply repay as much as the time the detailer devotes to its study.

The body of built architecture in Western traditions from antiquity to the present provides evidence of the importance of the link between art and craft. Classical Greeks originated the notion

Architectural Detailing: Function Constructability Aesthetics. Fourth Edition. Patrick Rand, Jason Miller, and Edward Allen.
© 2025 John Wiley & Sons, Inc. Published 2025 by John Wiley & Sons, Inc.

of *techne*, derived from the Greek verb *tikto*, meaning "to produce." This term means the simultaneous existence of both art and craft, deliberately avoiding any distinction between the two.

Architectural details can convey to the observer in literal terms the facts about the form and how it is made. They can also reveal what is latent within the form, features so subtle that they are not consciously noticed by the casual observer. In the following patterns, the term *aesthetics* will be used to describe features that recognize the inextricable link between art and craft, between the ideal and the circumstantial, and between the concept and its tangible embodiment. In architectural detailing, ideas must be made real.

The detailer is challenged to find solutions that solve the specific technical requirements of a given detail, while also reinforcing the building's central aesthetic themes. Some details may seem to have no solutions; others may seem to have too many. The most appropriate solutions are functional, convey meaning, and reward the senses.

Although this section emphasizes the visual qualities of a building and its details, the detailer should always look for opportunities to delight the other human senses. Tactile qualities of materials and details are important: the feel of a carpet or polished marble underfoot; the satiny smoothness of polished wood handles on a cabinet; deep, luxurious cushions on a bench; a nubby texture in a wallcovering. Auditory qualities are also vital: Should a particular architectural space seem hushed and quiet? Should it be vast and echoey? Should one's footsteps resound throughout a room, or would it be more appropriate that one tread softly, as if floating noiselessly? Would it enhance the architectural experience if one heard the sounds of splashing water, of birdsongs, of wind in trees, of children chattering, of machines working productively? And consider the opportunities for olfactory delight in a building: the fragrance of cedarwood, the perfume of flowers, the freshness of grass growing, the moist breezes off a pond, the waxy smokiness of candles, the musky scent of leather. The designers of the greatest buildings have considered these possibilities and have often used them to their advantage – transforming a building into a work of architecture.

CHAPTER 14 Aesthetics

Contributive Details

All details of a building should contribute to its formal and spatial themes. Contributive details articulate a waell-conceived building and convey an enduring message through carefully crafted combinations of material, assembly, and form.

1. Every detail has a style. The style may be the incidental by-product of practical actions, as might be found in good vernacular architecture, or the intentional expression of a particular language of architecture, such as the Doric order. A Doric temple is much more than just a low gabled roof supported by closely spaced columns that encircle a walled rectangle. It is also a particular set of subtle proportions with a consistent set of intentional details, each of which contributes to the overall appearance that we recognize instantly, not just as traditional, not just as classical, but as Doric.

The Gothic style was based on a desire to fill tall, long spaces with natural light from generous windows. It encompassed a structural ideal of elaborate stone vaulting supported on slender piers, its thrusts absorbed by delicate buttressing, and a set of details very different from those of Doric builders. Whereas the Doric order's details emphasized a thick, discontinuous,

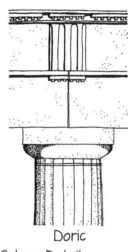  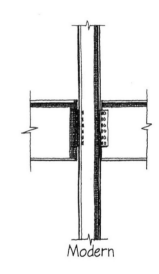

1. Column Details

sticklike constructional aesthetic, the Gothic featured thin, flowing members that all contributed to an apparent continuity of space, form, and structural action.

The modern style advocated the truthful expression of material and unornamented functionalism. The theme of continuous or universal space was well served by the minimalist steel frame and transparent glass skin, eliminating all that was not essential. Rather than carved stone, the modern column takes raw minerals and transforms them into manmade materials whose properties and shapes are rationally controlled.

In each instance, the aesthetic style of the structure reflected both the construction knowledge and the material technology available. The solid Doric, the ethereal Gothic, and the direct Modern expressed the values of the cultures or institutions that built them, attaching meaning to different methods of creating and enclosing space. ▷

Architectural Detailing: Function Constructability Aesthetics. Fourth Edition. Patrick Rand, Jason Miller, and Edward Allen.
© 2025 John Wiley & Sons, Inc. Published 2025 by John Wiley & Sons, Inc.

2. The details associated with any architectural style may be analyzed in a similar fashion: Craftsman style with its celebration of wood joinery; Prairie style with its details that emphasize horizontality (sometimes even to the point of turning all exposed screws so their slots are horizontal); various Brutalist or Minimalist styles, in which solids, slabs, and sticks of material seem to join or flow into one another without visible connectors; High-Tech style, in which the parts of a building are made to look like the pieces of a precision machine, joined with visible bolts and pins, or Contemporary styles in which layers of abstract materials and discrete connections prevail.

3. Try to imagine a building of "universal space" by Ludwig Mies van der Rohe articulated with Victorian Gothic details: The ornate surface embellishments of the latter clashing against the restrained structure of the former would create a compositional conflict too great to resolve. The minimalist spaces and forms of a building by Mies are appropriately enhanced by minimalist details; if they are not, it is not a Mies building. Now try to imagine a Romanesque building with High-Tech details or a Baroque building with Brutalist details. It is impossible for compositions of such varied attitudes toward details to be resolved. The dissonance would be jarring and would be so for a very long time. A building's details are integral to its style and critical to its compositional coherence.

4. Every designer of buildings works in their own manner; it may not have a name, but it has a consistent personality or a guiding ethic. This personality or ethic stems from an approach to space, to form, to light, to color, and to details. The style of the details must be integral with the style of the building. As a designer's manner evolves and changes with each project, so must the details. The details must contribute their proportional share to the character and content of the building. For some architects, a particular material or detail is the seed from which the building's design grows. Even if not the source of the central design concept, details are the voice of the concept, the means through which the concept is expressed.

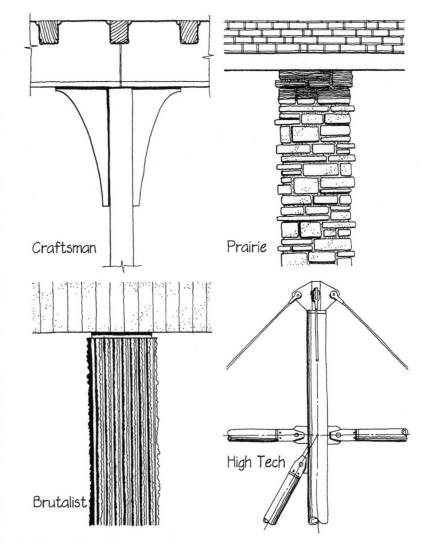

2. Column Details

238   PART 1 ■ DETAIL PATTERNS

5. Vernacular architecture past and present abounds with examples of contributive details, not driven by its intellectual rewards, but simply because building features, large and small, all come from common sources. This type of "architecture without architects" is possible because their makers share common cultural roots, common skills, and common material palettes that informed common building solutions. Vernacular buildings often reveal themselves honestly in straightforward, unembellished assemblies with unmasked features that are very slow to fall out of fashion. Forms of poetic expression are sometimes the residue of insightful work with limited means rather than stylistic preferences.

6. A building's details should be all of a family – that is to say, each detail should relate to others in a cohesive and well-considered building. It is inappropriate to copy individual details from multiples sources and patch together a set of details that function well but bear no visible resemblance to one another. The designer should develop a matched and organized set of a building's most important details as an ongoing part of the overall design process. This set of key details should then serve to guide the preparation of every other visible detail in the building.

Details can relate to one another by sharing a common compositional approach, which may be evident in their proportions, materiality, alignment, and orientation. These details become a meaningful language that can be understood by users. These related details can then be used to reinforce formal or programmatic objectives for the building as a whole. In a pragmatic, inexpensive building, a long, double-loaded corridor may be used to achieve a high space efficiency factor and provide clear wayfinding. But by detailing the resilient flooring material to change orientation at specified locations along the corridor, the length of the corridor can be modulated and zones of the program marked with a threshold. Several features of the building may be expressed simultaneously. When carefully coordinated with different wall, ceiling, and lighting treatments,

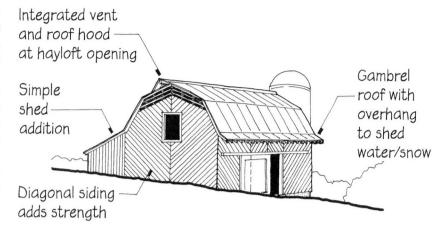

5. Features of a Vernacular Loft Barn

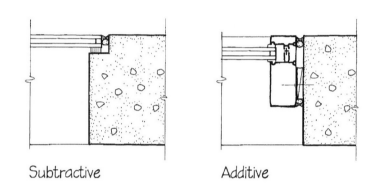

7. Fixed Window in Concrete Wall – Two Versions

prominent rooms of the building can be indicated without use of a second (or third or fourth) flooring material, simplifying initial construction and the post-construction inventories of "attic stock" for building maintenance.

7. Dissimilar elements and architectural palettes can also be joined. Special attention must be given to their technical and compositional compatibility. For instance, massive and skeletal forms can form an interesting duality in a building, but intuitively the massive portion should be below or beside the skeletal. Imagine a massive masonry volume supported by slender steel columns. Even though such a building might be structurally possible, the composition would be unsettling visually and, potentially, in other ways for building occupants.

At closer range, the detail between a thick concrete wall and a glass opening can be solved using various compositional approaches. A sleek subtractive detail may involve sliding the glass panel into a minimal offset cast in the face of the concrete, where a concealed sealant tape joins the fragile glass to the tough concrete. An additive detail may use a metal frame as a third compositional element, placed between the concrete and glass. Through choices such as these, the detailer expresses an attitude toward the dissimilar materials and an understanding of the project budget; each solution has its own economic and performance implications for constructability and functionality. ■

Timeless Features

Details embody knowledge, skills, and solutions earned from the past, they respond to the certainty of the present, and they will serve an unknown future. Building details should be designed to meet an aesthetic and performative purpose with this broad spectrum of time in mind, not focused too narrowly on the present or too broadly on the uncertain future.

1. Nothing expires faster than a trendy graphic look, a flashy detail, or material treatment. The longer the life expectancy of the building, the more timeless its materials and details should be. Many interior architecture projects, like the planned obsolescence of many consumer items, are constructed on the presumption of change. But a 100-year building should not be detailed using the fleeting "retail" fashion of the day. Computational design, digital fabrication, and artificial intelligence platforms offer additional tools to the designer's toolbox for inspiration and execution of a building detail that works. No matter the tools used in their development, well-designed details, made using durable materials, and installed using appropriate workmanship, possess a timeless quality.

2. Timeless details are more likely to be understood and appreciated by people in the future, much as good literature or music is appreciated by successive generations in a culture. A building with well-proportioned forms and spaces, an ordered plan, and meaningful and well-made details will live a long time, almost certainly longer than the initial program for which it was built. Owners in the future will become the building's agents, maintaining it as necessary, introducing new elements with care, and being respectful of its basic ordering principles. Such buildings should not be made with features that become aesthetically obsolete in a short period of time.

3. To be timeless, innovation remains essential. A detail does not need to have been done previously, or selected from a catalog of stock solutions. New details and materials will always be part of an architect's work. New details should be based on sound compositional principles, should demonstrate a grasp of the relevant physical phenomena, and should not waste human or material resources. If this is done, the new details will likely achieve this timeless quality.

4. The means of production often become the date or time stamp on the building. As industry introduces new materials and processes, or as new methods of construction are introduced at the construction site, eager designers explore their technical or aesthetic possibilities. Each designer nudges the envelope of authentic insights regarding the new material or process. Initial uses of new materials and tools are often artificial imitations of their predecessors. Insight follows imitation: Plastic was first used to imitate ivory products, such as billiard balls and piano keys; only later were the unique possibilities of plastics discovered. Anachronisms abound: Sophisticated CNC (computer numeric control) machines are used to carve Corinthian capitals out of plastic foam. Digital 3D printers can be used to make plastic replicas of rosettes made centuries ago out of carved stone or molded plaster.

Detailers should actively participate in the exploration of new materials and construction processes, striving to distinguish between formal possibilities that are timeless and those that are merely today's fashion.

Geometry and Proportion

Geometry and proportion have been used to achieve compositional order since the beginnings of architecture, and they are used by designers and detailers today at all scales. Formal relationships between elements of architecture have been used in countless variations to make aesthetically pleasing compositions. Designers have also used proportions of the human body to relate occupants, ergonomically and experientially, to architectural space and form.

1. Geometry is the most common compositional tool used by designers. It is embodied in the use of simple two- and three-dimensional shapes, but also in the relationship between these shapes. Symmetry, balance, grids, and proportions are examples of common themes based on geometry. Geometry and proportion have the potential to exert pervasive influence on many aspects of building design. These examples from different continents and nearly four centuries apart demonstrate the extent to which architects have employed geometry and proportion (adapted from *Precedents in Architecture*; Clark and Pause, New York: John Wiley and Sons, 2012).

2. The proportions and balance between important spaces and forms can express harmony – or any other expressive goal – throughout a building. The quality of a composition can be enhanced at no additional cost, simply by the placement and sizes of building elements. This idea extends to the spaces between individual buildings in a larger ensemble complex, or the relationships between individual components and detail elements within the building.

3. An example of a proportional system is the golden section, which is 1:Φ (phi) or 1:1.618. This proportional system occurs in many forms in nature and in the human body. It has been used in art, music, and architecture since Euclid formalized a durable system of geometry in Greece. The Great Pyramid, built

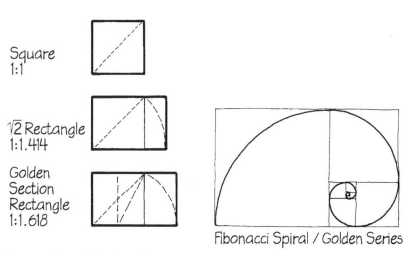

Redentore Church
Venice, Italy
Andrea Palladio
1591

Magney House
Bingie Point, Australia
Glenn Murcutt
1984

1. Geometry and Proportion: Two Examples

Square 1:1

√2 Rectangle 1:1.414

Golden Section Rectangle 1:1.618

Fibonacci Spiral / Golden Series

3. Proportioned Rectangles

in 2570 BCE, manifests phi in its ratio of height to base. The golden section's proportions are satisfactory aesthetically and preferred by the human eye. The Fibonacci series expresses the golden section: 0, 1, 1, 2, 3, 5, 8, 13, 21, 34, 55, 89, 144, 233, and so on. Each number is the sum of the previous two, and each number is roughly the previous number multiplied by the golden section.

Another mathematically significant proportion that has been said to have special aesthetic qualities is the √2 rectangle or 1:1.414. This is the length of the diagonal of a square whose sides are 1 unit in length. ▷

4. Civic and religious spaces are often designed and constructed of monumental dimensions compared to the size of occupants, symbolizing that these spaces are designed for an entity or entities grander and more significant than a human being. With this increased scale and implied gravitas, the architectural implications of such large spaces on structural design, acoustic quality, and many other factors – including the execution of details – merit careful qualitative attention.

5. The dimensions of the human body and human ergonomics influence functions and proportions of many building elements. For instance, window and door dimensions reflect the average sizes of people, but in most cases can be made to match the dimensions of a target population that is not average. A children's theme park or playhouse may intentionally use smaller dimensions than normal buildings, to be in proportion to its primary occupants. Adults also may enjoy the novelty of experiencing spaces designed to a child's proportions.

6. Proportions affect more than just the visual compositional features of a building. For safety and functionality, building codes set forth parameters for riser and tread proportions of stairs and for the slope of ramps. Fire stairs are usually near the steeper end of the allowed range (7 in. riser, 11 in. tread [178, 280 mm]) in order to perform their function with minimal floor space. Monumental stairs in the lobby of a symphony hall may have a shallower riser to tread ratio (5.5 in. riser, 14 in. tread [140, 355 mm]) to make traversing the stair more graceful and comfortable. No matter the application, effective stair design typically establishes and maintains a consistent ratio for its length of travel, because even minor

5. Openings Reflect Human Proportions and Activities

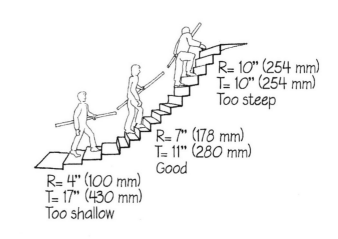

6. Optimal Riser and Tread Proportions

variations within a flight may be unsafe for users (*Safe Footing*, Chapter 9).

The maximum slope for a ramp accessible by the disabled should not exceed 1:12 (1 in. rise for every 12 in. of horizontal distance [25, 305 mm]). At this slope, level landings are required after a code-specified travel distance and at all instances in which a change of direction is made on the ramp. Like stairs, there are unique details to consider for ramp applications, including the provision of continuous handrails or guardrail assemblies, the texture of the travel surface, and the smooth transition between different surfaces. ■

Hierarchy of Refinement

When designing a building, architects usually establish a hierarchy of importance of rooms and elements, reflecting the importance of each part of the building in relation to the other parts. The level of detail refinement within the building should be consistent with this hierarchy.

1. Across different building types and uses, important spaces are often finished and detailed more lavishly or specially than other spaces of lesser stature. The City Council meeting room in a town hall will generally be more refined in its finishes and details than the work room down the hall. A public lobby in a corporate building is generally more refined in its finishes and details than the service entrance. On a smaller scale, the entry foyer and living room in a residence is typically better appointed and more carefully finished than a garage.

2. Details viewed at close range are generally more refined than those that will be seen from far away. Exterior materials at ground level are often more detailed, of higher quality, and made to closer tolerances than those on the upper floors of a tall building. They may also be designed for tactile qualities and anticipated wear because they are within reach.

3. In buildings with layered forms of construction, the visible outer surfaces are typically detailed with much more refinement than those concealed within the assembly, where only technical issues are relevant. For buildings with fewer layers of assembly, the designer responds to an added aesthetic challenge for the assembly detail and its specifications. For instance, a wall constructed of cast-in-place concrete

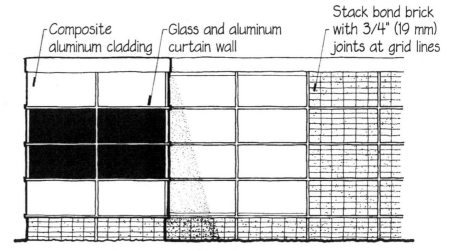

5. Consistent Compositional Features

as a structural back-up to a finish material addresses issues of function and constructability. When the cast-in-place concrete is intended as the exterior and/or interior finish for the wall, new agendas emerge about the incorporation of important wall functions, formwork selection, workmanship standards, control joints, admixtures, and finish textures.

The surface character, visual warmth, and indoor environmental qualities of wood offers an attractive option for interior surfaces in a mass timber structure. To achieve these aesthetic benefits, a variety of structural performance and fire-resistant assembly factors must be addressed across Type III, IV, and V construction types. The type of structural connections and the location or exposure of the structural mass timber components inform functional detailing decisions and impact the aesthetic experience. These two examples make one issue quite clear: The reduction of layers does not always result in a reduction of detailing challenges, particularly for a resilient and sustainable building (***Progressive Finish***, Chapter 13).

4. No detail should fail to meet its functional obligations, and all must be constructable, but the degree of refinement may vary in order to enhance the detail's symbolic or experiential content. Some details are to be celebrated in a building, while others are quietly competent, functional and simple. From an economy perspective – both financial and material – resources conserved in making routine details are then available for the special ones.

5. Differences between surface materials and details should be thought of as variations on a basic theme. This will make all the details part of a family, and it will make it easier for the observer to detect the intended relationship between them (see ***Contributive Details***, earlier in this chapter). ▷

6. At one time, refined building materials were formed from raw materials: Stone details were carved from rough blocks; a squared wood column was laboriously shaped with an adze and a plane from a log. High refinement was the mark of a skilled craftsperson, bestowing honor and respect on the material artifact. With injection-molded plastics, aluminum extrusions, and computer-controlled laser cutters or three-dimensional printers, the production of incredibly precise, refined building components is possible with unprecedented ease. A good question to ask might be: "How much precision and refinement is enough?"

If every surface and detail is equally refined, none is more important than another. Meaning is diminished when there is no differentiation of refinement. Architectural philosopher John Ruskin advocated in his *Stones of Venice*, first published 1851–1853: "There should be no refinement of execution where there is no thought, for that is slave's work, unredeemed. Rather choose rough work to smooth work so only the practical purpose be answered, and never imagine there is reason to be proud of anything that may be accomplished by patience and sandpaper." The human attraction to precision, crisp details, and smooth surfaces may be a vestige of the pre-industrial and pre-digital ages, when the means of production made such refinements rare to achieve and expensive to obtain. The detailer should continue to reserve the most refined, custom-made details for the most important elements in the building, making other details in a manner consistent in cost, quality, and thought with their level of importance.

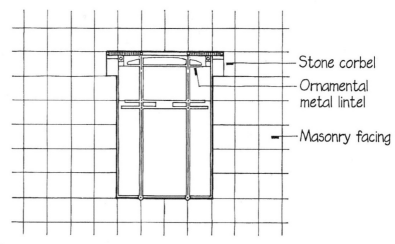

6. Refined Details

Intensification and Ornamentation

Details can be embellished to add to the visual richness of a building and to draw attention to its formal and, depending on the detail condition, its functional qualities.

1. Since the beginning of civilization, makers of things have demonstrated love of their work by adding nonfunctional elements to their forms. Weavers have added textures, colors, and patterns. Tile makers have added brightly decorated glazes. Carpenters have chamfered and carved their work. Shinglers have added scallops and sawtooth patterns. Masons have laid delightful patterns of headers, soldiers, rowlocks, and corbels in their walls. Iron workers have wrought elaborate tracery patterns and cast sculptural elements for columns, gates, and grilles. The results of these efforts are often very beautiful, sometimes because they reveal inherent beauties of material and craft, and sometimes because they are simply beautiful in the abstract.

2. Examining an ancient, decorated Greek vase, two sets of painted patterns are discovered. One set is made up of circumferential stripes and bands that were created by holding a paintbrush against the clay vase as it spun on the potter's wheel. These stripes generally were applied at locations significant in relationship to the curvature of the vase – a change in the radius or direction of curvature. This practice might be termed *intensification*, because it is purposefully related to the process of making the vase and to its form, and thus it intensifies the vase's aesthetic by further articulating its form and function. The bands and stripes express the pragmatic and formal qualities of the vase. The other set of patterns consists of scenes of animals, warriors, athletes, gods, and goddesses – whatever suited the mood or mission of the potter. These bear little or no relationship to the manufacture or form of the vase, and might be termed *ornamentation*. Both intensification and ornamentation contribute to the beauty of the vase, but they sprang from different aesthetic inspirations.

2. Analysis of a Greek Vase

3. Intensification and ornamentation have their places also in the work of the building trades. For example, the carpenter's chamfers reduce the likelihood of splinters along the edges of a post or beam, and they make the member slower to catch fire. In addition to these useful functions, they also bring the long, straight edges more prominently to view, and their beveled facets add sculptural interest to the timbers. A chamfer could not continue into a joint between members without creating unsightly gaps, so carpenters developed ways to terminate chamfers short of the end of the member, such as sinuous lamb's tongues or various angular notches. In the joints themselves, much of the carpenter's artistry was necessarily concealed in mortises, tenons, and laps, but pleasing patterns could be created of exposed pegs and brackets. All this might be considered intensification, because it sprang from necessity but went beyond it to create a delight that enhances an intuitive understanding of how the building was made. If the carpenter went on to carve scenes, patterned motifs, or mottoes on the sides of the beams, this would be viewed as ornamentation because, as attractive and contributive to the overall aesthetic of the building as it might be, it was not related directly or indirectly to necessity. ▷

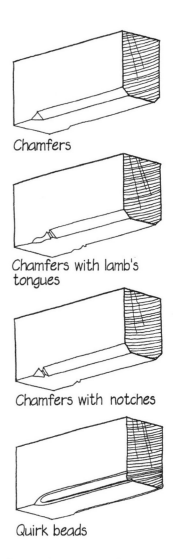

3. Intensification of Beam Edges

4. The detailer should look first to intensification as a way to enhance the aesthetic impact of details. The functional sources of inspiration for intensification are many: the need to put control joints into a stucco wall to manage surface cracks; the need to use form ties and rustication strips to create satisfactory surfaces of architectural concrete; the need to add brackets and bolts to connect members of steel or timber; the need to cover uneven and unsightly gaps where floors or soffits join walls; the need to install a lintel to support masonry over a window or a door opening; or the need to make closely spaced seams in a sheet metal roof.

Each of these conditions – and countless others – presents an opportunity to intensify the form of a portion or the whole of a building by such strategies as adding intentional lines or moldings to junctions between planes, creating rhythms and patterns of fasteners or seams, exaggerating sizes or numbers of things such as bolts or brackets, or adding contrasting colors. Each such effort is a celebration of the necessary, a virtuoso cadenza, a sharing of the joy of assembling a building with the viewer who was not involved in its construction but who comes to appreciate that process when it is made visible.

5. Ornamentation can be as effective as intensification; however, its application requires more dexterity and judgment, because it does not arise from a specific, tangible feature of the building but is instead derived from some other source or is created from scratch. Often, intensification alone is sufficient to carry the building into the realm of the special; however, applied ornament can look superficial, even awkward or tasteless if it is badly done or is at odds with the intrinsic features of the composition. ■

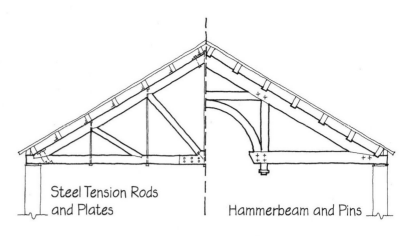

4A. Intensification of Heavy Timber Roof Trusses

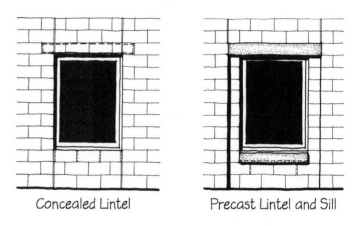

4B. Intensification of Window Opening in Masonry Wall

Sensory Richness

Building details and surfaces can engage all of the senses. Although perception relies chiefly on the visual realm, the other senses provide important content to the aesthetic experience of a form or space. The ways in which people experience buildings contribute to the meaning subsequently attached to them.

1. Varying textures and materials in a building can be used to designate functions and control the intimacy of spaces: cool, hard, polished, echoey surfaces for public spaces; warm, soft, quiet surfaces for private spaces; resilient surfaces for utility rooms; robust, durable surfaces for industrial areas; and resilient surfaces for healthcare facilities. A lifetime of past experience results in a shared set of associations between sensory qualities of a building and their usual purpose. Material and texture transitions can also mark thresholds between different realms within a continuous interior, helping visitors navigate spaces without assistance.

2. Materials meant to be comfortable to touch would not only be free of sharp edges or splinters (*Safe Edges*, Chapter 9), but also may be smooth, soft enough to respond to gentle pressure, and not so thermally conductive that they pull body heat from fingertips. Not all surfaces need to be comfortable to be safe. In a primary educational building, a durable wall made of concrete masonry uses bullnose units at corners to reduce risk of injury. The floor of a preschool classroom must be much more comfortable than the floor of the cafeteria. Washrooms and kitchens place a higher priority on sanitary qualities (*Cleanable Surfaces*, Chapter 10), so they are often hard, free of pores and crevices, and may even be coated with a microscopic coating that is self-cleaning to protect the surface from biological growth. A fire stair door handle is meant to be thermally conductive so firefighters know before opening the door whether there is a fire close to the other side.

3. Human contact alters almost all building materials. Even stainless steel darkens slightly from the oils in the hands that touch it (*Surfaces That Age Gracefully*, Chapter 10). Unyielding stone columns at the entry to a classical temple acquire a sheen and darker tone at the height of human reach, as a result of the countless hands that could not resist the temptation to feel the fluted stone column shapes. The minor changes in shape and appearance of building surfaces become a record of use patterns, and an experiential cue to future visitors about which surfaces are most engaging.

4. The sounds of rain on the metal roof, footsteps of someone walking down a hallway, and muffled conversations from behind a door are all examples of how sounds contribute to the sensory experience of a room, a series of spaces, or an entire building. Sounds reflected from or absorbed by building surfaces give an acoustic preview of things not yet visible. To an astute listener, and especially to someone who is visually impaired, the dimensions of a space and the texture of its surfaces can be detected simply by the way the space sounds. This is useful and sometimes enjoyable. The detailer controls the quality of these experiences by selecting materials and assemblies that coordinate effectively with the space in which they are used to achieve the desired effect (see Chapter 5).

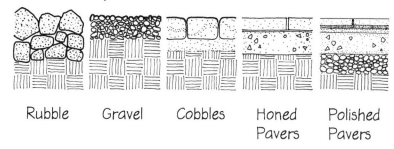

1. Same Material – Different Textures

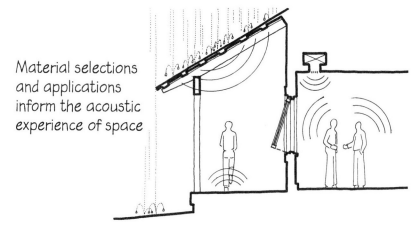

4. Sounds from Building Surfaces and Occupants

Formal Transitions

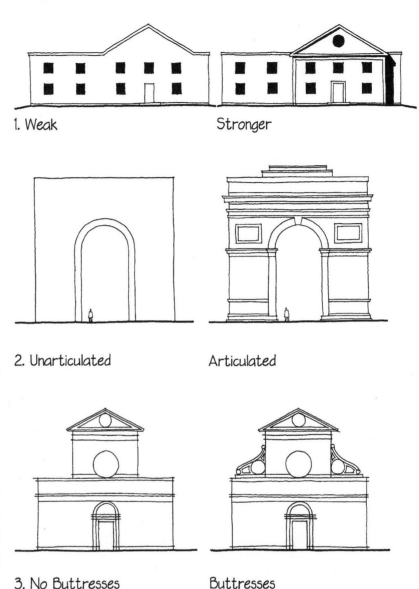

1. Weak — Stronger

2. Unarticulated — Articulated

3. No Buttresses — Buttresses

Details can help to clarify and unify the visual composition of building elements that might otherwise seem disjointed or unrelated.

1. The masses and forms of a well-designed building generally work together and require no further attention from the detailer, but occasionally a detail can help to correct the appearance of an awkward junction or transition. A gable-roofed mass incorporated into a larger flat-roofed volume can appear weak and lifeless, because the basic formal volumes that make up the composition are difficult to discern. Minor changes in detailing can create a stronger elevation that draws attention to the proportions of the basic volumes and establishes a clear hierarchy of elements.

2. An unarticulated transition from supporting piers to an arch appears indecisive. The addition of a string course and pier capitals provides a definite demarcation to the boundary between pier and arch. The addition of a thicker base and a profiled cap mark the transitions from the form to the ground and to the sky.

3. Many Renaissance and Baroque churches used ornate, nonstructural buttresses to make a smooth transition from the main mass of the church to a superimposed dome or vault. These elements took their cue regarding form and materiality from the building elements already established in the composition.

4. As materials and construction technologies advanced, tall buildings established a language of formal transition like that of classical columns to clearly define the base, middle, and top of the architectural composition. This basic formula ensures a clear aesthetic response to the ground level experience and distant viewed experience of these unique and often massive structures.

5. On a smaller scale, a timber beam that simply emerges from the plaster of a supporting wall looks disjointed even though it works functionally. An applied bracket and pilaster at this transition can establish a stronger visual connection between the two elements. Similarly, a structurally adequate connection between the beam and a column can appear weak and abrupt; brackets can ease this transition. The bracket also represents the wood blocking or shim that might have been used at one time to adjust the vertical position of the beam where it bears on the wall or column. ▷

6. Abutting or aligning two or more materials in exactly the same plane looks fake, as if the materials are just different colors of paint. Even a slight offset of their surfaces, perhaps expressing different material thicknesses, will help. If that is not possible, then a ***Reveal*** (Chapter 12) or the protruding edge of a neutral third material between them will help distinguish their unique properties.

When a single material turns a corner, the detailer must decide whether the transition is to appear seamless or should be articulated as a feature. Truly seamless corners on the exterior of a building are technically challenging because of many functional and constructability factors described in preceding portions of this book. The use of reveals and neutral intermediate materials can also be considered here.

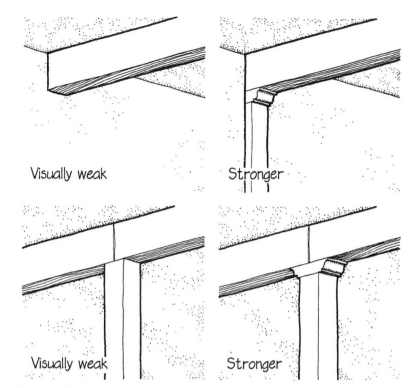

5. Formal Transitions in Wood Beams

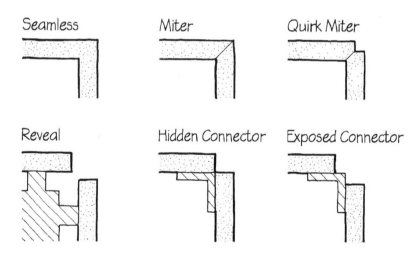

6. Detailing a Corner Transition – Several Alternatives in Plan

7. The transitional element may have a visual and functional presence that is created to assist constructability, not just acting as a neutral seam. In this example, the glass handrail is connected to the edge of the floor assembly overlooking an atrium. The transitional element is a unifying steel plate that has been fabricated for this project to perform several functions. It is a fascia that conceals the edges of the floor deck, suspended ceiling, and everything in between. It extends higher than the floor surface to become a kick strip and accepts the stainless steel fitting that holds the glass handrail.

8. There are many details that require the graceful termination of a form: a finial on a newel post, a volute at the termination of a handrail, a pendant beneath an overhanging second story, a cheek detail at the end of an eave. In none of these examples is it visually satisfactory merely to chop off the member that is being terminated. ∎

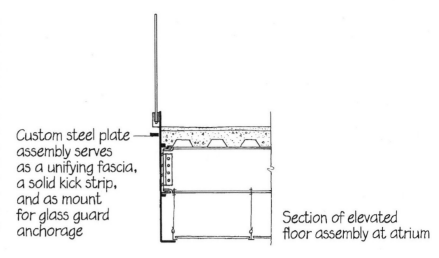

7. Transitional Detail Performs Several Functions

8. Terminations

Didactic Assemblies

Architectural details can be highly instructive about how the materials, assemblies, and service systems are used. Legible features make the building more understandable to occupants, satisfying curiosity and reducing confusion. For some people, order in the world around them is a source of beauty. Others may find it a meaningful or even entertaining way to connect to their architectural setting. Flaunting technical features may advance the "brand" or identity of the owner. The expression of technical systems may also reflect the increasing share of building costs of these systems or emphasize aspects of building performance as part of the building aesthetic.

Possible interpretations:

featureless	massive	layered	thin
abstract	coarse	refined	fragile
monolithic	structural	cladding	rainscreen

3. Surfaces and Details are Instructive

1. Making assemblies visible is a chance for workers to display their skills (***Pride of Craftsmanship***, Chapter 13), but it also has functional implications. Visible assemblies and details make it easier to detect and repair faulty components. This strategy may also reduce costs and environmental impact, because superficial covering layers may be reduced (***Minimum Number of Parts***, Chapter 11).

2. Exposed services demand careful advance planning to coordinate various subsystems to avoid conflicts and make the exposed elements attractive. The standards of workmanship for fabrication and erection of architecturally expressed structural steel (AESS) are higher than those for concealed steel frames, with commensurate cost implications. The same is true for exposed heavy timber and mass timber constructions. Codes may restrict the use of unprotected steel or wood structural elements, even in fully sprinklered buildings.

3. Surfaces often reveal what is behind that surface, simply by revealing intrinsic facts about its materials and connections. Very little can be known or inferred about a featureless monolithic wall. The introduction of seams between the pieces that make up the wall begin to provide clues about its basic composition and construction. Visible fasteners suggest that the facing material is not load-bearing. The type and frequency of fasteners used imply likely material properties, such as strength and thickness. This is because we have experienced similar materials or details in the past and are constantly comparing new designs to our personal inventory of experiences. Gaps between elements making up the surface lead to speculation that this is a rainscreen application, which correlates with possibilities for the wall section assembly used to produce that final appearance.

4. Legibility does not require that every feature or layer be exposed. Seams between elements of the wall may be shown to give the wall surface a pleasing scale or proportion, but it does not need all fasteners and other intrinsic features to also be shown. Exposing all of the elements making up the assembly may distract from the intended grasp of its basic formal or spatial qualities. Detailers have many options to consider when creating architectural products that match their intentions. Decisions about what to reveal and what to conceal – and when and where to apply those choices – are among those options. ∎

Composing the Detail

Aesthetic objectives are often catalysts for exploration of a detail's technical possibilities. The detailer fuses aesthetic composition and technical exploration to find the solution most appropriate for the architectural situation.

1. In the best architecture, details go beyond the technical realm to convey important compositional qualities and meaning. A well-composed detail can capture the essence of the building design in a vivid way and explain the relationships between the parts of the building they are joining. The wood siding scribed to meet the irregular face of the ashlar stone wall explains that the stone wall is the dominant element, anchoring the composition. The detail demonstrates the basic architectural concept while also revealing a material hierarchy informed by constructability (wood is easier to shape than stone) and a visual hierarchy responsive to fundamental material properties (the lighter material reacts to the heavier material).

2. Many buildings have one little feature that people can fall in love with. The potency of the detail as a memorable building feature is sometimes underestimated. Details that are seen up close or touched have the greatest potential to positively influence the observer. Grasping the door pull that was designed by the building's architect is as close as one can come to shaking that architect's hand.

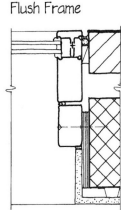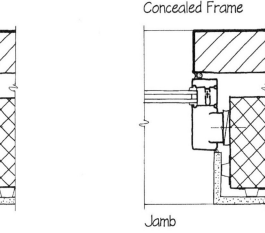

3. Window Frame in Masonry Wall—Two Versions

3. Compositional questions such as whether a shadow line is desired, whether the window should be flush or recessed, and whether or not a joint should have a piece of trim all provoke technical exploration. The detailer explores what must be done to produce a shadow line, for glass to be in the same plane as the exterior cladding, or for a joint to be trimless. What the detail looks like and how the detail is made are inseparable aspects.

4. A detail can join elements in countless ways, from an apparently seamless weld, as in a Mies steel frame, to the boldly expressed timber joints and wood fasteners of a Greene and Greene connection. As a result, countless questions emerge for the detailer: Does the connection want to be celebrated and objectified, or should it be quietly competent calling no attention to itself? If fasteners or splices are used to make the connection, should they be prominent in the composition, or should they be downplayed? Are the connections exposed for ease of disassembly and maintenance, or are they concealed from view?

5. Details must be visualized in three dimensions. It is wise to develop details in three-dimensional sketches or models to visualize completely their forms and implications. Three-dimensional development also helps the viewer to explore how each detail turns the corner or intersects another element. ■

PART II

DETAIL DEVELOPMENT

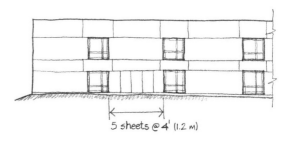

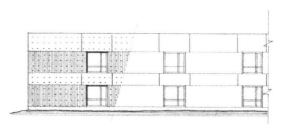

SECTION 1

APPLYING THE DETAIL PATTERNS

This section of the book consists of three illustrated narratives. These describe the process of designing the key details of specific building projects in wood light framing, architectural concrete, and masonry with a concrete frame. The intent of these chapters is to demonstrate how a hypothetical architect develops and designs the details of a building: to reveal something of their concerns, mode of thought, and way of working. Throughout these narratives, special emphasis is given to explain how the detail patterns presented in Part I are a natural and integral part of the architectural detailing process. Pattern names are shown in italics so they are readily identifiable.

Although these narratives reveal many necessary twists and turns, they have been simplified a good deal to reduce length and to make them easier to follow. The drawings, similarly, have been cleaned up and reduced in number from the innumerable freehand scribbles; countless tracing-paper overlays; and smudged, densely overdrawn sections that are the usual interim products of the detailer. An attempt has been made to relate the drawing styles on these pages to the qualities of the actual drawings that the detailer produces along the way, starting with freehand pencil sketches and ending with precise, computer-drafted details. Three-dimensional physical and digital model studies would likely also be used by the team of collaborators to carry out and support the work; these are not included because they are beyond the focus of this book.

What should be apparent in these narratives – in addition to a knowledge of the detail patterns and some conventions of drafting – is that detailing requires a ready familiarity with construction materials, tools, processes, and standards that must be acquired from sources other than this book. It is assumed the reader has at least a beginning understanding of these areas and that the reader's understanding is being augmented constantly by reading technical literature, consulting more experienced colleagues, and observing actual construction operations.

The three building designs presented here break no new stylistic ground. They aspire only to contribute to an initial understanding of detailing practice. As one acquires more experience, it is even more challenging (and a good deal more fun) to work on the detailing of an out-of-the-ordinary design. Building designs that push the envelope call for details that do this also, while still being functional and constructable.

There is a crucial theme that runs through these three examples: The design of the details of a building is a process that establishes with considerable precision both the technical means of its construction and its interior and exterior appearance. In each of the three examples, we begin the design of the details with only an approximate idea of the form and texture of the building.

Architectural Detailing: Function Constructability Aesthetics. Fourth Edition. Patrick Rand, Jason Miller, and Edward Allen.
© 2025 John Wiley & Sons, Inc. Published 2025 by John Wiley & Sons, Inc.

By the time this handful of key details has been developed to a preliminary stage of completion, the building has come alive, not only because it has become patently constructable, but also because it has assumed a character and a personality of considerable depth. It follows that the design of the details of a building should begin while its form and space are still fluid. In this way, the materials selected, the processes by which they are assembled, and the developing character of the details can inform the form-making process for the building as a whole.

There are few greater mistakes a designer can make than to create a finished form for a building and only then begin to consider how to build it. Buildings designed in this way are often unsatisfying to the senses, difficult to construct, and prone to performance issues. Every great building – ancient or contemporary, handcrafted or prefabricated – incorporates its handling of materials and processes as an integral part of its aesthetic, showing that its designer expended as much love and expertise on its details as on its space and form.

CHAPTER  Detailing a Building in Wood Light Framing

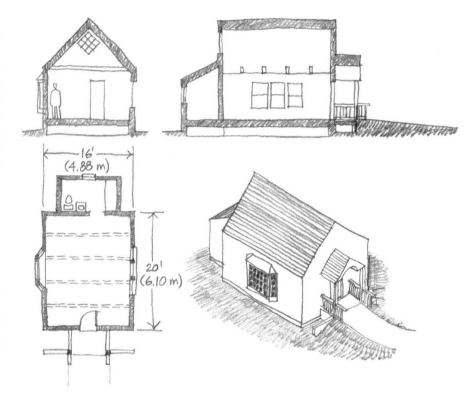

THE PROJECT

The project is a small sales office for a residential subdivision in coastal New England in IECC (International Energy Conservation Code) Climate Zone 5. The roof pitch is 12/12 (45°). Both the roof and the walls will be clad with red cedar shingles (*Surfaces That Age Gracefully*, Chapter 10). The interior will be finished with gypsum board walls and ceiling and a varnished oak floor.

SETTING PERFORMANCE STANDARDS

We want the building to convey the image of an uncomplicated cottage with a minimal, prismatic form (*Timeless Features*, Chapter 14). The details of the building should be as simple as possible to contribute to the minimalist, geometric architectural image, and they should relate closely to one another.

Although smaller than many residences, this is actually a commercial building in terms of the building and energy codes. We have the option of using whole-building energy performance as described in IECC energy code Section 407, but this process is more complex than using the prescriptive tables found in Chapter 4 of the IECC. We will proceed using the prescriptive minimum *Thermal Insulation* (Chapter 3) values that follow. Metric equivalents are shown in parentheses.

Walls: R-13 between studs + R3.8 continuous insulation *or* R-20 if only between studs (R-90 + R-26 *or* R-139)

Roof: R-38 if between rafters *or* R-25 if continuous insulation (R-264 *or* R-173)

Floor: R-30 (R-208) if above an unconditioned space.

We will exceed the minimum value slightly by using R-23 (R-160) mineral wool high-density batts for wall insulation between studs to reduce energy consumption and cost (*Life Cycle*, Chapter 10). The roof insulation must be done in a manner that allows the ceiling to follow the line of the rafters to create a tall interior space. ▷

Architectural Detailing: Function Constructability Aesthetics. Fourth Edition. Patrick Rand, Jason Miller, and Edward Allen.
© 2025 John Wiley & Sons, Inc. Published 2025 by John Wiley & Sons, Inc.

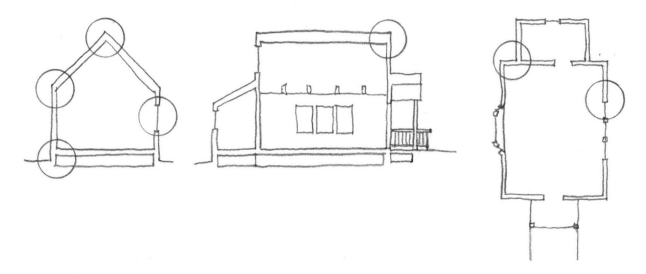

KEY DETAILS TO DEVELOP

The key details to establish the constructional and visual character of the building are those circled on the accompanying section and plan diagrams.

These must be developed as a consistent set of *Contributive Details* (Chapter 14) that work well with the building's architecture and with one another. They are the most general of the building's details. Details of special situations, such as the entry porch and the shed to the rear that houses the toilet room, will be developed using these general details as a point of departure.

EARLY WORK ON FORM, MATERIALS, AND DETAILS

The prismatic form we have envisioned presents an eave-detailing problem: Under most circumstances, storm drainage from the roof would be collected in gutters and downspouts, which would disrupt the clean geometry of the building. Gutters could be built into the roof surface at the top of each wall, but we discard this idea because built-in gutters often prove to be troublesome in use. When they become clogged with leaves or ice, water is likely to back up under the shingles (see *Unobstructed Drainage*, Chapter 1).

The building code requires water from the roof be collected in storm drainage systems such as gutters, or discharged onto ground surfaces such as paving or landscape surfaces, provided that the stormwater flows away from the building. If an eave overhang of at least 1 ft. (305 mm) is provided, no gutters are required because the overhang is an *Overhang and Drip* (Chapter 1) that protects the walls and

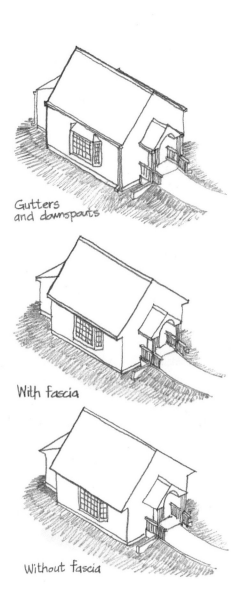

windows. If we adopt this alternative, however, we will want to detail a drip trench filled with crushed stone in the ground beneath each eave, to prevent erosion and to minimize splashing of water and mud onto the siding at the base of the wall.

Deep roof overhangs help create a sheltered feeling for the "cottage." And if they are deep enough, roof overhangs can contribute to the overall simplicity of the form by eliminating the need for a separate roof over the bay window. The bay window is 12 in. (305 mm) deep, so we adopt tentatively an 18 in. (457 mm) overhang.

We sketch the building exterior with this overhang. It is an intriguing formal idea to pursue, but the vertical fascia board appears as a complicating, extraneous surface separating the roof and walls. Could we eliminate the fascia? This would result in a purer, simpler form for the building, one more in the spirit of the original idea (**Composing the Detail**, Chapter 14).

Structure and Thermal Insulation

In addition to the R-38 discontinuous or R-25 continuous (R-264 or R-173) roof insulation, the building code also requires that if the roof is to be vented, then a continuous 1 in. (25 mm) ventilation space beneath the entire roof surface must be maintained (**Ventilated Cold Roof**, Chapter 1). Since this is a high snow-load location, we need the cold roof performance in order to minimize the risk of ice-damming. The code also requires a wide ice and water barrier sheet beneath the roof shingles at the eaves, to minimize potential damage from ice dams. This barrier must extend from the eave edge to a point at least 24 in. (610 mm) inside the exterior wall line. An R-38 (R-264) roof can be difficult to achieve when there is no attic, because the roof structure must be deep enough to contain the thickness of the insulating material required to reach this level of thermal protection. Unfaced batts with a separate vapor retarder sheet are generally the most economical way to insulate a small sloping roof. A check of insulation manufacturers' catalogs tells us the standard batt thicknesses and R-values, based on both normal- and high-density (HD) batting (see Table 15-1).

If we decide to use plastic foam insulating materials, a further look at the

TABLE 15-1: Thermal Resistance.

	(ft²-hr-°F/BTU-in)	m²-°C/W
3½" (89 mm) batts	R-11 and R-15 (HD)	R-76 and R-104
5½" (140 mm)	R-23 (HD)	R-146
6½" (159 mm) batts	R-19	R-132
6½" (171 mm)	R-22	R-153
7½" (184 mm) mineral wool batts	R-30 (HD)	R-208
8½" (209 mm)	R-30 (HD)	R-208
10½" (260 mm) batts	R-38 and R-44 (HD)	R-208 and R-264
12" (305 mm) batts	R-38	R-264

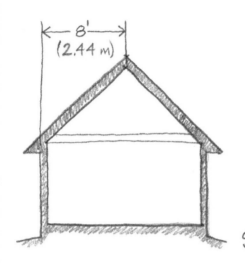

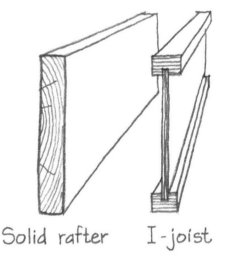

Solid rafter   I-joist

manufacturers' catalogs reveals the following possibilities:

Extruded polystyrene:
R-5.0 per in. (R-35 per 25 mm)

Polyisocyanurate foam:
R-6.0 per in. (R-42 per 25 mm)

Polyisocyanurate foam, foil faced:
R-6.5 per in. (R-46 per 25 mm)

We also discover from the American Society of Heating, Refrigerating and Air-Conditioning Engineers' *ASHRAE Fundamentals* that the R-value of a gypsum board ceiling and interior air film is only a bit over 1. The R-values of the ventilating airspace, sheathing, roofing, and exterior air film cannot be taken into account, because the ventilating airspace is assumed to be at outdoor temperature. Therefore, we must find space for R-38 (R-264) of insulating materials between the airspace and the gypsum board.

Structurally, the roof will consist of wood rafter pairs tied at intervals with horizontal wooden members. The building is 16 ft. (4.88 m) wide, so each rafter must span about 8 ft. (2.44 m), as measured in horizontal projection. We consult the National Forest Products Association's *Span Tables for Joists and Rafters* to find the necessary size for the rafters, reading from the table that gives values for members that carry a sloping gypsum board ceiling and a 30 psf (146 kg/m²) snow load.

Two by six rafters at a 16 in. spacing (38 × 140 @ 406 mm) can span more than 9 ft. (2743 mm), so they would be more than sufficient for this building. We recognize, however, that 2 × 6 rafters will probably not provide sufficient space for insulating materials, so we use the table to verify some other structural options to keep open:

2 × 8 rafters @ 24 in. spacing (38 × 184 @ 610 mm)

2 × 10 rafters @ 24 in. spacing (38 × 235 @ 610 mm)

2 × 12 rafters @ 24 in. spacing (38 × 286 @ 610 mm)

▷

From a structural standpoint, rafters deeper than 2 × 8 could be spaced more than 24 in. (610 mm) o.c., but we do not want to exceed this spacing for two reasons. One reason is for ease of insulating: Standard insulating batts are made only for 16 in. and 24 in. (406 and 610 mm) spacings. The other is that the required thicknesses of plywood roof sheathing and gypsum board ceiling panels become excessive at rafter spacings greater than 24 in. (610 mm).

As an alternative to solid wood rafters, we could use manufactured wood I-joists as rafters to create the depth we need. These come in standard depths of 9½, 11⅞, 14, and 16 in. (241, 302, 356, and 406 mm). The load-and-span tables in the manufacturers' literature tell us that I-joists in any of these depths could serve as rafters for this building at a 24 in. (610 mm) spacing.

Now we return in our thinking to the thermal insulation problem: What are some insulation options that would achieve an overall rating of R-38 (R-264) for the roof construction? We list a few possibilities:

1. 8¼ in. (209 mm) HD batt
R = 30 (R-208)
2. 6¾ in. (171 mm) batt + 2 in. (51 mm) of any foam plastic
R = 29 to 35 (R-201 to 243)
3. 7¼ in. (184 mm) mineral wool HD batt + 1½ in. (38 mm) of polyisocyanurate
R = 39 (R-270)
4. 6¼ in. batt + 3½ in. batt (159 + 89 mm)
R = 30 to 34 (R-208 to 236)
5. 6 in. (152 mm) of polystyrene foam
R = 30 (R-208)

We note that if we were to abandon the ventilated cold roof approach and fill the rafters with foam-in-place insulation, the rafters would need to be 2 × 12s to get the required insulation value. The higher framing cost and vulnerability to ice-damming discourage this approach.

Option 1, the 8¼ in. HD batt, has the advantage of simplicity. If we add the 2 in. (51 mm) airspace below the roof sheathing (*Vapor Ventilation*, Chapter 4), a rafter depth of 10¼ in. (260 mm) would be required, which is 1 in. (25 mm) less than the actual depth of a 2 × 12. The disadvantage of this option is that long 2 × 12s are heavy and hard to handle at roof level during construction (*Parts That Are Easy to Handle*, Chapter 11). Manufactured wood I-joists 11⅞ in. (302 mm) deep might be a good alternative, because they are somewhat lighter; however, they require a more elaborate, hard-to-make detail where they rest on the wall frame, so we decide to search for a solid-lumber solution if possible.

Looking at Options 2 and 3, we see that a 6¾ or 7¼ in. (171 or 184 mm) batt plus 2 in. (51 mm) of airspace would require a minimum rafter depth of 8¾ to 9¼ in. (222 or 235 mm). We round this up to the nearest standard lumber depth, 9¼ in. (235 mm), for nominal 2 × 10 rafters. The foam panels could be nailed across the underside of the rafters, and the gypsum board could be attached with long screws that would pass through the foam and penetrate into the rafters about ¾ in. (19 mm), the depth recommended by gypsum board manufacturers. For 2 in. (51 mm) thick foam, a bit of arithmetic shows us that the screws would have to be about 3¼ in. (83 mm) long to achieve a ¾ in. (19 mm) penetration into the rafters. We find from the U.S. Gypsum Corporation's *Gypsum Construction Handbook* that the longest recommended standard drywall screw is only 3 in. (76 mm), so Option 2 is not feasible.

Option 3 would work, however, because, with 1½ in. (38 mm) of foam insulation, a standard 3 in. drywall screw would achieve the necessary penetration. A side benefit of this construction would be that the foam panels would insulate the rafters as well as the spaces between them, acting as a **Thermal Break** (Chapter 3) for the more conductive wood.

Option 4 could be created by installing 2 × 4 furring on edge across the undersides of the rafters, as shown. This shares with Option 3 the advantage that thermal bridging through

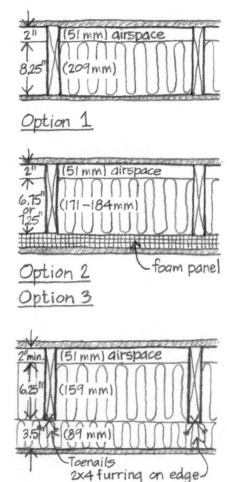

the wood of the rafters is minimized, and glass fiber insulation is generally cheaper per unit of thermal resistance than plastic foam. But this cost advantage would be negated by the additional expense of the 2 × 4s, and the toenailing of the 2 × 4s to the rafters would be somewhat difficult because of the awkward overhead position (*Accessible Connections*, Chapter 11).

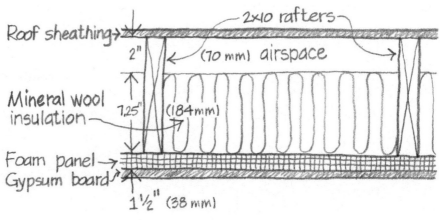

Option 5 involves using only foam plastic insulation, but it is problematic because it is difficult to fit the rigid foam panels tightly enough between rafters to eliminate thermal leakage. This problem could be eliminated by spraying polyurethane foam in place rather than using pre-foamed panels. This involves another subcontractor, however, and would probably be rather expensive for so small a building.

Thus, we tentatively adopt Option 3, consisting of 7¼ in. (184 mm) HD batts between nominal 10 in. rafters spaced 24 in. o.c. (235 @ 610 mm), with a 1½ in. (38 mm) thick layer of polyisocyanurate panels attached across the bottom of the rafters. We will proceed with the detail on this basis and see if everything works out satisfactorily.

DETAILING THE EAVE

We will begin our detailing of the building with the eave, because this one detail does the most to establish the appearance of the building and also seems to present the most challenges. We adopt the customary scale of 1½ in. = 1 ft. (1:8), which allows us to show all but the most intricate of features. Metric scales of 1:5 or 1:10 can also be used to examine details. In developing this detail, we follow step by step the process that the carpenters will use to construct it, *Rehearsing the Construction Sequence* (Chapter 13). We draw first the studs, top plate, and sheathing of the wall that supports the rafters, and add to it the rafters with their triangular bird's-mouth cut that allows them to bear on the top plate and sheathing.

Detailing the Exterior Features

To create the fascialess eave we sketched earlier, we will ask the carpenters to make a level cut on the bottom end of the rafters. For the moment, we draw this with a full 18 in. (457 mm) overhang on the rafter itself; later we may adjust this dimension, if the finished overhang dimension is too large or too small.

Next, we add roof sheathing panels. Plywood or oriented strand board (OSB) panels for a 24 in. (610 mm) rafter spacing can be as thin as 7⁄16 in. (11 mm), but experience with other buildings has shown us that a ⅝ in. (16 mm) thickness produces a roof plane that is less prone to show sagging between rafters (*Robust Assemblies*, Chapter 10). ▷

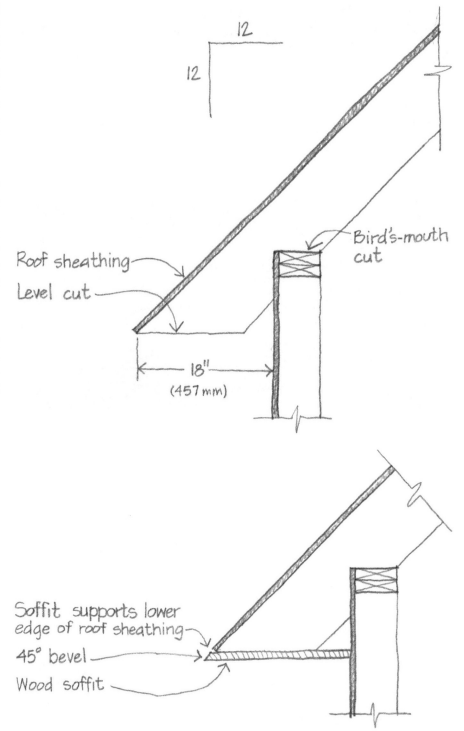

The lower edges of the sheathing panels will need to be supported at the eave to prevent an unsightly waviness from showing along the edge of the roof. The soffit can provide this support if it is stiff enough (***Small Structures***, Chapter 7). It could be made from ¾ in. (19 mm) plywood and/or nominal 1 in. (25 mm) boards. Again, experience comes into play here. Engineering analysis might show that a thinner plywood soffit would be strong enough and stiff enough, but hands-on experience and field observation tell us that thinner plywood will be too flimsy (***Refining the Detail***, Chapter 13). We could make the soffit from a single strip of plywood, but we would have to cut into it for ventilation openings, and the wide pieces of plywood would be heavy and hard to fit accurately into place (***Parts That Are Easy to Handle***, Chapter 11). Furthermore, the 45-degree (12/12) bevel on the outer edge would be hard to cut in a perfectly straight line with a hand-held circular saw, and its knife edge would be fragile because of the layered construction of the plywood (***Clean Edge***, Chapter 12). If we adopted a square edge rather than a 45-degree edge, the exposed edges of the laminations in the plywood would not be very attractive, especially because there tend to be voids in the interior layers.

A square-edged piece of solid lumber could make an excellent outer edge for the soffit. Soft pine would be adequate, but we know from experience that vertical-grain Douglas fir tends to be very straight and much stiffer than pine, and it could give good structural support to the lower edge of the roof sheathing. It could also support one edge of a formed aluminum continuous louver strip in the soffit to ventilate the roof cavities.

The building code requires that we install an ***Air Barrier System*** (Chapter 2) over the roof sheathing. For this we will use a tear-resistant polyolefin underlayment product that comes in rolls that are wider and longer than those of traditional roofing felt, reducing seams that might not be well sealed. This helps keep the wind from blowing water through the shingles and the joints in the roof sheathing (***Rainscreen Assembly and Pressure Equalization***, Chapter 1). It also serves as a backup layer

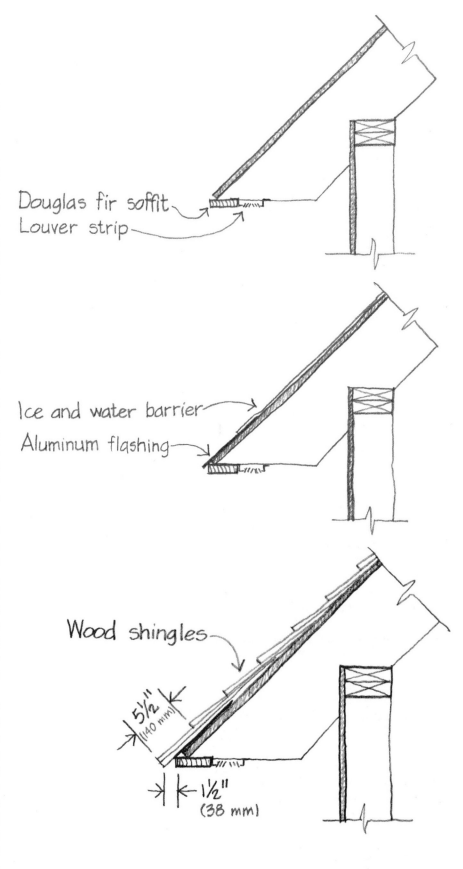

of waterproof material in case there should be a leak in the shingles (**Moisture Break**, Chapter 1). The ice and water barrier sheet is installed in place of the lowest strip of underlayment and should drain out over the edge of the soffit board. It is a very soft, flexible material that cannot support itself, however, so we add a narrow strip of aluminum flashing beneath it to carry any water drainage free of the soffit (**Small Structures**, Chapter 7).

The wood shingles of the roof are applied at the industry-recommended exposure of 5½ in. (140 mm), which gives so-called triple coverage, in which no portion of the roof is protected by fewer than two layers of shingle, giving considerable security against water leakage, even if a shingle should crack (**Expected Life**, Chapter 10). The undercourse and first course of shingles should overhang the soffit board by the 1½ in. (38 mm) dimension (measured horizontally) recommended by the red cedar shingle industry, to allow water to drip free and not run back under the soffit (**Overhang and Drip**, Chapter 1). It will be important to show this overhang dimension on the finished drawing, because carpenters need to be alerted to its importance, or they will often provide a smaller overhang.

This takes care of the roof edge in a way that is simple, attractive, and functionally satisfactory. Now we must finish off the soffit area. We prefer locating the soffit vent near the outer edge of the overhang, because experience shows that when it is located near the building wall, on sunny winter days warm air may rise off the wall below and enter the soffit and cold roof cavity, causing premature snowmelt and ice-damming on the roof.

To support the innermost portion of the soffit, we must provide horizontal framing all the way back to the wall sheathing (**Small Structures**, Chapter 7). We do this with a header strip nailed to the wall and short lookouts face-nailed to the side of each rafter tail, butting to the header. Working to scale, we see that the 2 × 4 stock normally used for such framing will not fit, but that 2 × 3 stock will. The span of the lookouts is extremely short – only a few inches – so 2 × 3s will be sufficiently stiff to nail against. ▷

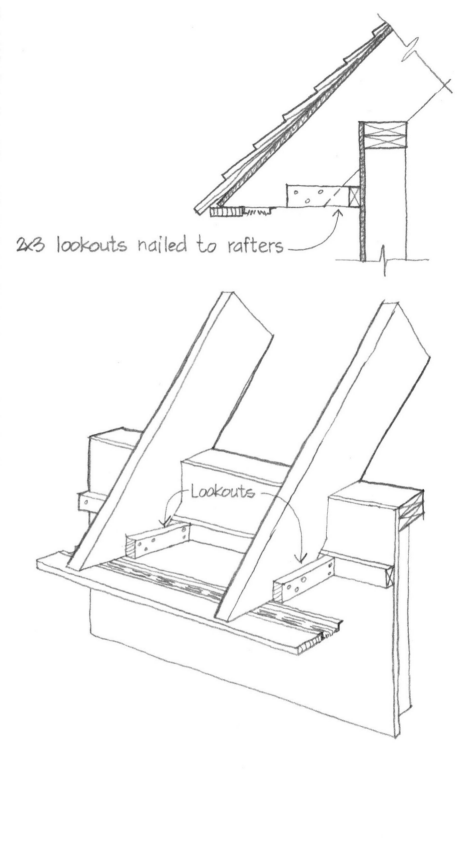

SECTION 1 ■ APPLYING THE DETAIL PATTERNS 263

We could close the soffit with fir or pine boards. These would look very handsome but would require finicky blind nailing in very tight quarters in a difficult overhead position (**Accessible Connections**, Chapter 11). A strip of A-face plywood with one edge planed perfectly straight could work well here: The planed edge would fit against the aluminum strip vent, which would conceal most of the raw edges of exposed plies. The other edge, with its slightly wavy cut, characteristic of hand-held circular saw work, can be held short of the siding by a comfortable margin of ±¼ in. (6 mm) to allow for inaccuracies (**Dimensional Tolerance**, Chapter 12). This gap will be covered by a trim strip that will be nailed in place after the siding has been installed (**Hierarchy of Refinement**, Chapter 14).

We add the building wrap **Air Barrier System** (Chapter 2) and wood shingles over the wall sheathing. We select a 7½ in. (190 mm) exposure for the wall shingles. The literature from the red cedar shingle industry allows an exposure of 8½ in. (216 mm) on walls, which should give the necessary double coverage, but our experience on prior projects has been that many shingles are far shorter than their nominal 18 in. (457 mm) length, leading to the exposure of small areas of building paper at the tops of the joints, unless the exposure is reduced somewhat. The top courses of shingles will have to be cut off where they meet the soffit board, leaving an exposed line of nail heads and a rough upper edge of shingles. We conceal the irregular edges of both the shingles and the soffit board with a red cedar 1 × 2 trim piece that forms an easy **Sliding Fit** (Chapter 12) to close the soffit detail tightly and attractively.

Thinking about Fasteners and Finishes

The soffit boards will be exposed to view. It is tempting to try to attach them with finish nails, but we must keep in mind that the Douglas fir 1 × 4 is semistructural, lending stiffness to the edge of the roof sheathing. Ladder pressure during construction might dislodge the 1 × 4 if it were finish nailed, pulling the lumber off over the headless nails. In service, under heavy snow loadings, the same thing might occur (**Expected**

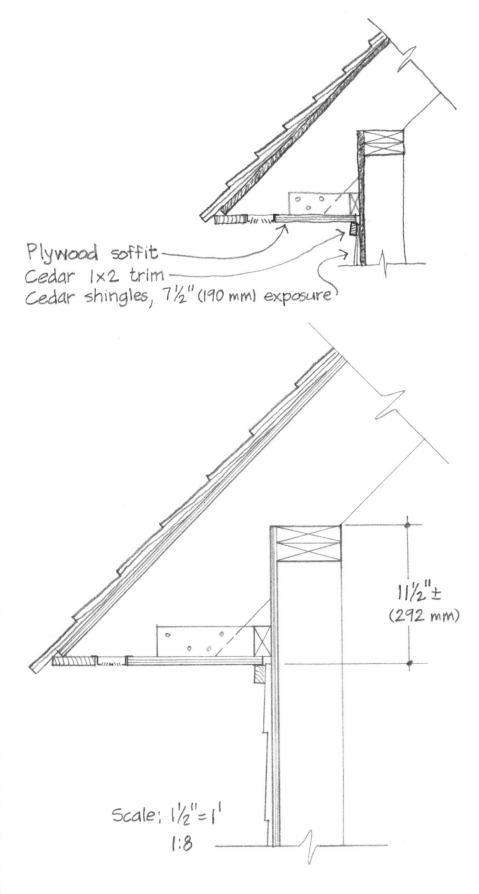

Life, Chapter 10). We need headed nails, but common nails with their large heads would look rather crude. Siding nails, which have smaller heads, are one good choice for fastening the soffit boards to the framing. Another good choice would be finish drywall screws, which have very small heads and which would draw the boards tightly to the framing. In either case, the fasteners should be stainless steel, aluminum, or hot-dip galvanized to minimize corrosion staining, because even a protected soffit attracts some condensation that wets the surface and corrodes metal fasteners (**Robust Assemblies**, Chapter 10). There probably will not be space on the drawings to indicate the fasteners, so we make a note to be sure that this information is in the written specifications for the project.

At this point, we need to be thinking also about how the soffit will be finished. If it will be painted, the heads of the nails or screws can be recessed and their holes filled and sanded before painting. Painting is generally a three-coat process – a primer plus two coats of latex paint – with sanding between coats to ensure a smooth finish. Staining, either with transparent or heavy-bodied stain, requires only two coats and no sanding, so it is more economical. We adopt a heavy-bodied stain finish and make a note to include this in the written specifications.

Checking the Spatial Implications of the Eave Detail

It is apparent that the steep roof pitch and the broad overhang place the soffit some distance below the top of the wall. Will this push the window heads too low? We construct the detail to scale and measure that the soffit lies almost 12 in. (305 mm) below the top of the wall plate. If the wall is framed at a standard 8 ft. (2438 mm) height, this will place the window heads at

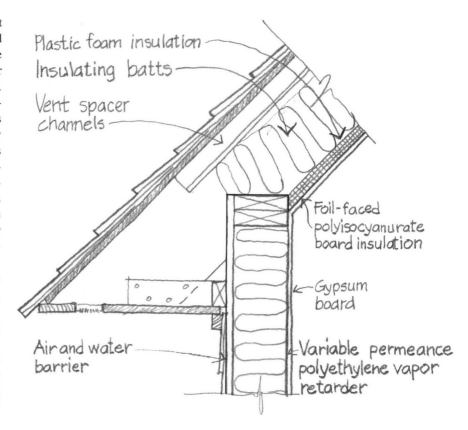

about 7 ft. (2134 mm), which is more than sufficient for a structure of this small scale.

Detailing Insulation, Ventilation, and Interior Finishes

We now add to our eave detail the plasticfoam insulating panels, gypsum board interior finish layer, and mineral wool insulating batts that we selected earlier. Where the insulating batts tend to push up into the ventilating airspace over the exterior walls, we provide short lengths of foam plastic vent spacer channels to maintain a free flow of air. We note on our drawing the continuous air and water barrier building wrap that is installed on the exterior side of the sheathing.

We note that the air and water barrier will extend over the double top plates and turn down a few inches on the inner face of the wall framing. At this junction, it will meet the foil-faced polyisocyanurate board insulation. In this cold climate, we will install a variable-permeance polyethylene-based vapor retarder to the inner face of the wall framing. In low ambient humidity such as wintertime, it will be a Class II vapor retarder, preventing interior water vapor from entering the wall assembly. In humid conditions, it will be vapor permeable to let vapor escape to the interior. It also extends to the top plates, where the foil-faced rigid foam insulation takes over as the Class II vapor retarder. ▷

DETAILING THE RAKE

The eave detail we have designed looks good to us, but it represents only one edge of each roof plane. The opposite edge of each roof plane is the ridge, and the two adjacent, sloping edges are the rakes. Until the ridge, rakes, and wall corners are designed and their details coordinated with the eave, we will not assume that the eave detail we have just developed is final. By "coordinated" we mean that the details should be consistent with one another aesthetically, that they should be a consistent set of **Contributive Details** (Chapter 14), and that they should meet gracefully and comfortably at the corners where they come together. With this in mind, we design the rakes next, with special reference to how the rakes join the eave.

Exterior Features of the Rake

The building that we are designing does not have a rake overhang. Our task therefore is simply to design a detail that will keep out rain and snow at the sloping edges of the roof while covering the rough edges of materials where the wall siding and roof shingles join.

We have already selected cedar shingles for both the roofing and the siding. We could finish the rake with a rake board; if we did this, we might want to use an unfinished cedar board to match the shingles, or, if it were pine, we might coat it with a heavy-bodied stain to match the soffits (**Hierarchy of Refinement**, Chapter 14). We could also finish the rake with a sloping trim course of shingles. In comparison to the stained trim board, this would minimize the prominence of the rake lines and

Rake board

Rake shingles

would in turn contribute to the minimalist aesthetic that we have in mind (**Composing the Detail**, Chapter 14). We decide to use shingles for the rake trim.

The sloping course of rake trim shingles could be applied directly over the top edge of the sidewall shingles, but this top edge is very irregular in thickness because of the sawtooth profile of the shingled wall. To provide a flat surface on which to nail the trim shingles, we attach over the top edge of the wall sheathing a concealed nailing strip, a narrow board whose thickness, ¾ in. (19 mm), is about the same as the maximum total depth of the sidewall shingles. To protect and conceal the cut shingle edges and nail heads along the very top edge of the sidewall shingles, we make this nailing strip about an inch narrower than the trim shingles, thus allowing the trim shingles to overlap the sidewall shingles by a generous amount (**Composing the Detail**, Chapter 14). We must specify a width for the rake trim shingles; 3 in. (76 mm) is perhaps the minimum that will allow for proper nailing to the nailing strip beneath. We select the actual width by studying the appearance of rake trim courses of various widths on the end elevation of the building. We select 3½ in. (89 mm), which results in a nailing strip 2½ in. (64 mm) wide (1 × 3, a conveniently standard size). (See

Uncut Units, Chapter 11.) Wood shingles are customarily furnished by the manufacturer in assorted random widths, ranging from about 3 to 12 in. (76–305 mm), so the builder will use a table saw to cut constant-width shingles for the rake from wider shingles.

The wood shingles on the roof must overhang the rake trim shingles by 1 in. (25 mm) or so, to prevent water from running under the rake edges. If we install a ¾ in. (19 mm) thick nailing strip, and the rake shingles are about ¾ in. (19 mm) thick at their maximum, the roof shingles must be laid with a total rake overhang of 2½ in. (64 mm) beyond the sheathing of the gable wall. It is wise to note this dimension on the final detail drawing, because the roof is usually shingled before the walls and rakes. The builder must have the foresight to provide a sufficient overhang or else face a difficult and expensive reshingling of the roof edges. The detailer should take precautions to avoid this potentially costly situation.

The lower corner of each rake must terminate gracefully at the triangular cheek area on each corner of the building. Probably the simplest way to finish the cheek is to extend the sheathing and sidewall shingles onto it. The spacing of the rake trim shingles can be matched to the spacing of the roof shingles for a neat appearance.

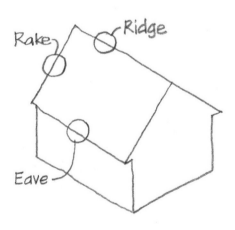

The last rake trim shingle at the bottom can be left square, as shown, or cut off level, as dictated by appearance considerations. At the ridge of the roof, the two rake trim courses can intersect with a miter. The two mitered shingles will be the only ones on the facade that will have exposed nail heads, unless a mastic construction adhesive is used to glue these two shingles in place, which may not bond well and would make future reshingling difficult (***Expected Life***, Chapter 10).

There is one other aspect of the rake detail that requires our attention, and that is the framing of the triangular wall of the gable. Carpenters are accustomed to building houses with attics, but our building has none. In houses with attics, the wall studs in the gable ends are normally interrupted at ceiling level by a double top plate, and short studs on top of this plate are used to frame the triangular gable. The top plate is supported laterally by the attic floor. In our building, which has no attic floor, this type of framing would not be strong enough against wind loads. The gable wall studs in our building must be single pieces that stretch from floor to rafter. We scale an elevation drawing to find that the longest stud will be about 15 ft. (4.6 m) tall. We are using 2 × 6 studs 24 in. apart (38 × 140 @ 610 mm). Are these strong and stiff enough for such a tall wall? We check a table in the building code and find that they are. We know from experience that carpenters will not frame the end walls with full-height studs unless we tell them to do so, so we make a note to call this out on the elevations and sections of the construction drawings. ▷

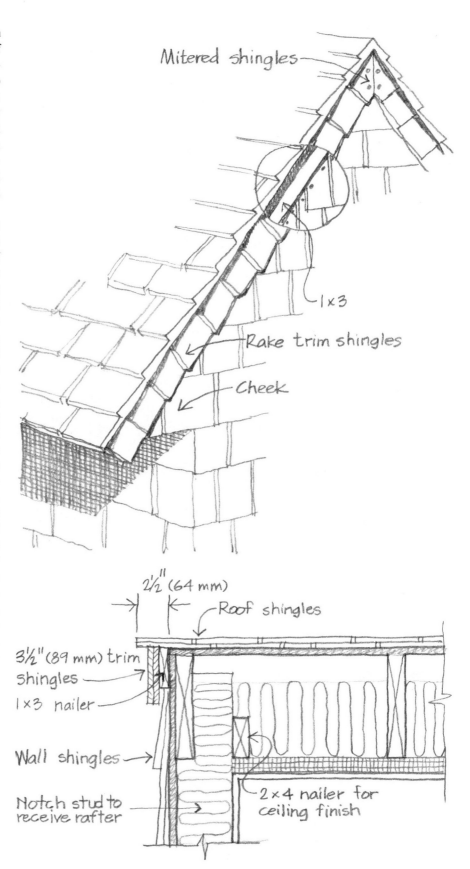

Developing the Soffit Termination

Looking up from beneath, the eave soffit must terminate neatly against the inside surface of the cheek shingles, which should hang down to form a drip 1 in. (25 mm) or so below the soffit. If the soffit boards and continuous vent strip were simply butted to the cheek, a somewhat rough appearance would result. The most finished appearance would result from mitering the 1 × 4 outer soffit piece to form a return at the end of the soffit (*Hierarchy of Refinement*, Chapter 14). This will work if the 1 × 4 is made of well-seasoned lumber, such as the kiln-dried Douglas fir that we have already chosen. If there is any uncertainty about the moisture content of the soffit lumber, it is better to use a butt joint to avoid the opening of the miter joint that will occur if the wood shrinks (*Butt Joint*, Chapter 12). Notice that the location of the butt joint is chosen to conceal the end grain of the wood against the vertical surface of the cheek shingles, rather than expose it under the sloping roof shingles.

Our design for the rake detail is now complete, pending a later check for consistency with the other details of the building.

DETAILING THE RIDGE

We must design a detail for the ridge consistent with the eave and rake details. We begin by drawing the structural elements of the ridge: the rafters from each side and a ridge board between their plumb cuts. The building code requires only a nominal 1 in. (25 mm) ridge board, but we know that most builders prefer to use a nominal 2 in. (51 mm) ridge board, because it usually leads to a straighter ridge (*Local Skills and Resources*, Chapter 13). Before we settle on the height of the ridge board, however, we must work out the ventilation opening at the top.

The functional requirements for the ridge detail are that it diverts water to the roof surfaces on either side and that it provides screened, water-protected openings for ventilation of the airspaces between the rafters. An easy way to satisfy both of these requirements is to use a manufactured aluminum ridge vent strip that is simply nailed over the top course of shingles on each side. The strip is designed with screened ventilation openings that are protected from gravity-driven water by overhangs and from wind-driven water by aerodynamic baffles. For our building, the disadvantage of the aluminum ridge vent is that we do not feel its appearance is up to that of a roof finished with a high-quality material such as wood shingles. We would prefer to finish the ridge either with a pair of cedar or redwood boards, or with a traditional "Boston ridge," composed of the same wood shingles that are used for the roofing. This leaves us with the problem of providing ventilation openings that are protected from water penetration and insects.

Some catalog research turns up several proprietary designs for protected ridge ventilation strips that can be covered with shingles or boards. We select one that we know is available locally (*Off-the-Shelf Parts*, Chapter 13), and we trace its catalog detail onto our developing ridge detail. We draw the plywood sheathing and hold the top edge of each slope back from the ridge line by the 2 in. (51 mm) dimension recommended by the vent strip manufacturer. We

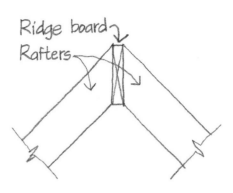

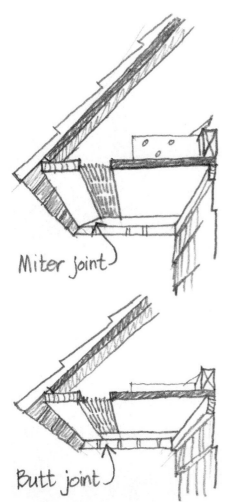

draw the courses of wood shingles leading up to the ridge, and we cut them off at the upper edge of the plywood. We add the vent strip with its flexible center portion that adjusts to any roof pitch. We look again at the size of the ridge and decide that, to keep the ventilation passages free, it can be only a 2 × 10 piece of lumber.

How will we finish over the vent strip? The catalog shows that there is only a narrow zone available for nailing on each side of the vent strip. This is not sufficient for shingles, which would require two lines of nails on either side of the ridge, so we decide to use ridge boards. We will specify that these be made of unfinished red cedar, to match the shingles. In drawing the ridge boards, we note that because of the taper of the shingles, the boards do not meet at right angles. On the final detail drawing, we will add a note to the carpenter to measure the angle and plane the edges of the boards to match it. Because of the difficulty of doing exacting cutting and fitting while standing on roof scaffolding, we will recommend in the written specifications that the ridge board pairs be assembled on sawhorses on the ground and then carried up and attached (*Simulated Assemblies*, Chapter 11). To minimize cupping of the boards, we show a *Relieved Back* (Chapter 6) on each board, and we specify brass screws for all of the fastenings (nails often pull out under cupping stress; screws cannot).

Moving to the interior of the ridge detail, we add the insulating batts. We see that the ends of the batts might push up against the ridge board and block the air passages, so we add foam plastic vent spacers. We complete the ridge detail by adding 1 in. (25 mm) of foil-faced plastic foam insulation and the gypsum board ceiling planes. To simplify installation of the foam, we adjust the vertical position of

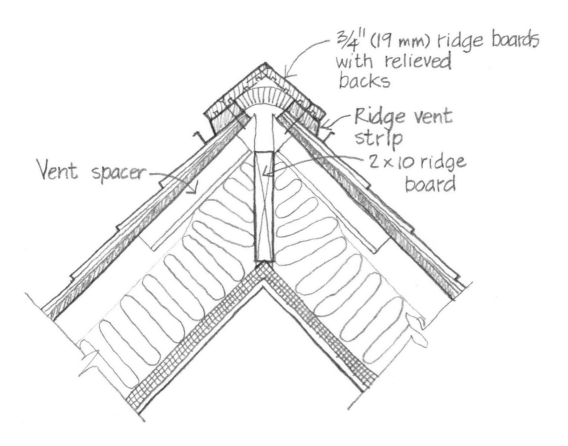

the ridge board to allow the panels to butt beneath it (**Butt Joint**, Chapter 12).

How will we terminate the ridge detail? If the detail that we have drawn simply runs to the ends of the building, there will be a raw end of vent strip to cover, and the raised profile of our ridge detail will not be consistent with the minimal geometry that we are creating. After some sketching of alternatives, we decide to stop the vented ridge detail 1 ft. (305 mm) short of each end wall, closing the vent strip with standard end caps. This should still provide plenty of ventilation for the last rafter space at each end, and the last foot of ridge boards can be applied directly to the shingled slopes (**Composing the Detail**, Chapter 14).

We must be sure that we have provided enough roof ventilation to meet the building code requirement of 1 square foot of ventilation per 300 square feet of floor area. Our building has a floor area of about 320 square feet (30 m²), so we need about square feet (0.1 m²) total of free ventilation openings. The code requires that this be divided approximately equally between the eaves and the ridge. If this were an unheated attic, we would intentionally pressurize it slightly by making ridge vents about 40% of the required area, and soffit vents about 60%. Slightly pressurizing an attic reduces suction of the conditioned air out of the occupied spaces below, saving energy and enhancing comfort.

Multiplying the catalog values for the free ventilation areas per foot of the soffit vent and ridge vent strips by the linear footages of each strip, we find that we have provided several times the legal requirement, so even the end rafter spaces will be adequately ventilated (**Robust Assemblies**, Chapter 10).

With the finishing of the designs for the eave, rake, and ridge details, we can now visualize completely how the roof will look. We make a freehand perspective to be sure that we like the way our details work with one another and with our design intentions for the form of the building (**Contributive Details**, Chapter 14). We note with satisfaction that our details are beginning to create a clear personality for the building. ▷

DETAILING THE GRADE CONDITION

There are three choices for the floor and foundation system: (1) a concrete slab on grade, (2) a basement with a wood floor structure above, or (3) a crawl space with a wood floor structure. In the New England climate, a slab on grade, even if properly insulated, tends to feel cold in winter, unless it is heated with hot water coils or electric resistance wires. In the humid days of summer, a slab will often be cool enough to condense moisture from the air, unless the room is continually air-conditioned or dehumidified (*Warm Interior Surfaces*, Chapter 4). We reject the slab option. We also decide against the basement option, because our client has no use for a basement in this particular building. We will detail a crawl space foundation.

We check the code requirements for a crawl space. It must be at least 18 in. (457 mm) high, with an access door at least 18 in. × 24 in. (457 × 610 mm). It must be continuously insulated around the perimeter to at least R-11 (R-19). Insulated crawl spaces are not required to have ventilation openings when the ground surface is covered with a sealed polyethylene vapor retarder and the space is treated in accordance with the International Energy Conservation Code as a semi-conditioned space. We will insulate the crawl space wall as planned and will provide small supply and return ducts in this space. The temperature and humidity will be stabilized within a moderate range at very little expense.

Structuring the Floor

Before we can draw the grade detail, we must also know the size of the floor joists. We consult the floor joist design table in *Span Tables for Joists and Rafters*, keeping in mind that the framing lumber most commonly available in New England lumberyards is spruce-pine-fir, a mix of several species that are rated at a modulus of elasticity (E) of 1,300,000 psi (9 000 MPa). From experience we know that joists designed to this E-value tend to feel a bit bouncy underfoot, so we customarily design joists as if their E were only 1,000,000 psi (17,000 MPa) (*Robust Assemblies*, Chapter 10). Following down this column in the floor joist table for a 40 psf (1.92 kPa) live load, and assuming a 16 in. (406 mm) spacing of joists, we find that a 2 × 6 can span 8 ft. 4 in.; a 2 × 8, 11 ft.; a 2 × 10, 14 ft.; and a 2 × 12, 17 ft. (38 × 140 mm: 2.54 m; 38 × 184 mm: 3.35 m; 38 × 235 mm: 4.27 m; 38 × 286 mm: 5.18 m).

We overlay some tracing paper framing diagrams on the floor plan.

We could span the floor with 2 × 6s across the 16 ft. (4.88 m) dimension with a beam in the middle; we could span it with 2 × 8s across the 20 ft. (6.10 m) dimension with a beam in the middle. However, 2 × 10s offer no new solutions, although 2 × 12s would allow us to span the width of the building without using a center beam. Without doing a detailed check of the comparative costs, we know that eliminating the beam would eliminate the need for beam pockets in the foundation, a line of joist connections across the middle of the building, as well as the cost of the beam itself. In other words, the 2 × 12s would greatly simplify the framing of the floor. There are two reasons for not wanting to use such deep members: They raise the floor another few inches above grade, and they are heavy and harder to handle. But the higher floor is of no consequence in this particular building, and the heavier framing members are not too hard to handle at ground level. We decide to use 2 × 12 floor framing. The builder may propose alternatives, such as truss-joists, if cost factors are advantageous.

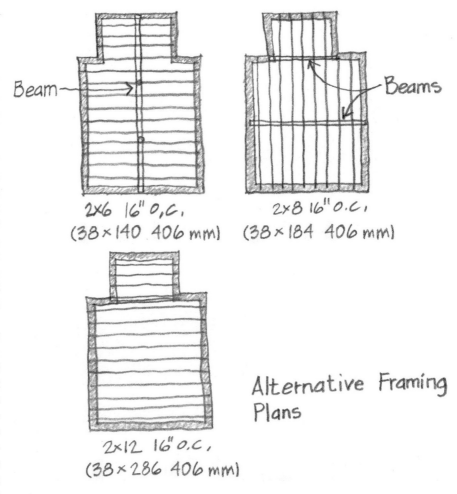

Alternative Framing Plans

Developing the Basic Detail

As we develop the grade detail, we are **Rehearsing the Construction Sequence** (Chapter 13) step by step. We draw a customary 16 × 8 in. (406 × 203 mm) concrete footing, whose bottom surface lies the code-mandated 4 ft. (1219 mm) below grade (**Foundation below Frost Line**, Chapter 6). Knowing that site-cast concrete foundations are the norm in this area (**Local Skills and Resources**, Chapter 13), we show an 8 in. (203 mm) concrete foundation wall on the footing. To reduce cracking of the wall, we insert pairs of #5 (16 mm) reinforcing bars top and bottom. (The size and number of bars is not based on rigorous engineering analysis in this case, but on conventional practice.) To tie the frame down to the foundation, we show an embedded anchor bolt every 4 ft. (1219 mm) around the perimeter of the building (**Small Structures**, Chapter 7). The code permits a single 2 × 6 sill, but we decide to double the 2 × 6 for greater stiffness and better nailing. We note the lower sill piece should be made of preservative-treated wood to avoid decay from soil moisture rising by capillary action (**Dry Wood**, Chapter 10).

Now we draw the framing and sheathing in order of construction: The 2 × 12 joists and header, the ⅝ in. (16 mm) plywood subfloor, the 2 × 6 stud wall, and the ½ in. (13 mm) wall sheathing. We have dimensioned the floor plan of the building so that the subfloor will consist entirely of full and half sheets of plywood (**Uncut Units**, Chapter 11). The exterior wall finish is drawn on the detail: an **Air Barrier System** (Chapter 2) and a weathering layer of cedar shingles. We show the undercourse and bottom course of shingles projecting 1 in. (25 mm) below the top of the foundation to form an **Overhang and Drip** (Chapter 1) that will help keep the sill dry. ▷

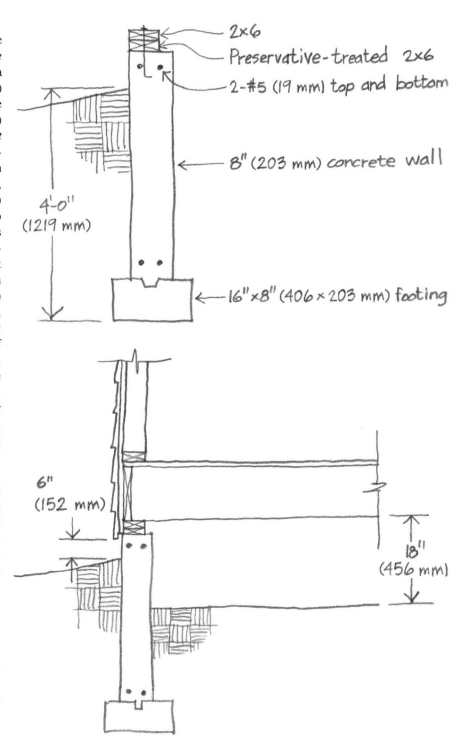

SECTION 1 ■ APPLYING THE DETAIL PATTERNS

Insulation in the walls will be the special R-22 (R-153) HD mineral wool batts with an inside variable-permeance vapor retarder. This leaves us with the problem of how to insulate the floor against heat losses and gains. We could insulate between the floor joists, above the crawl space. This would be simple and comfortable, but it would leave the crawl space cold in winter, which would lead to excessive heat losses from the ductwork and frozen water pipes below the toilet room. We must insulate around the crawl space so that it will remain relatively warm. A bit of library research tells us that the earth floor of the crawl space does not need to be insulated if we insulate its perimeter properly, because the protected earth within the crawl space will remain at a fairly high temperature throughout the winter.

There are two ways of insulating the perimeter. One is to install a couple of inches of foam polystyrene board on the outside of the foundation. The other is to spray an open-celled, vapor-permeable foam insulation to the inside of the framing and sill, and down the inside of the foundation wall to the floor of the crawl space. We try these options on tracing paper overlays: The outside insulation would require moving the foundation wall inward a couple of inches from the edge of the floor frame and cantilevering the sill by this dimension to create space for the boards of foam plastic. This is acceptable structurally, because most of the wall and roof load is transmitted to the sill through the joists anyway, and these would still have a firm bearing through the sill to the concrete wall. The insulation would also have to be coated above grade to protect it from sunlight and mechanical damage. This coating would be stucco with a reinforcing mesh. The inside insulation would be installed under somewhat cramped conditions (**Accessible Connections**, Chapter 11), but would require no special coating. It would probably end up being a little easier for the builder, and therefore less expensive. We draw the insulation on our sketch. We can use hygrothermal modeling to research its performance and will monitor it in winter and summer after the building is occupied. We finish the crawl space floor with a heavy 6 mil (0.006 in. or 0.15 mm) polyethylene vapor barrier on

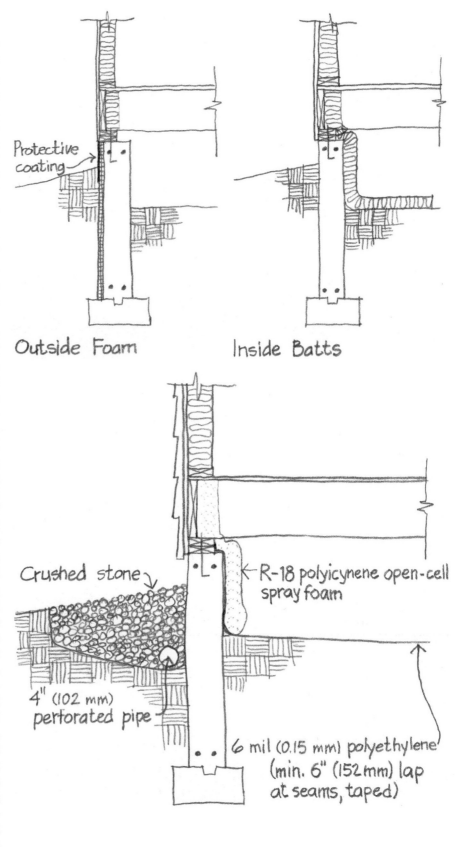

top of the soil. This is turned up at all edges and sealed with mastic against the face of the crawl space wall. This continuous membrane is a reliable barrier and is easy to install (**Robust Assemblies**, Chapter 10).

Outside the foundation, we keep the bottom of the siding at least 6 in. (203 mm) above grade level (**Dry Wood**, Chapter 10). We slope the grade away from the building for good drainage (**Wash**, Chapter 1). Under the drip line of the eaves, we provide a broad, shallow trench filled with coarse crushed stone. This will prevent soil erosion (**Building Armor**, Chapter 10) and keep dripping water from splashing mud up onto the siding (**Dry Wood**, Chapter 10). A thin, fluffy sill sealer, which is a glass fiber insulation, is placed on the top of the foundation wall before the sill plates are installed. This will fill the uneven top surface of the concrete and prevent air leaks. If groundwater was a problem on the building site, we would instead call for through-wall flashing to be installed in this location to prevent moisture from rising through the concrete to the wood superstructure (**Moisture Break**, Chapter 1).

We note that the floor of the crawl space lies a few inches below the outside grade. This could lead to flooding of the crawl space if there is a crack in the concrete wall. We add an asphaltic dampproofing layer to the outside of the wall below grade, but this will not bridge cracks that may form in the wall. We decide to play it safe and add a perforated drainage pipe around the foundation, below the level of the crawl space floor, laid in crushed stone (**Foundation Drainage**, Chapter 1). On our drawing, the crushed stone of the drip trench encroaches on the crushed stone in which we want to lay the pipe, so we simply combine the two into a single trench filled with stone. We examine the contours on the site plan and discover that we can slope the discharge pipe from this trench to drain by gravity into a nearby swale, avoiding the need for a pump (**Unobstructed Drainage**, Chapter 1).

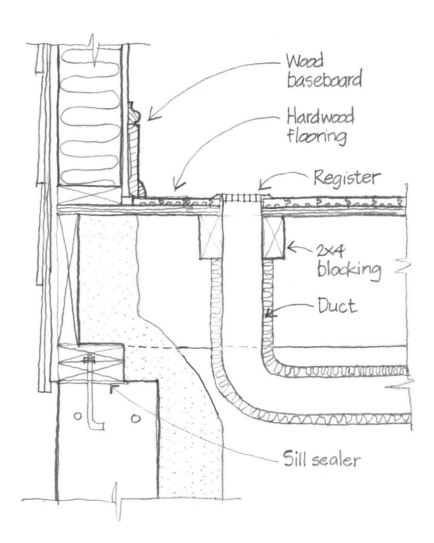

Detailing the Interior Finishes

The interior finishes are straightforward: a gypsum board wall, hardwood flooring, and a baseboard (**Building Armor**, Chapter 10). We notice that the standard patterns of flooring and baseboards all have **Relieved Backs** (Chapter 6) to reduce cupping problems. We decide this small showpiece building deserves the luxury of a three-piece baseboard, in which the shoe and cap moldings are slender, flexible strips that conform to the irregularities of the wall and floor with a **Sliding Fit** (Chapter 12). The **Reveal** (Chapter 12) at the junction of the cap and baseboard allows this to occur without creating unsightly misalignments of the two pieces.

We plan to heat and cool the building with a gas furnace and forced air. The floor registers for this system will be fed from insulated ductwork in the crawl space (**Horizontal Plenum**, Chapter 8). We add a typical floor register to our detail, showing structural blocking on either side to support the subfloor and flooring around the register (**Small Structures**, Chapter 7).

We have now solved the crawl space detailing, except for the required **Vapor Ventilation** (Chapter 4) and **Maintenance Access** (Chapter 10). For access, we decide to avoid exterior complications by providing a trapdoor in the floor of the toilet room. ▷

DETAILING THE CORNER

Working in plan view at the same scale as the other details (1½ in. = 1 ft. or 1:8), we construct details of typical outside and inside corners. As usual, we do this in order of construction as a way of **Rehearsing the Construction Sequence** (Chapter 13). One complete wall of the building will be framed to the full length of the building on the floor platform and tilted up into position. The other wall will be framed short of the corner by the depth of a stud so that it mates to the first wall with a simple **Butt Joint** (Chapter 12), and so on, around the building. As we draw this condition at the inside corner (the corner where the toilet room joins the main mass of the building), we provide a flat-framed 2 × 6 stud for attachment of the wall of the toilet room. We notice that the edge of the sheathing to the left of this flat stud has nothing to be fastened to. We add a 2 × 4 stud as a nailer; the 2 × 4 is less expensive than a 2 × 6, and it avoids thermal bridging. Although the wall between the main room and the toilet room would ordinarily be framed with 2 × 4s, in our building it must be framed with full-height 2 × 6s, as previously noted, because it becomes an exterior gable wall above.

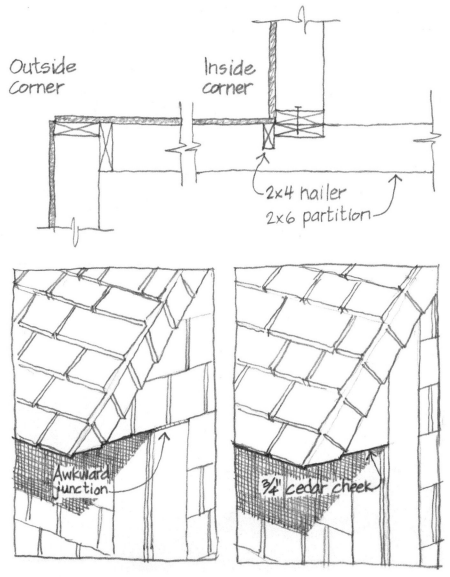

We must decide how we want the corner to look on the outside. We glance back at our early design sketches for the building and our three-dimensional sketches of the eave and rake details, looking for clues as to what we should do with the wall corners to create a consistent set of **Contributive Details** (Chapter 14). We are weighing two basic choices for the outside corner: to use vertical corner boards to which the wall shingles are butted, or to weave the shingles directly together at the corners. We have a slight preference for the first choice. Corner boards are the dominant corner finish on older buildings in the area, and they are simpler and quicker for the carpenter because of the simple **Butt Joint** (Chapter 12). A woven corner requires more labor, because the two corner shingles in each course must be planed to join one another tightly and neatly.

Our sketches of the area where the corner, rake, and eave join together show that there would be an awkward connection where the corner boards join the shingled triangular cheek area that we had envisioned earlier, because the end grain of the corner board is exposed and is very vulnerable to water penetration. We could avoid this by running the corner board on the gable end of the building all the way up to join the 1 × 3 spacer beneath the rake trim shingles. Then we would want to finish the cheek with a piece of ¾ in. (19 mm) cedar rather than shingles. We decide to do this (**Composing the Detail**, Chapter 14).

The traditional corner boards in the neighborhood are rather wide, usually around 7 to 8 in. (178 to 203 mm). We will use a cedar 1 × 8 on one wall and have the carpenter trim about 1 in. (25 mm) off the 1 × 8 that butts inside it, so the apparent widths of the two boards will be the same. We show a ¼ in. (6 mm) ***Reveal*** (Chapter 12) at the butt joint so that the carpenter can avoid some of the more finicky fitting that otherwise would be required. We also show shallow saw cuts in the back of each board, a ***Relieved Back*** (Chapter 6) detail that can be created with a table saw on the building site to reduce cupping of the wide boards. Eight-penny galvanized finish nails will be used to attach the boards, and the shingle courses will be butted tightly to them on either side. We will not paint the corner boards: They, like the cedar shingles and trim, will be left to weather naturally (***Surfaces That Age Gracefully***, Chapter 10).

Detailing the inside corner, we follow the standard practice of using a full 1 × 1 in. (25 × 25 mm) stick of cedar in the corner, butting both planes of shingles tightly against it.

Inside the building, the insulating batts will be installed between the studs and the vapor retarder across them. Then the gypsum board will be applied. We see that the gypsum board on two walls has no stud to which it can be nailed. There are several ways to provide such a stud at the outside corner; we choose to show a 2 × 4 that allows access for insulation to be stuffed behind it to the corner, eliminating a potential thermal bridge. A similar stud is required at the inside corner. ▷

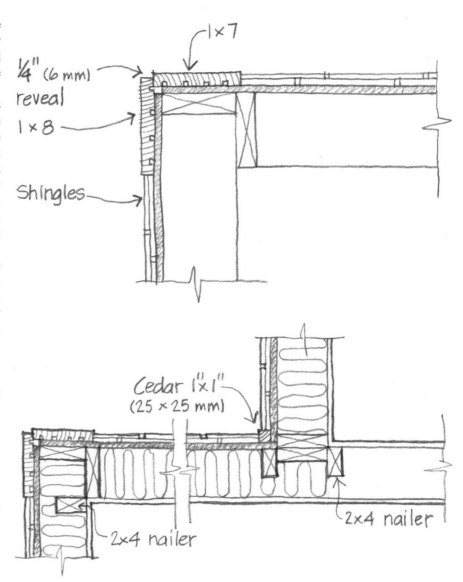

DETAILING THE WINDOWS
Selecting a Window

Again taking a cue from nearby historic houses, we decide to use double-hung wood windows in our building. We plunge into the catalogs of several reputable manufacturers to choose the windows for this project. We look for low maintenance and good appearance, and we decide to use a wood window that is clad with white vinyl on the exterior (*Surfaces That Age Gracefully*, Chapter 10). We look for good thermal performance and find that all of the manufacturers we are considering provide *Multiple Glazing* (Chapter 3) with selective coatings to achieve excellent insulating values (*Life Cycle*, Chapter 10). We look for *Rainscreen Assembly* (Chapter 1) details and find that, although all of the manufacturers use certain features of rainscreen detailing, none markets a true rainscreen design. We examine their details further and find that one manufacturer's details make more consistent use of *Overhang and Drip* (Chapter 1) features to protect the window and the surrounding wall. The tested performances of this window are impressive, too: The overall thermal resistance of the window unit, including the frame, is R-3.2 (R-22). It uses argon-filled insulating glass. Because of a clever *Weatherstripped Crack* (Chapter 2) detail, the air infiltration is only 0.05 cfm per foot of crack, and it is designed for a wind pressure of 40 psf (1.91 kPa). We also know this manufacturer has a good network of dealers in the area and a solid reputation for on-time delivery (*Off-the-Shelf Parts*, Chapter 13). We make a copy of the catalog details and slide them under a sheet of tracing paper to begin designing our window details. If we were developing our details using computer-aided drafting, or CAD, we could download the details directly into our drawing files from the manufacturer's online support. If constructing the project with a building information modeling (BIM) platform, a complete component model may be downloaded and used.

There is only one significant difference between the details that the window manufacturer furnishes and the details we want to draw: We are using studs that are 2 in. (51 mm) deeper. We will develop our details in order of construction and see how this affects our design.

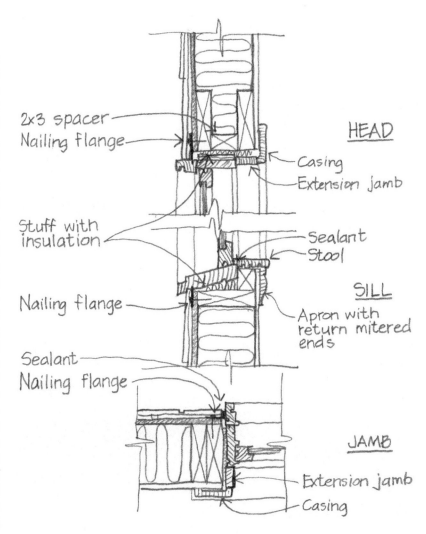

Developing the Basic Detail

We draw the studs, header, and wall sheathing of the rough opening in the standard head, sill, and jamb details. We space the two header pieces with a 2 × 3 to bring them out to full frame thickness, and we show insulation inside the header (*Thermal Break*, Chapter 3). The window unit is tilted up into the rough opening from the outside and pushed inward until the plastic nailing flanges lie flat against the air barrier and sheathing. At all boundaries of the opening, the air and water barrier is folded over the edges and layered shingle-style with flashing. There is a generous *Installation Clearance* (Chapter 11) and *Dimensional Tolerance* (Chapter 12) between the manufacturer-recommended rough opening dimension and the outside dimensions of the window unit that makes this potentially difficult five-plane fit into an easy *Sliding Fit* (Chapter 12). The window unit is held by hand while its sill is centered in the rough opening, leveled, and shimmed to its final position. Once checked, the sill flange is nailed to the sheathing and framing with galvanized shingle nails, whose broad heads offer a more secure bearing against the relatively fragile plastic (*Distributing Loads*, Chapter 7). One jamb of the window unit is then plumbed up, and its flange is nailed to the frame. The window is checked to make sure that it operates freely and that the cracks around the sashes are of constant width. Then the remainder of the flanges are nailed.

The exterior shingling presents no problems. There is a convenient notch in the underside of the sill to provide an *Overlap* (Chapter 1) with the shingles and create a *Clean Edge* (Chapter 12) where the two intersect. At the jambs, the shingles are held ¼ in. (6 mm) from the unit, to leave space for the sealant. These are "nonworking" sealant joints, in which very little movement is anticipated, so no backer rod is used. The plastic flange at the window head doubles as a flashing. The manufacturer's detail shows sealant between the shingles and the head of the window, but this makes no performative sense because the sealant would restrict the free drainage of water from the cracks between the shingles. We detail the head without sealant.

Moving indoors, the spaces between the window unit and the rough framing are filled with spray foam insulation. This is done primarily to provide an *Air Barrier System* (Chapter 2) that will reduce the leakage of air. The foam must be carefully installed to fill the cavity but not to excess, which could distort the window frame and cause the sashes to bind.

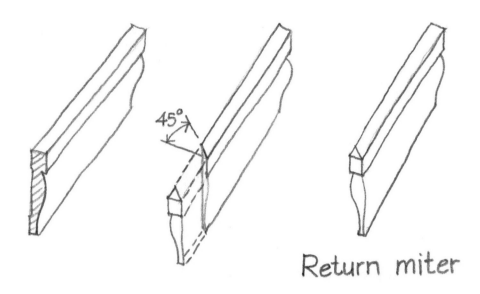

Return miter

Detailing the Interior Finishes

The first interior finishing operation around each window will be to install the stool, extending it past the opening on both sides so that the jamb casings can butt to it neatly. We show a strip of wood blocking to support the stool and the upper edge of the gypsum board. We rabbet the stool over the window sill and install a thin bead of sealant between them to provide a small *Upstand* (Chapter 1) against the penetration of wind-driven rain. We detail a *Relieved Back* (Chapter 6) to reduce cupping distortions and rounded *Safe Edges* (Chapter 9) on the inside. We make a note to specify back priming for all the interior window trim pieces. To cover the gap between the gypsum board and the stool, we install a wood apron. We decide to use very simple, flat casings and a simply molded apron to trim the window. At the two ends of the apron, the relieved back will show unless we ask the carpenter to do a return miter. This is easily done using a power miter saw. ▷

The greater depth of the framing of our building must be dealt with at the jambs and head of the window. This is done with simple, square-edged extension jambs that are nailed and glued to the window frame. Some plane work is usually required to adjust the exact depth of the extension jambs to match the level of the gypsum board all around. Then the jamb and head casings are applied, leaving a small **Reveal** (Chapter 12) where they meet the extension jambs, so as to simplify fitting. At the two upper corners, we have a choice between miter joints and butt joints. We select **Butt Joints** (Chapter 12) to avoid any chance that miters could open up in an unattractive way because of wood shrinkage, although this is a small risk with kiln-dried millwork of this relatively narrow width. The butt joints do require that return miters be created at the two exposed ends to conceal the relieved back.

There is always the danger with window details that we may design a feature that does not carry around the corner to the next detail in a satisfactory way. We avoid this in part by always showing with light lines the elevation of features that lie behind the plane through which the section is cut. Additionally, we prepare a couple of three-dimensional sketches to see how the corners look.

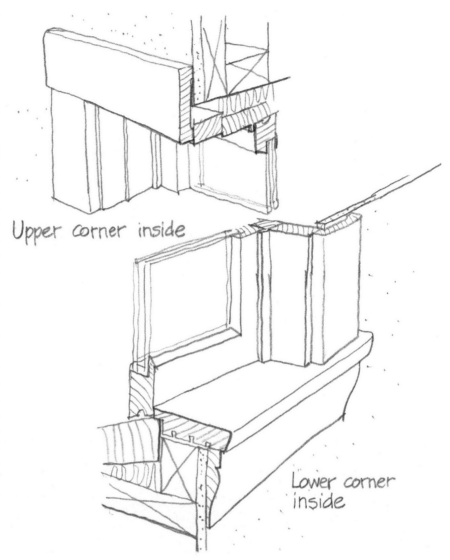

Upper corner inside

Lower corner inside

DESIGNING THE RAFTER TIES

Because this structure has neither an attic nor a ridge beam, exposed horizontal ties must be installed at intervals to keep the bottoms of the rafters from spreading. Some experimentation in plan and perspective leads us to decide tentatively on a spacing of 4 ft. (1.2 m) between ties. A simple mathematical analysis shows that, at this spacing, the tension in each tie will be 720 lb. (327 kg) under a full snow load. This is a very small force: A 1×3 could carry it safely. But there are reasons to use a larger piece of wood than this: Occupants of the building over the years are likely to hang things from the ties. Workers may lay planks across them to facilitate work on the ceiling. There would be difficulty making a 720 lb. connection at the ends of a 1×3 (*Robust Assemblies*, Chapter 10). A quick calculation shows that nine 10-penny nails are needed, or else a bolt; neither of these options would work with a member as small as a 1×3. We recognize the nails will be much cheaper to install than the bolt, because the required fasteners and installation tool will already be in the carpenter's belt (*Off-the-Shelf Parts*, Chapter 13). Perhaps the most compelling reason to use a larger tie is that a 1×3 would simply look too slender and weak (*Composing the Detail*, Chapter 14). We decide to try a pair of 2×8s with a 1½ in. (38 mm) space between. The 2×8s will be strong enough to support scaffolding planks and large enough to accept the required nails at the end.

The space between allows the twin ties to sandwich the end of a rafter, creating an easy connection. We make a note to dimension the rafter locations carefully on the roof framing plan so that the ties will occur at precisely the desired locations. ▷

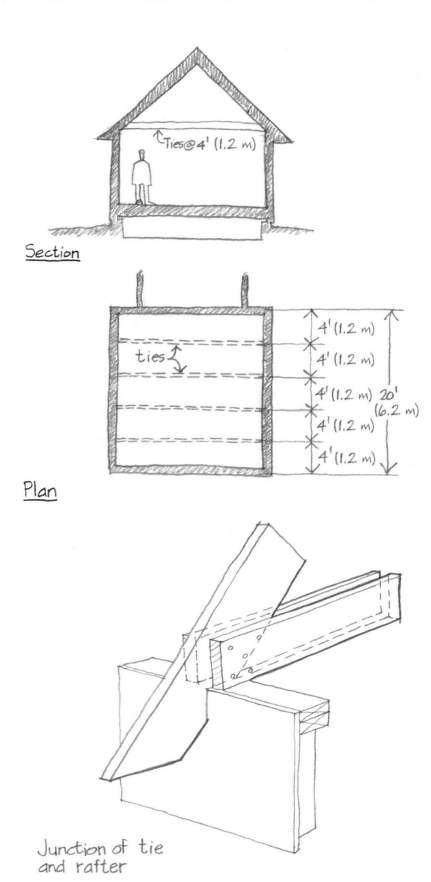

Junction of tie and rafter

We draw the 2 × 8 ties accurately on a ¼ in. scale (1:48) cross section of the building. They look heavy and overbearing, their horizontality seemingly negating much of the vertical quality of the roof space. They even appear to sag a bit, an optical illusion caused perhaps by their contrast with the upward-angling ceiling planes. After a series of experiments on tracing paper overlays, we decide to taper the ties from full thickness at the walls to a reduced thickness in the middle, making all the taper on the undersides of the members so as to create a slightly arched room space below (*Refining the Detail*, Chapter 13).

We also add a vertical member connecting the center of the ties to the ridge. The vertical member has little structural function but, together with the tapering, it seems to overcome the stodgy horizontality of the ties, relating well to the full height of the room. The tapers on all of the members express the structural tension in them, much as the taper in a strand of pulled taffy expresses its stretching (*Intensification and Ornamentation*, Chapter 14).

The vertical member will sandwich neatly between the twin ties but will have to butt to the underside of the rafters at the ridge – a difficult connection to make. We decide to make the vertical member of a pair of ¾ in. (19 mm) thick pieces that will spread and flex slightly as they rise from the ties so that they can be nailed to either side of the rafters at the ridge. The center of each of these pieces will have to be notched to go around the ridge board.

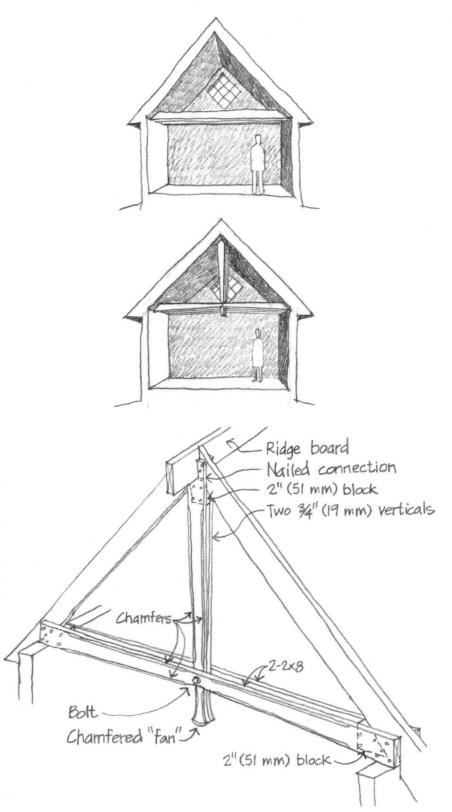

We will connect the vertical members to the horizontal ones at the center of the ties with a single exposed bolt. All the nailed connections will be buried in the roof and wall construction, making them invisible. In each of the three locations where paired members pass through the interior finish layer, we add a short block to close the gap between the members. We note that casing beads should be detailed around each of these penetrations to make a *Clean Edge* (Chapter 12) on the gypsum board finish.

To dress up the ties a bit, we decide to chamfer the edges, except in the zones near the ends and the center connection. This is a form of *Intensification* (Chapter 14) that will further bring out the tensile role of the members by making them appear thinner and more rounded in profile.

The lower end of the vertical member seems arbitrary and abrupt if it is merely cut off horizontally. We try many sketches of pendant designs before setting on a chamfered fan as a suitable termination (*Ornamentation*, Chapter 14).

In our notes for the written specifications, we record that ordinary framing lumber can be used for these members, but that the builder should select the pieces carefully so as to use wood of good visual quality. The grade markings and any other stray marks or scuffs should be sanded off (*Hierarchy of Refinement*, Chapter 14). Depending on our final decisions regarding interior finishes, we

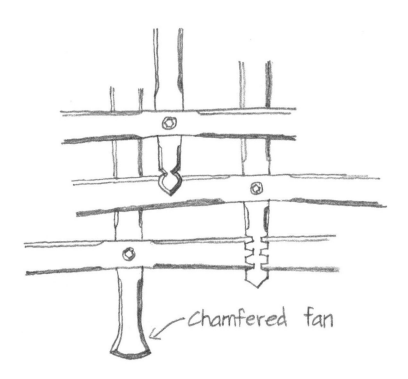

will either stain the wood members or sand, prime, and paint them. The wood will probably not be of such a quality that we would want to varnish it.

NEXT STEPS

We have now finished the preliminary design of the key details for the sales office. We draft precisely scaled, finished-looking versions of all these details for review. There are still a few important details to design: the bay window, the porch, and the intersection of the roof and wall where the main mass of the building joins the toilet room. When these have been completed, we will check all the details simultaneously to be sure that they are consistent in style and to see that the thermal insulation and vapor retarder are complete and continuous all around the building. ▷

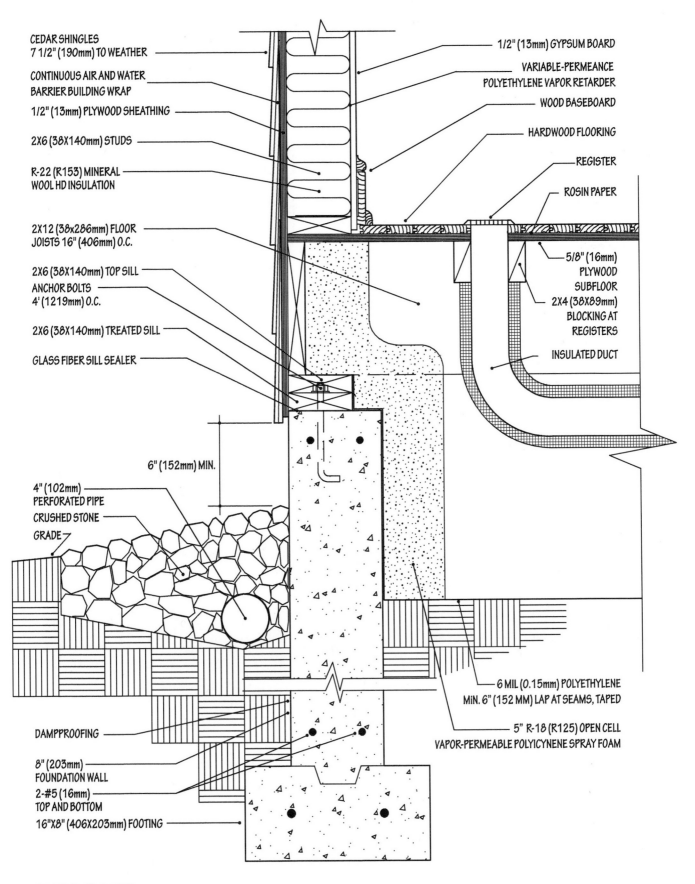

FOUNDATION DETAIL
Scale 1 1/2"=1' (1:8)

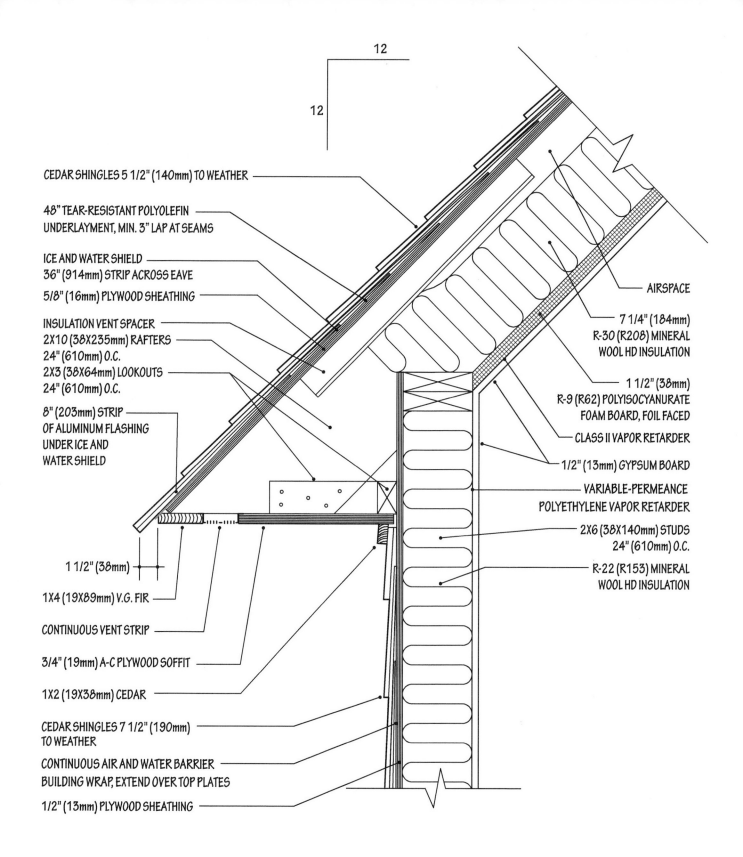

EAVE DETAIL
Scale 1 1/2"=1' (1:8)

SECTION 1 ■ APPLYING THE DETAIL PATTERNS

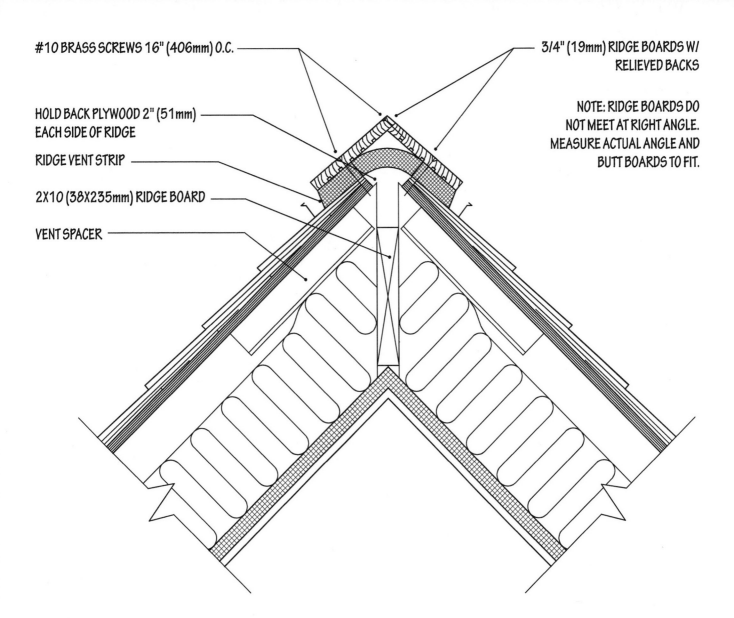

RIDGE DETAIL
Scale 1 1/2"=1' (1:8)

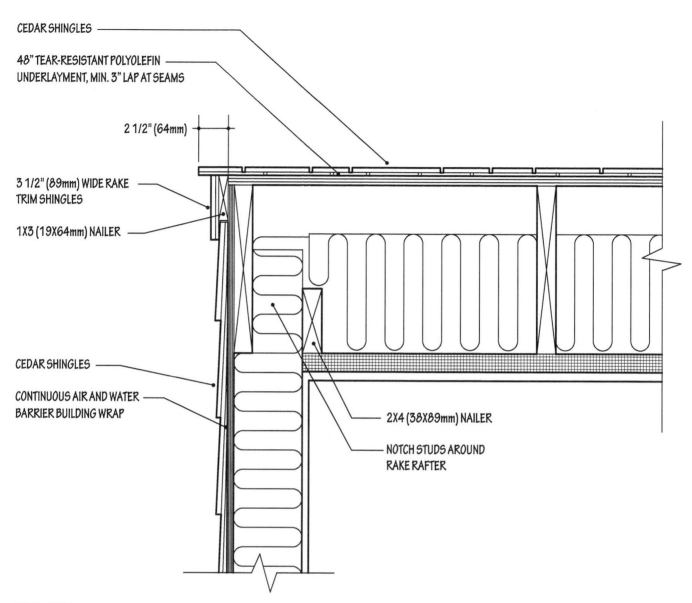

RAKE DETAIL
Scale 1 1/2"=1' (1:8)

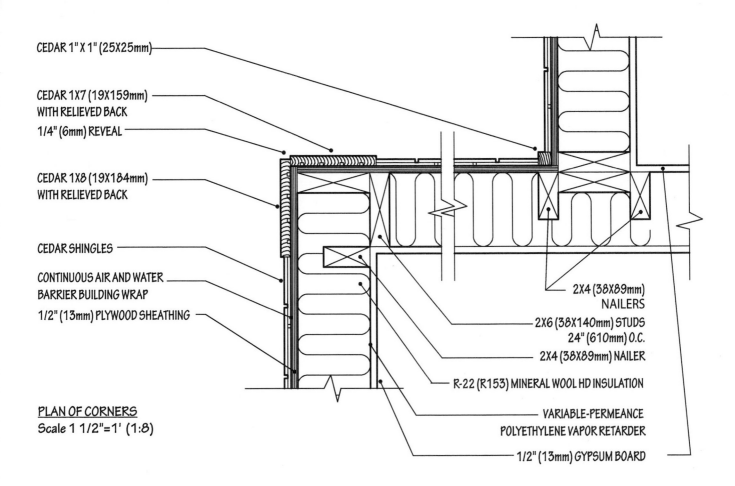

PLAN OF CORNERS
Scale 1 1/2"=1' (1:8)

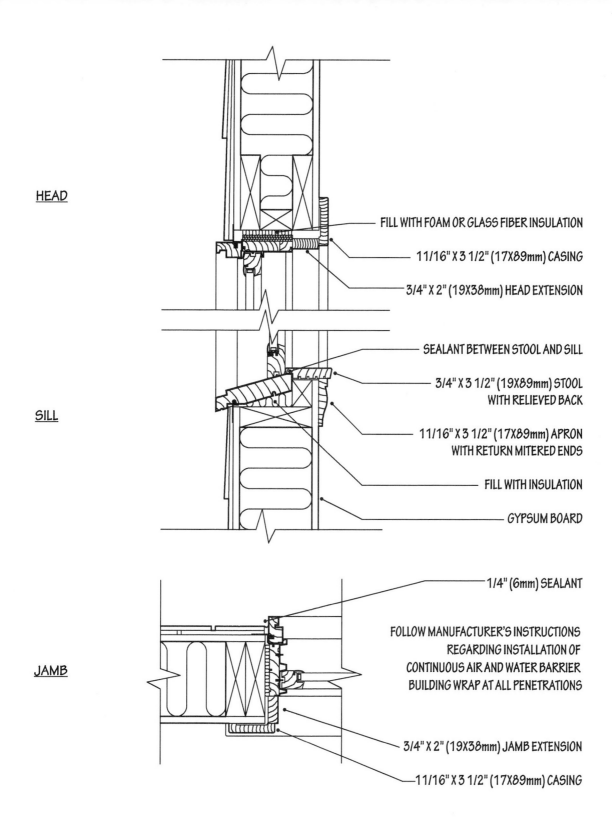

WINDOW DETAILS
Scale: 1 1/2"=1' (1:8)

SECTION 1 ■ APPLYING THE DETAIL PATTERNS

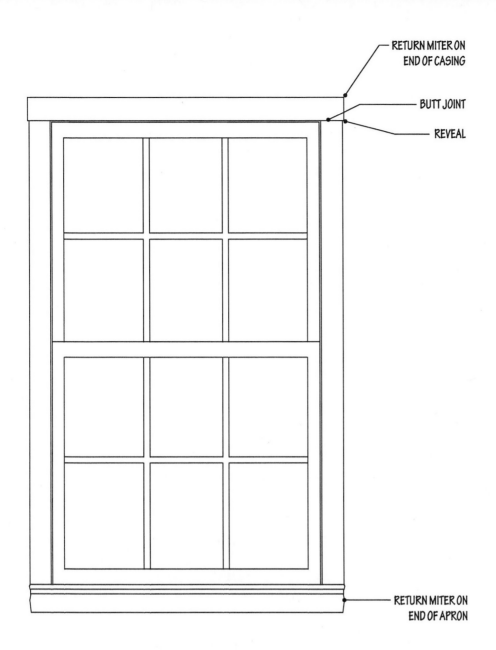

INTERIOR ELEVATION OF WINDOW FINISH
Scale 3/4"=1' (1:16)

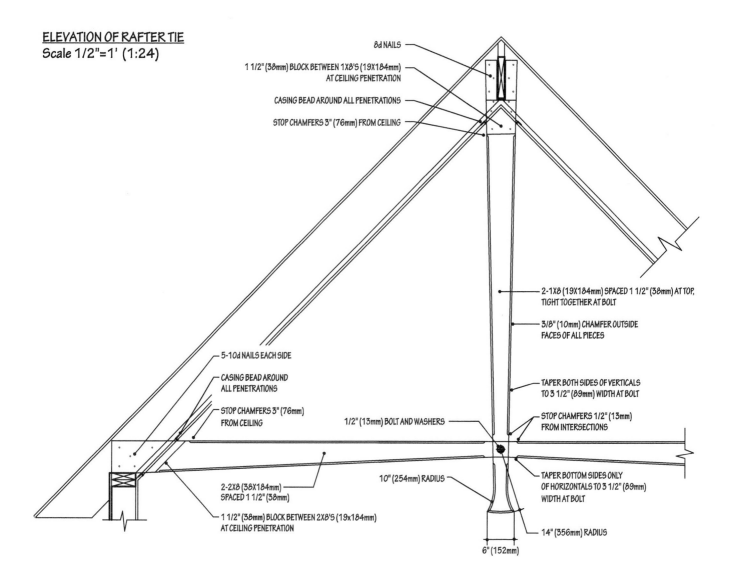

There has been an important aesthetic component to our work: The architectural character of the building has emerged in a pleasing way as we have developed these key details. Unsympathetic detailing can destroy the aesthetic of an otherwise well-designed building, while thoughtful detailing can make it even better, which is a point lost on architects who consider themselves to be designers but who are unwilling to consider and work on the detailing of their buildings.

As we prepare to draft the final drawings of all the details for this building, we gather and organize the notes that we made to help us remember key aspects of these details in other phases of the project work. We make a list that reminds us to include in the specifications such special items as the ridge vent strip, the soffit vent strip, the soffit boards, the ice and water shield, the insulation vent spacer channels, the flashing metal, the foam insulating boards, the thicker vapor retarder sheet, the longer screws for the gypsum board ceiling finish, and the hot-dip galvanized fasteners for the soffit boards, as well as the more usual components, such as shingles, sheathing, air barrier sheet, insulating batts, and gypsum board.

We also make some notes regarding things to keep in mind as we visit the site again and again during the construction process. Communication is a key component of translating the effort made in design detailing to the effort in construction. It would be good to call to the builder's attention in advance the need to frame the gable walls with full-height studs and to overhang the shingles at the rakes and eaves by the required amounts, thus avoiding some very costly potential errors. The ridge detail is complex enough that we should discuss it in detail with the builder before it is constructed. The crawl space vapor barrier and insulation could also benefit from an advance conference. The exposed roof ties will require extra attention from both architect and contractor. The first of these to be built will be carefully checked as the exemplar for the others (***Simulated Assemblies***, Chapter 11). Other than this, these details are largely based on common practice and probably need no special mention on the jobsite.

KEY REFERENCES

The following are important reference materials that were used in developing this set of details. Full bibliographic information on these publications is given in ***Appendix A, The Detailer's Reference Shelf***.

1. Relevant building and energy codes, including IBC, IECC, and IgCC.
2. Manufacturers' catalogs, including print and online resources.
3. APA, The Engineered Wood Association, Plywood Design Specification.
4. American Wood Council, *Span Tables for Joists and Rafters, and Design Values for Joists and Rafters*.
5. Rob Thallon, *Graphic Guide to Frame Construction: Details for Builders and Designers*.
6. Edward Allen and Rob Thallon, *Fundamentals of Residential Construction*. ■

CHAPTER 16
Detailing a Building in Architectural Concrete

THE PROJECT

The project is a classroom building for a public college on a small campus in southern Ohio, United States. It is located in IECC (International Energy Conservation Code) Climate Zone 4. The cast-in-place concrete structure is two-stories tall and uses a commercial low-slope roof assembly with a parapet wall. Interior finishes are limited to concrete, gypsum board and suspended ceiling grids. To facilitate long-term operations and maintenance, exposed building services are part of the interior aesthetic.

SETTING PERFORMANCE STANDARDS

Most of the existing campus is made up of nineteenth-century buildings finished in handcrafted gray granite. College officials would like a solid, well-crafted building; however, given the budget available for the project, granite is not an affordable or appropriate solution. The integrated design and construction team have determined with college administrators that a building with an exposed concrete exterior will both meet the project budget and fit the character of the campus. ▷

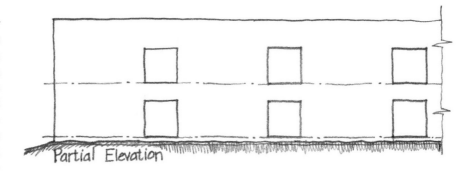

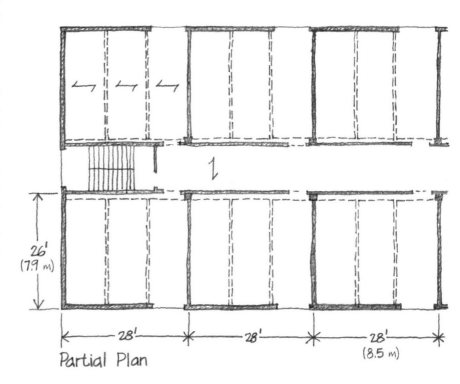

Architectural Detailing: Function Constructability Aesthetics. Fourth Edition. Patrick Rand, Jason Miller, and Edward Allen.
© 2025 John Wiley & Sons, Inc. Published 2025 by John Wiley & Sons, Inc.

The prescriptive International Energy Conservation Code (IECC) specifies minimum insulation values of R-9.5 continuous insulation for this building's mass walls, R-25 continuous insulation for the roof, and R-10 for 24 in. at slab-on-grade perimeters (metric equivalents are R-65, 173, and 69 for 610 mm). The college mandates higher insulation values of at least R-19 walls and R-30 roof (132 and 208 m²-°C/W), to reduce energy consumption and costs (*Life Cycle*, Chapter 10).

We will use these prescriptive requirements as a start, but will also collaborate with our mechanical consultant, who will model energy performance using compliant energy analytical software such as WUFI (acronym for the German terms for heat and humidity variable) or EnergyPlus (hosted by the US Department of Energy's National Renewable Energy Laboratory), and resources like ASHRAE Standard 90.1.

KEY DETAILS TO DEVELOP

We will begin the detailing process by designing the details indicated on the section and plan diagrams to the right.

These typical conditions will determine the most general details and serve as a base from which to design more special details, such as those of the main entrance. We want to develop these key details as a consistent set of *Contributive Details* (Chapter 14) that work well together. Like the early stages of the building's schematic design, early work designing details is best done using quick sketches on paper so that iterative alternatives and tracing paper overlays can be quickly produced. We start with the *idea* of the details, then move through stages to their technical conclusions.

EARLY DECISIONS CONCERNING MATERIAL, STRUCTURE, AND FORM

Each two-story wing of the building has evolved as two rows of classrooms flanking

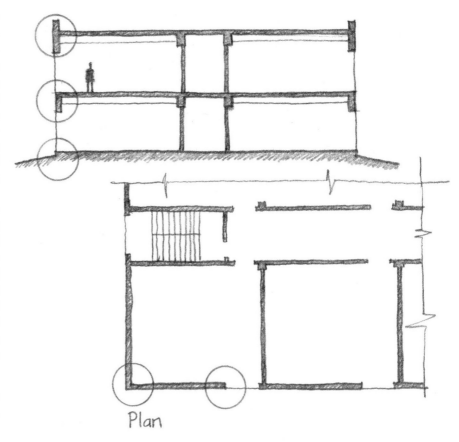

Plan

a double-loaded corridor. Working with the team's structural engineer, we have developed a one-way concrete slab and beam system for the upper floor and roof. Each structural bay of the building is 28 × 26 ft. (8.53 × 7.92 m) to match the desired size of the classrooms. The floor and roof slabs will be 6 in. (152 mm) thick and will span across concrete beams spaced 9 ft. 4 in. (2835 mm) apart. The outer end of each beam will rest on a concrete load-bearing wall that is 10 in. (254 mm) thick. The inner end will be supported by a concrete girder that spans between columns 28 ft. (8.53 m) apart. The floor-to-floor height has been tentatively fixed at 12 ft. (3658 mm) and the window head height at 8 ft. (2438 mm).

The classrooms will be heated and ventilated by a variable air volume system (VAV) whose primary ducts will run in a *Horizontal Plenum* (Chapter 8) above the central corridor, with secondary branches to diffusers in the classrooms. There will be no suspended ceiling grid, except in the corridors.

The tentative fenestration scheme for the building is based on a single, large window opening into a corner of each classroom. By locating and sizing the *Geometry and Proportion* (Chapter 14) of windows near an intersection of exterior and interior walls, natural daylighting will brighten the room and the interior wall while reducing glare. This results in a quietly direct but programmatically effective elevation.

EARLY WORK ON MATERIALS AND DETAILS

Working on a typical elevation of a classroom wing, we develop a mullion pattern for the window opening that will provide two opening sashes and a safety rail at waist height. ***Composing the Detail*** (Chapter 14) in this way balances the window composition with its asymmetrical interior location in each room. Checking the building code, we find tempered glass will be required in the lower lites of the window, because they exceed the area permitted for ordinary annealed glass so close to the floor (***Safe Glazing***, Chapter 9). We make a note to inform the specifications writer.

It will be necessary to construct the concrete wall in separate pours, starting from the ground and working up. In walls, concrete is typically placed in story height lifts, because to place it in taller dimensions may overburden formwork and workers. Remember: Concrete must be properly mixed to optimize strength and workability. Because it is somewhat fluid when freshly mixed, the placement of concrete is sometimes referred to as "pouring" the concrete. This does not suggest that its fluidity should be increased to make it easier to "pour" because that could alter the critical water/cement ratio intended. Care is taken to support the concrete as it is delivered into the formwork so that the still-fluid material mixture cannot drop unsupported more than 4 ft. (1219 mm). Dropping from a greater height would cause the coarse aggregate to separate from the finer aggregate and cement gel.

The seams between pours will be visible no matter what we do, so it seems logical to follow the standard practice of using recessed rustication strips at the pour lines to create a pattern of ***Reveals*** (Chapter 12) that will mask the seams with a regular grid of shadow lines. We must also anticipate the cracking that will occur in the wall as the concrete shrinks by designing a pattern of vertical ***Control Joints*** (Chapter 6) to channel this cracking in an acceptable manner (***Expected Life***, Chapter 10). Additionally, the formwork for the wall will need through-wall form ties at close intervals to prevent blowouts or spreading when placing the concrete; these ties will leave visible holes in the concrete that we will make as clean as possible (***Clean Edge***, Chapter 12) by using plastic cones to form neat recesses at the ends of the ties. From the pour lines, the control joints, and the form tie holes, we will create a detailed elevational composition for the building façade (***Intensification and Ornamentation***, Chapter 14).

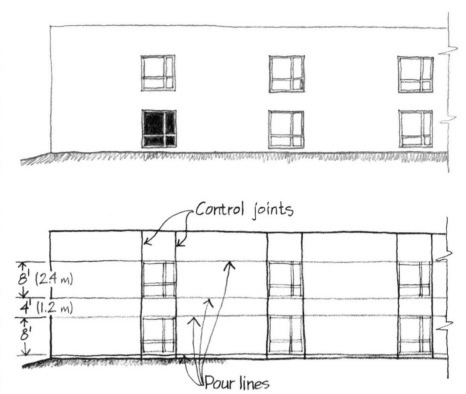

The concrete pours resolve themselves naturally into horizontal layers, one for each floor slab and spandrel, and one for each story height of wall. Each wall pour will be 8 ft. (2438 mm) high, requiring a form a few inches taller than 8 ft. The extra dimension is necessary to allow for overlap of the previously poured wall layer below and to prevent concrete from overspilling the form at the top (***Dimensional Tolerance***, Chapter 12). A check of some manufacturers' catalogs and online resources shows that formwork plywood up to 10 ft. (3048 mm) long is readily available (***Off the Shelf Parts***, Chapter 13), and the structural engineer tells us that an 8 ft. (2438 mm) pour height will not require unusually strong formwork to resist the pressure of the wet concrete. We will dimension the building repetitiously so that the sections of formwork can be used repeatedly as construction progresses (***Repetitious Assembly***, Chapter 11).

Control joints should be located to control cracking at points of weakness in the wall. Such points occur at each of the window openings. The American Concrete Institute (ACI) recommends a maximum joint spacing of 20 ft. (6.1 m), so we decide to place a control joint at each side of each window opening. We make a note to specify water-reducing admixtures to minimize the shrinkage of the concrete; admixtures like these will reduce the potential for cracking and will help minimize unattractive voids in the exterior surface of the concrete, by making the concrete flow more easily into the forms.

We look up the standard ***Dimensional Tolerance*** (Chapter 12) for cast in place concrete structures in ACI publication 117–10, *Standard Tolerances for Concrete Construction and Materials*. These indicate that the overall dimensions of the constructed building of this size may vary by as much as 1 in. (25 mm) either way, and that wall thicknesses may vary by as much as ⅜ in. (9 mm). Individual wall length dimensions may vary up to ½ in. (13 mm). We will detail accordingly to accommodate these constructional tolerances (***Robust Assemblies***, Chapter 10). ▷

Having made these tentative decisions, we construct an elevation drawing to see what the building face will look like with the rustication strips and control joints in place. After studying this drawing, we move the vertical control joints several inches outside the window jambs to give the lintel area of the spandrel an apparent bearing on the walls below (**Hierarchy of Refinement**, Chapter 14).

We must now consider how to integrate the pattern of form tie holes with the tentative pattern of rustication strips and control joints. The structural engineer tells us that form ties are normally spaced at about 2 ft. (610 mm) intervals, both vertically and horizontally. Looking at a piece of wall that runs from one window to the next, we see that it will require five sheets of plywood, each 4 × 9 ft. (1.22 × 2.74 m), with the long dimension oriented vertically. Consulting a book on formwork construction, we learn the plywood needs to be braced by studs running across the width of the sheet, which will be horizontal in this case. The studs are supported by walers running perpendicular to the studs, and the walers are supported by the metal ties that run through the formwork to the walers on the other side. If we space the form ties 1 ft. (305 mm) away from each edge of each sheet of plywood, this produces a regular pattern of holes that works well with the plywood joints and gives a 2 ft. (610 mm) spacing horizontally. Vertically, if we divide each sheet into three spaces between holes that are placed 1 ft. (305 mm) from the top and bottom, the tie spacing comes out to be 2 ft. (610 mm). The structural engineer does a preliminary check on the stiffness of the walers. He says the 2 ft. dimension will work and notes the importance of specifying stiff formwork to avoid unattractive bulges in the surface of the finished wall (**Small Structures**, Chapter 7). Formwork may be designed by the architect but is typically engineered by the contractor rather than the architect or structural engineer; however, we can specify maximum allowable deflections for the formwork components of plywood, studs, and walers.

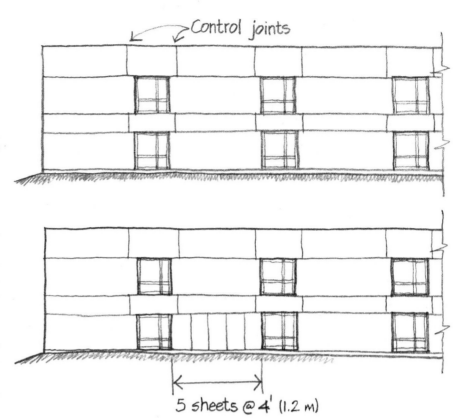

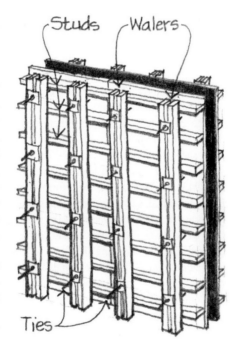

With form tie holes added to the drawing, we examine the pattern and proportions of the elevation: The pattern is orderly and well proportioned, but somewhat bland and monolithic in appearance overall. As we consider different design possibilities, the discussion turns to using different surface textures for the concrete. A texture might address the uniformity of the facade and would help conceal small defects in the concrete work (***Forgiving Surface***, Chapter 12) without introducing additional material assemblies or functional requirements. After considerable experimentation on tracing paper overlays, a decision is made to use a vertical board texture on the walls and to sandblast the spandrels lightly to create a matte surface that contrast nicely with the boards. The board texture will also obscure the marks of the vertical joints between panels of formwork, and the sandblasted texture will soften them considerably. We will note to ask the contractor to prepare a sample panel of this concrete treatment to verify it has the appearance we want for the building elevation (***Simulated Assemblies***, Chapter 11). ▷

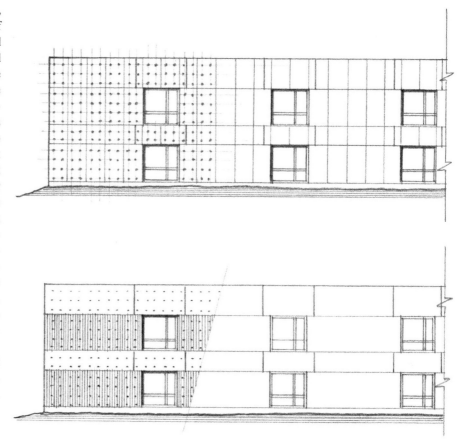

FORMULATING AN APPROACH TO THE IMPORTANT WALL FUNCTIONS

Water Leakage

Architectural concrete, because of its simple, massive geometry, does not adapt readily to a rainscreen approach to watertightness. Instead, we must detail it as best we can to eliminate the openings through which water can penetrate the wall. We will start by specifying a strong, dense concrete and by insisting on careful vibration of the concrete into the forms, to eliminate pockets and voids in the finished product. We will control cracking by designing a concrete mix that uses minimal water, by providing sufficient steel reinforcing for the wall, by insisting on long and careful wet curing, and by providing sealed control joints at appropriate intervals (*Moisture Break*, Chapter 1).

Thermal Insulation and Water Vapor

Concrete is a poor thermal insulator. We review some options for installing *Thermal Insulation* (Chapter 3): We could place it on the outside of the wall, using an exterior insulation and finish system (EIFS). This would give the building the advantage of an *Outside-Insulated Thermal Mass* (Chapter 3), and it would allow the concrete work to be done to a much less expensive level of workmanship (*Progressive Finish*, Chapter 12). We reject this option, however, because its external appearance would be that of a fuzzily defined stucco building, not a crisply delineated concrete one, and because we feel that EIFS is not sufficiently resistant to physical damage for use on a college campus. It would also deviate too much from the solidity desired by the college administration.

A second option would be to install plastic foam insulation within the formwork and to pour the concrete either around or against it. After some discussion among members of the

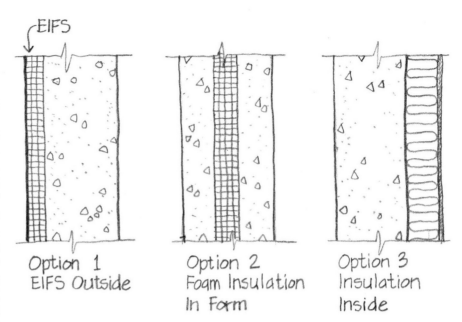

Option 1
EIFS Outside

Option 2
Foam Insulation In Form

Option 3
Insulation Inside

project team, we discard this idea, because the foam is fragile, tends to float, and would therefore create many potential complications during the forming and casting operations.

As a third option, we consider installing the thermal insulation on the interior side of the concrete wall, in a separate operation carried out later in the construction process. Metal furring strips or studs would be required to support an interior finish layer (probably gypsum wallboard or veneer plaster) over the insulation. The mechanical engineer does a few scribbles and announces that either 3¼ in. (83 mm) of polyurethane foam insulation or 4¾ in. (121 mm) of high-efficiency glass fiber insulation would be sufficient to meet the college's target for energy efficiency. The plastic foam alternative would create a bit more usable floor space but would be more costly and would not integrate as well with electrical work. The glass fiber alternative would provide ample space for electrical wiring. We decide tentatively to adopt a hybrid approach using a thin layer of polyurethane sprayed onto the inner face of the concrete and batts between the metal studs. This option is built in layers toward the interior of the building, allowing us to check that each layer is properly installed before installing the next (*Observable Assemblies*, Chapter 11).

We note with regret that the exterior walls cannot be a very useful part of the thermal mass of the building with the insulation on the inside but remind ourselves that considerable *Outside-Insulated Thermal Mass* (Chapter 3) remains in the floor and roof structures. And although we are losing the exposed concrete finish on the interior surfaces of the walls, the painted gypsum wall finish will contrast handsomely with the exposed concrete ceilings (*Hierarchy of Refinement*, Chapter 14), and the concrete workers can concentrate their attention on creating a perfect finish on just one side of the wall – the exterior. Our interior-side insulation strategy is also compatible with the functional approach the college facilities group is using to improve the thermal efficiency of several existing load-bearing masonry buildings on campus.

We now take up the problem of the thermal bridges that exist where the slabs and beams join the exterior bearing wall.

The structural engineer decides that there is no reason the one-way slabs must join the walls directly, and a **Thermal Break** (Chapter 3) detail is sketched out that involves simply inserting a strip of plastic foam insulation into the formwork at the edges of the slabs, prior to casting. This leaves only the beam intersections as thermal bridges, and the mechanical engineer estimates that the effect of these is negligible in the overall heat loss of the building. Furthermore, the potential for moisture condensation on the interior surfaces of a beam near the outside wall proves to be minimal, because calculations show that the insulating value of the 15 in. (381 mm) of concrete through which heat must travel to escape along a beam is sufficient to ensure a **Warm Interior Surface** (Chapter 4) – not warm to the touch but about as warm as the interior surface of a double-glazed window, which is good enough to avoid condensation under most conditions. There is a more serious and potentially problematic thermal bridge at the end walls of the building, where the slab is supported continuously by the wall. After much discussion with the engineer, we decide to support the slab edge on another beam in this location and to separate the beam from the wall by a foam **Thermal Break** (Chapter 3), like the one used on the side wall. We will have to provide reinforced concrete connections between the beam and the wall at intervals to provide lateral support to the wall; these bracing conditions will have to remain as thermal bridges.

The thermal breaks do raise a problem of code compliance based on the occupancy type. Given the use, height, and floor area of the building, the building code requires that the floors have a two-hour fire resistance rating. The plastic foam thermal breaks have no fire resistance. To solve this, we will specify that the foam thermal breaks be removed after the concrete has cured, and that they be replaced with mineral fiber safing suspended on sheet

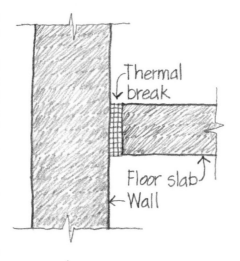

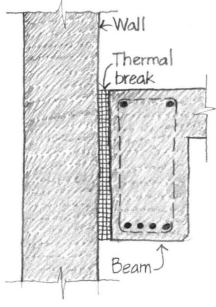

metal clips. The safing is a high-melting-point batt that is almost as good a thermal insulator as the plastic foam. The foam may be removed most easily by burning it out with a propane torch. The combustion products of polyurethane foam are similar chemically to those of wood smoke, but we will have to check to see if local air-quality regulations will permit this means of removing the foam. If they object, then we will use rigid mineral wool board insulation that can be installed prior to the casting of concrete, and can simply be left in place permanently. It is wise to have alternatives for detailing challenges that might arise during construction.

A particular make and model of aluminum window is adopted by the design and construction team because of its aesthetic, functional, and economic success in several previous buildings that the partnership has designed and built together. The design of this window incorporates many detailing patterns, the most important of which are **Multiple Glazing** and **Thermal Break** (Chapter 3). ▷

DETAILING THE WALL SECTIONS

With these tentative decisions made, we are ready to begin designing the construction assembly of the key details for a typical wall, working at a scale of 1½ in. = 1 ft. (1:8) so that we can visualize the details more completely. We pencil lightly the outlines of the slabs and walls for a spandrel detail and a parapet detail. The safing and an approximate pattern of steel reinforcing – obtained from the structural engineer – are added to the concrete work on the wall section. Given the required thickness of thermal insulation, we decide to add a full 3⅝ in. (92 mm) steel stud wall inside the concrete wall, instead of ordinary furring strips. Rather than place the studs directly against the concrete wall surface, we leave a 1 in. (25 mm) space between them. This will provide the space for applying the continuous polyurethane spray foam insulation, and it will also give a considerable **Dimensional Tolerance** (Chapter 12) to avoid conflict with occasional bulges or inaccuracies on the interior concrete surface.

The steel stud framing will be installed prior to the spray foam application so that the expanding foam approximates the dimension between the concrete and the steel studs. If the foam expands slightly into the stud cavities, that is of no harm. Unfaced batt insulation will be installed between the studs. The studs also provide a form of **Horizontal Plenum** (Chapter 8) for the electrical wiring.

The closed-cell, high-density polyurethane foam insulation is also an effective vapor retarder (**Warm-Side Vapor Retarder**, Chapter 4) and air barrier (**Air Barrier System**, Chapter 2) that will prevent interior vapor from reaching the concrete exterior wall, whose inner surface may be below the dew point in winter. All layers toward the interior of this foam must be chosen to have high vapor permeance to allow inward movement of vapor, so it is not trapped in the inner wall assembly.

Where the stud wall joins the ceiling, a **Structure/Enclosure Joint** (Chapter 6) is created by cutting the studs somewhat short of the inside of the metal runner track; this allows for the ¼ in. (6 mm) potential differential of combined slab deflection and creep from one floor to the next that the structural engineer has estimated (**Dimensional Tolerance**, Chapter 12).

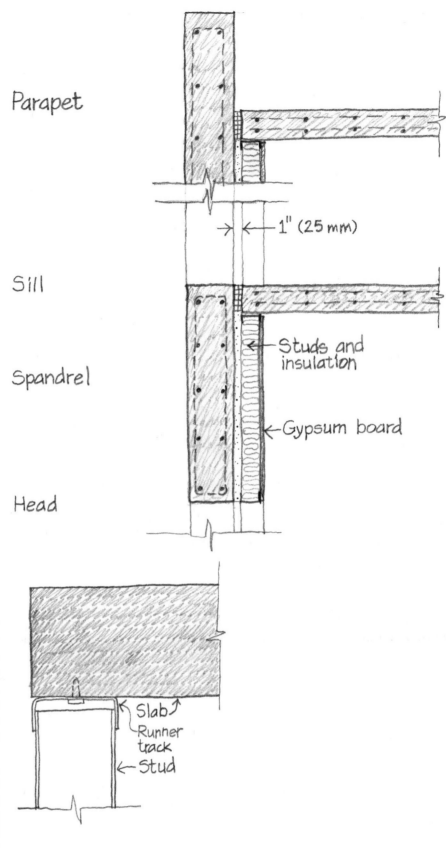

Detailing the Window Openings

After a considerable number of trial-and-error studies on tracing paper overlays, the window head and sill are added to the developing section. These details will have to be refined further after consultation with the window manufacturer. The window catalog "typical detail" shows rough jambs of wood; we are proposing tentatively that the head and jambs of the window unit be screwed to strips of plywood that are mounted to the concrete with screws and expansion anchors (*Refining the Detail*, Chapter 13). The plywood should be treated with a preservative so that it will not decay if it is exposed to water leakage or condensation (*Dry Wood*, Chapter 10).

A manufacturer-specified *Installation Clearance* (Chapter 11) between the plywood and the window frame will be taken up by shims. The nominal size of this gap, ⅞ in. (22 mm), will take into account the maximum expected inaccuracy in the concrete work (±½ in. or 13 mm) plus the space necessary to allow the aluminum window unit to slide easily into position (⅜ in. or 9 mm). Each plywood strip will extend into the building to stabilize the steel stud wall, to which it will be fastened with self-tapping screws. The gypsum wall finish will return around the plywood with a corner bead to finish against the window frame with a *Clean Edge* (Chapter 12) created by a metal casing bead. On the outdoor side, the thickness of the plywood will provide for installation of a generously sized *Sealant Joint* (Chapter 1) and backer rod. Except for the sealant joints, the windows will be installed from inside the building (*Accessible Connections*, Chapter 11).

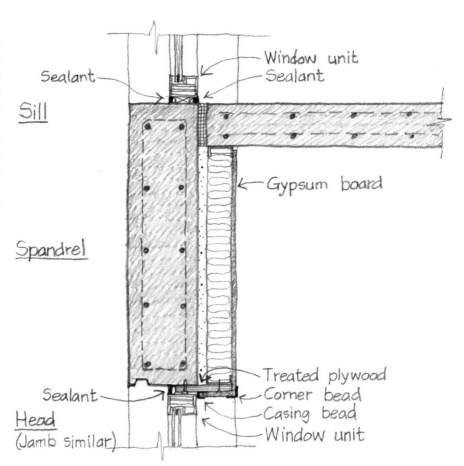

The joint at the head of the window is well protected from water by the drip groove and overhang of the spandrel above, so a defect in the sealant is unlikely to create a water leak. The sealant joints at the jamb and sill are likely to be wetted during rainstorms, however, and can leak if they are defective. We decide to treat the exterior sealant joint as a deterrent seal, and to provide a second sealant joint along the interior edge of the window unit as an air seal. If the exterior sealant is flawed, the interior seal and the space around the window unit will create a *Rainscreen Assembly and Pressure Equalization* (Chapter 1).

We recognize that the head and jamb details of our design are virtually identical, so for now we will develop the head detail only. Because the window unit extends to the floor, the sill detail must be developed differently from the head and jambs to accommodate the surrounding conditions. ▷

Detailing the Interior Finishes

The interior details are finished with a standard vinyl casing bead that has compressible wipers to provide for ceiling slab deflection along the top edge of the gypsum board, a standard vinyl base as *Building Armor* (Chapter 10) at the foot of the wall, and an aluminum box extrusion with a *Sliding Fit* (Chapter 12) at the window sill to cover the foam plastic thermal break.

The box extrusion will be screwed to the floor only, not to the window, forming a *Structure/Enclosure Joint* (Chapter 6) that allows the floor slab to deflect without stressing the window. To cushion the box section against the hard, slightly irregular concrete slab, we bed it in sealant. This is a nonworking sealant joint (meaning that the slab and the aluminum box will have little or no movement between them), so we do not provide a backer rod or worry about the exact thickness of the sealant. The sealant will simply be applied to the underside of the aluminum piece just before it is screwed down, and the excess sealant that squeezes out of the joint as the screws are tightened will be wiped off. To create a soft, quiet joint between the window frame and the box extrusion, we show a synthetic rubber gasket (*Quiet Attachments*, Chapter 5). We make a note to consult with the window manufacturer about furnishing these extrusions in a finish to match the window frame. We draw an interior perspective sketch of a typical window opening to see how our details will look and to check how the pieces will meet at the corners. While *Rehearsing the Construction Sequence* (Chapter 13) with this sketch, we realize the vinyl base should be installed after the gypsum board but before the box extrusion to avoid tedious trimming around the aluminum component.

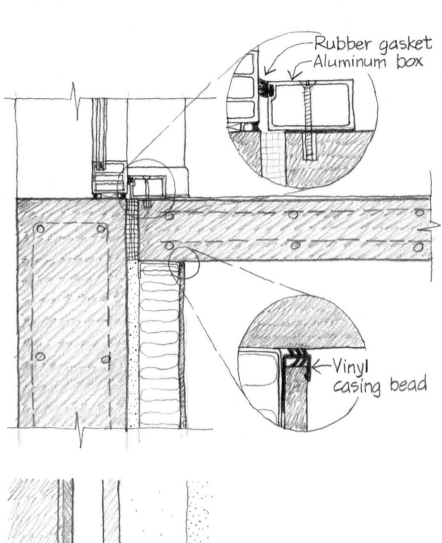

Detailing the Exterior

Outdoors, much of the wall detail for exterior exposure remains to be designed. We begin by creating an *Overhang and Drip* (Chapter 1) with a groove at the head of the window. This will be made with a simple strip nailed into the formwork. At the sill we make a sloping *Wash* (Chapter 1) to conduct water away from the window. The termination of the wash at the jambs will have to be studied later in an elevation sketch.

Checking the building code, we discover that a parapet is not required on this building because of the wide spacing between buildings on the campus. We decide to construct one anyway, because we want to imply a greater apparent thickness for the roof while concealing building services such as vent stacks or condensers that are functionally necessary but aesthetically extraneous to the project (*Hierarchy of Refinement*, Chapter 14). We put a wash on the top of the parapet to shed water toward the roof. This will help prevent unattractive water staining of the concrete facade. For the roofing system, we adopt an inverted roof assembly, with polystyrene foam insulation, in a thickness specified by the mechanical engineer, installed above the roof membrane (*Warm-Side Vapor Retarder*, Chapter 4). A heavy layer of stone ballast anchors the insulation boards in place and protects them from degradation by sunlight.

A reglet insert in the formwork of the parapet provides an *Overlap* (Chapter 1) between the concrete wall and the metal counterflashing. The bend in the counterflashing allows it to clamp tightly against the upturned edge of the roof membrane by spring action, and the underlying airspace that this creates acts as a *Capillary Break* (Chapter 1). The bottom of the counterflashing turns outward to form an *Overhang and Drip* (Chapter 1).

We add the rustication strips to the section, tapering the edges of each strip at least 15 degrees, as recommended by the ACI, so that they can be removed easily and without damage to the concrete. A wall pour will terminate at the top of the rustication strip beneath the spandrel. The spandrel formwork will be placed after the wall formwork has been removed and will contain an identical rustication strip that will mate with the profile of the concrete at this location. This decision will also help the builder align the formwork for the higher pour. Notice that here, as in many other parts of this detail development process, we are *Rehearsing the Construction Sequence* (Chapter 13) as a way of understanding the basis for our design decisions. ▷

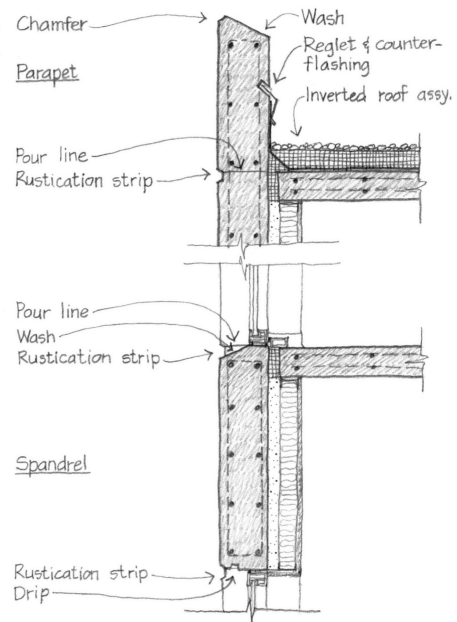

DETAILING THE GRADE CONDITION

We develop the grade detail quickly on a tracing paper overlay of the typical spandrel detail. The ground floor will be a concrete slab on grade, which the structural engineer figures should be 6 in. (152 mm) thick and reinforced with bars in both directions. We will place a 6 mil (0.15 mm) polyethylene vapor barrier beneath the slab to prevent groundwater from rising into the building (**Moisture Break**, Chapter 1). After soil testing has been completed, the geotechnical engineer will assist in working out a detailed specification for compacted backfill and a layer of crushed stone beneath the slab. Between the slab edge and the concrete wall, we insert a 2 in. (51 mm) thick layer of polystyrene foam extending to 4 ft. (1219 mm) below grade, to retard the passage of heat through the slab and soil to the outdoors. We choose to run the slab down the wall rather than fold it back under the slab, as is sometimes done, because we do not want the soil under the slab to freeze and heave. This nearly continuous insulation strategy on the interior side of the concrete wall system will exceed the minimum requirement of the code to conserve resources and will make the floor surface warmer in winter (**Life Cycle**, Chapter 10).

DETAILING THE CORNER OF THE BUILDING

Working now in plan view, we develop the detail for an exterior corner of the building. We chamfer the concrete corner to avoid breakage (**Clean Edge**, Chapter 12). We create vertical **Control Joints** (Chapter 6) 4 ft. (1219 mm) from the corner on either wall. These will absorb the concrete shrinkage stresses that are likely to accumulate at the corner by inducing controlled cracking in the concrete. As recommended by ACI, we discontinue half the horizontal reinforcing bars at each control joint to help create a plane of weakness. ACI also recommends that a control joint have grooves on both sides of the wall to a total depth of one-quarter the thickness of the wall, which is 2½ in. (64 mm) in our building. We decide to use a standard ¾ in. (19 mm) deep rustication strip on the inside face and a

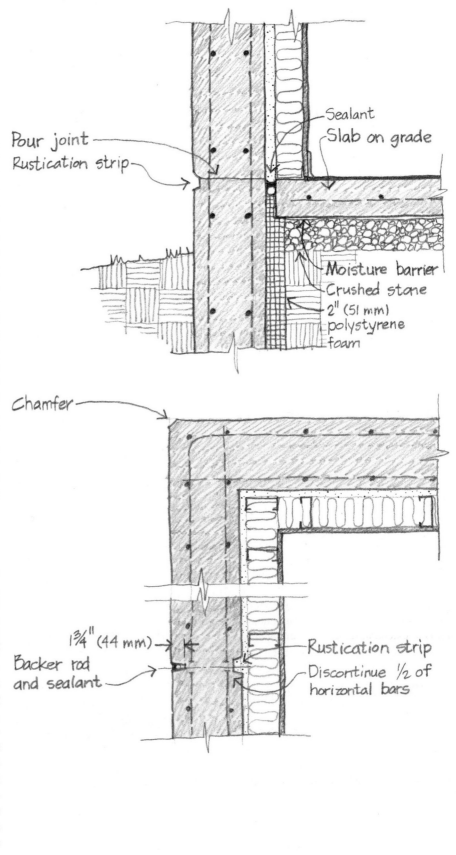

1¾ in. (44 mm) deep strip on the outside. This deeper strip must be narrower to accept a backer rod and sealant; the sealant will keep water and air from penetrating the expected crack in the concrete (*Expected Life*, Chapter 10).

The studs, gypsum board, and insulation are detailed in the standard way, holding the studs away from the corner several inches, in the manner recommended by the manufacturers of the studs and boards. We contemplate placing a control joint in the gypsum board in the same plane as the control joint in the concrete wall, but we realize that the gypsum board is supported on the floor slab, which has no joint at this location and is not connected in any way to the concrete wall. We do not need a control joint in the gypsum, although choosing to add a control joint or *Reveal* (Chapter 12) might be viewed as an opportunity for *Intensification and Ornamentation* (Chapter 14) of the interior finishes.

ELEVATION STUDIES

We need to study at larger scale the relationships of the rustication strips, the terminations of the various pours, the window openings, and the control joints. For this purpose, we construct a larger-scale elevation view, showing the form tie holes, rustication strips, control joints, and sill wash. After some tracing paper studies of alternatives, we decide to terminate the wash with a sloping end plane. The pattern of the recessed strips and form tie holes strikes us as neatly organized and satisfying.

The control joint around each window lintel, like the control joints at the corner, needs to extend at least one-quarter of the way through the wall, or 2½ in. (64 mm). Again, half the reinforcing bars should be discontinued at this plane (we make a note to coordinate with the structural engineer to see that this is detailed properly on the structural drawings). But the detailing of the exterior slot of the control joint gives us some difficulty because of the way it is tied in with the horizontal rustication strips and the sloping sill. Ideally, we would like to make the control joint slot as wide as the rustication strip, for visual simplicity, but this would result in an excessively wide joint that would waste sealant. Forming a narrower, deeper slot at the bottom of the recessed strip seems a bit fussy and difficult.

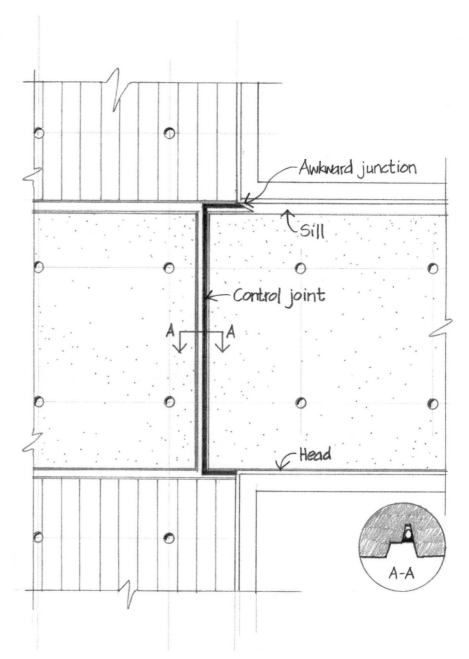

We also realize that the line of the control joint as we have drawn it in elevation is not satisfactory. Any shrinkage in the concrete is likely to cause ugly diagonal cracks at the corners of the lintels, rather than cracks that follow obediently along the difficult path we have laid out. Furthermore, the top end of the control joint joins the sloping sill in a very awkward way that will be hard to construct (*Clean Edge*, Chapter 12).

We must try again. ▷

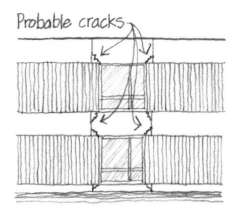

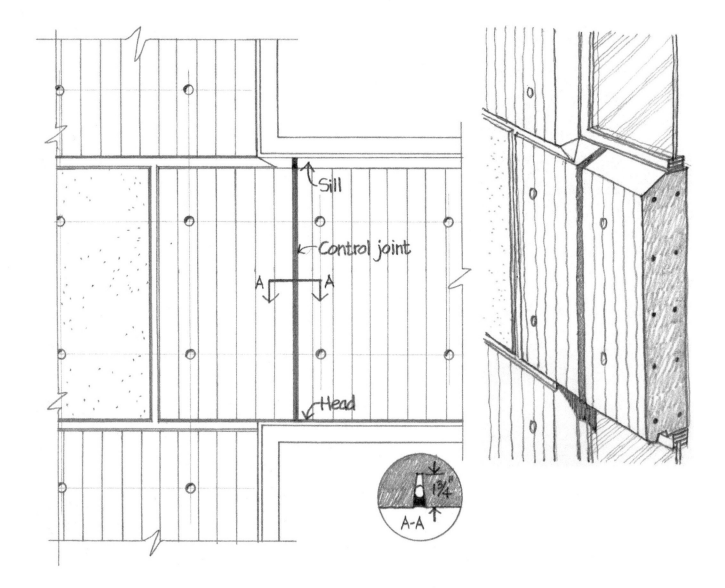

After much exploration of alternatives on tracing paper overlays, we arrive at a solution that we like much better for performance and aesthetic management reasons.

We move the control joints several inches out onto the lintel and give them the narrower width they require, creating a simple, straight-line path along which cracking can occur.

The control joint with its sealant will have to continue up over the sloping sill until it joins the sealant beneath the aluminum window frame. To retain the visual identity of the lintel, we set it off from the rest of the spandrel with a vertical rustication strip at each end. To reinforce the visual integrity of the lintel further, and to minimize the appearance of the control joints, we give the lintel a board texture, while retaining the sandblasted texture on the rest of the spandrel. By *Refining the Detail* (Chapter 13), this small detail enhances a strong aesthetic pattern on the facade, locates the control joints where they will do the most functional good and remains easy to construct.

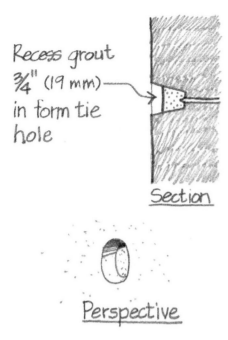

The holes left by the form tie cones must be sealed in some way, to prevent the broken ends of the metal ties from rusting and staining the facade. This could be done with sealant, with a plastic or rubber plug, or with stiff grout compacted into the hole. We avoid trying to fill the holes flush with grout, because the grout would smear onto the wall surface in a messy way and would inevitably contrast in color and texture with the cast concrete around it. After weighing the options, we elect to use the grout and to recess it well into the conical hole, using a large wood dowel and mallet to compact the surface. The recess constitutes a shadow-casting **Reveal** (Chapter 12) that will conceal any messiness in the grout work. As a repetitious operation on the elevations of the building, this strategy offers the contractor a well-informed solution that can be completed with a ***Pride of Craftsmanship*** (Chapter 13).

As our preliminary details near completion, we run an eye counterclockwise around the perimeter of the heated and cooled space of the building on our details, starting in the middle of the roof, looking for thermal bridges. If the cant strip were made of plastic foam, the insulating layer of the building would wrap neatly around the roof wall junction without a thermal bridge, except for the intermittent concrete beams that we have already considered and decided to accept as inevitable. We make a note to specify a foam plastic cant strip. The floor edges are well broken thermally, and the window openings will offer no thermal bridges if we add a strip of glass fiber batting to the inch-thick gap behind the steel stud furring at the jambs.

NEXT STEPS

We have recorded a long list of items to communicate to the project specifications writer. Notes on the exact qualities of the materials to be used for the formwork are needed. Air entrainment in the concrete must be specified to minimize weathering damage. Selection of a nonstaining form release agent for the walls is vital, as well as specification of the *same* agent for use in the slab and beam forms to ensure visual uniformity for all exposed concrete surfaces. If two different release agents are in use, there might be confusion that would lead to the wrong release agent being used on the exterior surfaces. Specification of noncorroding or plastic-tipped spacers and chairs for the reinforcing bars, to avoid rust stains, is also necessary. The cement color must be selected carefully. Because the project relies on architectural concrete as both structure and finish surface, we want the specifications to require that all the cement be from the same kiln batch, and that all the aggregates come from the same part of the same quarry, to avoid color variations.

The concrete casting, vibrating, curing, and sandblasting procedures must be standardized. We must specify measures to protect finished concrete surfaces from gouging and staining during subsequent construction operations, using tarpaulins, mats, and wooden corner guards. A certain amount of repairing of exposed concrete surfaces will undoubtedly be required; we must specify the materials and procedures very carefully to avoid garish patches (***Expected Life***, Chapter 10).

We will specify that a full-scale sample wall be erected on the site in advance by the contractor, using a representative sample of the workers who will construct the building, not an elite team of the best workers. This will allow the building owner, the contractor, the contractor's on-site project supervisors, and all the design team professionals to work out any remaining problems with materials and details. We will require that the specified patching procedures be tried out and refined on this sample wall. We will also specify a preconstruction conference of all parties, during which materials and procedures can be discussed in detail; this will help avoid false starts and inconsistent workmanship (***Simulated Assemblies***, Chapter 11).

Architectural concrete work is not forgiving of errors or sloppiness. Though we have made it somewhat more forgiving in this building by a judicious use of rustication strips and textures, it would still court disaster to use an inexperienced contractor on the project. As representatives for the design and construction team, we will work with the owner to assemble a list of qualified contractors and subcontractors who have built architectural concrete buildings successfully previously. Unqualified contractors will not be allowed to bid.

At this point in the process of designing the details, we can prepare a clean and accurate set of drawings to summarize clearly all the design decisions we have made. The sketches and analog drawings we have already done were quickly produced. They will make the upcoming transition to digital drawings speedy. These details are still only semifinished; they cannot be completed until some of the loose ends that we have already identified have been cleaned up, until they have undergone more extensive review by other members of the project team, and until the rest of the working drawings and specifications for the project have been brought to a similar stage so that inconsistencies can be identified and corrected.

A logical next step will be to develop other important details of the building, including special conditions such as entrances and stairwells, to discover if the aesthetic established in this set of details can be applied consistently to the entire building (***Contributive Details***, Chapter 14). It is reasonable to expect that some adjustments will be required. ▷

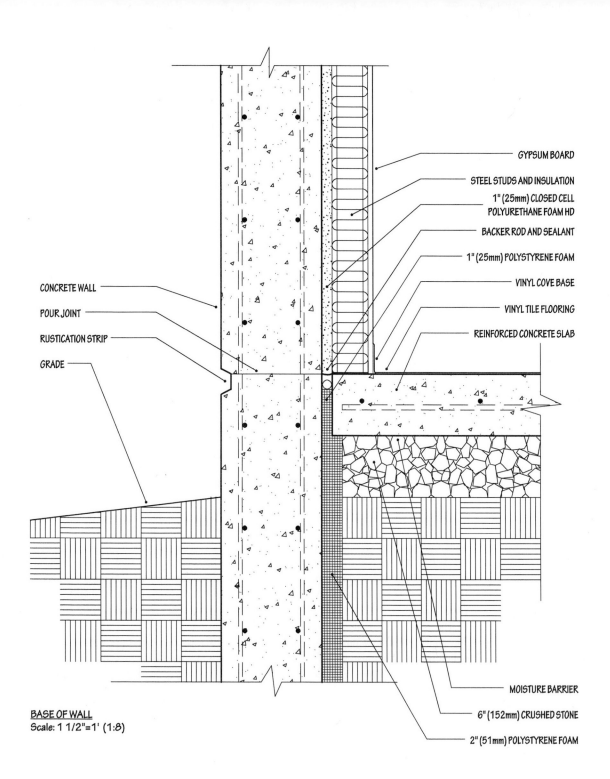

BASE OF WALL
Scale: 1 1/2"=1' (1:8)

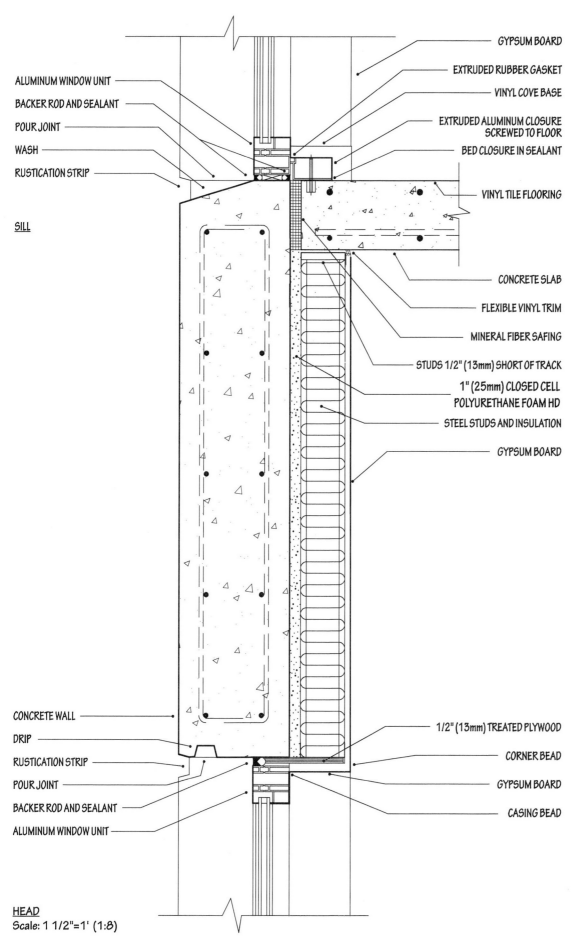

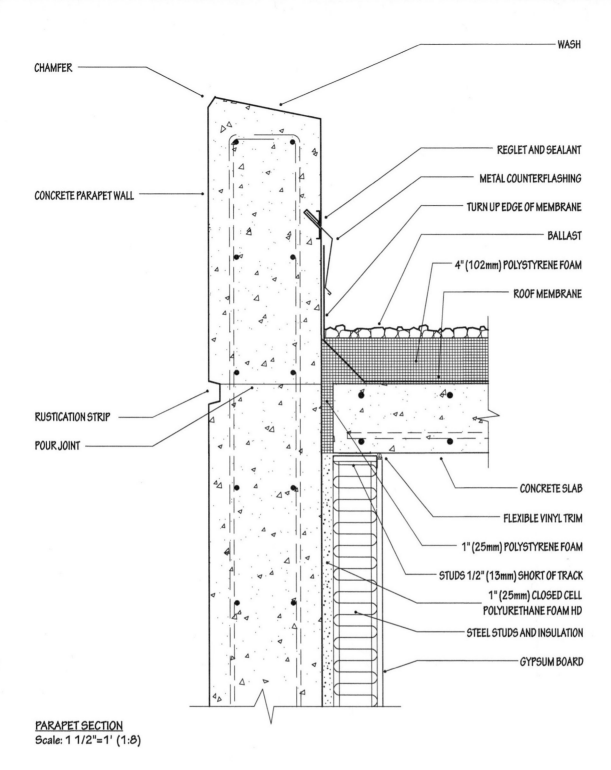

PARAPET SECTION
Scale: 1 1/2"=1' (1:8)

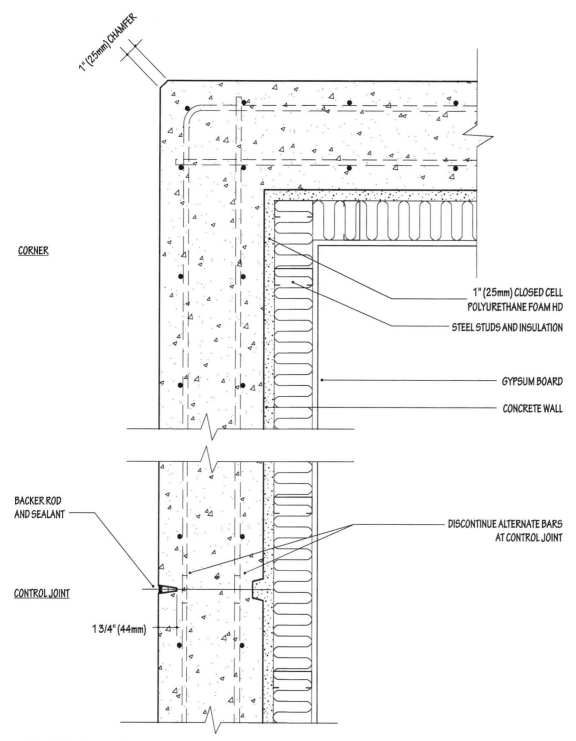

PLAN OF CORNER AND CONTROL JOINT
Scale: 1 1/2"=1' (1:8)

SECTION 1 ■ APPLYING THE DETAIL PATTERNS

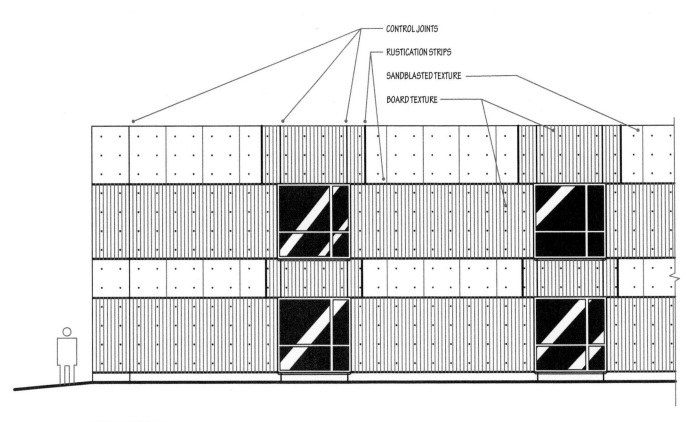

TYPICAL ELEVATION
Scale 3/32"=1' (1:128)

KEY REFERENCES

The following are important reference materials that were used in developing this set of details. Full bibliographic information on these publications is given in *Appendix A*, *The Detailer's Reference Shelf.*

1. Relevant building and energy codes, including IBC, IECC, and IgCC.
2. American Concrete Institute Committee 303R-12, *Guide to Cast-in-Place Architectural Concrete Practice.*
3. American Concrete Institute 117–10, *Standard Tolerances for Concrete Construction and Materials.* 2015.
4. M. K. Hurd, *Formwork for Concrete.*
5. United States Gypsum Company, *Gypsum Construction Handbook.* ∎

CHAPTER  Detailing a Building in Masonry on a Concrete Frame

THE PROJECT

The project is a 17-story luxury apartment cohousing condominium building in a mountainous area of northern California. This location is in Seismic Design Category D and in IECC (International Energy Conservation Code) Climate Zone 4. The concrete and masonry building is designed to accommodate the potential for differential movement as a series of joined yet independent structures. Building services are localized in each dwelling unit; interior finishes are selected for long-term resilience and easy repairability.

SETTING PERFORMANCE STANDARDS

The cohousing community owners desire a well-finished, smartly appointed, and durable building to further their shared commitment to sustainable living. The applicable national code specifies minimum values of R-9.5 continuous insulation in mass walls, an R-25 continuous insulation on the roof, R-10 for 24 in. at slab-on-grade perimeters (metric equivalents are R-65, 173, and 69 for 610 mm), and high-performance, low-emissivity double-glazed windows. The owner's sustainable design objectives call for higher insulation values than these, to reduce future energy consumption and costs. We comply by designing R-16 walls and R-30 in the roofs (R-111 and 208), *Life Cycle* (Chapter 10). Seismic requirements of the International Building Code (IBC) apply to the design of the structure and cladding. Each private dwelling unit must have a high degree of acoustical privacy from one another and from shared common areas throughout the building. ▷

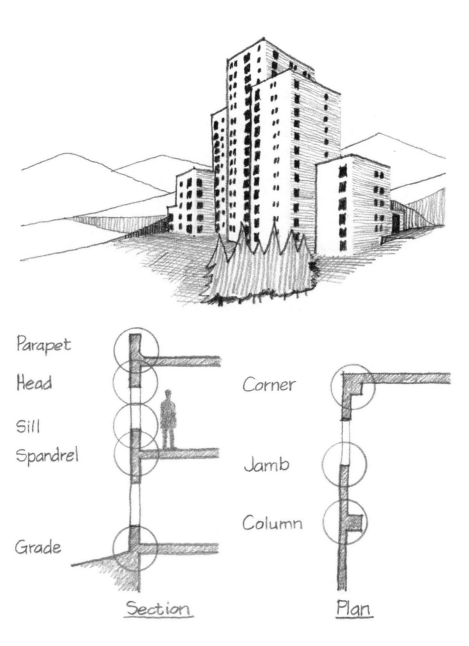

Architectural Detailing: Function Constructability Aesthetics. Fourth Edition. Patrick Rand, Jason Miller, and Edward Allen.
© 2025 John Wiley & Sons, Inc. Published 2025 by John Wiley & Sons, Inc.

KEY DETAILS TO DEVELOP

The key details that will establish the visual character and mode of construction of the building are those circled on the section and plan diagrams to the right. These must be developed as a consistent set of *Contributive Details* (Chapter 14) that work well with the building's overall architecture and with one another. These conditions are the most general and, in many ways, the most critical of the building's details to develop. Details of special situations, such as the entrance, lobby, roof terraces, and junctions between towers of differing heights, will use these general details as a point of departure. Of these key details, the spandrel is the detail from which the other key details will be derived. We will begin our detailing work at that location.

EARLY DECISIONS CONCERNING MATERIAL, STRUCTURE, AND FORM

Working together with the structural engineer, we have made a preliminary choice for the structure of the building: A two-way flat-plate concrete system supported by concrete columns typically spaced on 24 ft. (7.32 m) centers. To maximize the number of floors and housing units, in response to a regulatory overall height restriction, floor-to-floor height is approximately 9 ft. (2743 mm). The floor plates will be 10 in. (254 mm) thick. Multistory spaces will be possible by cutting out sections of the flat plate between columns. Column size will vary – large at the bottom of the building and small at the top. There will be perimeter beams around the edges of all the floor plates; the role of these beams will be partly to strengthen the edge of each floor plate, partly to stiffen the frame against lateral loads, and partly to support the weight of the cladding system.

The apartments will be heated and cooled by energy-efficient, variable-speed fan-coil units with integrated energy recovery ventilators (ERV) at the exterior walls. The pipe risers that feed these units with heated and chilled water from the basement mechanical room will have to be housed in *Vertical Chases* (Chapter 8) at various locations. Each fan-coil unit will require an exterior louver for air intake and exhaust.

After considering several options, we decide to face the building structure with brick masonry. A brick exterior is an attractive solution for this project for a number of reasons. Brick gives an impression of quality, strength, and permanence, the more so because it is a *Surface That Ages Gracefully* (Chapter 10). The wide array of brick unit colors, textures, and bond patterns available offers us compositional opportunities for *Formal Transitions* and *Hierarchy of Refinement* (Chapter 14) between different building elements in a system of *Parts That Are Easy to Handle* (Chapter 11). Windows in the cohousing towers will be a combination of casement and fixed units constructed of wood with a vinyl cladding on the exterior. These will occur in varying sizes and in somewhat random locations that suit the interior configurations of the studio, two-bedroom, and three-bedroom units.

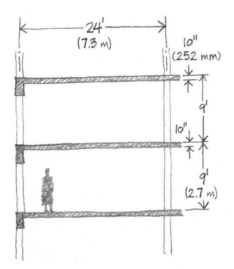

Inside, floors will be carpeted except for ceramic tile floors in private baths, communal kitchens, and shared laundry facilities. Made from recycled materials, a modular carpeting system has been selected partly because it is a desirable material for resilient interiors and partly because it will contribute to acoustic privacy (*Cushioned Floor*, Chapter 5). Selected for its surface durability and its clean, monolithic appearance, the non–load-bearing partitions will be veneer plaster mounted on steel studs. Ceilings will be the painted undersides of the slabs. Because the building structure – and exposed building services – are also interior finishes, we make a note to communicate a performance specification for *Pride of Craftsmanship* (Chapter 13) to the project contractor prior to the commencement of work.

EARLY WORK ON MATERIALS AND DETAILS

We find from Table 12–2 (see *Dimensional Tolerance,* Chapter 12) that the standard dimensional tolerance for a concrete frame is ±1 in. (25 mm) from a vertical plane for the lower nine stories and ±1¾ in. (44 mm) at the building's maximum height. Our details will have to take this into account.

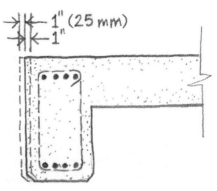

There are three different approaches we might consider using to apply a brick exterior to this building. One is to shop-fabricate the brickwork components in large, reinforced panels that can be trucked to the site, lifted, and attached to the building with relatively little on-site work (*Factory and Site*, Chapter 13). This is an intriguing option, but we discard it on this particular project for two market-specific reasons: (1) there are few such fabricators nearby, and (2) there are a number of excellent masonry contractors in the area who will be able to construct the cladding in place at an economical price (*Local Skills and Resources*, Chapter 13).

Another option is to construct the cladding in place as a brick masonry facing, or veneer, over a concrete masonry backup wall.

We must weigh this against a third and potentially cost-saving option, which is to construct the cladding in place but to use a steel stud backup wall rather than concrete masonry. We have studied this question in some detail, partly by observing constructed buildings of both types, and partly by reading many current articles in technical journals. We conclude that there are unanswered questions concerning the long-term durability and safety of brickwork attached to steel stud walls. These questions stem from the relative flexibility of the studs, which may allow cracking of the brick facing, and from the potential for corrosion and disintegration of the steel and gypsum components of the system. For this building, in which durability is a major design criterion, and in this context, where seismic design is required, we choose to design an all-masonry wall that will be constructed in place (**Robust Assemblies**, Chapter 10).

The backup wall will be made of nominal 8 in. (203 mm) hollow, lightweight concrete blocks, reinforced horizontally with steel wire joint reinforcement and vertically with reinforcing bars in grouted cores. Lightweight concrete blocks are selected primarily for their fire and sound resistance. As their name suggests, these units are lighter than other concrete masonry products, which makes it easier for skilled masons to lift and lay block efficiently.

We have decided to use modular bricks, which measure 2¼ in. × 3⅝ in. × 7⅝ in. (57 × 92 × 194 mm), because their dimensions will coordinate well with the dimensions of the building and the backup masonry, thereby avoiding costly cutting of masonry units (**Uncut Units**, Chapter 11). We will use standard ⅜ in. (9.5 mm) mortar joints. Given the high wind loads on the walls of this building, we will need to use very stiff metal ties to give lateral support to the brick facing. The building code requires that the ties in this location be spaced so that each supports no more than 2³⁄₁₆ sq. ft. (0.25 m²) of wall area. It also requires that the ties connect to joint reinforcing of ³⁄₁₆ in. (4.8 mm) wires in the brick facing. To prevent deflection and cracking of the facing, we decide to avoid adjustable masonry ties, which tend to

TABLE 17-1: Thermal Resistance of Wall Components

	R (ft²-hr-°F/BTU-in)	R (m²-°C/W)
Outside air film	0.17	1.18
3½ in. (89 mm) of brick @ R-0.20/in. (R-25/25 mm)	*0.70*	*4.85*
2 in. (51 mm) cavity	*0.90*	*6.24*
8 in. (203 mm) lightweight CMUs	2.00	13.87
1 in. (25 mm) furring space	1.01	7.06
½ in. (13 mm) plaster or gypsum	0.45	3.14
Inside air film	0.68	4.72
Total thermal resistance (excluding items in *italics* above)	**4.31**	**29.97**

have excessive dimensional play. Instead, we will specify use of three-wire joint reinforcing that includes the ties and the reinforcing wires for both brick and block in a single welded assembly.

FORMULATING AN APPROACH TO THE IMPORTANT WALL FUNCTIONS
Thermal Insulation and Water Vapor

For maximum security against water leakage, we will detail the exterior wall as a cavity wall. We sketch it freehand in section, working from outside to inside. It will consist of a brick facing, a cavity, a concrete masonry backup wall, and a furred interior wall facing of veneer plaster.

The wall assembly will probably need some additional thermal insulation to achieve the client's target value of R-16 (R-111). Using values from *ASHRAE Fundamentals*, we determine the thermal resistance of the wall components shown in Table 17-1. The thermal resistances of the brick veneer and 2 in. (51 mm) cavity are shown in the table, but when considering the actual performance

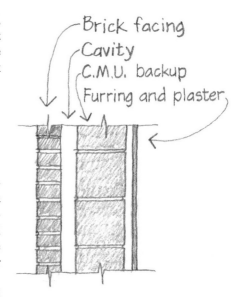

of the assembly, these components are not included in the total R-value calculation of the wall (see *italics*). The rationale is that outside air moving through vents into and out of the cavity may negate the value of these two layers. We feel confident in the total value as shown and believe the wall's actual performance will exceed this value.

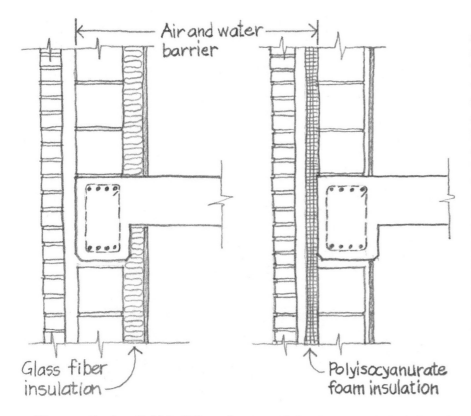

We must add at least R-11.7 of ***Thermal Insulation*** (Chapter 3) to the wall to meet the objective of R-16 (add R-80 to meet R-111). Consulting again the list of R-values in *ASHRAE Fundamentals*, we see that we can do this with either 3⅝ in. (93 mm) batts of glass fiber or 2 in. (51 mm) of rigid polyisocyanurate boards. This type of rigid insulation is more costly than polystyrene but is a better insulating product. We use it to keep the brick veneer relatively close to the backup wall in this seismically active area. We make freehand sketches of both options.

To remain dry, the glass fiber would have to be on the interior side of the concrete masonry wall, which would require very deep furring strips and would reduce the available floor space in the apartments. It would also leave the edges of the floor slabs uninsulated. The polyisocyanurate foam, which is resistant to moisture, can be installed by the masons in the wall cavity. This would wrap the concrete structure and the concrete masonry walls in a virtually unbroken blanket of insulation, avoiding thermal bridges and creating an ***Outside-Insulated Thermal Mass*** (Chapter 3) that would make the building easier to heat and cool, as well as ***Warm Interior Surfaces*** (Chapter 4) that would not condense moisture in cold winter weather. It would have the added advantage of sheltering the structure of the building from outdoor temperature extremes. We decide to try the continuous foam insulation in the cavity.

The vinyl-clad wood windows we have selected for the building easily meet the energy requirements of the code. With the relatively low conductivity of the wood frame, there is no need for ***Thermal Break*** (Chapter 3), and the ***Multiple Glazing*** (Chapter 3) of the window achieves the necessary R-value and a sufficiently ***Warm Interior Surface*** (Chapter 4) to avoid condensation. ▷

Water Leakage

The cavity wall will operate as a ***Rainscreen Assembly*** (Chapter 1) if we detail it with a proper rainscreen, air barrier, and pressure equalization chamber (PEC). The brick facing will serve as a satisfactory rainscreen. The cavity will serve as the pressure equalization chamber, and we will ***Drain and Weep*** (Chapter 1) the cavity with weep holes and appropriate flashings. Horizontal shelf angles at each story will compartment the cavity vertically, and L-shaped sheet metal pieces will be installed into vertical movement joints to compartment the cavity horizontally. We will make a note to calculate PEC cavity and vent sizes suitable for this climate.

The air barrier will consist of the concrete masonry wall and the portions of the perimeter beams and columns exposed to the cavity. To maintain the integrity of the air barrier, we will apply a ***Sealant Joint*** (Chapter 1) where the concrete masonry joins the frame, but some air will diffuse through the concrete blocks themselves, so we need to apply an airtight membrane or coating to the blocks to create an ***Air Barrier System*** (Chapter 2) that will both contribute to thermal comfort and prevent water leakage through rainscreen action. We will choose an air and water barrier material that is relatively impermeable to water vapor, but the mechanical engineer assures us that, because it will be on the inside surface of the insulating foam boards, its temperature will always remain above the dew point. It will act as a ***Warm-Side Vapor Retarder*** (Chapter 4) and will not trap any condensate.

Acoustic Privacy

Acoustic privacy and the mitigation or reduction of noise transmission between condominium units are extremely important issues in multiple-unit dwellings The design team has hired an acoustical consultant to assist development of acoustic solutions based on the material assemblies and floor to floor heights of structure. The consultant suggests that a padded carpeting system installed over the concrete slabs will provide a ***Sound-Absorbing Surface*** (Chapter 5) and will contribute significantly to the management of noise transmission through the floors (***Cushioned Floor***, Chapter 5). They will propose ways in which to cushion floors beneath the ceramic tile areas, which would otherwise generate and transmit too much impact noise. Between units on the same floor, the consultant recommends that the non-load-bearing walls between units be framed with double rows of studs with acoustic batts and extra layers of gypsum board (***Airtight, Heavy, Limp Partition***, Chapter 5). Walls within units can be made of a single row of steel studs with double layers of gypsum panels; the consultant will make more precise proposals for these as the details develop. The choice of fan-coil units for heating and cooling is applauded, because these units avoid the ductwork that might furnish a flanking path for sound between apartments, but they note that penetrations of the piping through floors and walls will have to be sealed very securely. The consultant suggests coordinating with the mechanical engineer to select fan-coil assemblies that are inherently quiet and have *Quiet Attachments* (Chapter 5) to the structure of the building.

Movement

Because of the physical site location and mixed assemblies used in the building, the accommodation of movement will be an extremely important function of the details we are drawing. The concrete masonry backup walls will shrink slightly after installation and must have **Control Joints** (Chapter 6). Because the backup walls are interrupted at approximately 22 ft. (6.71 m) intervals by the concrete columns, this function can be served by the perimeter sealant joints we are already planning to provide as part of our air barrier strategy. The brick masonry facing will expand slightly after installation. It will also expand when heated by the sun and air and will contract when cooled. The concrete frame of the building, insulated with the expanded polystyrene foam, will remain constant in dimension.

We note that thermal expansion and contraction of the brickwork wythe will occur, while the outside-insulated concrete masonry wythe to which it is tied remains constant in dimension. If we divide the brick facing into small panels with movement joints, the relative motions between the two wythes will be small and can be absorbed by small amounts of flexing in the metal ties.

It is important, however, that we use ladder-type joint reinforcing and ties rather than truss-type; diagonals crossing the cavity in truss-type reinforcing could cause the two wythes to act as a single structural unit, bending when exposed to temperature extremes like the bimetallic spring in a thermostat. This phenomenon is shown in exaggerated form in the accompanying plan views. We will ask the structural engineer to verify the joint reinforcement gauge and select the seismic clips that are appropriate for this location.

The columns and beams of the building frame will deflect under gravity loads. Because the frame is made of concrete, there will also be creep – a small but significant, irreversible, long-term shortening of the columns and sagging of the beams. Wind loads and seismic loads will cause the concrete building frame to flex and drift. All these structural movements will apply loads to exterior and interior walls, unless the walls are separated FROM the frame by **Structure/Enclosure Joints** (Chapter 6). The most important of these will be the soft joints that must be provided under the shelf angles supporting the brick facing.

Locating and Sizing Movement Joints

We look at possible patterns for dividing the brick facing into panels. The facing will be supported on a steel shelf angle at each floor, so we will provide a horizontal movement joint beneath each angle. In the vertical direction, we recognize that vertical or diagonal cracking tends to occur at the corners of the window openings, where the facing is weakest. However, it is difficult to organize vertical joints at the window openings in a visually satisfactory way, and the end bearing details of the steel window lintels in the brick facing create certain technical uncertainties in this approach. It would be much simpler to install a movement joint at the center line of each column, thus dividing the facade into story-height panels 24 ft. (7.32 m) long – a dimension so short that it will minimize potential cracking forces at the windows. We try this pattern as an overlay sketch on the building elevation and decide it is acceptable visually.

We size the vertical joints by following the procedure outlined in the section "Determining Widths of Sealant Joints," Chapter 1:

$$W = \frac{100}{X}(\varepsilon L \Delta T + M_o) + t$$

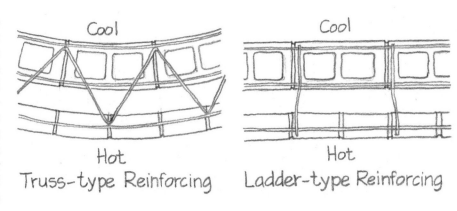

Truss-type Reinforcing   Ladder-type Reinforcing

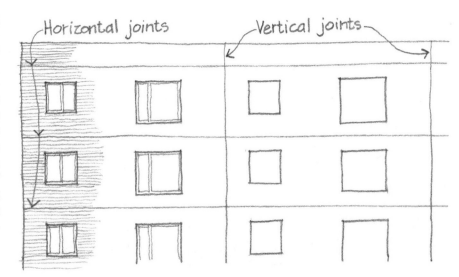

Assuming a silicone joint sealant with a movement capability of ±50% (an assumption that we will later communicate to the specifications writer):

$$W = \frac{100}{50}[(0.0000036 \text{ in./in./°F})(288 \text{ in.})(180°\text{F}) + 0.06 \text{ in.}] + 0.125 \text{ in.}$$

$$W = \frac{100}{50}[(0.0000065 \text{ mm/mm/°C})(7315 \text{ mm})(82.2°\text{C}) + 1.52 \text{ mm}] + 3.17 \text{ mm}$$

$$W = 0.62 \text{ in. } (16 \text{ mm})$$

Use a ⅝ in. (16 mm) sealant joint at each column line.

In this calculation, 0.0000036 in./in./°F (0.0000065 mm/mm/°C) is the coefficient of thermal expansion of brickwork, taken from Chapter 1. Length (*L*) equals 288 in. (7315 mm), the same as 24 ft. (7315 mm), the distance between joints. The maximum range of temperature that the brick facing

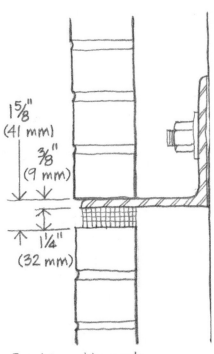

Section through Soft Joint

will experience is 180°F (82.2°C). This may seem large, but research has shown that dark-colored masonry in summer sunlight can easily reach 140°F (60°C), and winter night-time temperatures in this region can go well below zero (–18°C). The 0.06 in. (1.52 mm) is a calculated value for moisture expansion (see **Seasoning and Curing**, Chapter 6). The **Dimensional Tolerance** (Chapter 12) for the brickwork is 0.125 in. (3 mm), a relatively small amount, because we know the masons can easily make small dimensional adjustments in the head joints of mortar to maintain a constant-width expansion joint. ▷

We apply the same formula to sizing the horizontal joint, the soft joint that must be provided below every shelf angle. The structural engineer wants to allow a full ½ in. (13 mm) for deflection and creep in the concrete structure, and we include the same ⅛ in. (3 mm) tolerance:

$$W = \frac{100}{50}[(0.0000036 \text{ in./in./}°F)(107 \text{ in.})(180°F) + 0.5 \text{ in.}] + 0.125 \text{ in.}$$

$$W = \frac{100}{50}[(0.0000065 \text{ mm/mm/}°C)(2718 \text{ mm})(82.2°C) + 12.7 \text{ mm} + 3.17 \text{ mm}$$

$$W = 1.26 \text{ in. (32 mm)}$$

Use a 1¼ in. (32 mm) soft joint beneath the shelf angle.

The engineer also tells us that the shelf angle will have to be ⅜ in. (9.5 mm) thick, so the overall height of the horizontal joint at each story will be 1⅝ in. (41 mm).

DETAILING THE SPANDREL

With these essential wall function parameters established, we begin our detail development at the typical spandrel condition. Once the spandrel has been worked out, the remainder of the key details can be developed with comparative speed on tracing paper overlays over the spandrel section.

Horizontal Brickwork Dimensioning

As we begin laying out a preliminary spandrel section, we confer with the structural engineer on several important points. First, we would like for the floor-to-floor variation in column size to occur entirely within the building footprint, so that the outside face of the structural frame will lie in a single flat plane. Our engineer readily agrees with this proposal.

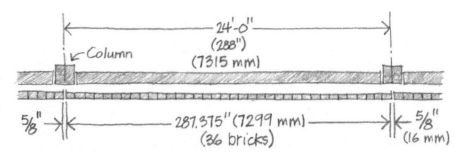

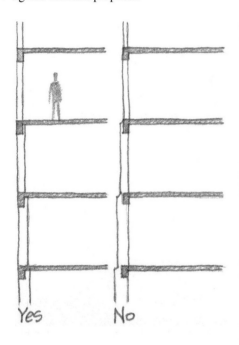

Second, we would like to coordinate the dimensions of the frame with the dimensions of the masonry work to minimize cutting of masonry units (*Uncut Units*, Chapter 11). This will result in as much of a *Repetitious Assembly* (Chapter 11) process as possible.

We do some calculations of masonry dimensions: In the horizontal direction, the center-to-center column spacing has been set at 24 ft. (7315 mm), and we have already determined there will be a ⅝ in. (16 mm) sealant joint at each column.

Thus, the space available for brickwork in each bay will be:

(24 ft.)(12 in./ft.) − 0.625 in. = 287.375 in.
7315 mm − 16 = 7299 mm

Each brick is expected to be 7⅝ in. long and 3⅝ in. wide (194 × 92 mm), and mortar joints are ⅜ in. (9.5 mm) thick. Brick industry standards limiting size variations make this a good expectation. There will be one fewer mortar joints than bricks in each course. The number of bricks needed to occupy this space can be approximated as:

Thirty-six modular bricks with their mortar joints would ordinarily occupy an exact length of:

36 (7.625 in. + 0.375 in.) − 0.375 in.
= 287.625 in.

36 (194 mm + 9.5 mm) − 9.5 mm
= 7316 mm

Because we have only 287.375 in. (7299 mm) of length available between expansion joints, the course of bricks will have to be squeezed by a dimension of:

287.625 in. − 287.375 in. = 0.25 in.
7306 mm − 7299 mm = 7 mm

We will suggest on our construction drawings that the masons make the first two head joints at each end ¹⁄₁₆ in. (1.6 mm) narrower to accomplish this, lining up the rest of the head joints accurately with those of the concrete masonry backup wall so that openings will be easy to create.

Vertical Brickwork Dimensioning

The brick coursing must be coordinated vertically with the floor-to-floor height. If the floor-to-floor height is 108 in. (2743 mm) and the total height of the soft joint plus shelf angle thickness is 1⅝ in. (41 mm), the space to be filled with brickwork is:

108 in. − 1.625 in. = 106.375 in.
2743 mm − 41 mm = 2702 mm

Each course of brickwork, with its mortar joint, is 2⅔ in. (67.7 mm) high. This works well with the block coursing in the backup wall, because three courses of brickwork are the same 8 in. (203 mm) height as one course of block work.

In calculating the height of the brick courses, we must take into account that the bricks will not have a mortar joint on the shelf angle; nor will they have one under the soft joint. As a result, there will be one fewer mortar joints than courses, and we must add a nonexistent mortar joint to our story height to be able to calculate the number of courses:

$$N = \frac{106.375 \text{ in.} + 0.375 \text{ in.}}{8/3 \text{ in. per course}}$$

= 40.03 courses

$$= \frac{2702 \text{ mm} + 9.5 \text{ mm}}{67.7 \text{ mm per course}}$$

= 40.05 courses

We cannot ask the masons to build 0.03 or 0.05 courses, so we calculate the height of an even 40 courses, remembering to deduct the height of one mortar joint:

Height =
(40 courses)(8/3 inches/course) − ⅜ in.
= 106.29 in.
(40 courses)(67.7 mm/course) − 9.5 mm
= 2699 mm

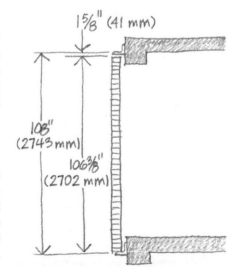

This is slightly less than the 106.375 in. (2702 mm) we were shooting for. Suppose we try to make up the difference in the soft joint:

Height of joint beneath shelf angle:

= 108 in. − 106.29 in. − 0.375 in.
= 1.34 in.
= 2743 mm − 2699 mm − 9.5 mm
= 34.5 mm

The 0.375 in. (9.5 mm) in this calculation is the thickness of the shelf angle. We wanted a joint that is 1.25 in. (32 mm) high, so the 1.34 in. (34.5 mm) dimension is only about 0.10 in. (2.5 mm) more, which is reasonable.

Concrete Masonry Dimensioning

The concrete masonry backup wall must fit between columns in each bay; it will increase the efficiency of the masonry work (and reduce its cost) if we minimize the number of blocks that have to be cut. With uncut blocks, masons can produce wall lengths in any multiple of 8 in., less ⅜ in. (203 mm, less 9.5 mm), to account for the fact that a wall contains one fewer mortar joints than blocks. The center-to-center column spacing is 24 ft. (7315 mm), which is an even multiple of 8 in. (203 mm). Therefore, any column size that is a multiple of the module of 8 in. (203 mm) would minimize cutting of blocks. We ask the structural engineer if the columns could be standardized in width at either 16 or 24 in. (406 or 609 mm), letting the depth vary as needed. After reviewing the preliminary figures and calculations, the engineer reports that 24 in. (609 mm) width will be needed on the lower floors, but a transition to 16 in. (406 mm) on the higher floors is possible.

Meanwhile, we have noted the need to provide a movement joint at each end of each segment of the backup wall, to allow for block shrinkage and seismic motion of the frame. If the columns were a full 16 or 24 in. (406 or 609 mm) in dimension, this would allow only ⅜ in. (9.5 mm), the dimension of a standard mortar joint, for sealant at each end. If we squeezed the

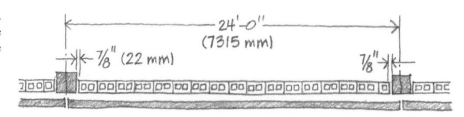

columns to 15 or 23 in. (381 or 584 mm), this would permit a generous ⅞ in. (22 mm) joint at each end. After a quick consult, the engineer agrees this is acceptable.

In the vertical direction, the backup wall of concrete masonry units will have to fit between the top of the floor slab and the underside of the perimeter beam. The floor-to-floor height is 9 ft. (2743 mm).

The engineer would like the depth of the perimeter beam to be about 18 in. (457 mm), measured downward from the top of the slab, but says that there is some flexibility on this dimension because the width of the beam or the reinforcing schedule of the beam can change if necessary to achieve the same strength and stiffness. We will install a soft joint between the top of the concrete masonry wall and the bottom of the beam to allow for deflection and creep. Working from the calculated dimension of the exterior soft joint and subtracting the portion attributable to temperature movement, we decide to make this joint ¾ in. (19 mm) high. Thus, the height available to be filled with concrete masonry is:

(9 ft)(12 in. / ft) − 18 in. − ¾ in. = 89.25 in
2743 mm − 457 mm − 19 mm = 2267 mm

Because each course of standard concrete blocks, including mortar, is 8 in. (203 mm) high, we see that it would take about 11 courses to fill this space. We calculate the beam depth required to accommodate an even 11 courses of blockwork:

Beam depth + (11 courses)(8 in./course) + 0.75 in. joint = 108 in.

Beam depth = 19.5 in.

Beam depth + (11 courses)(203 mm/course) + 19 mm joint = 2743 mm
Beam depth = 491 mm

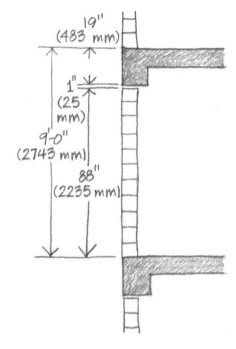

The structural engineer says this would be fine, and suggests we round off the dimension to 19 in. (483 mm) for ease of formwork fabrication. This would provide a soft joint of 1 in. (25 mm), which is acceptable based on our analysis. Before we conclude this exercise, we also need to check the headroom under the perimeter beam. The building code does not permit a soffit height of less than 7 ft. (2134 mm), and we must allow an extra 1½ in. (38 mm) for finish beneath the beam.

Headroom =
  108 in. − 19 in. − 1.5 in. = 87.5 in.
  = 7 ft. 4 in. > 7 ft. 0 in. (OK)
  = 2743 mm − 483 mm − 38 mm
  = 2222 mm > 2133 mm (OK)

The preliminary dimensioning of the bricks and the concrete masonry units is complete. ▷

Starting the Spandrel Detail

We can now proceed with the construction of our preliminary spandrel detail for the building. Working at a large enough scale of 1½ in. equals 1 ft. (1:8), we can see all the important features, including thicknesses of mortar joints and positions of flashings. We pencil in the slab and the perimeter beam. We show chamfers on the two lower edges of the beam to prevent breakage of the edges when the forms are removed (*Clean Edge*, Chapter 12).

We draw the concrete masonry units and their soft joint beneath the beam. We add a vertical layer 2 in. (51 mm) thick against the outside of the backup wall and perimeter beam to indicate the polyisocyanurate foam insulation in the cavity. We add another 2 in. (51 mm) for the open portion of the cavity, which is the minimum width that masons can keep clean of mortar droppings (*Installation Clearance*, Chapter 11). If the cavity is not clear, excess mortar can clog the weep holes at the bottom and form a water bridge between the wythes. This would negate the actual performance benefits of detailing a cavity wall assembly. Outside the cavity we lay out the 3⅝ in. (92 mm) thickness of the brick facing wythe.

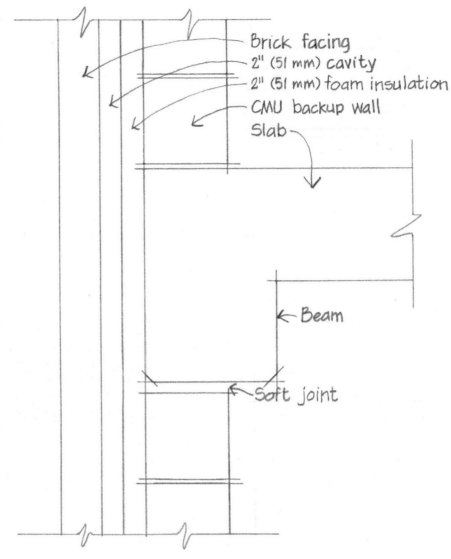

We need to choose an exact vertical position for the shelf angle. This component must be positioned immediately beneath a course of bricks, which in turn must match the concrete block coursing for the ties to connect, so we begin by working downward from the horizontal mortar joint where the blockwork rests on the floor slab. We would like to keep the shelf angle high on the concrete beam for several functional reasons. First, a high shelf angle position will minimize the amount of flashing material required and eliminate the need for masonry ties to penetrate the flashing – a situation that would have the potential for performative failures like water leaks or galvanic corrosion. Second, a high shelf angle position will also minimize interference between the shelf angle and the flashings that occur over window heads. Finally, to achieve the code-mandated density of masonry ties, we must place ties 16 in. (406 mm) apart both horizontally and vertically. This means there will be ties in every second horizontal mortar joint in the backup wall. It is unwise to place ties and flashing in the same mortar joint: There is not space for both, and galvanic corrosion could result from contact of the dissimilar metals. For these reasons, a convenient location for the top surface of the shelf angle should be no lower than one block height below floor level, so the first row of ties can be placed on top of the first course of blocks, one course above the flashing. After trying this to scale on the drawing, we decide to place the shelf angle three brick courses (equal to one block course) below the top of the floor slab. ▷

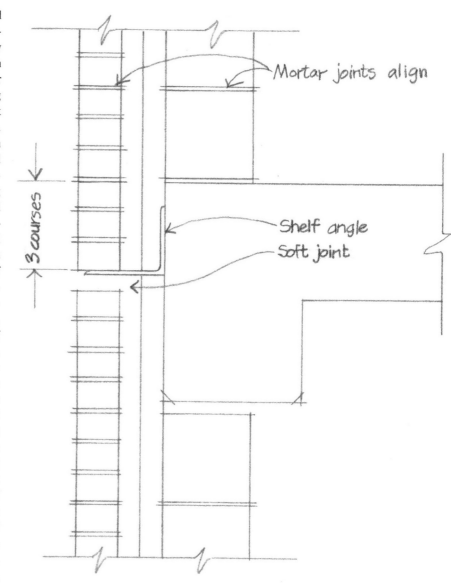

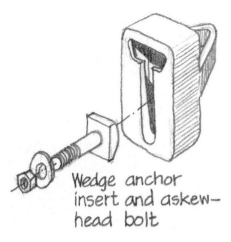

Wedge anchor insert and askew-head bolt

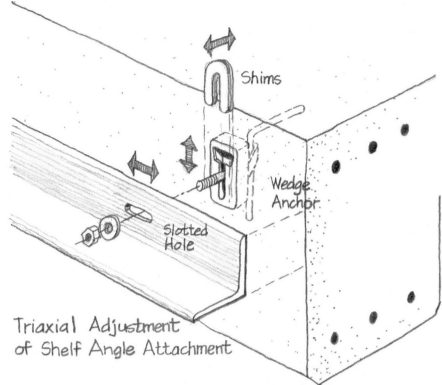

Triaxial Adjustment of Shelf Angle Attachment

We now turn our attention to the problem of fastening the shelf angle to the concrete structure. The structural engineer has proposed to do this with malleable iron wedge anchor inserts cast into the face of the concrete beam at 6 ft. (1829 mm) intervals.

In addition to having a high load-bearing capacity, this type of anchor allows for vertical dimensional adjustment by means of a sliding bolt with an askew (sloping) head that locks securely against the wedge-shaped front of the insert at any height. The shelf angle and its fasteners constitute a very important **Small Structure** (Chapter 7), designed by the engineer to be strong and stiff enough to support the facing safely. The angle itself is a 7 in. × 6 in. × 3⅜ in. (178 × 152 × 9.5 mm) steel shape that falls about ⅜ in. (16 mm) short of the outer face of the brickwork, leaving space for sealant.

This shelf angle passes through the thermal insulation layer of this wall assembly, making it a small thermal bridge. There are several proprietary adjustable thermal break shelf angles on the market, but their literature does not state explicitly that they are viable in seismic zone D, where our building will be located. Our consulting engineer recommends that we use a conventional shelf angle in this location.

While the wedge anchors provide ample *vertical* adjustment for inaccuracies, we must also address this question: What about the ±1 in. (25 mm) tolerance in the *horizontal* location of the beam?

If the beam falls short of its correct location, we can make up the small difference with steel shims inserted between the angle and the face of the concrete (***Dimensional Tolerance***, Chapter 12). If it falls far short, we can use an angle with an 8 in. (203 mm) leg rather than a 7 in. (178 mm) leg to avoid having to use a thick stack of shims. If the beam lies outside its correct location, an angle with a shorter leg may be required. The structural engineer will determine whether the longer and shorter angles need to have different thicknesses than the normal angle so that their stiffnesses will match. The shelf angle locations should be accurately marked by surveyors as the formwork is stripped from each floor, allowing ample time for the contractor to special-order angles if necessary. The angles will be punched or drilled for the bolts at the fabricating plant, and we detail the holes to be horizontal slots that will allow considerable leeway for wedge inserts that were not accurately placed. Thus, we have provided a fully triaxial ***Adjustable Fit*** (Chapter 12) that will compensate for expected levels of inaccuracy in the making of the concrete frame: vertical adjustment with the wedge anchors, in-and-out adjustment with shims and different sizes of angles, and lateral adjustment with horizontally slotted bolt holes in the shelf angles. We make a note, nevertheless, to have the construction administrator from our office see that formwork and wedge anchor locations are checked before the concrete is poured (***Observable Assemblies***, Chapter 11). The inspector should also be sure that all the wedge anchors are installed correctly, because a wedge anchor is only secure against loading in a direction that drives the askew head of the bolt more tightly against the wedge.

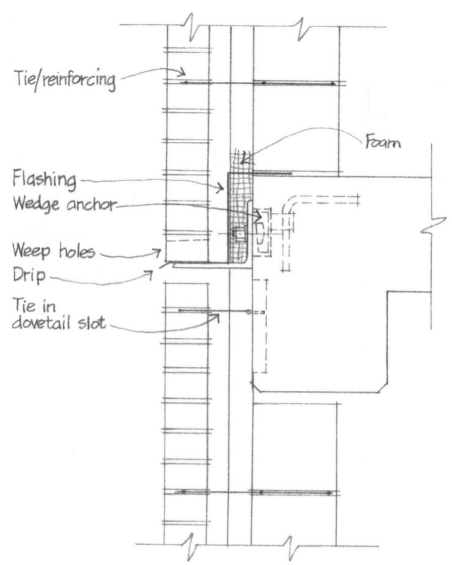

Ties and Flashings

Returning to our drawing, we add the masonry courses and ties. We notice that ties are needed to connect the brick facing to the spandrel beam above the top of the concrete masonry backup wall. We provide for these by installing vertical dovetail slots 16 in. (406 mm) apart on the face of the concrete beam so that the masons can insert dovetail ties to the brick facing. The slots are small metal channels filled with low-density plastic foam. They are nailed to the inside of the formwork before the concrete is poured. The foam keeps the concrete from filling the slot but is easily removed by the masons as they install the ties.

We add to our drawing the continuous sheet of flashing that comes from beneath the backup wall, over the shelf angle (***Moisture Break***, Chapter 1).

This catches any water that may enter the cavity, and drains it through weep holes to the outdoors. There are several details of importance here: The flashing should go over the foam insulation, rather than under, so that the foam cannot work loose and block the weep holes. This arrangement has the side benefit that the foam can serve to protect the flashing from puncture by the bolt ends on the shelf angle. Notice that the flashing forms an ***Upstand*** (Chapter 1) about 8 in. (203 mm) high to prevent the wind from driving water up into the backup wall. From this section of Chapter 1, we see that this 8 in. (203 mm) dimension is sufficient to prevent leakage at a wind velocity of about 125 mph (200 km/h), far higher than occurs in this region. The flashing should project well beyond the toe of the angle at a downward slope of 45 degrees to form an ***Overhang and Drip*** (Chapter 1) that will shed water free of the wall instead of allowing it to seep back in. This means that the flashing should be made from a material that is (a) sufficiently stiff to form the drip and (b) unaffected by sunlight. This rules out most plastic and synthetic rubber flashings. Copper sheet would be the best material, but in order to prevent galvanic corrosion, it needs to be protected from contact with the zinc coating on the shelf angle (***Protected and Similar Metals***, Chapter 10). We make a note to research and specify a flashing material that laminates copper between layers of inert materials for this purpose.

There are many ways to form weep holes: plastic tubes laid in the mortar joints, cotton rope wicks, and so on. Believing in the virtues of simplicity and the efficient use of construction resources, we choose to create large weep openings 2 ft. (610 mm) apart by simply omitting the mortar from every third head joint of the brick course immediately above the flashing. These tall, vertical openings allow for some accidental accumulation of mortar droppings at the base of the cavity, and they are easy for masons to make.

Open-mesh products designed specifically for this purpose can be inserted into the cavities to keep mortar droppings from clogging the weeps at the bottom of each cavity. However, we have not seen test data proving that water drains out of cavities any better when this product is installed. It is possible that water draining downward inside the cavity is absorbed by mortar droppings suspended on the mesh. Until reliable test data is available, we will continue to call for masons to follow the workmanship standards described in masonry industry technical notes (***Accepted Standards***, Chapter 13). It is better to minimize mortar droppings in the cavity than it is to catch them as they fall (***Minimum Number of Parts***, Chapter 11, and ***Unobstructed Drainage***, Chapter 1). ▷

Detailing the Soft Joint

We need to look more closely at the construction of the shelf angle, soft joint, and flashing. For this we find that we need a larger scale of drawing, so we prepare a detail at 6 in. equals 1 ft. (1:2). The soft joint that we propose is 1¼ in. (32 mm), which is unusually thick. The traditional standard ⅜ in. (9.5 mm) joint is grossly inadequate for a concrete frame building. We have made the joint this thick because we are being extremely careful to allow for expected creep and deflection in the concrete frame (*Expected Life*, Chapter 10). We make a note to check the availability of low-density rubber compressible filler strips in the thickness needed. We will select a type that has a factory-installed sealant applied to the exposed face, reducing the height of the field-installed sealant to two beads of about ⅜ in. each. This solution avoids specifying and installing a very tall sealant joint that is very likely to sag out before it cures.

Many architects try to hide the soft joint by: minimizing its thickness; by recessing the outer lip of the flashing into the mortar joint; and by using L-shaped bricks to conceal the additional thickness. From a performance standpoint, these efforts to minimize functional requirements of the building envelope are misguided and potentially dangerous expedients to maintain façade uniformity. A constructively simple and aesthetically appealing alternative is to select a different color of brick and perhaps mortar for the first course to be laid on the shelf angle (*Intensification and Ornamentation*, Chapter 14). Because the eye is drawn to the horizontal band of differently colored brick, minor features such as joint thickness and weep holes are much less noticeable.

A soft joint that is too thin will not be able to absorb all the movement that occurs, and the brick facing may be put under a structural load that will cause it to crack and buckle. A recessed flashing leads to a wet shelf angle that can corrode. The lips of L-shaped bricks are fragile and subject to freeze-thaw spalling. These predictable detail-to-material failures can result in costly and tedious maintenance repairs requiring specialist restoration contractors.

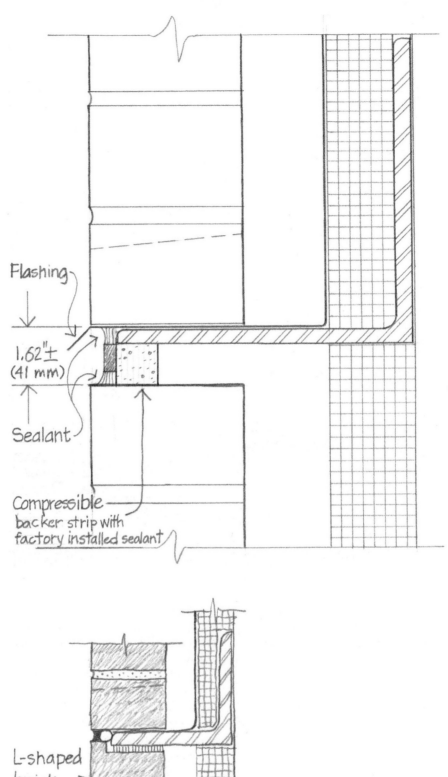

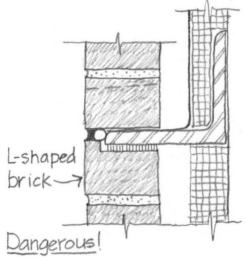

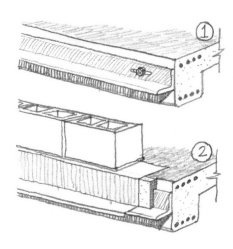

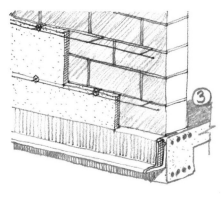

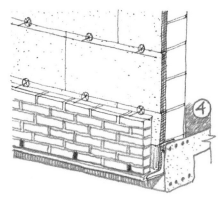

Detailing the Air Barrier

Returning to the original section drawing, we try *Rehearsing the Construction Sequence* (Chapter 13) to see if it makes sense.

First, ironworkers will install the shelf angles, setting them to accurate alignment marks that surveyors have left on the perimeter beams (1). Next, the masons will begin their work by installing the foam strips and flashings over the shelf angles, lapping and sealing the flashings at end and corner junctions. Then they will lay the first course of concrete blocks in the backup wall, which brings them to the height at which the first strip of metal joint reinforcing and ties must be placed (2). This strip, once in place, will obstruct any further work in the cavity. We realize immediately that the air barrier, insulation, sealant at the column faces, and brick facing must be completed up to this level before the strip is installed. This forces us to think more deeply about these components of the wall.

A bit of catalog research reveals two general types of air barrier materials available for cavity walls: flexible sheet materials that are adhered or fastened mechanically to the backup wall and synthetic or asphaltic fluid-applied mastics that are troweled or sprayed onto the wall. We make a note to verify that the air barrier material is chemically compatible with the flashing, insulation, and other products it will be in contact with; asphaltic materials often are not.

We note that some of the sheet materials are available in widths designed to match the every-second-block-course spacing of ties that we are using. This is potentially useful, but with further research, we find that the sheet materials must be cut to fit around the ties, and a mastic must then be used to seal these penetrations. We also see that for the adhered systems, the blockwork must be primed with a coating that takes at least an hour to cure before the sheet material can be adhered. These additional requirements and steps seem like severe disadvantages – especially the curing time – which might delay the progress of the work. Fluid-applied mastics appear to have none of these disadvantages. Compared to the sheet materials, they would simplify the masons' work. However, if some mastic should slop onto the top surface of the concrete masonry, it would destroy the adhesive bond of the mortar to the blocks and weaken the wall. We decide to use a mastic air barrier, but we make a note to specify that it be held back 1 in. (25 mm) from the upper edge of the blocks until the next two courses have been laid. We also note that the sealant joint where the backup wall meets each column must be completed before the mastic is spread, to avoid mastic contamination of the surfaces to which the sealant must adhere.

To rehearse again the masons' work thus far: They must install the first strip of foam insulation over the shelf angle, place the flashing, and lay the first course of concrete blocks in the backup wall. The waterproofing subcontractor would then install backer rod and sealant on the outside face where this course meets the columns at either end (the inside sealant joints can be done later), and spray on the air barrier mastic. Then the masons must install the next strip of foam insulation, only 8 in. (203 mm) high, pressing it against the mastic. This raises a problem: We were going to specify that the mastic coating be held 1 in. (25 mm) below the top of the concrete masonry, to be continued from that level after the next block courses have been laid. But once the foam insulation is installed, it will be impossible to get behind its top edge with a trowel to continue the mastic work as an unbroken air barrier membrane. We must rethink the sequence.

Suppose that we have the masons do everything as we have already planned, but leave out the foam for the moment, constructing the first six courses of brickwork instead. Then they could place the strip of foam insulation loosely in the cavity, install the joint reinforcing and tie strip above the insulation (3), and lay the next two courses of backup blocks. At this point the backup wall would be 16 in. (406 mm) higher than the brick facing. The waterproofing subcontractor could then apply the sealant at the junction between the columns and the backup wall and spray on the next strip of mastic, being careful to seal around the ties and over the top edge of the previous strip of mastic. All of these steps can be observed by the office's construction administrator (*Observable Assemblies*, Chapter 11).

Next, the masons could reach through the ties into the cavity to push the 8 in. (203 mm) strip of insulating board into position, locking it in place with standard plastic clips that snap over the ties (4). This would seem to work more smoothly than the first scenario, presenting fewer problems of worker access. Each clip is designed to hold the top of one sheet and the bottom of the next. The strip of foam just above the flashing would have no bottom restraint, but we could solve this problem by asking the masons to daub mastic onto the back of the foam with the tip of the trowel just before pushing it into place and installing the clips (*Accessible Connections*, Chapter 11).

▷

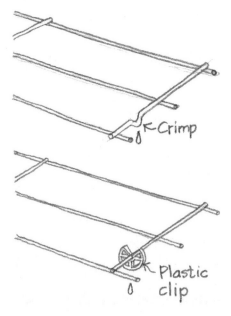

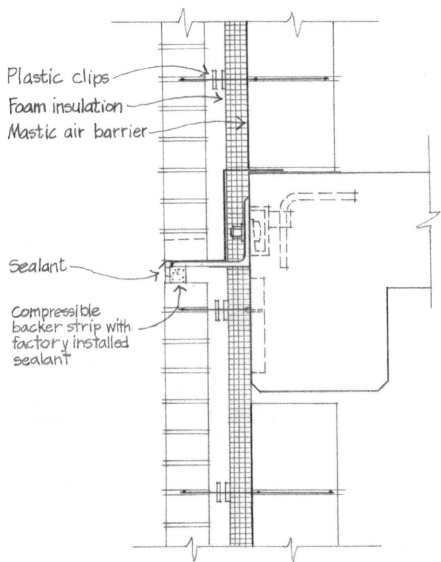

This option is more appealing but is still less than ideal. The mortar colors for the block and brick wythes will likely be different, and they may get confused by the masons on the scaffold. Another concern is that the crews of masons and mastic installers may be crowded on the scaffold, each crew trying to carry out its work at the same time (*Minimum Number of Parts* and *Repetitious Assembly*, Chapter 11).

We adjust our thinking accordingly and now plan to construct the inner concrete block wall first. Next, the fluid-applied air and water barrier will be sprayed over its surface and allowed to dry. Later, the masons will install the rigid insulation between the protruding joint reinforcement wires, and then lay the brick veneer (*Progressive Finish*, Chapter 12). They may need to flex the wire joint reinforcement slightly to place the brick. An experienced mason from this area (*Local Skills and Resources*, Chapter 13) assures us that this option would be much better than building both the block and brick wythes at the same time, because that process would require exceptional coordination of materials, time, and space by different subcontractors.

Many types of masonry ties have a V-shaped crimp located at the midpoint of the cavity. Its function is to act as a drip (*Overhang and Drip*, Chapter 1) to keep adhering drops of water from working their way across the tie from the outer wythe to the inner wythe. Because the crimp reduces the structural stiffness of the tie, our structural engineer proposes that we do not include it in the ties we are using in this seismically active location. We note in the tie manufacturer's catalog, however, that the clip we are using to retain the insulation boards may also be used to create a drip on each tie. This will require a second clip on each tie, because the clip that is pushed up tightly against the insulation cannot drip free into the cavity.

The combination of joint reinforcing and dovetail tie strips we have selected neatly solves the problems of reinforcing the backup wall in a horizontal direction, providing ties between the backup and face wythes of masonry, reinforcing the face wythe, and creating the code-mandated mechanical connection between the face wythe reinforcing and the ties. These strips are welded from steel wire and then galvanized (zinc coated) to retard rust. But galvanizing is not a permanent cure for rust. If the outer wythe leaks water into the cavity, if vapor condenses in the cavity, or if the mortar joints allow moisture to reach the embedded wires – all of which are likely to occur during the life of the building – then the zinc coating will gradually disintegrate and the wires will ultimately rust (*Expected Life*, Chapter 10). Given the owner's insistence on durability and our own desire to construct a building that will not start to fall apart a few decades from now, we will specify stainless steel wire rather than galvanized carbon steel. The added initial expense expressed as a percentage of the overall cost of the building will be very small (*Robust Assemblies*, Chapter 10). We will specify a very heavy zinc coating for the shelf angles, which are sheltered by the overhanging flashing and sealant joint and are less likely to be exposed to water.

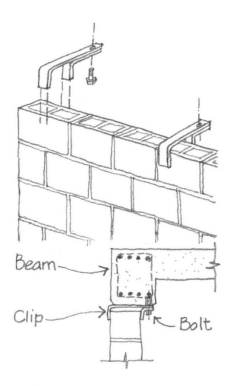

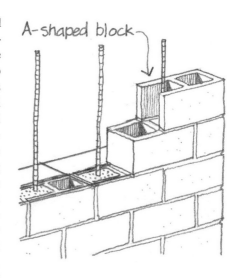

Detailing the Backup Wall

The backup wall must be engineered very carefully because it supports the air barrier mastic and the brick facing against wind and seismic loads (***Small Structures***, Chapter 7). Our structural engineer has chosen the type of concrete masonry units, the thickness of the wall, the size and frequency of the horizontal joint reinforcement and ties, and the size and frequency of the vertical reinforcing bars in this wall based on wind and seismic load calculations. The determined friction between the base of the backup wall and the floor slab is sufficient to transmit the lateral loads between them. At the top, where the wall joins the perimeter beam, a mechanical connection must be made to transmit lateral loads from the wall to the beam. The engineer furnishes a sketch of a clip being designed for this purpose. There will be several such clips in each bay. Each will be bent from steel plate, drilled, galvanized, and attached with a machine screw and expansion sleeve into a hole drilled into the underside of the perimeter beam. The clip joins the beam in a ***Sliding Fit*** (Chapter 12) that easily accommodates any inaccuracies. The engineer will furnish exact numbers and dimensions of the clips later, as the details develop.

Rehearsing the next portion of the construction sequence, we visualize the masons laying the first few courses of concrete blocks, inserting joint reinforcement as they go, and applying the air barrier coating and brick facing as previously described. Then they will insert the vertical reinforcing bars into the cores of the blocks as directed by the structural drawings and grout the cores that have bars in them. These bars will project upward and extend almost to the bottom of the perimeter beam, making it impossible to thread succeeding courses of blocks over them. From this point up, the masons will have to use A-shaped blocks that can be installed easily around the reinforcing; these are a standard shape that is readily available. If each core of the block was to be vertically reinforced, we would use H-shaped blocks, which are also standard shapes. After the backup wall has been erected in each bay, the lateral load clips will be installed. Then the soft joint will be created between the top of the wall and the underside of the perimeter beam, using a compressible joint filler strip in the center of the wall, and a backer rod and sealant on each face. ▷

Detailing the Interior Finishes

We turn our attention now to adding the interior finishes to our detail of the spandrel. Vertical, galvanized steel, hat-shaped furring strips (a stock item) will be fastened to the wall 16 in. (406 mm) apart with powder-actuated fasteners, and a foil-backed veneer plaster base will be screwed to the furring strips. (Veneer plaster base is commonly called "blueboard." It is a gypsum board that is designed to serve as a base for a thin coating of veneer spackling compound or plaster.) Electrical wiring for wall receptacles will be run in a metal conduit; we note that a gap should be left at reasonable intervals in the furring strips for this purpose (***Horizontal Plenum***, Chapter 8). A standard 1½ in. (38 mm) deep electrical box will just fit in the thickness provided by the furring and plaster.

The clips restraining the top of the backup wall must be covered with a finish layer, so we furr and plaster the beam as well as the wall. Because of the potential for movement in the soft joint between the perimeter beam and the backup wall, we use a resilient vinyl trim bead – a stock item from the gypsum supplier's catalog (***Off-the-Shelf Parts***, Chapter 13) – to provide a movement joint between the plaster wall and the plaster soffit under the beam.

At the base of the wall, we install a wood baseboard (***Building Armor***, Chapter 10) using finish screws that, like finish nails, are almost headless, to attach it through the plaster to the metal furring strips. To keep the plaster flat and firm behind the baseboard, we indicate a horizontal furring strip at the base of the wall.

After the baseboard is in place, the pad and carpet can be installed, using a tackless strip to form a neat edge against the baseboard. A call to our acoustic consultant brings bad news: A floor detail that consists of a carpet and thick pad over a 10 in. (254 mm) concrete slab has an impact insulation class of about 70, which is excellent, but its sound transmission class (STC) is only about 53, which is below standard for a building of this quality. To address this,

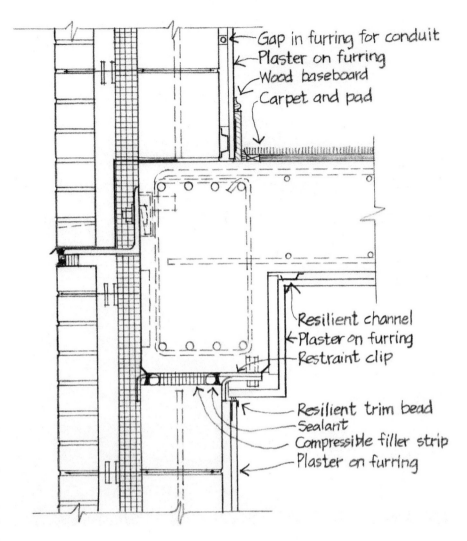

the consultant asks us to install suspended plaster ceilings with acoustic batts on top. We would like to avoid doing this, if possible. Adding a suspended ceiling system creates a cascade of additional costs to the project. The ceiling itself is only one added expense. In order to accommodate the ceiling grid, the height for each story of the building would have to increase by several inches to maintain an acceptable floor-to-ceiling height. Changing the floor-to-floor height adds column height and exterior wall area, requiring a more heavily braced structure for the taller building. After a few calls back and forth, we settle on a compromise: Rather than painting the underside of the slab, we will install a ⅝ in. (16 mm) veneer gypsum board and plaster ceiling, screwing it to resilient metal channels that are fastened directly to the underside of the slab. This will raise the STC to approximately 60, which our acoustic consultant considers acceptable for this type of occupancy and use. Because the channels are only ½ in. (13 mm) deep, we can accommodate the entire ceiling assembly in the story height already established.

After a great deal of study, coordination, and collaboration with consultants, we have completed the design of the typical spandrel detail. A fully annotated, accurately drawn version of this detail is shown at the end of this chapter.

Detailing the Window Openings

Our basic spandrel section is now complete and becomes the base drawing from which we can prepare the other detail sections. On the first of these, we will work out the installation of windows, which, in turn, might inform a future detail for exterior doors. For this detail we rely heavily on the window manufacturer's suggested details and installation recommendations, which are conveniently presented in its online catalog at the same scale that we are using: 1½ in. equals 1 ft. (1:8). We download these details from the manufacturer's website for use in our digital working drawings, but we also photocopy selected catalog details to use as an underlay with our drawing paper and quickly trace them during the design process.

The window selection process began early in the building design process, based on the client's expressed preference for casement windows and a satisfactory set of building elevations that uses a combination of casements and fixed sash units. We selected a manufacturer who is reputable, makes a good product, and has good technical representatives to help with design, ordering, and installation problems. Also important is the manufacturer's willingness to make custom window sizes, because it is very difficult to fit stock window sizes into brickwork without cutting bricks or using exposed filler strips around the window units. We will work out masonry opening dimensions for windows that fit the brick and block coursing, and the windows will be manufactured to fit these openings. Using the standards of the National Fenestration Rating Council

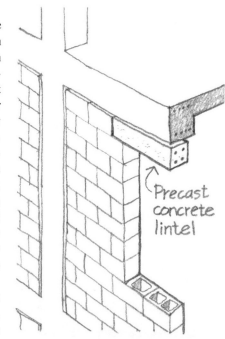

Precast concrete lintel

(*Accepted Standards*, Chapter 13), we choose a certified, insulated, low-E window appropriate to the weather exposure in the area where we are building.

Before beginning our window details, we think about the installation process. We could have the masons build the window units into the walls as they go, but this has serious disadvantages. The masons are already working with several different materials and components – blocks of several sizes and types, bricks, mortar, flashings, two different kinds of ties, insulation boards and clips, air barrier mastic, backer rod, sealant, compressible filler strips, lintels – and we should not complicate their task any further (*Minimum Number of Parts*, Chapter 11). The inevitable mortar droppings from masonry work above could damage the glass and frames. And undoubtedly the masons will find it very convenient to use the unobstructed window openings as access and supply points. So we will detail in such a way that the windows can be installed after the masons have finished their work.

The head of the window falls one block course below the perimeter beam. We could support this line of blocks across the window opening on a steel lintel, but this seems both laborious and expensive. Instead, we could show a precast concrete lintel identical in cross-sectional dimensions as the course of concrete masonry and 16 in. (406 mm) longer than the width of the masonry opening for the window. This extra length gives a good bearing on the wall at each end and exactly replaces a half-block on each end.

The masons could lay the lintel into the wall as if it were simply a long concrete block. There is an issue with this seemingly elegant solution, however: We calculate that a typical lintel weighs approximately 300 pounds, requiring at least four masons to lift it into place unless a small, hand-operated hoist can be used from inside the building. The precast lintel is not an example of *Parts That Are Easy to Handle* (Chapter 11). Perhaps the masonry contractor would prefer to use a steel lintel after all or make a reinforced block lintel using temporary centering, U-shaped blocks, rebars, and grout, all of which are easy to handle. We will offer these as alternatives and let the contractor choose. ▷

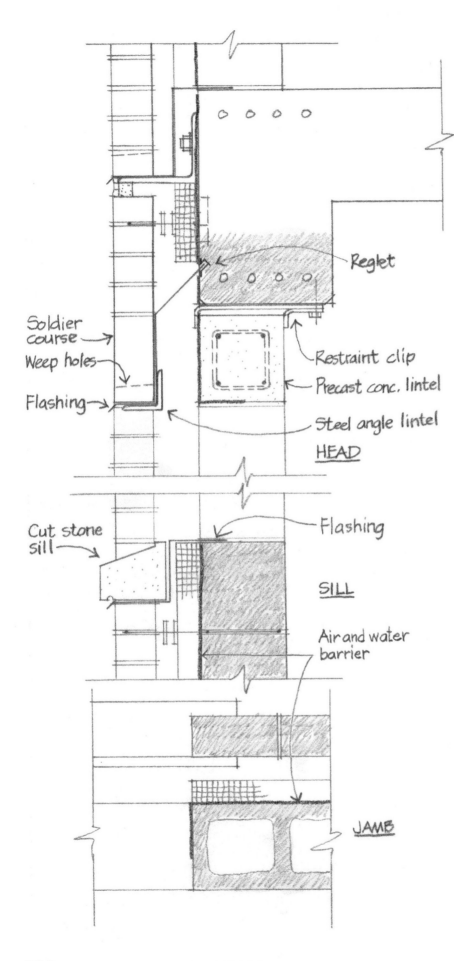

To express the window openings more prominently on the exterior of the building and allude to the structural requirements at these openings, we decide to place a soldier course of bricks over each lintel (***Formal Transitions***, Chapter 14).

We use a steel angle lintel to support the brick facing across the window opening. As with any horizontal interruption of the cavity, we must flash and weep over the window unit and lintels to catch and drain any water that may leak through the brick facing. This necessitates a reglet (***Overlap***, Chapter 1) in the face of the beam. From our typical spandrel detail, we see that the dovetail slots will need to be shortened above the windows to accommodate the reglet. We decide to use a cut limestone sill to avoid the leakage and deterioration of rowlock brick sills that are likely in this severe climate (***Robust Assemblies***, Chapter 10). This decision adds a functional touch of ***Intensification and Ornamentation*** (Chapter 14) to the fenestration. We install another flashing beneath the sill to deal with leakage between the sill and the window unit or through any defects in the sill (***Moisture Break***, Chapter 1). Both the head and sill flashings must be continued longitudinally past the jambs of the window and terminated with an effective end dam. We will show this with a pictorial view in the final working drawings and mention it in the specifications; if omitted, spillage of water off the end of the flashing can cause severe leakage.

Both flashings must also terminate at the outdoor side in an ***Overhang and Drip*** (Chapter 1), and we must provide weep holes over both flashings. The weeps over

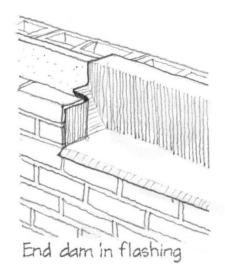

End dam in flashing

the sill flashing are created by laying pieces of clothesline or sash cord rope into the mortar under the stone sill and then pulling them out after the mortar has hardened a bit, leaving a ⅜ in. (9.5 mm) diameter void through which water can drain.

The easiest installation process for wood windows is one that mimics the installation of windows in a wood-frame dwelling. Builders use an area-specific method to install window frames (***Local Skills and Resources***, Chapter 13). After the window unit has been leveled and shimmed, nails are simply driven through an exterior flange or through the window frame itself, into the wood framing to attach the unit. We must modify this procedure for our brick cavity wall, fastening through the frame rather than a flange and using screws rather than nails to avoid the impact of hammering, which might crack or dislodge masonry units from the wall. We will mimic the wood frame of the house by installing a rough frame of preservative-treated wood in the cavity between the brick facing and concrete masonry backup wall.

Once the rough frame is installed, the window unit can be placed into the frame from inside the building, leveled and shimmed, and attached with finish screws.

We decide to fasten the rough frame to the backup wythe only. This will avoid a rigid connection between two wythes that need to be able to move independently. In addition, the backup wythe is designed to bear the wind load, including the wind load from the window itself. We design the rough wood frame for easy installation.

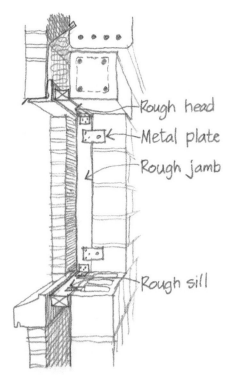

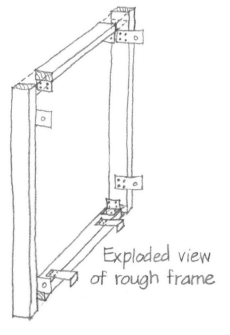

Exploded view of rough frame

A piece will be installed in each of the jambs first, attached to the backup wall with powder-driven fasteners through sheet metal plates.

Then the sill piece can be lowered into the cavity by holding onto two metal clips and can be attached to the jamb pieces with screws driven through perforated sheet metal angles at the corners. The metal clips, besides offering convenient installation handles, also join the sill to the backup blocks. Glass fiber insulation is stuffed lightly beneath the head flashing. The head piece goes in last and is fastened to the jamb pieces in the same manner as the sill.

Once the rough frame is complete, the window installation becomes easy. Two carpenters slide the window unit into the opening and center it carefully between the jambs; the masonry and the rough frame have a generous ***Installation Clearance*** (Chapter 11) all around with which to work. Next, the carpenters align and level the sill, shimming as necessary with wedges of composite plastic or wood shingle (***Adjustable Fit***, Chapter 12), and screw down the sill to the rough frame. They square the frame of the window unit and check to see that each jamb is shimmed plumb before fastening the jambs and head (***Simulated Assemblies***, Chapter 11). The last task is to insert backer rods and sealant around all four sides of the window unit, outside and inside, to create effective air and water seals. If a water leak should occur inside or around the window unit, the water will be caught and drained by the sill flashing. ▷

We construct an outside elevation of a typical window at the same scale as the section to see how our details look from another orthographic vantage point. In this drawing, we see that the stone sill will need to project a half-brick length at either end to visually lock-in to the surrounding wall.

This will also place its flashing end dams sufficiently outside the jamb of the window to catch any leakage from the vertical sealant joints. It will necessitate a sill design with level lugs that project above the sloping **Wash** (Chapter 1) of the sill to support the brickwork at the jambs.

We lay out all the bricks carefully on the elevation and notice that only masonry openings that are multiples of a full brick length will be symmetrical – something we make a note to consider when we are finalizing the schedule of window dimensions. We also see that the lintel looks best if the course just below it terminates with full bricks at the window opening, thus eliminating a weak-looking vertical alignment of head joints. We will work backward from this observation to specify how the first brick course should be laid out on the shelf angle. We experiment with the idea of using specially molded bricks, such as quarter-rounds, for the jambs (**Hierarchy of Refinement**, Chapter 14). They add a good deal of subtlety and character at relatively little cost, but their use necessitates more expensively shaped lugs on the sill. We will continue to think about that joint between window and wall as the overall design progresses.

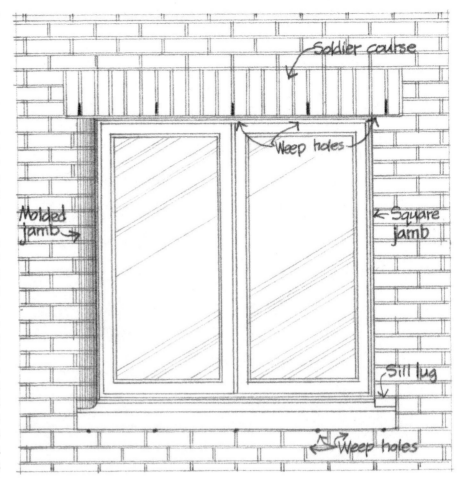

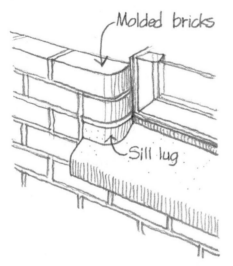

334 PART II ■ DETAIL DEVELOPMENT

We return to our window sections.

Inside, we continue the plaster at the window head to meet the frame of the window – a simple, elegant, and inexpensive detail that reduces the number of parts needed and is easily maintained (***Minimum Number of Parts***, Chapter 11 and ***Repairable Surfaces***, Chapter 10). We do the same with the jambs. At the sill, we decide to install a marble stool for its durability and appearance in lieu of wood. A wood stool, though a less expensive option, is likely to cup because of the width required. A wood apron molding finishes the gap between the stool and the plaster. We make a perspective sketch to be sure that the interior finish details of the window will give the desired appearance and feel confident in the levels of ***Progressive Finish*** (Chapter 12) achieved. The preliminary version of the window details is now complete. Before moving on to other conditions, we check carefully to ensure each element lies in the same plane in head, jamb, and sill details. ▷

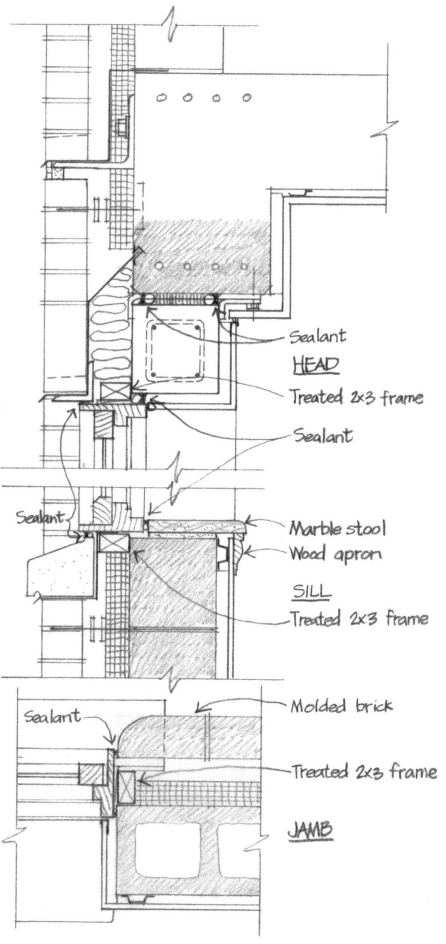

SECTION 1 ■ APPLYING THE DETAIL PATTERNS

DETAILING THE CORNERS AND COLUMNS

Now we develop a detail of the wall at the same scale, but in horizontal section (plan view), examining what happens at the columns and at the corners of the building. The basic arrangement of the components follows almost automatically from the spandrel detail developed earlier. We add dovetail slots and anchors to tie the ends of the brick wall segments to the columns. In accordance with the joint pattern worked out earlier in elevation view, we show the *Expansion Joint* (Chapter 6) in the brick facing at the centers of the columns. At each outside corner of the building, we must add an expansion joint to allow a generous dimension for differential expansion and contraction of the adjacent wall planes as the sun moves around the building. We try first to do this with a single joint at a half-brick length from the corner, but this seems weak both physically and visually. Instead, we settle on two joints at each corner, centered on the adjacent faces of the column. We add to the detail the *Structure/Enclosure Joints* (Chapter 6) where the backup wall meets the columns. L-shaped sheet metal pieces are installed into one of the two movement joints at each corner to compartmentalize the pressure equalization chamber. We do not bother to insert movement joints in the foam plastic insulation boards, because the foam is so weak and pliable that it simply compresses or expands very slightly as movement occurs.

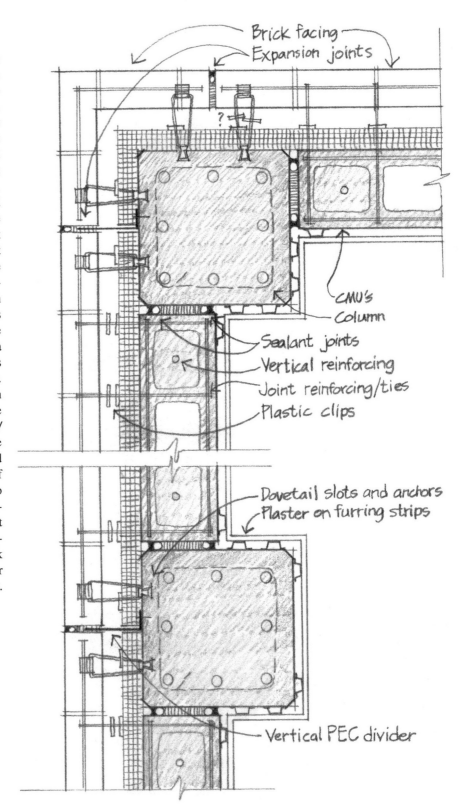

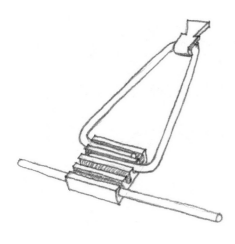

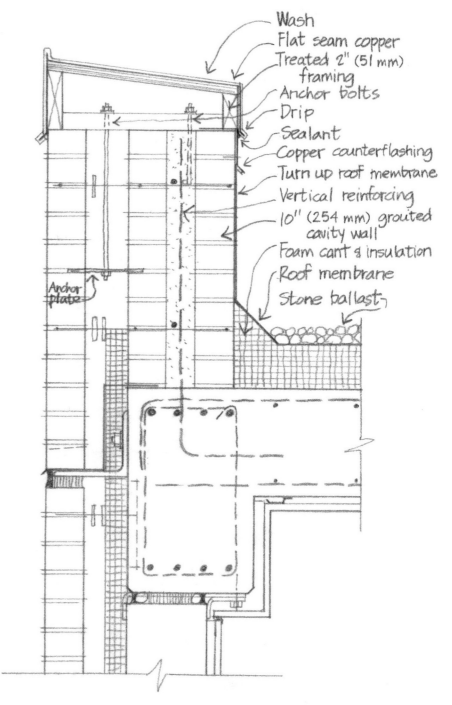

We recognize in this drawing that the dovetail anchors do not satisfy the building code requirement of tying mechanically to reinforcing in the joints of the brickwork. We find in the catalogs a tie manufacturer who can furnish seismic clips that lie in the mortar joint and accomplish this purpose. It is unclear whether it will be feasible to install two drip clips on each dovetail tie because of the close spacing of the two wires. We will have to obtain samples and try them out.

DETAILING THE PARAPET

Masonry parapets should be avoided whenever possible. Because they are exposed to the weather on both sides, they tend to leak, and they experience more thermal expansion and contraction than the walls below. This often leads to severe cracking between the parapet and the walls of the top story. On this project, however, we are required by local code and building ordinances to include a parapet on a structure with a low-slope roof assembly. Working on a tracing paper overlay of the basic wall section, we make a horizontal mark 30 in. (762 mm) above the roof slab, the code-required minimum height for a parapet. We use the standard shelf angle support and extend the brick facing course by course near this mark. We also extend the backup wall but, to avoid problems of differential expansion and contraction, will build it entirely of brickwork rather than concrete masonry. To keep the parapet in place against wind and seismic loads, we build the backup wall as a reinforced brick wall: Dowels of reinforcing bar that emerge from the roof slab are grouted into the cavity. Horizontal reinforcing for the wall is provided by the same wire joint reinforcement and tie combination that is used in the walls below. Both the facing and the backup wall are cut completely by sealed expansion joints at the column lines. ▷

A standard coping detail for this parapet would feature cut stone or precast concrete coping sections placed on top of a continuous flashing at the top of the wall and held in place by dowels that project through the flashing. This detail does not satisfy us, because we are afraid that mountain storm winds or earthquakes could dislodge the stones. There are proprietary aluminum coping systems available, but we don't think they would look appropriate on this building. We design instead a coping that is built in place of preservative-treated wood and plywood and sheathed in copper; we will have to compare its cost with the heavier alternatives. It features a **Wash** (Chapter 1) that directs water back toward the roof to prevent staining of the facade, an **Overhang and Drip** (Chapter 1) on each side, and anchor bolts that fasten the whole coping assembly securely to the masonry. One bolt is embedded in the grouted core of the backup wall; the other reaches deep into the open cavity – through a galvanized steel anchor plate – to engage enough weight of brickwork to avoid being pulled off by high winds. The copper sheets that cap the parapet are applied with ordinary flat-seam roofing technology. The copper counterflashing beneath the coping overlaps the turned-up edge of the roof membrane to protect the back of the parapet completely from water.

It is impossible to eliminate the thermal bridge that occurs where the masonry parapet joins the roof slab. To minimize the thermal transfer, we run the foam in the cavity well up into the parapet, creating a rather long path that heat must travel through concrete and masonry in order to move in or out of the building. This solution is more durable and stronger than using an insulated steel stud assembly to support the brick veneer in the parapet.

DETAILING THE GRADE CONDITION

Having developed details for the floor edges, windows, corners, columns, and parapet, we must now address how the building meets the ground. We would like to get the brickwork close to the ground to avoid showing large expanses of the foundation walls. At the same time, we want to provide a clear material transition at this important condition that works as a **Contributive Detail** (Chapter 14). The foundation walls must have **Thermal Insulation** (Chapter 3), preferably located on the outside to provide **Outside-Insulated Thermal Mass** (Chapter 3). We have a rough detail from the structural engineer that shows the structural slab of the ground floor supported on the top of the concrete foundation wall and doweled to it with reinforcing bars. We begin the design of this intersection by sketching a freehand detail on tracing paper laid alternately over the typical spandrel detail and the structural engineer's detail, trying to bring the two together. We rest the backup wall on the structural slab and the brick facing on the top of the wall, but we must increase the engineer's 12 in. (305 mm) wall to a 16 in. (406 mm) thickness to make this work. We bring 2 in. (51 mm) of polystyrene foam insulation up the outside of the foundation wall and find that it meets the

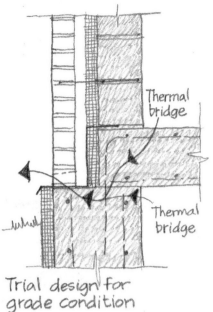

Trial design for grade condition

flashing at the bottom of the brick facing in an awkward way. There is also a large and seemingly unavoidable thermal bridge through the edge of the slab and the top of the foundation wall.

Looking for a better-performing alternative, we abandon this sketch for the moment and try another, this time using the same shelf angle detail deployed in the rest of the wall assembly. Suddenly, the specifics of the detail all fall into place: The concrete wall drops back to the desired 12 in. (305 mm) thickness; the insulation that emerges from the ground can be turned back under the shelf angle to form a **Thermal Break** (Chapter 3).

We adopt this detail and finish it: The basement wall must be dampproofed before the insulating boards are applied. Where the insulation is exposed above ground level, we can protect and finish it with galvanized stucco lath and a two-coat cement-based stucco application. We leave a space between the foam and the angle, protect it with an **Overhang and Drip** (Chapter 1) on the flashing, and seal it with a backer rod and sealant. We make a note to be sure that grade never approaches closer than 6 in. (152 mm) to this joint, to protect the angle from corrosion and to keep the weep holes clear at the base of the brick facing. We ensure good **Foundation Drainage** (Chapter 1) by sloping the ground away from the building (**Wash**, Chapter 1) and by installing a porous drainage panel on the outside of the insulation that will conduct groundwater to a system of drainage pipes around the footings. Knowing that the stucco cladding is vulnerable to impact by landscaping equipment such as mowers, we call for a gravel apron 24 in. (610 mm) wide to make an attractive, low-maintenance transition at the base of the wall. This will also minimize staining and weathering of the stucco from splashing rain.

Checking for Thermal Bridges

We examine the perimeters of the conditioned spaces on all the exterior details, looking for thermal bridges. The polystyrene foam insulation does a remarkably good job of wrapping the building. The only serious breach in this insulating layer, as we noted earlier, is where the backup wall emerges through it at the parapet. The masonry ties and shelf angles throughout the wall are also thermal bridges, but they constitute such small cross sections of metal that they conduct very little heat. The cost and embodied energy of the added features to eliminate this minor amount of thermal loss would represent diminishing returns to the overall building performance. ▷

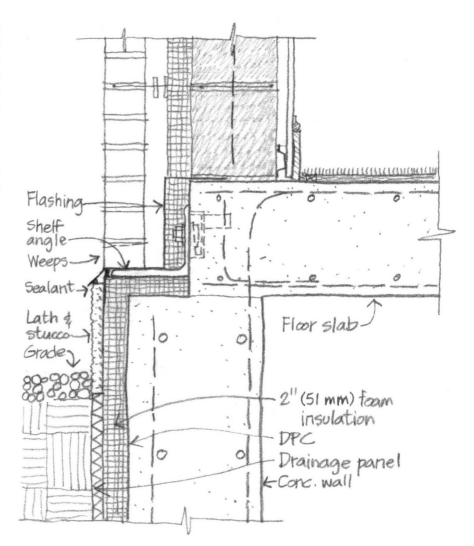

Elevation Studies

In designing these preliminary details, we have made many decisions that affect the appearance of the building both inside and outside. We have laid a grid of movement joints onto the facades, have designed a parapet coping and window surrounds, and have detailed the way in which the building meets the ground. Now we visualize the cumulative effect of these decisions by overlaying a tracing paper sketch on one of the original design elevations. When we first drew the design elevation, before the design of the details began, we had only a vague idea of how the building would be put together. Now we are working with a tangible and buildable reality. We find ourselves in the powerful position of knowing how the building is put together and how to adjust it to accommodate the project budget and building program. We summarize our work on the design of the details in a set of accurately constructed drawings.

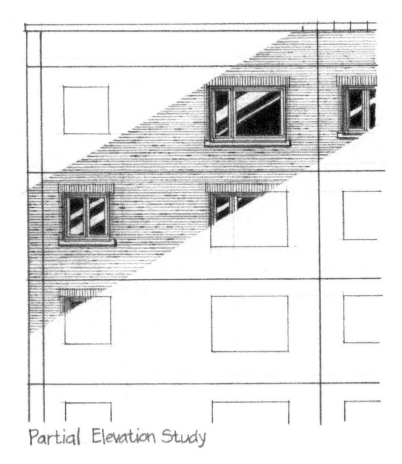

Partial Elevation Study

NEXT STEPS

Although we are well along in the process of detailing the building, much remains to be done. We have not yet addressed such special details as the main entrance, the lobby, the corridors and elevators, fire exit stairways and doors, and the service areas of the building.

Working with the acoustical consultant, we must develop details for a set of interior finishes, including walls between dwelling units, corridor walls, stairway and elevator enclosures, interior partitions of dwellings, and flooring details. The primary functional criteria to which we will be working are acoustical privacy and fire safety.

Working with the mechanical engineer, we will design details of **Vertical Chases** (Chapter 8) in which to run the pipe risers for the heating and cooling systems, coordinating these with the locations of the fan-coil units in each apartment. At the same time, we will determine the size and proportions of the external air louvers for the fan-coil units, develop a detail for installing the louvers, and experiment with various arrangements of louvers on the elevation drawings. We still have unfinished business with the structural engineer concerning such matters as final sizes of beams and columns and details of the grouted reinforcing in the backup wall and parapet.

We must still examine the overall size and massing of the building to see how many **Building Separation Joints** (Chapter 6) are needed. We will review the position of movement joints through the brick veneer and calculate the sizes of pressure equalization cavities and vents. We will investigate further the feasibility of our copper parapet coping detail. We will use various three-dimensional sketches, drawings, and models to visualize alternative ways of detailing both the exterior elevations and the interior spaces of the building to achieve a consistent architectural expression. And we will do more research into the provisions of the International Building Code that relate to our details, making sure that we are in complete conformance, with special consideration given to **Fire-Safe Materials** (Chapter 9), **Fire-Resistant Assemblies** (Chapter 9), and seismic provisions. We must take care to provide at least the mandated number of condominium units that are of **Barrier-Free Design** (Chapter 9). This code research will lead eventually to a meeting with the local building inspector to discuss the code conformance of the design and to correct any problems before construction begins.

Soon we will meet with the project specifications writer, taking with us all the notes we have made concerning items that need to be mentioned in the specifications, such as the thick joint filler strip and the stainless steel joint reinforcing. Much of our meeting will center on the task of selecting **Accepted Standards** (Chapter 13) by which to specify the bricks, concrete masonry units, mortar, masonry ties and reinforcing, grout, sealants, galvanizing, flashing, roofing, and other building materials for the project. We also want to be sure we specify **Nontoxic Materials** (Chapter 9), paying particular attention to off-gassing from materials used inside the building, such as carpets, carpet adhesives, particle-board interior components that may give off formaldehyde, and paints and varnishes. This is not just a matter of altruism; many prospective tenants will not rent or buy condominiums that have strong odors of organic chemicals (**Life Cycle**, Chapter 10). Because the cohousing community owners are planning to seek certification from several sustainable design and healthy environments rating systems, our sourcing of all building materials and products will be deeply informed by those criteria.

We also begin to organize our notes that we will pass on to the construction administrator concerning things that need to be checked especially closely during the construction process, such as the dimensional accuracy of the formwork; the accuracy with which wedge inserts, dovetail slots, and reglets are placed in the formwork; whether the wedge inserts and reglets are installed right side up; lap joints and end dams on flashings; the cleanliness of the cavity behind the brick facing; the integrity of the air barrier coating of mastic; the spacing of the masonry ties; and the construction of the horizontal soft joints. Recognizing the intricacy of the wall we have designed and the extent to which its functional success hinges on such matters as these, we decide to hold an extensive preconstruction conference with the successful bidder to go over these concerns one by one. We also decide that it would be wise to specify that the successful bidder construct a small, full-scale mockup of the wall on the construction site, using actual materials (**Simulated Assemblies**, Chapter 11). This will give everyone involved in the construction an advance opportunity to work out any problems in the construction sequence we have designed, to get used to its complexities, and to see how the wall will look. We can also use the mockup to experiment with alternative brick and mortar colors, sealant colors, joint toolings, and special brickwork details around the openings, and the contractor can use it to teach masons and other craftspeople exactly how the work must be done for the building's construction to be successful. ▷

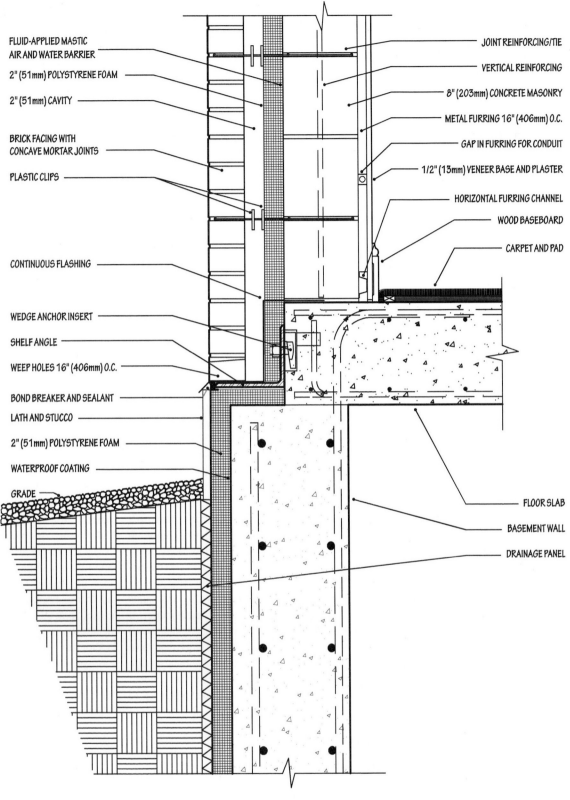

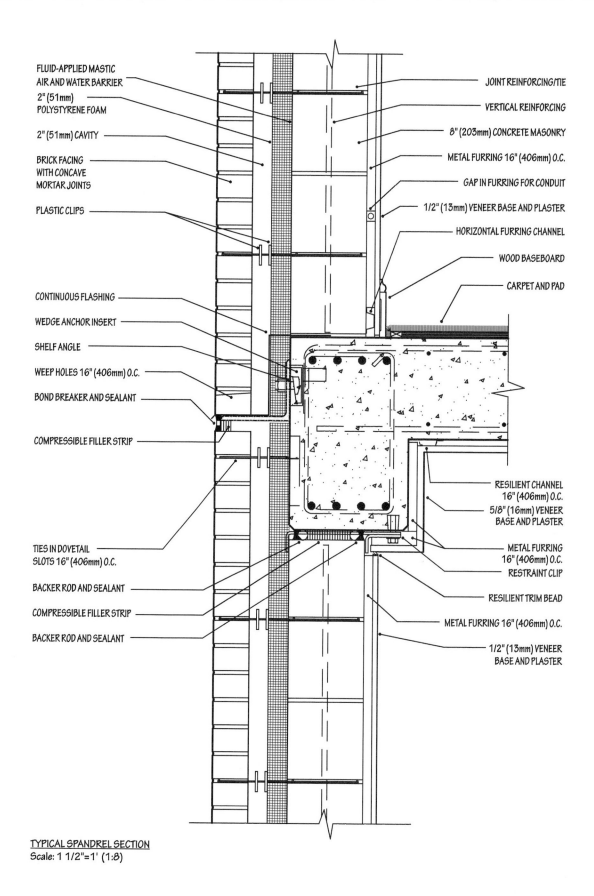

TYPICAL SPANDREL SECTION
Scale: 1 1/2"=1' (1:8)

SECTION 1 ■ APPLYING THE DETAIL PATTERNS

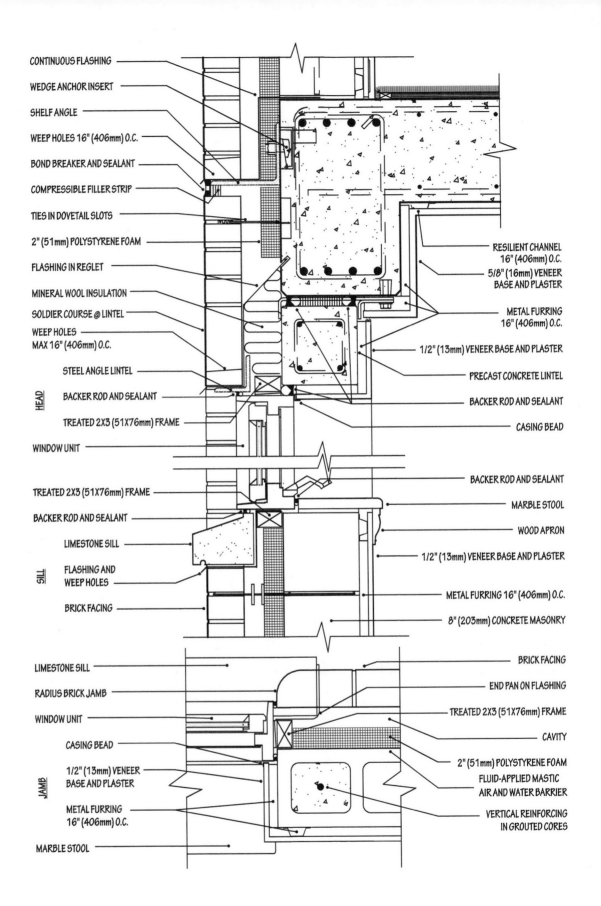

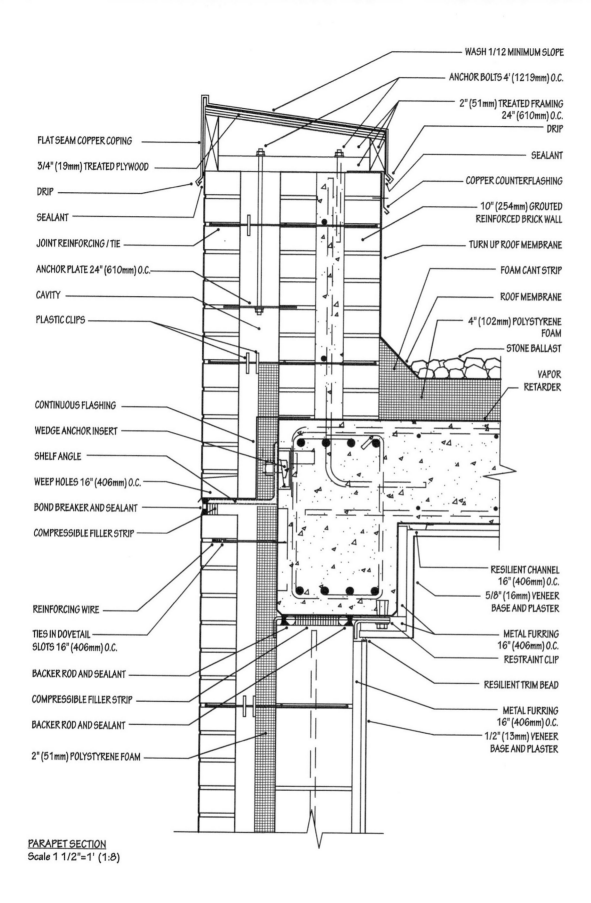

SECTION 1 ■ APPLYING THE DETAIL PATTERNS   345

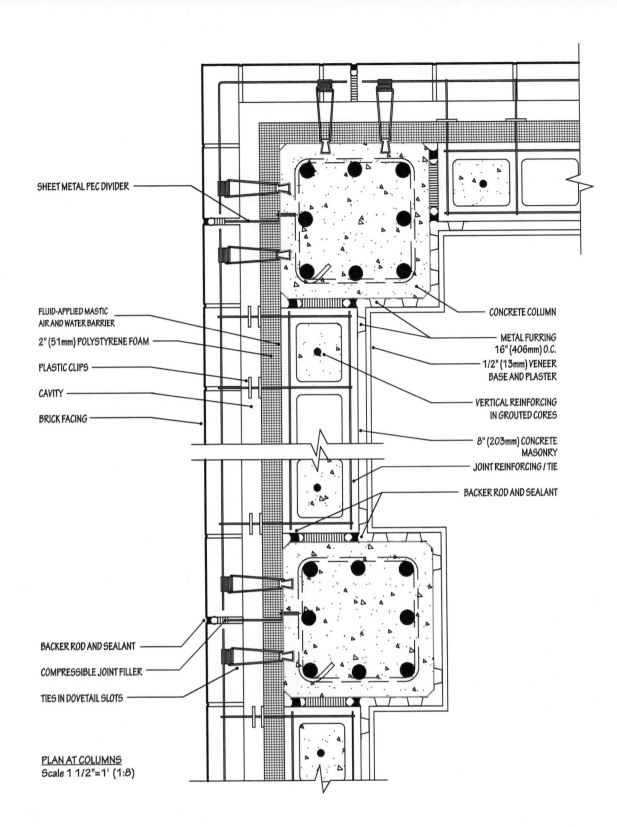

ELEVATION OF TYPICAL WINDOW
Scale 3/4"=1' (1:16)

KEY REFERENCES
The following are important reference materials that were used in developing this set of details. Full bibliographic information on these publications is given in *Appendix A, The Detailer's Reference Shelf*.

1. Relevant building and energy codes, including IBC, IECC, and IgCC.
2. Christine Beall, *Masonry Design and Detailing*.
3. Brick Industry Association, *BIA Technical Notes on Brick Construction*.
4. National Concrete Masonry Association, *TEK Manual for Concrete Masonry Design and Construction*.
5. Sheet Metal and Air Conditioning Contractors National Association, Inc., *Architectural Sheet Metal Manual*.
6. United States Gypsum, *Fire Resistance Design Manual*. ∎

SECTION 2
GETTING STARTED

Designing details is not a neat, linear, fully logical operation. Like any design process, it is engagingly messy and complex. It involves false starts, wrong turns, mental blocks, dead ends, backtracking, and moments of despair as well as purposeful progress, intelligent decisions, creative synthesis, and gratifying moments of inspiration, insight, and triumph.

Begin the process of detailing a building by clarifying your ***aspirations*** for the project in terms of function, constructability, and aesthetics. If you have been involved in the project's schematic design, it should be easy to outline these goals.

Next, set specific ***performance standards*** for the project. Summarize relevant standards, such as the code-defined type of construction and fire resistance, the client's expected level of durability and environmental performance, any special considerations such as seismic, wind, or flooding conditions, and so on. The stated aspirations and performance standards for the project constitute the relevant basis for the design of details.

Identify the key details from which other details of the building are likely to be derived. Develop these details in sketch form, preferably on inexpensive tracing paper, with a pen or soft pencil. Most digital media are too hard-edged and rigid to be appropriate for this stage of detail development. No matter how sharp the pencil or how exact the digital modeling tool, these early studies of details will begin with the broad ideas and the general architectural approach. It is better to save the more precise and technical media for later in the process, while remembering that even then they work to much closer tolerances than most construction processes.

Begin by drawing the "given" features, such as the building's skeletal structural frame, its load-bearing walls, and the approximate locations of the building's exterior enclosure systems. Begin by addressing sectional details where the exterior wall meets the ground, a floor, and the roof. Add plan studies where the wall meets a window or door opening, or turns a corner, or where two different cladding systems intersect. The first ideas for the key details will emerge logically from these fixed elements, perhaps as you follow the detail pattern, ***Rehearsing the Construction Sequence*** (Chapter 13).

At this early stage of detail development, it is best to think freely and not to be too constrained about the regulatory, economic, or logistical challenges associated with the project; they will be addressed soon enough. It is more important to work rapidly to establish a tentative set of key details that share a common tectonic approach.

At this point, rigorously assess each detail in terms of the particular criteria you stated at the outset. How does each meet the broad aspirations you stated regarding function, constructability, and aesthetics? How does each compare to the more specific performance standards that you set for the detail? Beyond those criteria, now look at the compositional or spatial implications of your first efforts. Refine your aesthetic goals to make them more precise than they were previously.

Architectural Detailing: Function Constructability Aesthetics. Fourth Edition. Patrick Rand, Jason Miller, and Edward Allen.
© 2025 John Wiley & Sons, Inc. Published 2025 by John Wiley & Sons, Inc.

Make notes graphically or in writing, summarizing important items in each detail that may have bearing on other parts of the building or that may need to be investigated further. These notes may also record items that need to be incorporated into the final working drawings or into the project's written specifications.

Repeat this process for all the key details. Carry the findings from each detail investigation forward to positively inform the next detail in the series. Be sure that all of the building's details grow from a common source, with each detail influencing the others.

After bringing all of the key details up to a fairly advanced level of development, test them in greater depth. Explore their less typical conditions. How does the detail turn an angled corner? How does it terminate at an unusual opening or against the far wall? How does it meet another intersecting material? How is an opening made in it for a horizontal or vertical chase, or for a window or roof aperture?

Perhaps your studies to this point have been done at a relatively small scale, such as ¾ in. equals 1 ft. (1:16), a scale at which it is impossible to draw the smaller features of a detail. If so, then step up to 1½ or 3 in. scale (1:8 or 1:4, or the more customary metric scales of 1:10 or 1:5) to study the detail more closely. All detail studies must include three-dimensional sketches or a study model. Each change in scale and medium will bring with it new challenges. Expect to use an iterative process to probe multiple alternatives before finding the best solution.

Though the detailing process is seldom neat and linear, it should not be chaotic or wander pointlessly. It should always focus firmly on the objectives that were established at the outset and with reference to the detail patterns explained in this book.

Standard details can be used, but so can new ones, provided each addresses the basic principles described in this book. Be willing to challenge and adapt standard details to meet the specific needs of the project.

As with your learning of the architectural design process in general, with experience you will become more efficient in the process of designing details. The design of a building's details, like the design of its form and spaces, is never finished. Expect to continue to refine the details as the project evolves, including at the construction site.

APPENDIX A
The Detailer's Reference Shelf

APPENDIX B
Formulating Exercises for Self-Study, Studio, or Classroom Use

APPENDIX A: The Detailer's Reference Shelf

Every detailer will have his or her favorite selection of essential references. These are ours. The list is selective rather than exhaustive.

It would be unwise and expensive to try to assemble this entire shelf of references at one time. It is better to acquire references one or several at a time, as they are needed, and the collection will gradually fill itself out. If you are determined to acquire a minimum shelf of detailing references immediately, start with the most essential publications, indicated by an asterisk (*). Ordering information is given for all references, except books by recognized publishers. There is a charge for most of these publications; the main exceptions are manufacturers' catalogs, most of which are free.

The internet is usually the most powerful, immediate, and direct path to detailing information. A robust browser and reliable internet access will enable detailers to access a full range of resources, locally and globally. Most resources that were formerly available only through personal correspondence and catalogs are now available for download in PDF (portable document format) as well as other formats.

1. CODES

Contact the building department of the city or state/province in which a building will be built to determine the relevant codes. The building codes in most states in the United States are now derived from the International Building Code and other documents published by the International Code Council. Note that each state/province can choose which version of a code to adopt. In some cases, they choose to use a version other than the "current" one.

1. *International Building Code.* International Code Council, 500 New Jersey Avenue, NW, 6th Floor, Washington, DC 20001. This code and others are produced typically at 3-year intervals by ICC. They are available online at http://www.iccsafe.org, and can be viewed free online at http://publiccodes.cyberregs.com/icod/.

2. *International Energy Conservation Code* (IECC) and International Green Construction Code (IgCC). These codes and their commentaries are important in their influence on building energy management and envelope design and detailing. They are produced by ICC; see #1 in this list for contact information and websites.

3. *National Building Code of Canada* (NBC). Institute for Research on Construction, National Research Council, 1200 Montreal Road, Ottawa, Ontario, Canada, KIA OR6. Online at http://www.nrc-cnrc.gc.ca/eng/solutions/advisory/codes_centre_index.html. Also found here is the *National Energy Code of Canada for Buildings* (NECB).

4. Lathrop, James K. (ed.). *Life Safety Code Handbook.* National Fire Protection Association, 1 Batterymarch Park, Quincy, MA 02269–7471. Available online at http://www.nfpa.org. This book, updated frequently, sets forth and illustrates the life-safety and egress provisions that are common to all the building codes.

5. Ching, Francis D. K. *Building Codes Illustrated: The Basics.* Hoboken, NJ: John Wiley & Sons, 2022. A visual introduction to the fundamentals of the 2021 International Building Code. Useful commentaries and examples that guide to the application of code provisions.

2. STANDARDS

1. **Accessible and Usable Buildings and Facilities.* ICC A117.1. International Code Council, 500 New Jersey Avenue, NW, 6th Floor Washington, DC 20001. Also available from American National Standards Institute, Inc., 25 West 43 Street, New York, NY 10036. Available online at https://codes.iccsafe.org/content/icca117-12017P4.

   This book contains standards for making buildings and sites accessible to and usable by people with disabilities.

2. *ASTM Standards in Building Codes.* American Society for Testing and Materials International. 100 Barr Harbor Dr. PO Box C700, West Conshohocken, PA 19428–2959. Available online at http://www.astm.org. This compilation, updated frequently, covers all the ASTM standards under which building materials and assemblies are specified and detailed.

3. CSA Group (formerly the Canadian Standards Association); 178 Rexdale Blvd., Toronto, ON, Canada M9W 1R3. http://www.csagroup.org. Accredited standards development organization.

Architectural Detailing: Function Constructability Aesthetics. Fourth Edition. Patrick Rand, Jason Miller, and Edward Allen.
© 2025 John Wiley & Sons, Inc. Published 2025 by John Wiley & Sons, Inc.

3. GENERAL REFERENCES ON DETAILING

1. *Allen, Edward, and Iano, Joseph. *Fundamentals of Building Construction: Materials and Methods*. 7th ed. Hoboken NJ: John Wiley & Sons, 2019. This is a solid, general reference on how buildings are put together and gives a basic set of details for each type of construction.

2. Iano, Joseph. *Iano's Backfill*. Available online at https://jiano.typepad.com/. This website is maintained by the authors of *Fundamentals of Building Construction* to provide information, extensive weblinks, updates, supplementary information, resources for the classroom, and ideas for further study or research. It increases the value of the text to students, teachers, and practicing professionals and fosters a stronger community among all those dedicated to building well.

3. MasterSpec Published by ARCOM. Available online at https://www.designguide.com/products/47840/ARCOM-Architectural-Computer-Services?pcid=01. Updated continually, this is an encyclopedic reference on selecting and specifying materials and components for buildings. Individual sections on specific materials can be downloaded separately.

4. Construction Specifications Institute. *The Project Resource Manual – CSI Manual of Practice*. 5th ed. New York: McGraw-Hill, 2004. This is the standard by which nearly all construction specifications are written.

5. Construction Specifications Institute. *U.S. National CAD Standard*. Alexandria, VA. This resource establishes standard symbols and electronic data conventions for use on construction drawings and details, including standards for building information modeling/BIM. Developed in collaboration with AIA and National Institute of Building Standards/NIBS.

6. *Ramsey, Charles, and Sleeper, Harold. *Architectural Graphic Standards*. 12th ed. Hoboken, NJ: John Wiley & Sons, 2016. This large and useful handbook, which is updated frequently, is the standard reference for architectural detailing. Also available as CD and online at https://www.wiley.com/en-us/Architectural+Graphic+Standards%2C+12th+Edition-p-9781118909508.

7. Underwriters Laboratories. *Fire Resistance Design Directory*. Northbrook, IL: Underwriters Laboratories, Inc. Updated annually, this directory lists and illustrates all the building assemblies that UL has tested and gives their fire resistance ratings. Online UL resources at https://code-authorities.ul.com/architectural-engineering-and-construction-aec-ul-fire-rated-search-resources/

8. Watts, Andrew. *Modern Construction Handbook*. 5th ed., New York: Springer Wien, 2018. Vividly illustrated survey of constructions systems in all materials, with emphasis on contemporary methods and on cladding.

4. COLLECTIONS OF ARCHITECTURAL DETAILS

1. *Ballast, David Kent. *Architect's Handbook of Construction Detailing*. 2nd ed., Hoboken, NJ: John Wiley & Sons, 2009. Reliable collections of details are rare; this book is based on reliable sources and is referenced to MasterFormat section numbers for convenient specifying.

2. *Ford, Edward R. *The Details of Modern Architecture*. Vols. 1 and 2. Cambridge, MA: The MIT Press, 1990 and 1996. Much more than just a collection of details, this volume analyzes dozens of details of acknowledged masterworks. Volume 1 covers the years 1890–1928, and Volume 2 the years 1928–1988.

5. DETAILING WOOD

1. *Allen, Edward, and Thallon, Rob. *Fundamentals of Residential Construction*. 5th ed. Hoboken, NJ: John Wiley & Sons, 2022.

2. *American Institute of Timber Construction. *Standard Specifications for Structural Glued Laminated Timbers of Softwood Species: Design and Manufacturing Requirements*. 2010. Order online at https://www.apawood.org/ansi-117 This is a good general reference on the topic, including section properties, span tables, and typical details. It is updated frequently. Many AITC publications are available for download online at no cost at https://www.plib.org/aitc/resources/publications/design-standards/

3. American Institute of Timber Construction. *Typical Construction Details*. 2003. See #2 in this list for AITC URL address. This pamphlet contains dozens of examples of how to detail heavy timber frames. Available for download online at no cost.

4. *The Engineered Wood Association (APA). *Plywood Design Specification*. This thick document is filled with the authoritative data needed to select and to detail plywood and other wood panel products. Order this and other resources online at http://www.apawood.org.

5. American Wood Council. *National Design Specification for Wood Construction*. Order or download online at http://www.awc.org. This is the basic reference from which wood structures are engineered, and it is updated frequently. It is especially useful to the detailer for working out structural connections between wood members.

6. Architectural Woodworking Institute. *AWI Architectural Woodwork Standards*, 2nd ed. Technical and design illustrations regarding architectural woodwork from raw lumber and veneers all the way through factory-finished and installed product. Order or download online at http://www.awinet.org.

7. Canadian Wood Council Website. http://www.cwc.ca. Publications, software, and design tools regarding all types of wood construction, including heavy timber, glue-laminated, and light wood frame. The site has typical details for download in CAD format; it also has Environmental Product Data for wood products.

8. *American Wood Council. *Span Tables for Joists and Rafters* and *Design Values for Joists and Rafters*. Order or download online at: https://awc.org/codes-and-standards/span-tables/. Using these references, you can easily design structures for floors, ceilings, and roofs.

9. Kaufmann, Hermann, Krotsch, Stefan, and Winter, Stefan. *Manual of Multi-Story Timber Construction.* Basel, Switzerland: Birkhauser, 2018. One in a series by the publishers of DETAIL magazine, this manual has in-depth coverage of the material properties of wood, its history in construction, and numerous contemporary examples of heavy timber detailing.

10. *Simpson Strong-Tie Company, Inc. *Wood Construction Connectors.* Order online or download free at http://www.strongtie.com/. This annual catalog is the best single reference on metal framing connectors for wood light framing and heavy timber framing.

11. *Thallon, Rob. *Graphic Guide to Frame Construction: Details for Builders and Designers.* Newtown, CT: The Taunton Press, 2016. This is a complete, exhaustive collection of reliable details for almost every conceivable situation in a wood frame house.

12. *Western Wood Products Association (WWPA). *Dimensional Stability of Western Lumber Products.* Available online at http://www.wwpa.org. The charts in this booklet are extremely useful in estimating moisture movement in wood. Digital downloads on a variety of wood applications can be found at this website.

6. DETAILING MASONRY

1. *Beall, Christine. *Masonry Design and Detailing.* 6th ed. New York: McGraw-Hill, 2012. This is the best general detailing reference for masonry of all types.

2. *Brick Industry Association. *BIA Technical Notes on Brick Construction.* Available online at https://www.gobrick.com/resources/technical-notes. Updated frequently.

3. Indiana Limestone Institute of America, Inc. *Indiana Limestone Handbook.* Address for ordering: Indiana Limestone Institute of America, Inc., 1502 I Street, Suite 400, Bedford, IN 47421, or available online at https://iliai.com/pages/handbook/. Updated frequently, this manual gives complete information for detailing limestone.

4. *International Masonry Institute. IMI Masonry Detailing Series. Online resources at: https://imiweb.org/detailing-series/ Vivid technical 2D and 3D drawings of most types of masonry materials and assemblies; also includes plaster/stucco, terrazzo, AAC, and tile details. Drawings are linked to relevant IMI Technical Briefs, and can be downloaded as pdf files. Many recently completed case study documentations are also available at: http://www.imiweb.org/design_tools/case_studies/index.php.

5. Natural Stone Institute. *Dimension Stone Design Manual.* Order online at https://pubs.naturalstoneinstitute.org/resources/library. This resource is updated frequently; addresses the detailing of marble, limestone, granite and other architectural stones.

6. *National Concrete Masonry Association. *TEK Manual for Concrete Masonry Design and Construction.* NCMA, 13750 Sunrise Valley Drive, Herndon, VA 20171. Available online at http://www.ncma.org/. A complete manual of facts on designing and building with concrete masonry and related concrete units. Updated continuously; over 140 titles to date.

7. Kummer, Nils. *Basics Masonry Construction.* Basel, Switzerland: Birkhauser, 2021. One in a series by the publishers of DETAIL magazine, this manual has in-depth coverage of the material properties of masonry, masonry's historical uses, and numerous examples of masonry detailing.

7. DETAILING STEEL AND STRUCTURAL METALS

1. The Aluminum Association. *Aluminum Standards and Data.* Address for ordering: The Aluminum Association, 1525 Wilson Boulevard, Suite 600, Arlington, VA 22209. Updated every two years, this is a basic reference on aluminum alloys and product forms. Order online at https://www.aluminum.org/aluminum-standards-and-data.

2. *American Institute of Steel Construction. *Steel Construction Manual.* 16th ed. Chicago: AISC, 2023. Order online at https://www.aisc.org/publications/steel-construction-manual-resources/. This contains basic information on available steel shapes, their properties, and steel connections. From same source: *Detailing for Steel Construction.* 3rd ed. Chicago: AISC, 2002. Order online at https://www.aisc.org/Detailing-for-Steel-Construction-3rd-Ed.

3. *Boake, Terri Meyer. *Understanding Steel Construction.* Basel, Switzerland: Birkhauser, 2011. Exemplary projects are analyzed and presented in terms of materials, connections, framing techniques, fabrication, and construction. Thorough discussion is provided on exposed steel structures, curved steel, castings, diagrids, tension systems, and sustainable design considerations. Order online at https://birkhauser.com/books/9783034610483.

4. Schulitz, Helmut C., et al. *Steel Construction Manual.* Basel, Switzerland: Birkhauser, 2000. One in a series by the publishers of DETAIL magazine, this manual has in-depth coverage of the material properties of steel, its historical uses, and numerous contemporary examples of steel detailing. Order online at https://birkhauser.com/books/9783955531621.

8. DETAILING SITECAST CONCRETE

1. *American Concrete Institute Committee. 303R-12, *Guide to Cast-In-Place Architectural Concrete Practice.* 2012. Order online or download at http://www.concrete.org. This is an excellent guide to detailing and specifying exposed concrete surfaces.

2. *American Concrete Institute. 117–10, *Standard Specifications for Tolerances for Concrete Construction and Materials.* 2015. Order online or download at www.concrete.org. Dimensional tolerances for concrete work are spelled out in detail, with commentary.

3. *Architectural Concrete Form Liners.* Available for download online at www.greenstreak.com. This is an online catalog that illustrates standard form-liner textures. Rustication strips, chamfer strips, and waterstops are illustrated in other catalogs online from the same source, as is a discussion of 3D printing of concrete.

4. Hurd, M. K. *Formwork for Concrete.* 7th ed. Detroit, MI: American Concrete Institute, 2005. This is an excellent and comprehensive general reference on the detailing of concrete.

5. Peck, Martin, et al. *Modern Concrete Construction Manual.* Munich, Germany: DETAIL, 2014. One in a series by the publishers of DETAIL magazine, this manual has in-depth coverage of the material properties of concrete, its history in construction, and numerous contemporary examples of concrete detailing; includes digital fabrication and sustainability considerations. Order online at https://birkhauser.com/books/9783955532062.

9. DETAILING PRECAST CONCRETE FRAMING

1. *Precast/Prestressed Concrete Institute (PCI). *Design Handbook: Precast and Prestressed Concrete.* 8th ed. Chicago: PCI, 2021. Order online at https://www.pci.org/ItemDetail?iProductCode=MNL-120-17 This manual contains industry standards for component design, fabrication, handling, tolerances, performance attributes, and specifications.

2. Precast/Prestressed Concrete Institute (PCI). *Design Resources.* Online resources available at: https://www.pci.org/ArchitecturalResources. A substantial online compendium of publications covering most facets of precast concrete design, detailing and construction.

10. DETAILING ROOFING

1. *National Roofing Contractors Association. *The NRCA Roofing and Waterproofing Manual,* Four-volume boxed set. Rosemont, IL: NRCA, 2021-2024. Order online at http://www.nrca.net. These volumes contain roofing details, in isometric and section views. Includes details for low-slope membranes and for steep roofs in asphalt shingles, wood shakes and shingles, clay and concrete tiles, and slate.

2. Revere Copper Products, Inc. *Copper and Common Sense.* 9th ed. New York: RCP. Order online at https://reverecopper.com/architectural/ This is an excellent manual of sheet copper design principles and construction techniques.

3. Schunk, Eberhard, et al. *Roof Construction Manual.* Basel, Switzerland: Birkhauser, 2003. One in a series by the publishers of DETAIL magazine, this manual has in-depth coverage of the technical issues in sloped roofing, sloped roofs in history, and numerous contemporary examples of sloped roof detailing using many different materials. Order online at https://birkhauser.com/books/9783034615631.

    From same source: *Flat Roof Construction Manual.* 2010. Brief historical perspective and thorough discussion of contemporary methods of low-slope roof design and detailing; includes glazed, habitable, and green roof applications. Order online at https://birkhauser.com/books/9783034615655.

4. Sheet Metal and Air Conditioning Contractors National Association, Inc. *Architectural Sheet Metal Manual.* 7th ed. Vienna, VA: SMACNA, 2012. Order online at http://www.smacna.org. This is the standard reference for details of metal roofing systems and also for flashings, copings, fascias, gravel stops, and other sheet metal roofing details.

11. DETAILING CLADDING

1. *Straube, John. *High Performance Enclosures.* Westford, MA: Building Science Corporation, Building Science Press, 2012. This and many other excellent resources by John Straube, Joseph Lstiburek, and others that combine advanced scientific analysis with practical application are available at: http://www.buildingscience.com/index_html.

2. *American Architectural Manufacturers Association. *Aluminum Curtain Wall Design Guide Manual.* Schaumburg, IL: AAMA, 2019. Order online at http://www.aamanet.org/. This is the best general reference on detailing cladding systems that are based on aluminum extrusions.

3. Anis, Wagdy. *Air Barrier Systems in Buildings.* Whole Building Design Guide (WBDG), 2016. Review of the problems created by infiltration and exfiltration in buildings, and the design considerations of an air barrier system to control the problems. Order online at https://www.wbdg.org/resources/air-barrier-systems-buildings.

4. *Brock, Linda. *Designing the Exterior Wall: An Architectural Guide to the Vertical Envelope.* Hoboken, NJ: John Wiley & Sons, 2005. This book presents current concepts regarding cladding components and detailing strategies. It also includes practical case studies. Order at https://www.wiley.com/en-us/Designing+the+Exterior+Wall.

5. National Glass Association with GANA. *GANA Glazing Manual.* Topeka, KS; 2023. Order online at https://www.glass.org/news/2023/nga-publishes-updated-gana-glazing-manual This booklet shows standard methods of supporting and sealing glass in windows and cladding systems.

6. Herzog, Thomas, et al. *Façade Construction Manual.* Basel, Switzerland: Birkhauser, 2017. One in a series by the publishers of DETAIL magazine, the manual has an in-depth discussion of the technical issues in cladding construction, including numerous details from contemporary buildings. Order online at https://birkhauser.com/books/9783955533700.

7. PPG Industries, Inc. *PPG Architectural Glass Catalog.* View online at https://sweets.construction.com/swts_content_files/510/393454.pdf Updated frequently, this catalog includes valuable information on specifying and detailing glazing.

    An online tool for custom designs of insulated glazing units is available at: https://construct.vitroglazings.com/.

    An online energy modeling tool is available at: http://glassenergyanalysis.vitroglazings.com/.

8. Precast/Prestressed Concrete Institute (PCI). *Architectural Precast Concrete.* 3rd ed. Chicago: PCI, 2007. Order online at http://www.pci.org. This is a complete, lavishly illustrated guide to detailing precast concrete cladding.

9. Precast/Prestressed Concrete Institute (PCI). *Recommended Practice for Glass Fiber Reinforced Concrete Panels.* Chicago: PCI. This is a complete guide to designing GFRC cladding. Order online at https://www.pci.org/ItemDetail?iProductCode=MNL-128-01.

10. Schittich, Christian, et al. *Glass Construction Manual*. Basel, Switzerland: Birkhauser, 2007. One in a series by the publishers of DETAIL magazine, this manual has in-depth coverage of the material properties of glass, its history in construction, contemporary glazing technology, and numerous contemporary examples of glass detailing. Order online at https://birkhauser.ch/books/9783034615549.

11. *Whole Building Design Guide. *Building Envelope Design Guide*. Online resource, 2021, updated frequently. Developed with guidance from the Federal Envelope Advisory Committee to serve as a comprehensive guide for exterior envelope design and construction. Order online at: https://www.wbdg.org/guides-specifications/building-envelope-design-guide .

12. Zero International, Inc. *Sealing Systems for Doors and Windows*. View catalog of resources at no cost at http://www.zerointernational.com. This is Zero's catalog of weatherstripping and other ingenious devices for sealing around doors and windows.

Note: Also see the references on brick masonry, concrete masonry, and stone masonry listed in Section 6 of this bibliography, which contain information on detailing cladding assemblies in these materials.

12. DETAILING INTERIOR CONSTRUCTION

1. Armstrong Architectural Building Products. Catalogs of a wide range of acoustic ceiling systems and wall, flooring, and cabinet products. Armstrong Architectural Building Products, Lancaster, PA., https://www.armstrongceilings.com/.

2. *Gypsum Association. *Gypsum Fire Resistance Design Manual*. 2021. Updated frequently, this booklet gives fire-resistance ratings and sound transmission classes for a large number of wall and ceiling assemblies, using both plaster and gypsum board. Order online at http://www.gypsum.org.

3. *National Association of Architectural Metal Manufacturers. *Recommended Selection and Usage Guide for Hollow Metal Doors and Frames*. Chicago: NAAMM. This is a complete set of guides to hollow metal interior doors and frames, including soundproof and fire-rated doors. Order online at https://www.naamm.org/store/product/42/recommended-selection-and-usage-guide.

4. The National Terrazzo & Mosaic Association, Inc. *Terrazzo Systems Reference Guide*. 2021. Fredericksburg, Texas. The resource contains detailed information on installing, detailing, and specifying terrazzo floors, bases, and stairs. Online at https://terrazzco.com/wp-content/uploads/2021/03/2021-Terrazzo-Systems-Reference-Guide.pdf.

   NAAMM also publishes online a wide range of technical data on metal stairs, pipe railings, metal gratings, and metal finishes.

5. Stagg, William D., and Pegg, Brian F. *Plastering: A Craftsman's Encyclopedia*. New York: Crown Publishers, 1984. This classic resource is a complete guide to all the intricacies of ornamental plastering. It is especially useful in restoration work.

6. *Tile Council of North America (TCNA), Inc. *Handbook for Ceramic Glass and Stone Tile Installation*. Anderson, SC: TCNA, 2023. This book contains all the standard details for ceramic tile and quarry tile installation in every type of construction. Order at https://tcnatile.com/products/publications/2023-tcna-handbook-for-ceramic-glass-and-stone-tile-installation/.

7. *United States Gypsum Company. *Gypsum Construction Handbook*. 7th ed. Chicago: USG, 2014. This is a superb reference, packing into 500 well-illustrated pages everything one needs to know to specify and detail plaster and gypsum board walls and ceilings. View or order online at https://www.usg.com/content/usgcom/en/resource-center/gypsum-construction-handbook.html.

APPENDIX B

Formulating Exercises for Self-Study, Studio, or Classroom Use

Learning how to detail well is impossible without repeated practice. Even still: Practice does not make a perfect detail. Practice makes better details. Practice is most effective when the resulting details are used to construct actual buildings, because then it is possible to experience and assess the results of one's detailing decisions. A critical approach to see what turned out well and what could be done better in the next building is how architectural details – and the construction of them – evolve to improve the performance of the built environment.

This *actual* and real-world experience may not be fully available to students and interns, and one may wish to become more expert before attempting details that will be built. In these cases, several types of exercises can be formulated to help develop detailing skills.

1. ANALYZE AND MODIFY EXISTING DETAILS

A good way to begin the study of architectural detailing is to analyze existing building details from available sources, such as direct observation of the built work, actual working drawings, books of details, details in architectural journals, details in manufacturers' catalogs, and details in this book.

Revisit an Existing Work

Select an existing building from published accounts or from your present city, analyze how it has performed, and closely examine the details that led to that performance. Prepare remedies to deficiencies and propose improvements that would equip the building to meet contemporary performance criteria, noting that expectations creep ever higher during the life of a building. The new features should not sacrifice the original intentions of the designer.

An instructor can choose an exemplary building and go over its details with students to point out their flawed or unforgiving features. Students can then be asked to develop a new set of details that will perform better or be easier to construct, while retaining the appearance that was originally intended. Sketches of changes can be quickly made using photocopies or overlay tracing paper.

Identify the key details from which other details of the building are likely to be derived. Search for and decode the building's DNA. These details are often where the exterior wall meets the ground, a floor, and a roof. A secondary set would be associated with openings, typically including details at the head, jamb, and sill of an opening such as a window or door. The most important details might be crafted as 3D analog or digital models.

Students can work individually or in small teams to do the same type of analyses and design for a building of their choosing. Students can make a list of the patterns employed in their redesign. Consider whether there are patterns that should have been considered that were not. They can also indicate whether the revisions proposed could be implemented as repairs of the existing building or be necessary in the original construction.

2. DESIGN VARIATIONS ON EXISTING DETAILS

A logical next step in this progression of exercises is to start with a photocopy, print, or electronic image of an existing detail and then arbitrarily change one important parameter and redesign the detail accordingly. A simple example would be to start with a detail of a carpeted floor intersecting a gypsum plaster wall in a wood frame house, and then to change the flooring material to oak and the wall material to cherry paneling. A somewhat more challenging exercise in the same building would be to change a flat ceiling with an attic overhead to a sloping ceiling beneath a heavy timber roof.

Other exercises on the same set of details might be to change the floor from a wood platform over a basement to a concrete slab on grade, and then to change the wall construction from wood framing to concrete masonry. A variant of this exercise is to design an additional detail that is not present in the given set of details, such as a balcony railing or a porch roof that will harmonize with the rest of the design.

Exercises of this type can be as difficult as you wish. A tough one is to take a spandrel detail for brick veneer cladding over a reinforced concrete building frame (such as the one in Chapter 17), assume a steel frame instead, and redesign the detail accordingly. Less demanding would be to change the window type in a masonry wall, to design an alternative roof edge detail to achieve a different appearance, to develop a grade-level detail from an upper-floor spandrel detail, and so on.

Architectural Detailing: Function Constructability Aesthetics. Fourth Edition. Patrick Rand, Jason Miller, and Edward Allen.
© 2025 John Wiley & Sons, Inc. Published 2025 by John Wiley & Sons, Inc.

3. DESIGN NEW DETAILS FROM SCRATCH

Difficult, but the most realistic, are those exercises that involve developing details for a new building design. Three examples of this process are illustrated in the *Detail Development* (Part II) portion of this book.

Starting from a basic concept of the space and form of a building, a good plan of action would be the following:

1. Create a list of appropriate materials.
2. Select the key details to be developed.
3. Check the applicable building code for provisions relevant to the detailing process. Keep the code book close by for ready reference.
4. Obtain the necessary information on the building's structural and mechanical systems. This might be done by using consultants in an office, by using other technical teachers in a school, or by consulting *The Architect's Studio Companion: Rules of Thumb for Preliminary Design,* by Joseph Iano and Edward Allen (Hoboken, NJ: John Wiley & Sons, Inc., 2022).
5. Develop the details in stages, aided by studio-style critiques at frequent intervals from a teacher or a senior colleague.

This exercise is most effective if the original building design can be modified as the details are developed. This teaches the positive effect that detailing can have on the form and space of a building—a lesson that will be lost if the original building design is considered complete and inviolable.

Some examples of exercises of this type used in the authors' classes are the key details for a small, two-story branch bank building in an urban location; a façade for an urban infill building that serves as a masonry promotional bureau; and a masonry bearing wall for a suburban school.

The most comprehensive pursuit of this approach is to apply the methodology to the student's current studio project. This is most viable when the student has already carried the studio project nearly to the schematic design level, so that they have already formulated a basic building configuration, tentatively selected a material pallet, and envisioned the architectural qualities. This approach has been successfully carried out in a technically oriented design studio, and in a detailing seminar in which students were concurrently enrolled in a variety of studios taught by others. Applying the detailing principles to engage the design development of the project will empower the student to carry forth their design concepts to yield tangible building proposals. In the authors' experience, infusing design with technical content is often synergistic, enhancing the results both in the studio and in the seminar class.

4. USE THE PATTERNS TO DO BUILDING DIAGNOSTIC WORK

Once the patterns have been reviewed, learned, and understood, they can become a powerful basis for figuring out the causes of various building failures. Problems in real buildings make the most effective vehicles for these exercises. As practice exercises and problems for classroom discussion, you can invent situations that provide applied learning opportunities:

1. Narrow, parallel bands of dampness occur at 2 ft (600 mm) spacings on the ceiling of a single-story industrial steel–frame building in the winter. What is the likely cause? Can you draw a detail that represents the probable existing condition that causes the problem? Can you modify this detail to eliminate the problem?
2. A brick facing is buckling on a six-story classroom building. . . .
3. A stucco wall is cracking badly. . . .
4. People in the waiting room can hear conversations between a therapist and her clients. . . .
5. The plaster immediately beneath a window stool becomes damp after a prolonged wind-driven rainstorm. . . .
6. During renovation work, carpenters discover that the insulation in a 10-year-old wood-frame wall is saturated with moisture, and the framing is beginning to decay. . . .
7. Ice dams are occurring on a roof. . . .
8. An outdoor deck floored with pine lumber traps puddles of water during rainstorms. . . .
9. The flashings in a masonry chimney are corroding. . . .
10. A brick paving is spalling badly. . . .

5. TRY SOME FREESTYLE DETAILING EXERCISES

It can be refreshing and instructive to step outside the world of building now and then to attempt to detail other kinds of useful objects. Imagine designing and detailing an end table, a child's wagon, a garden trellis, an improved nail hammer, a refrigerator container system, a shelving system, or an automobile trash container. Materials can be mixed and matched as desired: Within a class, for example, everyone might attack the same design problem, but students could be assigned different materials to work with. Limitations on the types or the quantity of materials that can be used or how materials may be joined are other strategies to consider. Comparisons of design solutions and details then become even more meaningful.

This approach can be useful in exposing students to the experience of designing with materials and systems that are too complex for them to face in normal building situations, such as aluminum and glass curtain walls. A very useful (and popular) exercise that has yielded excellent results is the design of a coffee table with a glass top supported by a structure of aluminum extrusions. Success with simple projects will build confidence to engage more complex projects.

INDEX

Note: Detail patterns are in ***bold italics***.

A

Abutment Joint*, 102*
Accepted Standards*, 233, 325, 331, 341*
Accessible Connections*, 124, **184**, 221, 260, 264, 272, 299, 327*
Accessible routes, 131, 140
Acoustical tiles, 87, 173, 194
Acoustic privacy, 79, 314, 316–317
Acoustics, 45, 79–87, 100, 127, 242, 247, 312, 330, 341, 355
Activity series for metals, 158
Adjustable Fit*, 195, 200, **201–203**, 324, 333*
Adobe, 64
Advanced framing technique, or optimum value engineering, 228
Aesthetics, 223, 237–252, 347
Aging of the building, 145–167
Air barrier, 11, 20, 28–32, 34, 45–46, 53, 74, 114, 182, 223, 276, 290, 314, 327, 329, 331, 341
Air Barrier System*, **47–48**, 75, 231, 262, 264, 271, 277, 298, 316, 354*
Air leakage, 34, 45–47, 49, 74, 169
Airtight drywall approach, 74
Airtight, Heavy, Limp Partition*, **80–82**, 127, 316*
Aligning Forms with Forces*, **226–228***
Alignment, planes of, 198
All-Weather Construction*, **230–231***
American National Standards Institute (ANSI), 140, 233, 351
American Society for Testing and Materials (ASTM), 233, 351
Americans with Disabilities Act (ADA), 140–143
ANSI A117.5, 140, 351
A-shaped concrete block, 329
Asphalt-saturated felt, 47, 71, 73, 262
Astragal, 28, 177
Attic ventilation, 22–23, 76–77, 268–269

B

Backer rod, 36, 38, 277, 299–300, 303, 327, 329, 331, 333, 339
Back facing, 98
Back priming, 98, 277
Backup wall, 32, 48, 101, 114, 184, 314–323, 325, 327–330, 333, 336–339, 341
Baffle, 20, 28, 268
Barrier-Free Design*, **140**, 141, 341*
Baseboard, 47, 95, 98, 164, 173, 197–198, 211, 222, 273, 330
Bathtub, 135, 140, 188
Bookshelf, 115
Brick facing, *See* Cavity wall
Brick masonry, expansion joint, 33, 42–43, 92–93, 97, 101, 103, 105, 319, 320, 324–328, 336–337
Bricks
 freeze-thaw deterioration, spalling, 161, 210, 326, 358
 specially molded, 210, 334
Brick, size and weight, 92, 172–174, 176, 315, 320
Brickwork
 dimensioning, 172–173, 316–319
 patterns, 172, 174, 179
 repetitious, 179
Building Armor*, **164–165**, 273, 300, 330*
Building Separation Joint*, **111–112**, 341*
Building services, passages for, 7, 121–127
Butt Joint*, 38, 173, 200, 204, **206–208**, 268–269, 274–275, 278*

C

Capillary Break*, 13, 17, **26–27**, 29–31, 156, 271, 301*
Carpet, 66, 84, 86, 131, 137, 147, 153, 212, 236, 314, 316, 330, 341, 357
Casing bead, 210, 222, 281, 299–300
Casing, door or window, 47, 95, 98, 199, 207, 277–278
Cathedral ceiling, 77
Cavity wall, 13, 19, 20, 32, 47, 52, 57, 163, 316–322, 327, 333
 air barrier, 11, 20, 28–32, 47–48, 53, 74–75, 114, 182, 223, 231, 316, 327

Architectural Detailing: Function Constructability Aesthetics. Fourth Edition. Patrick Rand, Jason Miller, and Edward Allen.
© 2025 John Wiley & Sons, Inc. Published 2025 by John Wiley & Sons, Inc.

361

Ceiling
  directly attached, 77, 84, 268, 290
  furred down, 127, 217
  interstitial, 126
  suspended, 66, 86–87, 115, 125–126, 154, 173, 189–190, 194, 212, 250, 291
  textured, 86, 213
Cellular raceway, 121, 125, 127
Cellular steel decking, 127
Chair rail, 164
Chamfer, 134, 209–210, 245, 281, 302, 322, 353
Cheek, 250, 266, 268, 274
Chemical change movement, 89, 145
Chimney, 97, 358
  cap, 7, 162, 209
Cladding, See also Curtain wall; Moisture break; Thermal break
  clearance to frame, 188, 189, 193–195
  installation, 35, 54, 108, 149, 152, 153, 175, 177, 182–185
  panel anchor, 101, 114, 152, 160, 178, 202–203
  panel connections, 40, 104, 114, 120, 158–159, 171, 184–185, 187, 251, 352
  panel fitting, 185, 193–194, 196, 200
  panel joints, 31, 35, 174, 205, 210, 211
  storefront, 110, 155
  wind pressure, 32, 34, 35, 46, 89–90, 114, 274
  zone of installation, 189, 193–195
Cleanable Surfaces, 153, 247
Clean Edge, 7, 209–210, 262, 277, 281, 293, 299, 302–303, 322
Climate zones, 59, 61, 66, 70, 72, 257, 291, 313
Coefficient of friction, 130, 161
Coefficient of thermal expansion, 42–43, 89, 103–105, 318
Color of exterior surface, 43, 60, 103, 105, 150–152, 160, 165, 174, 179, 181, 213, 219, 231, 246, 249, 319
Column
  base plate, 192
  concrete, 134, 189, 194, 219, 314
  connections, 116, 119, 185–186, 188, 237–238
  movement, 89, 96–97, 100
  steel, 188, 192, 194, 196, 223, 227, 237
  wood, 96, 232, 244
Combustible materials, 52, 124, 135, 137–139
Composing the Detail, 252, 259, 266, 269, 274, 279, 293
Composite cladding, 28, 31–32, 82, 120, 182, 200, 205, 218
Computer aided manufacturing (CAM), 216–217
Computer numeric control (CNC), 119, 169, 191, 194, 216–217, 240, 244, *See also* **Factory and Site**
Concrete
  acoustic properties, 80, 84
  aging of surfaces, 150, 152, 161, 165, 213
  control joints, 92, 106, 108, 293–295
  edge details, 7, 209, 239, 247, 301–302
  formwork, 13, 57, 92, 107, 169, 178, 180, 205, 209, 211, 213, 219, 226, 293–295
  foundations, 24, 99–100, 156, 271–273, 302
  freeze-thaw damage, 161–162
  lightweight, 52
  pours, 57, 178, 183, 189, 211, 230, 293–310
  shrinkage, 92–93, 103, 106, 107, 110–112, 293, 302–303
  slab finish, 86, 130, 182, 211–212
  slab on grade, 71, 99–100, 106, 270, 292, 302, 313, 357
  surface texture, 134, 150, 152, 165, 181, 205, 213, 243
  wall, 51, 57, 64–66, 123, 204, 211, 212, 291–310
  wall control joints, 40, 102, 107, 291–310
Concrete masonry, 47, 56, 57, 64–66, 80, 81, 89
  absorption rate, 153, 161–162
  acoustic properties, 81, 86
  control joints, 107, 108
  dimensioning, 172–173, 176, 219, 319–323
  glazed, 86, 153, 161
  installation, 175, 224, 230
  manufacture, 219
  shrinkage, 92–93, 107
  wall, 123, 246, 313–346
Condensate Drainage, 19, 78
Condensation, 21, 25, 47, 51, 54, 67–78, 231, 265, 297, 299, 316
Connecting Dissimilar Materials, 116–117
Constructability, 169–236
  general guidelines, 169
Continuous control layers, 6, 25, 46, 47, 51, 55, 58, 70, 117, 174, 231, 272, 282, 298, 316, 327
Contributive Details, 237–239, 243, 258, 266, 269, 274, 292, 305, 314, 338
Controlling air leakage, 34, 45–50, 70, 74, 169, 277, 296
Control Joint, 92, 106–108, 243, 246, 293–294, 296, 302–304, 309, 317
  spacing, 108
Coped joint in molding, 208
Coping, parapet, 8, 17, 25, 93, 162, 337, 338, 340–341, 345
Corner block, 207
Corner board, 98, 274–275
Corner detail, 274–275, 286, 302, 309, 336
Corrosion, 67, 145, 150, 158–160, 163, 265, 315, 323, 325, 339
Cranes and hoists, 175–177, 331
Crawl space, 11, 24, 45, 136, 156, 270–273, 290
Creep, structural, 42–43, 89, 101, 110, 196, 227, 298, 314, 318, 319, 321, 326
Crown, 11
Curtain wall, 20, 31, 32, 35, 43, 59, 60, 65, 74, 78, 90, 135, 154–155, 173, 174, 212, 219, *See also* Cladding
  aluminum, 20, 31–32, 43, 115, 155, 159, 173, 174, 176, 194–195, 212, 219, 223, 354, 358
  brick, 101, 203
  expansion joints, 42–43
  glass replacement, 152, 154
Cushioned Floor, 83–84, 314, 316
Customized repetitive manufacturing (CRM), 217

362 INDEX

D

Dampproofing, 273, 339
Decking, 95, 127, 177
Deflection, structural, 8–9, 42–43, 89, 100–101, 111, 114, 135, 192, 196, 227, 294, 298, 300, 315, 319, 321, 326
Detail as process, xi–xii, 5–6, 220–222, 229, 239, 245, 255
Detail Development, 255–348
Detailer's Reference Shelf, xii, *351–355*
Detailing a Building in Architectural Concrete, 291–311
Detailing a Building in Masonry on a Concrete Frame, 313–348
Detailing a Building in Wood Light Framing, 257–290
Detailing for Disassembly, 146, 152, *186–187*, 187, 222, 252
Detail patterns, 5–252
    aesthetics, 235–252
    constructability, 169–234
    definition of, xi–xii
    function, 7–167
Didactic Assemblies, *251*
Digital fabrication, *See* Computer numeric control
Dimensional Tolerance, 57, 173, 188, *192–196*, 202, 222, 233, 264, 276, 293, 298, 314, 319, 324
Distributing Loads, *118–120*, 276
Doors, 5, 18, 28, 34, 49, 50, 79, 81–82, 115, 134, 140, 172, 173, 177, 188, 216, 246, 252
    accessible, 140–143, 242
    aluminum, 32, 134
    armor, 164
    closer, 85, 115, 140
    fire, 138–139, 247
    glass, 34, 135, 151
    sill, 7, 16, 31, 32, 34, 130
    weatherstrip, 32, 45, 47, 49–50
    wood, 95, 98, 109, 156
Drainage, internal, 19–21, 24, 25, 35, 38, 78, 175
Drain and Weep, *19–20*, 33, 78, 148, 316, 325, 332
Drip strip, 16, 31
Dry Wood, *156–157*, 271, 273, 299
Ducts, air conditioning, 68–70, 79, 82, 84, 85, 121–127, 136, 154, 190, 216, 270, 292
    exposed, 212

E

Ease of assembly, 20, 171–190
Eave, 10, 17, 22, 23, 114, 197, 250, 258–269, 274, 283
Efficient use of construction resources, 215–233
EIFS, *See* Exterior insulation and finish system
Elevation studies, 103, 174, 248, 266, 267, 290–292, 303–305, 310, 318, 331, 334, 340
Embellishment, xi, 238, 239, 245
Embodied energy, 147, 228, 339
End dam, 35, 332, 334, 341
Environmental Product Declarations (EPD), 136, 147
Equalizing Cross Grain, *96–97*, 206
Ergonomic factors, 134, 141–142, 176, 242, 247
Exercises in detailing, formulating, 357–358

Expansion, coefficients of thermal, 42–43, 89, 105, 318
Expansion Joint, 33, 36, 42, *103–105*, 106, 108, 111, 196, 318–321, 336–337
Expansion joint spacing, 105
Expected Life, 146, *148–149*, 186, 222, 229, 263, 267, 293, 303, 305, 326, 328
Exterior details, 17, 158, 261, 339
Exterior insulation and finish system (EIFS), 57, 65, 108, 157, 165, 296
Extreme Event Protection, *166–167*

F

Factory and Site, 57, 59, 173, 175, 180, 184, 200, *216–217*, 218–219, 314, 326
Fall Protection, *132–133*
Fascia, 17, 114, 197, 250, 259, 261
Fasteners, 54, 91, 100, 116–120, 158–160, 184, 187, 195, 201–203, 220, 251, 252, 264–265, 279, 290, 324, 333
Feather edge, 7, 209
Fire damper, 124, 127, 139, 154
Fire resistance ratings, 80, 124, 137–139, 297, 347, 348, 352, 355
Fire-Resistant Assemblies, 137, *138–139*, 243, 341
Fire-Safe Materials, *137*, 341
Fit, planes of, 109, 198, 204
Flame Spread Rating, 137
Flashing, 12, 13, 17–19, 22, 25, 27, 47, 71, 97, 134, 148, 156, 157, 160, 163, 231, 233, 263, 273, 276, 301, 316, 322–327, 332–334, 338, 341, 354
Floor, 80, 82–85, 138–139, 194, 222
    framing shrinkage, 92, 96–97
    raised access, 82, 126, 127, 190
    repair of, 148, 151, 153
    slab, 10, 24, 100, 106, 126, 127, 189, 194, 302, 306, 338
    structure, 84, 111–112, 180, 270
Flooring, 95, 130–131, 140, 152, 247, 257, 271–273
Forgiving details, 191–213
    definition, 191
Forgiving Surface, *213*, 295
Formal Transitions, 102, *248–250*
Form tie holes, 293–295, 303–305, 310
Foundation
    detail, 100, 282
    insulated shallow, 52, 66, 69, 99
    settlement, 89, 90, 102, 111, 194
    wall and footing, 40, 270–272, 338–339
Foundation Below Frost Line, *99*, 271
Foundation Drainage, *24*, 69, 272, 282, 339
Fuel-Contributed Rating, 137
Furring, 56, 62, 69, 87, 117, 122–123, 211, 260, 296, 298, 305, 315, 330

G

Galvanic corrosion, 158–160, 323, 325
Galvanic series of metals, 158
Galvanized steel, 60, 158–160, 265, 275, 290, 328, 329, 338

Gasket, 5, 19, 20, 31, 32, 34–41, 46, 49, 74, 81, 82, 100, 110, 111, 114, 119, 134, 135, 152, 160, 174, 196, 200, 300
   lockstrip, 39
Geometry and Proportion, 140, 235–236, 238–240, *241–242*, 251, 292, 341
Glass, 42, 59, 61, 67, 78, 82, 86, 115, 150, 176, 194, 218, 237, 239, 250, 276, 354
   fiber, foam insulation, 52–54, 71, 74, 75, 77, 260, 296, 316
   fitting to frames, 38, 39, 82, 104, 110, 115, 154, 200, 201, 239, 252
   low-emissivity (Low-E), 59, 61, 150, 313, 331
   maintenance of, 150–154
   reflective, 61
   repair of, 152, 154
   safety, 129, 133, 135, 139, 218, 250, 293
   smart, electrochromic, 155
   spandrel, 74, 75, 104
   wired, 129, 135, 139
Grade condition detail, 270–273, 282, 302, 306, 338–339, 342
Greenhouse rafter, 19
Guards, 115, 129, 131–135, 165, 242
Gutters, downspouts, 10, 19–22, 78, 114, 258
Gypsum
   board, 42, 47, 62, 71, 74, 80–81, 86–87, 92, 103, 222, 257, 259–260, 296, 316, 355
   uncut sheets, 172–173
   wall finish, 210–213, 265, 273, 275, 277, 281, 296, 299, 300, 303, 330

H

Handrails, 130, 132–135, 140, 242, 250
Health and safety, xi, 7, 67, 129–143, 145, 176, 247
Heat, conduction, radiation, thermal mass, 51, 54, 60–66
Heat flow, controlling, 51–66, 117
Hierarchy of Refinement, *243–244*, 248, 252, 264, 266, 268, 281, 294, 296, 301, 314, 334
Horizontal Plenum, 82, *125–127*, 154, 189, 190, 273, 292, 298, 330
House wrap, building wrap, 47–48, 71, 75, 264, 265, *See also* Air barrier
Humidity, 45, 67–78, 136, 156–157, 204, 230, 231, 265, 270, 292

I

Ice and water barrier, 259, 263, 290
Impact Insulation Class (IIC), 83–84, 330
Installation Clearance, 123, *187*, 222, 276, 299, 323, 333
Insulated glass, *See* **Multiple Glazing**
Insulation, thermal, *See* Thermal insulation
Intensification and Ornamentation, *245–246*, 280, 281, 293, 303, 326, 332
International Building Code (IBC), and
   International Code Council (ICC), 9, 22, 34, 59, 61, 70, 76, 77, 99, 115, 124, 129–135, 137–140, 242, 258, 293, 313, 341, 351, 358
International Energy Conservation Code (IECC) and

International Green Construction Code (IgCC), 70, 71, 257, 290, 291, 313, 351
Interior finish details, 96, 137, 173, 194, 212, 265, 273, 277, 281, 300, 330, 335
Inverted roof assembly, 73, 301
Isolation joint, 100, 106

J

Joint cover, 111, 112
Joint, wall panel, 8, 14, 26, 28–32, 35, 42–43, 173, 175, 176, 187, 194

K

Key details to develop, 182, 239, 255, 258, 281, 290, 292, 298, 314, 320, 347, 357–358

L

Labyrinth, 26, *28*, 29, 31
Lattice, snow support, 23, 114, 259
Less Absorbent Materials, *161–162*
Life Cycle, 58, 129, 145, *146–147*, 148, 185, 222, 257, 276, 292, 302, 313, 341
Lintel, 13, 19, 246, 294, 303–304, 318, 331–332, 334
Local Skills and Resources, *224–225*, 268, 271, 314, 328, 333
Lookouts, 263
Low-slope, flat roofing, 8, 9, 21, 23, 72, 73, 77, 111, 149, 175, 230, 248, 291, 337, 354
   at building separation joint, 111
L-shaped brick, 326
Lumber, distortions, 91, 94–98, 156, 204, 259–260
   framing, 96, 118, 156, 228, 270
   glue-laminated, cross-laminated, 77, 87, 91, 96, 119, 172, 173, 194, 218, 224, 231, 252
   laminated veneer, 91, 96, 172
   parallel strand, 91

M

Maintenance Access, 121, 126, *154–155*, 212, 273
Masonry, 19, 25, 32, 42, 56, 65, 71, 80–81, 103, 137, 163, 182, 194, 230, 246, *See also* Cavity wall; Flashing
   deterioration, 150, 152, 160–162, 213
   dimensioning, 92, 172–173, 176, 194–196, 219, 320–322
   edge details, 33, 102, 134, 209, 210, 334
   movement in, 42–43, 89, 92, 93, 97, 103, 105, 107, 108, 112, 314–321, 325
   parapets, 17, 93, 337–338
   partitions, 81, 86, 123
   repair of, 120, 152, 153
   thermal control, 51, 52, 54, 56–58, 64–66, 68, 317
   ties, 93, 97, 116, 120, 163, 315, 317, 323, 325, 327–328, 337, 345–346
   veneers, 25, 33, 47–48, 112, 174, 182, 183, 202, 313, 314
   walls, mechanical and electrical services in, 123, 189, 329
Mass production, mass customization, 180, 216–218
Metals

deterioration, 149, 150, 152, 158–160, 163, 265, 305, 325, 355
fastener combinations for, 158–159
Minimum Number of Parts, **174–175**, 251, 325, 328, 331, 335
Mitered corner, 204, 206, 208, 210, 267, 268, 277–278
Mockup assemblies, 160, 181–183, 229, 305, 341
Modular coordination, 172–173, 187, 314, 315, 320
Moisture Break, **25**, 148, 263, 273, 296, 302, 325, 332
Moisture movement, 89–90, 92, 102, 109, 111, 156, 192, 204
Mortar joint profiles, 161–162, 181, 315
Movement, accommodating, 89–112
Movement joints, *See Sealant Joints and Gaskets, Expansion Joint, and Control Joint*
Multiple Glazing, **59**, 61, 67, 69, 276, 297, 316

N

Noise Reduction Coefficient (NRC), 86
Nonconflicting Systems, **189–190**
Nontoxic Materials, **136**, 341
NRC, *See* Noise Reduction Coefficient

O

Observable Assemblies, **183**, 296, 324, 327
Off-the-Shelf Parts, 81, **223**, 268, 276, 279, 330
Open-web steel joists, 125
Outside-Insulated Thermal Mass, 51, 56, **64–66**, 296, 316, 338
Overhang and Drip, **15–20**, 29, 31, 161, 258, 263, 271, 276, 301, 325, 328, 332, 338, 339
Overhanging story, 18, 248, 258
Overlap, **12–14**, 109, 174, 197, 266, 277, 301, 332, 338

P

Paint, 60, 71, 86, 98, 136, 150, 152, 153, 156, 211, 213, 230–231, 265
Painting, exterior, 98, 150, 156, 230, 265
Panel anchor, 160, 184, 201–202
Panel joint, 8, 26, 28–32, 35–38
Parapet, 13, 17, 33, 93, 298, 301
coping, 8, 17, 93, 162, 338, 340
detailing, 16, 25, 27, 93, 149, 337–339
Partitions, 79–83, 100, 127, 148, 187, 196, 216, 314
fire resistance of, 138
services in, 122–124
Parts, sizes of, 174–176, 223
Parts That Are Easy to Handle, **176–178**, 260, 262, 314, 331
Patterns, detail, *See* Detail patterns
Paving, pavers, 9, 10, 24, 99, 161, 233, 258, 358
PEC, *See* Pressure equalization chamber
Phase change movement, 89–90, 99, 161, 302, 326
Pitch to drain, 10, 257, *See also* **Wash**
Plaster, 67, 71, 81, 86, 134, 137, 199, 209, 296, 314, 315, 330, 355
air barrier, 47, 84
casing beads and corner beads, 199, 210, 330
ceilings, 84, 87, 115, 213, 335
expansion joint, 42, 89, 103, 105, 108
illumination of surface, 213
ornament, 145, 232, 240
repair of, 152, 164
Plastic laminate, 98, 137, 153
flaws in, 213
Platform framing, 96–97, 228
Plenum above dropped ceiling, 82, 125–127, 190, 212, 292, 298, 330
Plywood and oriented strand board sheathing, 22, 47, 63, 70, 71, 75, 96, 120, 166, 199, 259–262, 266, 268, 276
Post base, 201
Preconstruction conference, 138, 181–182, 305, 341
Prefabrication, 14, 85, 87, 175, 184, 187, 192, 194, 196, 199, 216, 220, 231, 256
Pressure equalization chamber (PEC), *See* **Rainscreen Assembly and Pressure Equalization**
Pride of Craftsmanship, **232**, 251, 305, 314
Product Category Rules (PCR), 136, 147
Progressive Finish, **211–212**, 221, 243, 296, 328, 335
Proportion, *See* **Geometry and Proportion**
Protected and Similar Metals, 32, 60, 148, **158–160**, 265, 325, 328

Q

Quiet Attachments, **85**, 117, 300, 317
Quirk bead, 232, 245
Quirk miter, 204, 208, 210, 249

R

Radiant barrier, *See* **Reflective Surface and Airspace**
Radiant heat and energy, 51, 60–63, 66, 89
Rafter ties, 279–281, 289
Railing cap, 98, 204
Railing, stair and ramp, 115, 130–134, 140, 156, 242, 250, *See also* Handrails; Guards
Rainfall angle and intensity, 15, 21
Rainscreen Assembly and Pressure Equalization, 11, 20, **29–33**, 262, 276, 299, 316
Rainscreen panel joints, 20
Rake, 266–268, 274, 290
Refining the Detail, **229**, 262, 280, 299, 304
Reflective Glazing, 51, **61**
Reflective Surface and Airspace, 51, **62–63**
Reglet, 13, 14, 178, 301, 332, 341
Rehearsing the Construction Sequence, 177, 184, 212, **220–222**, 261, 271, 274, 300, 301, 327, 329, 347
Relieved Back, **98**, 268, 273, 275, 277, 278
Repairable Surfaces, **152**, 335
Repetitious Assembly, **179–180**, 218, 293, 320, 328
Repetitious Fabrication, 179, 216–217, **218–219**, 305
Resilient channels, 81, 84, 330, 343, 345
Return miter, 277, 278, 288
Reveal, 108, 162, 173, 200, **204–205**, 207, 208, 210, 222, 249, 273, 275, 278, 293, 303, 305

Ridge detail, 266–269, 280, 284, 289, 290
Ridge vent, 14, 22, 76, 268–269, 284, 290
Robust Assemblies, 30, ***163***, 261, 265, 269, 270, 273, 279, 293, 315, 328, 332
Roof
   low-slope, 8, 9, 21, 23, 72–73, 77, 111, 149, 175, 230, 248, 291, 337, 354
   membrane, 8, 9, 13, 17, 23, 60, 67, 71, 73, 117, 149, 301, 338
   sheet metal, seams, 105, 246
   shingle, 5, 8, 12, 17, 22, 60, 77, 95, 120, 152, 167, 176, 197–198, 245, 257, 262–269, 271, 274, 283, 290, 333, 354
   steep or sloping, 8, 22, 162, 265, 354
   terrace, 9, 314
   ventilation, 22, 23, 63, 67, 72–73, 75–77, 269
Roof assembly, inverted, 73, 301
Roof drains and drainage, 8–9, 21–24
Rustication strips, 108, 205, 246, 293–310

S
Safe Edges, ***134***, 247, 277
Safe Footing, ***130–131***, 161, 242
Safe Glazing, 133, ***135***, 139, 293
Safety, 129–143, 148, 176, 233, 242, 351
Sample panel, *See **Simulated Assemblies***
Sealant, 5, 8, 13, 14, 16, 19, 30–32, 36–43, 46, 47, 74, 81, 89, 100–103, 136, 148, 151, 277, 327, 341
   preformed tape, 5, 40, 239, 326
Sealant joints, 36–41, 45, 100–103, 112, 188, 196, 299–300, 303–304, 316, 327, 330
   proportioning widths, 41–43, 105, 318–321
Sealant Joints and Gaskets, 5, 31, ***36–40***, 46, 135, 200
Seasoning and Curing, 89–90, ***91–93***, 94, 95, 319
Sensory Richness, 79, 132, 141, 233–234, 241–242, ***247***
Seismic factors, details, 89, 90, 111, 114, 313, 315, 318, 319, 324, 328, 329, 337
Service life, tiers, 46, 146–149, 166, 186, 222, 229, 231
Shading coefficient, 61
Sharp edges, 129, 134, 206–210, 247
Shelf angle, 58, 101, 114, 202, 203, 316–319, 323–330, 337, 339
Shingle siding, 12, 197, 266–269, 274–276, 282–283, 286
Sidewalk crack, 106
Siding, wood, 12, 109, 162, 252
Similar metals, *See **Protected and Similar Metals***
Simulated Assemblies, ***181–182***, 183, 268, 290, 295, 305, 333, 341
Skylights, 19, 48, 59, 78, 135, 153, 223
Sliding Fit, 109, ***197–200***, 221, 222, 264, 273, 276, 300, 329
Sliding Joint, ***109–110***
Sloped glazing, 78, 135
Slotted holes, 202–203
Small Structures, 101, 113, ***114–115***, 118, 133, 262, 263, 271, 273, 294, 329
Smoke, 45, 50, 124, 126, 129, 136, 139
Smoke-Developed Rating, 137

Soffit, 17, 18, 76, 114, 197–198, 246, 262–269, 290, 319, 330
Soft joint, 101, 318–326, 329, 330, 341
Solar radiation, reflection of, 51, 61, 62
Sound Absorbing Surfaces, 79, 82, ***86–87***, 316
Sound, controlling, 79–87
Sound isolation criteria, 80, 83
Sound Transmission Class (STC), 80–84, 330
Spandrel, 101, 104, 114, 185, 189, 195, 196, 202, 293, 294, 298, 299, 301, 303–304, 320, 322, 357
Specifications, 42, 98, 122, 129, 181, 223, 224, 229, 233, 265, 268, 281, 290, 293, 302, 305, 314, 318, 332, 341, 347, 352, 353
Splinters, 134, 245, 247
Spun-bonded polyolefin (SBPO), 47–48, 71, 75, *See also* House wrap; Air barrier
Stairs, 85, 115, 129–132, 134, 135, 140, 142, 165, 223, 226, 242, 305
Standard products, 58, 61, 115, 129, 153, 173, 187, 223, 224, 233, *See also **Off-the Shelf Parts***
STC, *See* Sound Transmission Class
Steel dowels, 106, 107
   self-tapping, 119
Steel frames, 58, 116, 139, 177–179, 186, 193–196, 212, 226–227, 237, 251, 252
Steel stud frames, 32, 48, 54, 81, 100, 114, 122, 194, 298, 314, 316, 338
Stool, window, 31, 277, 335, 358
Structural creep, 42–43, 89, 101, 110, 196, 227, 298, 314, 318, 319, 321, 326
Structural deflection, 8, 9, 42–43, 89, 100, 101, 110, 111, 114–115, 135, 192, 196, 227, 294, 298, 300, 315, 319, 320, 326
Structural support, 7, 111, 113–120, 163, 262
Structure/Enclosure Joint, ***100–101***, 106, 196, 298, 300, 318, 336
Structure, wood roof, 259–260
Stucco, 57, 92, 103, 105, 108, 113, 152, 162, 210, 224, 230, 246, 339
Style, 135, 237–238, 281
Sump pump, 24
Supervision, construction administration, 224, 229, 290, 305, 341
Surface finishes, cleaning of, 152, 153
Surfaces That Age Gracefully, ***150–151***, 247, 257, 275, 276
Suspended ceiling, *See* Ceiling, suspended
Sustainable, resilient design, 51, 59, 136, 146, 150, 152, 216, 225, 239, 243, 313, 341
Swale, 24, 273

T
Temperature movement, 65, 89–90, 103–105, 110, 189, 205, 209, 317–318
Termination of form, 250
Thermal Break, ***54–58***, 59, 67, 69, 260, 276, 297, 300, 316, 324, 338
Thermal bridge, 54–58, 275, 297, 305, 316, 324, 338, 339

Thermal expansion, coefficients of, *See* Coefficients of thermal expansion
Thermal "flywheel," 65
Thermal Insulation, **52–53**, 56, 58, 63, 65–77, 111, 122, 123, 163, 228, 257, 259–260, 272–273, 282, 296, 298, 316, 324, 338
Thermally modified timber (TMT), 91
Thermal mass, 51, 56–57, 64–66, 68, *See also* **Outside-Insulated Thermal Mass**
Thermal movement, *See* Temperature movement
Thermal resistance, 52–53, 59, 62, *See also* **Thermal Insulation**
Timber connections, 249
Timeless Features, **240**, 257
Tolerances, dimensional, *See* **Dimensional Tolerances**
Topside roof vent, 73, 75
Toxic materials, 52, 59, 129, 135, 137, 341, *See also* **Nontoxic Materials**
Triaxial adjustment, 202, 324
Trucking and transportation, 146–147, 175, 177, 216, 219, 225, 314, 351

U
Uncut Units, **172–173**, 266, 271, 315, 320
Underfloor plenum, 126, 190, *See also* **Horizontal Plenum**
Unitized assemblies, 173, 175, 176, 219
Universal Design, 129, **141–143**, 176
Unobstructed Drainage, **21**, 258, 273, 325
Upstand, **34–35**, 277, 325

V
Vapor retarder, vapor permeance, 22, 47–48, 53, 63, 67–77, 111, 259, 269, 272, 290, 298, *See also* **Warm-Side Vapor Retarder**
Vapor Ventilation, 73, **75–77**, 260, 273
Vegetated surfaces, 8–10, 66, 114, 152
Vent spacer, roof, 22, 77, 265, 268–269, 290
Ventilated Cold Roof, **22–23**, 45, 76, 259, 260, 263
Vertical Chase, **122–124**, 139, 189, 314, 341, 348
Vertical-Grain Lumber, 91, **94–95**, 98, 134, 262
Vinyl wallcovering, 74, 152, 165
Volatile Organic Compounds (VOC), 136

W
Wainscoting, 152, 165
Wall cavity, 21, 25, 47, 75, *See also* Cavity wall
Wall detailing, 298–301
Wall, repair of, 152, 153
Warm Interior Surfaces, 45, 67, **68–69**, 70, 270, 316

Warm-Side Vapor Retarder, 53, 63, 67, 68, **70–74**, 75, 298, 301, 316
Wash, **7–11**, 13, 16, 24, 29, 31, 162, 209, 273, 301, 303, 334, 338, 339
Water leakage, 5–43, 175, 263, 296, 299, 316, 323, 333
  conditions and strategies, 5
  forces that can move water, 5
  barriers, 25, 48, 163, 223, 231, 259, 263, 265, 276, 316, 328, 332
Waterproofing, 28, 29, 71, 73, 161, 163, 263, 273, 327, 354
Waterstop, 40, 112
Water table molding, 17
Water vapor, controlling, 67–78, 163, 265, 296–297, 315
Weather-sensitive operations, 230–231
Weatherstripped Crack, **49–50**, 82, 276
Wedge anchor insert, 178, 202, 324, 341
Weep hole baffle, 20
Weep holes, 13, 19–20, 25, 32, 35, 78, 163, 316, 322, 325, 326, 332, 339
Weep tube, 35, 78
Wheelchair access, 130, 131, 140, 165
White and Bright Surfaces, **60**
Window, 45, 51, 59, 61, 82, 166, 216, 223, 242, 246, 252, 293–295, 345, *See also* Glass
  cleaning and repairing, 152, 154, 155, 166
  detailing, 5, 12, 26, 49, 70, 81, 110, 175, 186, 187, 196, 199, 204, 252, 276–278, 287, 288, 299, 300, 304, 307, 331–335, 341, 344
  frame, 55, 69, 110, 155, 199, 252
  installation, 154, 175, 188, 196, 199, 331–335
  sill, 7, 26, 27, 31, 34, 90, 162
Wood, 94–98, 150–151, 156, 162, 206–208
  engineered, 47, 91, 96, 194, 216, 218, 352
  decay of, 150, 153, 156–157, 160, *See also* Thermally modified timber
  repair of, 152
  seasoning, 91, 94–96
  shrinkage of, 206–208
Wood-destroying insects, 99, 150, 156–157
Wood frame construction, *See also* Wood light framing
  economical dimensions, 172, 173
  finishes, 152, 153, 162, 212
Wood light framing, 56, 63, 173, 194, 212, 220–222, 255–290
Worker, 136, 169, 171–190, 192–196, 220–222, 224, 232
  access, 8, 121, 126, 154–155, 184–185, 190, 327
  craftsmanship, 78, 182, 196, 213, 232, 251, 294, 305
  productivity, 154, 169, 176–180, 191, 216–218, 327